CASH COPY
How To Offer Your Products And Services So Your Prospects Buy Them . . . NOW!

Dr. Jeffrey Lant

Published by JLA Publications
A Division of Jeffrey Lant Associates, Inc.
50 Follen Street, Suite 507
Cambridge, MA 02138
(617) 547-6372

CASH COPY
How To Offer Your Products And Services
So Your Prospects Buy Them . . . NOW!

Dedication

I offer this book to my clients, past and present. I thank you for working with me and for continually challenging my thinking about the best way to get the results you wanted. Your constant prodding has continually forced me to reexamine my assumptions, remain open to new possibilities, and — most importantly — to grow. The information I share in this book — information that will help so many others — would never have been either possible or perfected without you!

Acknowledgements. As always, many people have been generous with their time and knowledge. You will see their names dotted throughout the text, and I hope you will use them in their areas of expertise. When I recommend people, I know they're good!

Three people, however, deserve a special mention. John & Lorraine Hamwey of ABC Publications, Inc. have again assisted me in producing this book, as they have now for many years. And my dear and good friend Professor Robert Dobson has, as usual, applied his lynx-eye to the text. As a result it is a better, stronger one. Thank you all.

Table of Contents

Special Foreword For The Second Printing

Dear Friend,

You're holding in your hand a bona fide American classic...the kind of book that will be read and used for decades to come. Why? Particularly for these three reasons:

1. People like you want to sell more products and services faster. CASH COPY helps. Used consistently and conscientiously, CASH COPY delivers the greater sales you want. *Starting today.*

2. By the same token, you want to stop wasting your marketing dollars. *Today.* Right now, like most people you're probably wasting over 98% of your marketing dollars producing communications that just don't work. From this moment on, you can stop this foolishness. CASH COPY makes you money in two ways: more sales, less waste.

3. CASH COPY works. I keep inviting my readers to get in touch and tell me how they're doing using the CASH COPY techniques. Working with my clients for years, I've known that what's in this book makes people money — often astonishingly large amounts of money. Now my readers are regularly telling me just how well they're doing by systematically following these guidelines.

Because of these three reasons, I say unequivocably: CASH COPY is a book that will change your life. Neither your marketing nor your business will ever be the same when you've finished it . You'll know just what to do to get people to buy your products and services *immediately*...and you'll be doing it. Every single day.

Knowing how much you get from CASH COPY, I'm truly delighted to offer you this volume from the second printing. Read it. Use it. Profit from it. Like thousands are already doing. Then, contact me and brag about your success. I love success stories...especially when I've had a hand in creating them!

Your continuing profit maker,

Jeffrey

Cambridge, MA
November, 1989

Introduction

What's In This Book, How To Use It, Why I Wrote It

I have written this book, my ninth, with a single objective in mind: to provide you with information that gets your prospects to respond to your marketing communications. That is, to motivate them to respond to your brochures, cover letters, annual reports, media kits, flyers, ads, catalogs, free client newsletters . . . and anything else you use to present your products and services.

Each day the bulk of the money that marketers invest in these marketing formats is wasted, as over 98% of what is used to stimulate sales fails to do so. The collective cost of these activities is astronomical, numbering in the billions and billions of dollars. But more than just this money is at stake:

- people who need your products and services to improve their lives, don't get them;
- resources that would be better utilized in other ways are squandered, and
- you don't make the sales you need to develop your business.

In large measure this dismaying situation is the result of the shocking inadequacy of the marketing materials being used today . . . marketing materials that you, too, may well be creating and distributing.

These materials — and I don't care what they are —:

- don't target people who need you;
- don't speak directly to these people;

- don't tell these people precisely what you can do for them;
- don't work to allay their anxieties about taking immediate action;
- don't use persuasive offers to stimulate the prospect to buy;
- don't use past buyer testimonials indicating specific results attained to get prospects to buy;
- don't hammer home a consistent, believable, client-centered message.

In short, millions of people selling products and services are engaged in a mockery of marketing, swiftly pursuing devastatingly self-defeating behavior that benefits no one, including themselves.

This must stop.

That's why I wrote this book.

Here, for the first time, the focus is on one thing and one thing only: creating marketing documents that get your prospects and your customers to buy NOW!

Not at some undefined period in the future.

Not next week.

Not tomorrow.

But NOW!

Throughout this book I'll be pushing you, prodding you, insisting that you do what is necessary to turn your marketing into NOW! marketing. For just one reason: so more of your prospects and past buyers buy more of what you're selling faster.

And, after all, isn't this what you really want?

What You'll Find In CASH COPY

This book includes 19 chapters, and, quickly, I'd like to introduce them to you.

In *Chapter 1*, you'll find 21 egregious copy errors you're probably making right this minute, errors that doom your marketing communications to failure.

Speaking broadly, this book is my attempt to make sure you never make these self-defeating errors ever again.

Having made sure you understand these errors, in *Chapter 2* the discussion proceeds to the important matter of how to run a client-centered business. It is my earnest conviction that you cannot write client-centered cash copy until you are running a business that's centered on your buyers. This chapter tells you how to do that. It's no good, you see, saying you're interested in delivering benefits to buyers unless your business practices confirm this.

Successful marketers, as you learn from *Chapter 3*, have a certain attitude and skills that assist them in creating client-centered cash copy. Here you learn how to develop both.

With *Chapter 4*, you begin to find out about your prospects, the most important people in this book . . . and your business. Here are the suggestions you need to follow to learn about them . . . because if you don't you cannot possibly write cash copy that motivates them to act.

In *Chapter 5*, we take up one of the most significant topics in marketing: how to transform your marketing communications from documents about you . . . to documents about your buyers, that is, how to transform features into benefits. Much has been written on this crucial topic; I cannot claim to be the first to recognize its importance. But I can show you, and do, just how to stop talking about what you're selling and transform your marketing into benefits that get prospects to buy.

Chapter 6 takes up the matter of testimonials, a subject most marketers never get right. Here you learn how to turn your past buyers into sales representatives and use the results they've achieved from using your product or service to both soothe the anxieties of your prospects and stimulate their excitement. After you master this chapter, you'll never again wonder how your past buyers can help you attract new ones. You'll know.

In *Chapter 7*, you learn about the crucial importance in marketing of NOW! That is, you learn how to create the irresistible offer that gets your prospect to act immediately. One of the crucial failings of far too many marketers is that they leave it to their prospects to decide when to respond, instead of making them want to act *immediately*. But that's rubbish! The practiced marketer understands that the prospect must be stimulated to act NOW! And he carefully crafts his marketing communications so that the prospect wants to act immediately to acquire the benefits. Mastering just this single chapter will dramatically improve the response to all your marketing communications.

In *Chapter 8*, we take up the question of competitors . . . and how to gather what you need to know about them to blast them out of the water! There is no polite discussion in this book about competitors; just a frank realization that competitors are people who absorb the discretionary money of your prospects and that you must do what you can to stop that from happening. Here's where you learn how you can . . . and how to outmaneuver your competitors so *you* get the discretionary money instead.

Whether you know it or not, your prospects have anxieties about accepting your offer. That's why *Chapter 9* is devoted to helping you understand their anxieties and answer them . . . so you can get them to buy what you're selling faster!

Chapter 10 is of particular interest to service sellers, especially to professionals who rely on their resumé credentials to get clients. In this chapter, you learn how to stop talking about where you've been (items of no interest to your prospects) and start using your past successes to justify present prospect investment in you. In my experience, almost all professionals fail to understand how to transform their experience (features) into benefits that make prospects want to use their service. Prospects don't want to hire you because of where you've been but because of what you've done for others. Your achievements, not your resumé, are what's important. With the information in this chapter, you can't make this mistake and can give prospects what they need to stimulate their excitement about hiring you.

Chapter 11 takes up the crucial matter of motivating through your prospect's pain. Here you learn how to take your prospect's pain . . . and desire to be without it . . . and motivate him to take action. You also learn how to overcome your aversion to using this kind of marketing. This chapter reinforces a crucial tenet of this book: what *you* feel is unimportant. What matters is focusing on your prospect and his condition and thereby getting him to act.

Chapter 12 is a potpourri of cash copy ideas . . . it tells you the rules you must follow to write cash copy and is where you'll return for brief refreshers when you're in the midst of preparing any marketing document.

In *Chapter 13*, we examine crucial components of your marketing communications, including envelope messages, headlines, opening paragraphs, and more. You not only learn that to create a compelling marketing communication *each* part must work to stimulate the prospect, but you learn how to make each part work. This is a detailed look at cash copy components.

In its turn, *Chapter 14* focuses on different marketing formats you'll be using: flyers, brochures, proposals, ads, postcards, annual reports, media kits, free client newsletters, and catalogs. Here you learn how to use these formats to excite immediate prospect response. These are the kinds of formats you'll be using over and over to get your prospects to respond, so it follows this is a chapter you'll use again and again to make sure you do it right.

Chapter 15 takes up the matter of the writing process, and gives you information you can use to become a stronger, more client-centered writer. Most adults find the writing process distasteful. If you expect to use it to generate more prospect and customer responses — and to generate them faster — *you* cannot. This chapter gives you what you need to know so you can write the strong, client-centered action-oriented prose cash copy requires.

Chapter 16 gives you copy lay-out and production tips. Here's the information you need (and resources for further reading) to put lay-out and design in the service of getting prospects to act quicker.

Because many people selling products and services don't really understand marketing and how to make it work for them, I've included crucial information on this subject in *Chapter 17*. Cash copy, you see, is a part of marketing; but to understand how to create cash copy without understanding how to use it seems futile to me. That's why I've included this information.

In *Chapter 18*, I take up the question of how to tinker with your copy and improve it as you gauge your marketing response. One of the clear messages of this book is that both marketing and cash copy are ongoing processes. This is not a business set in cement. It's organic, fluid. Here you find out how to keep your copy up-to-date and reusable.

Finally, *Chapter 19* takes up the question of how to find and work with a copywriting consultant. My objective in writing this book is obviously to help you write cash copy yourself. But I know that, for many valid reasons, you won't always be able to do this; you'll need assistance. This chapter tells you how to find the right consultant for you and how to work with him to get the best possible response to your marketing activity.

How To Get Your Money's Worth
From This Resource

CASH COPY is not a book to be lightly read and shelved. It is a book to be used
. . . each time you go back to create — or update — *any* of your marketing
documents. While a first reading will undoubtedly change your perspective on
marketing and improve your ability to produce cash copy, you can't get full
benefit from this resource by only one reading. That's why you should keep this
book close at hand and refer to it often as you produce your own cash copy.

To get the most from this book, let me give you some candid advice:

- Understand that my job is not to mince words with you. My job is to tell
  you, in the most direct language possible, what works and what doesn't
  work in producing cash copy. Most readers like this direct approach;
  some find it abrasive. If you're one of the latter, let me tell you something
  very important. Right now, very likely over 98% of the money you invest
  in your marketing is being wasted, because your prospects throw away
  what you give them and don't bother to respond to it. If this is acceptable
  to you, don't even bother to consult this book. You're beyond help.

But if you don't like the fact that so much of your money is continually wasted,
then pay close attention. Consider the fact that your marketplace, like all
marketplaces, is jaded and uncaring. It has an enormous capacity to ignore you
and whatever you attempt to sell it . . . even when what you're selling is
manifestly in its own best interest.

It's because I want you to overcome this difficulty . . . and get your prospects
to buy sooner and your clients to buy again faster that I've approached this
important topic in my characteristically relentless and hard-hitting fashion. You
may not like the insistent tone of this book. But I can assure you, you'll like even
less having 98 or 99 people (or more) out of 100 throw your marketing materials
away without bothering to read them, much less respond.

I know how hard it is to capture the attention of the overfed, slothful, sluggish,
spoiled, capricious, whimsical and demanding American public and get them to
buy. It isn't easy, but it *is* possible . . . if you follow the suggestions I lay out in
this book.

- You may find this book occasionally less than easy going. Yes, the truth is this is a book that makes you work! In this sense, it's an apt representation of the success process itself. For most people success isn't easy to achieve, either; they aren't overnight sensations. Success takes constant application and continuing oversight. I'm not a member of the "Get Rich Quick" School of American how-to writers, and I wish that lazy and facile critics (who seem to me incapable of making the distinction) would learn the difference between those of us offering seasoned advice on how to get ahead and the charlatans who make advancement sound like a breezy interval between martinis.

It isn't.

CASH COPY tells you what to do . . . but you've got to be the one to do it. You may not like knowing how much there is to do . . . and how assiduously you must approach the task of selling your products and services. For all I know, you may be a secret flatworm, one of those people who talks a good game about wanting to be successful, but can never quite get it together to do what it takes to succeed. If so, you're hardly going to find this book to your taste.

As I see it, as I've seen it for a decade now, my job is to tell you precisely what you need to do, give you precisely what you need to do it, and provide the details on precisely how to do it to achieve your objectives. Your job is to get out there and do it. Any other approach to this subject just doesn't make sense.

- Finally, don't let the masculine pronoun used in this book affront you. This book is an extended conversation between you and me, whether you are a man or a woman. I've used the masculine pronoun in most, but not all, places, because this still constitutes common usage. Don't make a big deal out of what is nothing more than a grammatical convention. My objective is to help you, whoever you are. Don't grumble about the insignificant things, when there is so much of very real value at your fingertips.

A Few Words About Who I Am And My Role In Your Life

As you will see as you work your way through this resource, I am not the standard how-to author, nor do I approach my work in the usual way. This infuriates many people — be they critics, reviewers, marketers or peers — who have set ideas about how things should be done. I have only one idea: to help you sell more of your products or services faster, in this instance by assisting you to create and use client-centered cash copy.

Established rules and canons of behavior are not important to me. Selling products and services is. This kind of focused attitude galls certain people who have come to the preposterous conclusion that there are set ways to sell things and that we marketers should adhere to them. Such a view, of course, is not only narrow and unhelpful; it's absurd.

I am a marketer, and this is a marketer's book, focused on one thing only: doing what it takes to motivate people to respond to offers and acquire products and services. Nothing else matters. Everything else is certainly beside the point, and probably pompous, too.

Some people dislike this attitude. They focus on how things are done . . . not the end results; on the process, not the objective. To give just one illustration, there are people who regard a book as a sacred thing and wish to keep it an arm's length, or more, from the taint of commercialism. Books and marketing are antithetical, they say.

Not to a marketer, they aren't. A book, in itself, is an opportunity to connect with new prospects and transform them into buyers. It is simply another way of connecting with people and motivating them to act.

The obstructionists in the first category condemn innovations like the Sure-Fire Business Success Catalog appearing in the back of this book. It's book anathema! It's unheard of! It's never been done before! What foolishness.

The marketer, as you will come to learn from this book if you don't know it already, always focuses on the main objective: how to connect with people and motivate them to act. No means that help achieve this objective are wrong; any means that foster it are right. Thus, your choice as you read this book — and work with me — is plain: either adhere, to your cost and that of your prospects, to senseless conventions, or learn to use any means available to connect you with your prospect and motivate him to act.

I warn you: as you move ever closer to becoming the consummate marketer (with the dazzling results this ensures), you will arouse envy, resentment and mindless criticism. But consider the ringing advice from England's rule-breaking King Edward VII: "They say. So say they. Let them say." Where did he put these words of wisdom? Why, he had them carved into the woodwork of the lovenest he built for his mistress Lily Langtry. You, too, must learn to consider the petty, carping, picayune source of such criticism — and ignore it. Get on with the real business of mastering marketing and connecting with the maximum number of your prospects and past buyers, motivating them all to buy as quickly as possible.

If this is what you want to achieve, you've come to the right place. And what is more, I can help you not just here, but throughout your marketing career. For I invite you to enter into a relationship with me, just as I invite all my get-ahead friends and readers.

Unlike other resource specialists, my telephone number — (617) 547-6372 — is printed in my books and in the Sure-Fire Business Success columns that run these days in about 100 publications and electronic data bases. While yet another innovation the obstructionists bemoan, this method now connects me to over 1,500,000 people monthly in several countries. Unlike authorities who place a barrier between you and them, I do not. I answer my own telephone and am ready to help you . . . if you have done what you can do to help yourself.

But if you haven't read the book . . . haven't attempted to solve your problem yourself . . . and are just looking for an easy out, don't expect me to be particularly sympathetic, much less agreeable. I am not a magic pill; I am and wish to be a valued member of your cash copy team, helping you master the skills and do what is necessary to get more people to buy what you're selling faster! Even to the extent of being your cash copy consultant, if that is what you want.

If you didn't get this book directly from me, you have to take the initiative to get in touch. There's a good reason for doing so: quarterly, I publish my Sure-Fire Business Success Catalog with recommendations on the best materials I've found to build profitable businesses and efficient non-profit organizations. A copy is in the back of this book, and if you'd like to keep getting it, let me know. It's free.

A Few Final Words

When you've finished this book, if you've followed the directions, you'll be ready to write cash copy and create the kinds of marketing communications that get your prospects to respond faster and your clients to buy again sooner. I guarantee it.

Doing so is for your own good, of course; it should deeply irritate you that so many of your marketing dollars . . . dollars that are so precious and could be used so profitably elsewhere . . . are regularly wasted. This kind of waste infuriates me. And it should cheer you up no end that you can stop this maddening process and get a much better return on your investment.

But even more than your own benefit, you should be glad for the benefit cash copy will help you make in the lives of your prospects. For with it, more and more of these prospects will buy what you're selling . . . and lead better lives as a direct result. All because you took the time and trouble to learn what it takes to write copy that focuses on them and gets them to respond NOW!

After you've had the opportunity to study this book and not only to write but to use your new cash copy, I'd like to hear how you're doing. And if you're making refinements on these methods, I'd love to hear about them. After all, I have much to learn, too. And there is no one I'd rather learn it from than you, my new friend and fellow cash copy practitioner.

Chapter 1

Twenty-One Egregious Copy Errors —
And Why You Make Them

You are going to be writing marketing documents — flyers, brochures, cover letters, cards, media kits, response coupons — and all the rest — for as long as you're in business. Even if yours is a micro-business, the tiniest around, you'll still spend thousands of dollars producing these documents.

Why?

You do it because you think you have to. Because everyone else does it. Because you expect it of yourself. Because your prospects expect it of you. Because it's the done thing, and you feel somehow inferior if you don't have what everybody else has. Without them, you reckon you're not *really* in business.

STOP!

The *only* reason for having marketing literature, literature that talks about your company, your products and services, is to sell those products and services. To get a prospect to connect with you (so you can do what's necessary to sell him what you've got), to get a prospect to buy what you're selling, or to get a customer to buy again.

There's no other reason for creating marketing materials. NONE. So drop any foolish notions that there are other reasons: "reasons" like prestige, or showing the flag, or keeping up with the professional Joneses. These aren't reasons for creating marketing materials. They are the expensive evidence of overweening human pride and as such have no place in running a profitable business.

From now on, from this moment, you're in the business of selling products and services, pure and simple. And hence in the business of producing marketing materials that'll help you reach this objective. DO YOU UNDERSTAND THIS?

To reach this objective, day in, day out. To make sure you never backslide. To succeed in reaching it, you've got to understand how to create cash copy, copy that sells. And this means understanding what is currently blocking you from writing this copy, so that, when you have to write this copy again (as you most certainly will), you'll do what it takes to write the only kind of copy that matters: copy that sells your product or service. Hence this list of twenty-one egregious mistakes you are currently making in your marketing documents.

BEWARE!

This list isn't exhaustive. There are other errors. Like these, however, they are dealt with in this guide. But I guarantee you this: if you stop making *these* mistakes, you'll notice an immediate improvement in prospect responsiveness to what you're distributing — and an increase in your sales, too. Which is, I repeat, the *only* reason you're doing all this in the first place.

Egregious Error #1. Your Copy Focuses On Yourself, Not The Prospect

Your selfishness is what kills most of your marketing copy and the marketing documents that that copy is in.

"But how can you possibly say that?", you wail. "I'm a good person. A decent person. The kind of person mothers love and dogs wag their tails for. How can you call my copy selfish?"

Easily, thank you.

More than 90% of the marketing documents I review are about the seller rather than the buyer. By this I mean that they lead with the seller and what he is selling; that they talk about the seller and what he is offering. That they inundate the prospect with information about who the seller is, what the seller is doing, why the seller is doing it, how long the seller has been doing it, the extent to which the seller is doing it, and on and on. One selfish fact piled high upon another. Boring us to death with their irrelevance. While simultaneously estranging us with their breathtaking arrogance and condescension.

Who cares about the seller?

Isn't the answer obvious? The seller cares about the seller.

The seller thinks the seller is swell.

The seller thinks that what the seller is doing is important and worthwhile.

The seller thinks that the prospect would be better off if he, the prospect, bought what the seller is selling.

But all this — every worthy thought about the seller, by the seller, for the advantage of the seller — is irrelevant. And you had best discard such thoughts now. Because this is not a book about sellers. It is a book about buyers. It is a book about the only people who can make you rich — your prospects. Not about that no doubt inestimable person who will get rich if you learn these lessons — that's to say, you.

I'll drive home this point throughout this guide, because it's a point that's daily overlooked by well-meaning marketers who think themselves good and kindly people. Perhaps they are. But as the merest glance at their marketing documents can attest (and I assure you you shall have that glance), their marketing materials mark them as consummately selfish. They write selfish copy about themselves and wonder why the needy of the world fail to respond. *Noblesse* has *obliged* — but nothing has happened except that that aristocrat is measurably poorer by the attempt, and the rest of us more justly cynical.

The first thing that a prospect should see when reviewing a piece of your marketing literature — be it a garden-variety business card or a four-color annual report — is himself, something about himself, something of use to himself, something that makes him feel good about his favorite subject — himself. *Not something about you.*

You will succeed in reaching your sales objectives, succeed in selling more of your products and services, to the extent that the prospect feels you exist for him, that you can help him, that you care for nothing so much as for him. The extent to which you succeed in achieving this objective is the extent to which you will have the lifestyle, with all its bounteous prizes, that you desire. Thus, the outside of your envelope should be about the prospect — not about you. Not about your product. Or your service.

The headline that opens your material should be about the prospect and what he wishes to achieve.

The salutation should speak to the prospect.

The opening line of anything you write should address the prospect directly, his hopes, fears, wants, aspirations and desires.

The body copy should pile on benefit after benefit of direct, compelling interest to the prospect.

The offer should be something that interests the prospect and motivates him to act NOW!

Get this point!

In short, never again — NO, NEVER AGAIN — must you ever focus on yourself. Your interests. Your company. Your products. Your services. From this moment on, *stop being selfish.*

Because selfishness is nothing more than a soma pill (remember your *Brave New World*) that gives you, just for a moment, a deeply false feeling of well being and self-contentedness. But client-centered marketing copy gets you daily reinforcement that others, a world of others, feel you are special. For who is more special to you than the person who exists to lavish care on you?

Take these lines of character Marguerite Blakeney from *The Scarlet Pimpernel* and apply them to marketing. "Sir Percy (her husband) seemed to worship me with a curious intensity of concentrated passion, which went straight to my heart. I had never loved any one before . . . so I naturally thought it was not in my nature to love. But it has always seemed to me that it *must* be *heavenly* to be loved blindly, passionately, wholly . . . worshipped, in fact. . . . And I was ready to respond."

As your prospects must be ready to respond to your passionate, intense worship of them. For after all, who in their lives is there to take such an interest in their desires, their foibles, their anxieties and their aspirations — as you! And what is mere money by comparison with this kind of adoration, which they crave, and cannot get elsewhere?

If nothing else, let this book dispel your corporate selfishness and smite it hard. Grievously hard. So you will move into the exalted sphere of double self-realization: for insofar as you succeed in helping your prospects realize their wishes, you will succeed in realizing yours.

Egregious Error #2. You Think Your Prospects Are As Interested In What You're Selling As You Are.

This is the error of projection, and it leads to a very false deduction.

Here is the dreadful business syllogism.

1) The product or service you are selling is important to the prospect.

2) You are interested in your product or service.

3) It follows that your prospect must be interested in your product or service.

Admit it, this is how you feel, isn't it?

If so, you are quite, quite mistaken.

Your prospects are not interested in your products or services. They are interested only in themselves, in their (all too often) petty aspirations, flawed desires, crack-brained anxieties and foolish fears. Thus it is to these — not the manifest wonders of your product or service — that you must appeal.

No one will ever be as interested in what you are selling as you are, particularly if you are the inventor of said wonder. Expect no one to be as interested as you are.

Take pleasure from the fact that you are the genius who has conceived such a marvel. But take your pleasure quietly, individually. Or gather clandestinely with other such wonder workers to beat the collective drums of hubris for your unrivalled, unbelievable, astonishing and surpassing marvelous creation.

Then go back to the real business of business: focusing on the wants, needs and aspirations of the severely flawed people who are the only people who can provide you with the lifestyle you desire: your prospects.

Of all that relates to you, they are right to sing out, "So what!"

All that has no immediate benefit for them, they are right to dismiss.

Every sentence that deals with you and not with them, they are right to despise and ignore.

They have only one constant question. And it is a question that you must answer every day, simply, candidly, thoroughly, persuasively: "What's in it for me, bub?"

Thus, all the fine rhetoric that you have labored to perfect. The rhetoric that rolls so grandly across the page about:

- the size of your company;
- the wealth of your company;
- the grandeur of your products and services;
- the importance of what you're offering, and
- the ways in which you are enriching the world thanks to what you're selling.

And all the rest of this nonsense is justly dismissed by the rightly doubtful prospect as entirely beside the point.

All that matters to this prospect.

All that ever matters.

Is just one thing, "What's in it for me, bub?"

What, indeed?

Do you know?

Do you care?

Will you take the time to say, directly, thoroughly, candidly, persuasively?

Or are you, like so many people purportedly in business, actually in the business of pleasing yourself? Of reassuring yourself, at the expense of your sales, that you are a clever person? A worthy person? A person the world should extol each day of your life and through immemorial cycles beyond?

YOUR PROSPECT WILL NEVER CARE AS MUCH ABOUT WHAT YOU ARE SELLING AS YOU DO.

Nor should he.

HE IS RIGHT TO ASK JUST ONE QUESTION OF YOU — AND ASK IT INSISTENTLY. AND HE IS RIGHT TO REJECT YOU — PEREMPTORILY — IF YOU CANNOT, IN AN INSTANT, ANSWER THIS QUESTION CREDIBLY, SOLIDLY, BELIEVABLY.

"What's in it for me, bub?"

But I'll wager you that now — right at this precise moment — you don't know the answer to this question. You cannot give a straightforward, simple, meaningful response. And thus your marketing copy shows your inability to answer this question. If you can't answer it, how can you — how possibly can you — think that anyone, any prospect, will ever think the answer you do give an adequate one? You poor self-deluding creature, you.

Egregious Error #3. You're Trying To Be Clever.

Every day I see the results of the thin, if febrile, imaginations of many marketers.

They think they are selling the bank by showing a boy on a skateboard gyrating outside an automatic teller machine. (BayBanks).

They think they are selling their training course by talking about golf and picturing a golf ball going into a hole. (Dale Carnegie Training.)

They think they are selling God knows what by showing a man with a button on his forehead saying "Video Arts" staring out at us grave and severe. (Video Arts.)

And every marketer, in every one of these marketing documents, thinks he's being clever. Is certain, dead certain, that he's just produced the most clever piece of marketing ever conceived. Why? Because it's different. Because it gets the attention of the reader. Because that reader laughs. Because that reader doesn't simply pass by oblivious to the important creative statement at his fingertips.

But does this marketing work?

Do people take action — buy something — as a result of seeing it?

Does the creator care?

He has the pleasing certainty that he has been — is seen to be — clever.

And if this isn't enough, well, the client will market again — in other ways — in order to achieve his (the client's) objectives.

You see, rather than create believable, client-centered benefits for his products and services, the "clever" creator of such marketing materials relies on his deep pockets (or, more often, his client's) to create familiarity. Such a person bets that familiarity is more important than real prospect benefits and an immediate incentive for action.

THIS IS MARKETING MADNESS.

Now hear this: the aim of your marketing materials is not to be clever. Is not to dazzle your prospects. Is not to convince them that you are the brightest little boy or girl on the block. Even if you are. All that — for marketing purposes — is irrelevant.

The only purpose for marketing.

The only purpose for your marketing materials.

The only point at all of any kind of marketing — is

SELLING YOUR PRODUCT OR SERVICE.

Nothing else matters.

Certainly not being clever.

Instead of cleverness, I appeal to you to consider the following:

- Have you — in whatever marketing materials you are producing — stressed prospect benefit after prospect benefit?
- Does the prospect feel, truly feel, that you are on his side, that you understand his problem? That you can help him?
- Have you made it easy for the prospect to take action — NOW! — to solve his problem?

Or have you filled up the screen with a gyrating teenager on a skateboard? (Of course, because this marketing message is doomed to fail — since it provides no discernible benefit to the prospect and no reason to do anything except laugh — it necessarily begets more gyrating teenagers on more senseless skateboards.)

Or a golf ball rolling through the picture that has no purpose there whatsoever? (Really, I ask you: what connection does a golf ball have with a Dale Carnegie course?)

Or used an idiot wearing a button on his forehead for no conceivable purpose except to make the rest us feel superior because we don't look as odd and uncomfortable?

Such marketing is not about sales. It is about being clever. About being different. About taking up space and time. About a lack of understanding of marketing. About day after day of bored marketers writing flaccid copy on deadline for the undiscerning. And not for what marketing is all about.

Which is to say, ABOUT SALES.

SELLING IS NOT MERELY AN IMPORTANT PART OF MARKETING.

IT IS THE ONLY PART OF MARKETING.

The objective of *every* marketing document you produce — be it a radio ad or a postcard in a direct response deck — is to get:

- someone who knows you — your customer — to buy again. NOW!
- someone who's never bought from you before — your prospect — to give you money in exchange for your product or service. NOW!
- your prospect — and future customer — to take action to put

himself in touch with you, so that you can move the selling process to a successful close. NOW!

"Hear and obey", as the ancient Manchu emperors said.

Egregious Error #4. You're Trying To Educate Your Prospects.

If, on the one hand, your copy fails because you are trying to show your prospects how clever you are, it fails, on the other, because you are trying to educate them so they understand their need for you.

Let's be very clear about this.

Marketers are not in the education business.

They are in the selling business.

You may feel you are trying to make the world a better place. (I certainly do.) But what has that to do with sales?

Your objective in marketing is not to find a market and educate it to an understanding of what you can do for it. But to identify a market with screaming wants and needs — and the means to pay for satisfying them — and feast upon it enthusiastically like a cormorant upon a freshly-caught fish.

Over and over again well meaning entrepreneurs ask me about what they should do to educate a market. And as frequently, I tell them, with profound seriousness, "Don't bother."

They are hurt.

Chagrined.

Angered by my callousness and insensitivity.

For is not teaching a good thing? Is not an educator a munificent benefactor of the world?

No doubt.

But such an educator has nothing to do with marketing.

And I am only interested in meeting the wants and needs of my market — by selling to my prospects. Not in educating them up to a level where, then and only then, will they be ready for what I am selling.

The aim of all marketing is not to enlighten. Is not to teach. Is certainly not to dazzle your still benighted prospects with your astounding brilliance.

The aim of marketing is to sell.

It is to understand what your prospects — in all their often ridiculous moods and with all their often hilarious humors — wish to achieve. And then to let them know — in no uncertain terms — that that is precisely what you can do for them. Now. With speed. Certainty. Ease. In comfort. With their guaranteed happiness. Is this what you do?

You will, reader, you will. Or you will not be marketing for long.

Egregious Error #5. You Don't Have A Major Client-Centered Message That You Hammer Home Again And Again.

In school we were all taught by Miss (never "Ms.") Grinch about the sin of written redundancy. She was, of course, our harridan of an English teacher, and, above all our instructors, remains a constant presence deep within us, a correctional stick ever ready to rap over our offending knuckles if we trifle with her draconian regulations.

Her legacy? An abiding fear of immediate perdition for those of us who don't begin each new paragraph with an original thought, something quite different from the paragraph above. To Miss Grinch, creativity and originality were infinitely more important than hard-hitting persuasiveness. And devil take the creature who hit the same point over and over and over again — from every conceivable angle — in a determined attempt to move his reader to do something.

But that's exactly what we must do.

Move someone to do something — a certain quite specific something that we inspire and command.

Someone who is besieged with other marketing offers. Up to 7,500 a week, if you live in a major metropolitan area. If our special someone were to do nothing more than pay attention to these messages, that person would do nothing more, period.

Someone who is half-distracted (if not worse) at the time our marketing message comes to his attention. Who is doing something else. Thinking about something else. Or just so comfortable that the thought of doing anything else now is anathema.

Someone who has lots of other responsibilities and calls upon his resources. Who might well admit that what we are talking about, offering, is just what he needs. But who knows that getting this will mean giving up something else. Even if he doesn't yet know what that something else is.

To get this person to take action NOW means:

- hitting the prospect's self-interest;
- piling prospect benefit on prospect benefit to create a rich layer cake of desirabilities;
- fostering a sense of urgency — of acute need — to take action NOW;
- getting the prospect to feel not only what he'll get by taking action but what he'll lose by failing to do so.

By orchestrating, in short, a client-centered crescendo that leaves our hitherto besieged prospect, overwhelmed by other marketing messages, fearful of taking action, uninterested in taking action now, no choice — no choice whatsoever — but to act NOW. Or face unbearable regret and gnawing discontent that he failed to do so.

By acting now our prospect gets the benefit that the magic marketing words promise:

- youthfulness
- friends
- security
- money
- power
- luxury
- prestige
- an end to a host of fearsome anxieties.

These, and all the rest of such profoundly human motivators. For these motivators are our certain enchanters.

But if you need any other reason for hitting your single point hard and hitting it again and again and again, consider this. Though Miss Grinch writes a graceful (if uninspired) essay, her salary was never more than $17,000 a year. Now in retirement, she finds her pension increasingly sparse while the unarguable delights of a perfectly turned sentence do sometimes pall. I've heard on good authority that she's been heard to regret she never mastered the essentials of copywriting. You'll find this book (shockingly corrosive to her life's work though it is) tucked under her virginal pillow. Though she'd sooner die than let her friends know of this septuagenarian sedition.

Egregious Error #6. You're Trying To Be "Professional".

I suspect, gentle reader, that you are an advocate of Professional Behavior as a means of getting ahead. That you give considerable thought to which socks give you the best chance of achieving success. Which look. Which mode of behavior. Even, which vegetables you should eat — and how. For I am appalled to discover that John Malloy, the jumped-up haberdasher who brought you *Dress For Success,* has put out a sequential tome called *Eat For Success.* I am pleased to tell you it has not done very well, readers apparently not glimpsing the careerist possibilities in a properly consumed zucchini or Brussells sprout that are so obvious to them in wearing a red tie with a power blue suit.

In the face of so much idiocy, I feel compelled to weigh in with some constructive thinking.

What matters in marketing is relentlessly focusing on your prospect — in each and every way. Your own professional image should always be secondary to your ability to convince your prospect that you place his welfare first; that you can deliver benefit after benefit he'll find meaningful and that persuade him to buy what you're selling.

Thus, nothing matters that is not directly related to your prospect.

The prospect does not care about the logo that you spent weeks creating and which gave you several fitful nights. The prospect cares only about what you can do for him, what compelling benefits you can offer.

The prospect does not care about the color of your stationery and the reasons which impelled you to select a silky gray over an antique ivory laid. The prospect cares only about what you can do for him, what compelling benefits you can offer.

The prospect does not care about the rotund inanities that spew forth without end from corporations. Where "the featured speaker is a pioneer and leader". Where "tax changes will be discussed." Where "there's a challenging opportunity available." (All quotes from a cover letter in front of me produced by a leading Saint Louis financial planning firm.)

Lines like this — and the millions of others that are pushed forth daily into a justly uncaring world — are bloated and gaseous. They say nothing. To no one. About anything.

They are just words. They are not the magic words of marketing that:

- are directed to a real person about something that that real person is interested in doing, achieving, having.
- excite this person (or frighten him) so that he takes action — NOW — to get the promised benefit.

No, they are just words. And nothing more. And for the sake of these paltry, pointless words forests groan and die. No wonder I have days when, in a rage, I dance the demented dance of the dervish, certain that an evil sprite is at the lever of our universe, spitting out a mean spirited laugh as he savors our inanity.

Thus, remember this:

- If what you write doesn't speak directly to the prospect and his want or need, what you have written is the antithesis of marketing.
- If what you write doesn't give specific reason after specific reason for the prospect to take action NOW, what you have written is the antithesis of marketing.
- If what you write is dull and ponderous, however true, and focuses on you and not on your prospect and his need, what you have written is the antithesis of marketing.
- If what you write does not give your prospect an immediate incentive for action, then what you have written is the antithesis of marketing.

There can be no justification for writing marketing documents — however "professional" they appear to you, seemingly cogent in their dull pomposity — that fail to excite the prospect with what you can do for him and fail to tell him what he should do NOW to get the benefit you can deliver.

Egregious Error #7. You Haven't Frightened Your Prospect.

Those who have graduated from Professional University, with its curious programs so deleterious to successful marketing, like to write bland, soothing, vapid, and uninspired prose. They think these hallmarks of the uncaring mark them as the consummate professional, eminently worth heeding because they are above the wearing fray of daily life. "Heed me," they seem to say, "because I am above the mess that you're in. My hands are quite clean and will stay that way. Because I'm a professional."

Reader, tell me: why have millions of people adopted this ridiculous code of behavior? And why do they think it will help them sell anything to anyone?

Professionals who operate in this cold-blooded and altogether detached fashion seem to believe that people make their decisions in an entirely rational and objective fashion. "I have only to state the truth about myself as I understand it— free from anything as demeaning as sordid supporting evidence — and surely, because of who I am, my education, my standing, and, if truth be known, my noble soul, I must get the prospect's account." So they reckon.

Nothing, of course, could be further from the truth.

Just as we humans love people who are manifestly inappropriate for us by any rational deduction (how else can we account for the staggering numbers of perfectly obvious mismatches that we all see?), so we make our decisions in ways that are hardly rational.

Which means we must assess the other motivators that are available to us. Which is, of course, where fear comes in.

In the marketing business, we have known for a good long while that fear is among our most potent prospect motivators. Particularly fear of loss. In case you are doubtful consider this.

In the middle of the night, an insurance salesperson calls to let you know that you can get a great deal on fire insurance — the best deal ever. If only you'll act before 6 a.m. Your reaction? Unprintable in a respectable publication like this.

But say at the same unnatural hour, a horror-stricken voice screams, "Quick! Your house is on fire!" You do act, do you not? Not only with promptness but with gratitude.

Which is why you must motivate your prospects through fear in general, and fear of loss in particular.

Now I admit the creators of many of the marketing documents I review seem to have heard this truth about using fear, for I see telltale signs of this knowledge. But that's just the point: it's only telltale.

Take this headline in a recent cover letter I received from a brokerage firm. "Tax Laws Have Changed Again Your Financial Plan Must Adapt." (*sic*) That line was followed by this: "Why Pay Money To The I.R.S. Which You Are Allowed To Keep?"

Now the hint of loss is there. But that's the point. It's just a hint.

As will become clearer and more compelling as the astonishing panorama of this book unfolds, to truly frighten people, the fear you use must be:

- specific
- immediate
- palpable
- grounded in reality
- sustained by credible specialists, and
- reinforced, time and again.

On this basis, the fear suggested by the two headlines above is feeble indeed, and so unpersuasive.

Graduates of Professional University, where all is rationality and calm discussion, do not like looking into the Pandora's box of humanity. They prefer things hygienic and sanitized — and hence unreal.

For marketing to work, you must touch the anxious nerves (as well as excite the deepest hopes and wants) of real people. People who are complicated, irrational, breathtakingly stupid, profoundly inspirational, fascinatingly unpredictable and altogether infuriating. The game is to get these people to send you a check. To contact you faster. To buy again sooner. Touching them and compelling them to act is what you must do.

This means leaving the detached unreality of Professional University and its languid lingo behind. For it is crippling you, preventing you from reaching out, touching, and moving the people who need you.

You must use every dark fear of every prospect as a lever to get that person to take action and connect with you — so that you can remove the cause for the fear and make that person's life better.

It is not enough to stand back and spout orotund professional clichés. Instead of saying something as vapid as "Tax Laws Have Changed Again. Your Financial Plan Must Adapt", tell your prospects:

- which laws have changed;
- in what ways the laws have changed;
- how their specific interests will be specifically threatened;
- what experts say will happen to them because of these changes;
- when they must act;
- what happens if they don't act.

Get the idea?

Pontius Pilate was a deeply rational and cultivated man, an eminent alumnus of the Professional University of his day. He looked out upon the Judean mob with disdain and disgust. Were these people? And were they about to crucify their Messiah. So be it. "I wash my hands of this," he said in what stands as the motto of every detached marketer in history.

But you, you who wish to sell to your prospect. You who want to improve their lives — and so help yourself improve yours, *you* cannot afford to be seen as detached and merely professional.

You need to use fear to excite anxiety. So that with this anxiety you can compel prospect action. For it is only when the prospect acts that you can do what is necesssary to improve his life.

For that is precisely what you want to do.

For some time to come you may feel queasy about using fear in this way. You may feel it somehow beneath you, beneath the uplifting standards you've set for yourself as the accomplished professional. Well, listen to this: GET OVER THIS DEBILITATING AND INANE POINT OF VIEW.

Your job is to sell. And so improve your prospects' lives.

If you cannot move them, you cannot sell. And if it takes the lever of fear and prospect anxiety to move them, why that is what you must use.

But remember this. When at last all the evil in the world had flown out of Pandora's box to frighten and unnerve her and everyone else, there remained one last thing behind. That, of course, was Hope.

And that hope is now represented by your product or service. For it is with this product or service that your prospect will take dead aim at reaching his objective and combatting his enervating fears.

For this hope and the product or service that embodies it, your prospect will thank you. And be truly grateful. As well he should be, for you are saving him from all the fears that you have so aptly rendered for him. You wily fox, you. For remember, without fear, hope is meaningless and without hope people do not buy.

Egregious Error #8. You Drone On About Product And Service Features, When All The Prospect Wants To Know About Is The Benefits He Gets By Using It.

Let's start with definitions. A feature is a characteristic of a thing. Size, color, weight, speed, availability, special conditions of use — all these are features. Taken all in all, features completely describe any individual product or service. Features pertain to the product or service. They are all about the thing — or service — itself and, by definition, have nothing to do with the specific person for whom the product or service is intended.

Which, of course, is just their problem.

And is why the consummate marketer is far more interested in prospect benefits — that is advantages or helpful results — than in product or service features. For it is benefits that sell, not features.

Now, if you're like most of the people who come to me in a consulting capacity, people who want to sell more of their products and services, you'll see this statement, confirm its significance, and assure me that you do understand and will abide by it.

But they don't.

And you won't either.

That's because it is easy to write down the features of what you're selling. And hard to translate these features into prospect benefits.

Still, it astonishes me even now to think how few marketers actually know the benefits to their prospects of what they are selling.

Which is why most marketing documents open with features — facts about the product or service.

Which is precisely what I want you never, never, never to do.

LEAD WITH BENEFITS. FOLLOW WITH FEATURES.

Presenting a feature is like saying "me."

Stressing a benefit is like saying "you."

You must keep in mind that client-centered marketing, and the cash copy that expresses this marketing, is all "You Marketing" — you the prospect, your interests, your wishes, your fears, your aspirations, — you, you, you!!!

In all honesty, do you feel the prospect is more interested in hearing about you — or about himself? Put this way, it's obvious, isn't it? Why, then, do companies insist on sending marketing letters that begin like this:

"ABC is a systems engineering and systems management firm, and has the ability to provide subcontracting services in several disciplines. These include: systems integration, systems development. . . ."

This opening says, as clearly as it can, that the writer:

- is more concerned about himself than his prospect;
- is more interested in being seen as a professional than in getting the prospect's work done;
- is wedded to jargon and the stale, meaningless language which stamps him as a graduate of Professional University;
- knows nothing whatsoever about the problems of the individual prospect and hasn't bothered to find out, and
- has no idea what's bothering the prospect and what the prospect would like to accomplish.

In short, a disastrous, futile, but textbook perfect example of what a graduate of Professional University considers accomplished marketing copy.

YOU MUST CONSIDER SUCH COPY THE PROFESSIONAL EQUIVA-LENT OF THE BUBONIC PLAGUE. EARNESTLY AVOID IT.

Here is how a Cash Copy Letter should open:

> Immediate benefit to you for letting me help you.

Attributed testimonial from someone like you who has successfully benefitted by using my services.

Dear you,

Here's a terrible problem you are facing.
Here's a raging desire you want to achieve.
Here's a want you are obsessed about.

Here, in short, is something very definitely about you. You. You.

THIS IS HOW CASH COPY MARKETING DOCUMENTS OPEN.

And how they continue. For "you" is the most important word that appears in any marketing document and the most important concept underlying any marketing document.

Yet, in the example quoted above, an example being used by a Maryland computer company, this key word doesn't appear. Instead, it's all "me, me, me, me". This might be a good warm up for a singer, but is a useless beginning to a piece of client-centered marketing copy.

Another way of looking at the same problem, another way of starting your marketing copy is this:

> Immediate benefit to you for taking action NOW.
> Benefit you get by connecting with me today.

Testimonial by someone like you who got a benefit you want by letting me help him.

Dear you,

Major, *specific* benefit to you.

Ways in which you'd be better off if you had this specific benefit. See the difference?

"ABC is a sytems engineering and systems management firm . . . " (a selfish line) can never pack the wallop and the client-centered punch of even the weakest "you" line. Because when you start using "you", the chances are much, much better that you'll use more benefits. And as you use more benefits that are significant to the prospect, that prospect must get interested and — the benefits being sufficiently compelling — take action.

Egregious Error #9. You Write in Jargon That Makes It Difficult For Your Prospect To Understand You.

Jargon means language understood by a select group. As such, by definition, jargon cannot be understood by everyone. Therefore, to write jargon is damnably foolish and self-defeating.

If you want to write cash copy, copy that will sell your products and services, your objective should be to write the cleanest, clearest, crispest copy possible. Nothing — not even jargon that seems common in an industry — must stand between you and your prospects. Nothing.

You must not ask, and cannot depend on, the prospect to take even an extra split second to attempt to understand your meaning. The prospect must know at once — immediately — what you've got for him.

But, you'll say, doesn't jargon enable people to do this? No, it most certainly does not.

To begin with, jargon often changes quickly. That means it's difficult to keep current on what words actually mean. They are not common words, not words ordinarily used, and as such even specialists in a field often have to consider what such a word actually means. Such consideration deflects attention from what the marketer is trying to accomplish: a sale. When the prospect is focusing on the word and its meaning, he cannot focus on your principal desire, to solve his problem by selling your product or service.

Then, too, many people — whatever they say to the contrary — never actually know what the jargon really means. Try asking people to define some jargon phrase of the moment. The results would be hilarious, if they weren't so pathetic. Most, not surprisingly, cannot provide a definition. Jargon is designed by the *cognoscenti* to include themselves, and exclude others. They use jargon like a fence, to keep the right people in, and the wrong people out. This is not what the marketer wants to do: he wants to sell his solution, be it product or service, to whoever has the problem, whether that individual understands the prevailing jargon, or not.

Finally, jargon is weak language, overfed and ponderous. Here's a jargon phrase right in front of me: "validated training." No doubt someone knows what it means, but this phrase is dull, pompous, condescending, impenetrable. Good marketing language is sleek, easy to understand, discernible in an instant, packed with prospect benefit, open to all who have the problem your product or service can solve.

Can you really afford to kill your marketing with jargon?

I think not.

Make it your objective to:

- talk to a specific person who has the problem your product or service can solve;
- tell him, candidly, directly, honestly, specifically what you can do for him;
- speak to him in words and phrases that he immediately understands, that he doesn't have to think about, certainly that are not beyond him.

You cannot lose bright and knowing people by speaking to them about benefits in words they easily understand. But you most assuredly will affront, insult and lose other prospects who have the same problems and can buy the same solutions if you talk to them in ways they must ponder about and wade through.

SO STOP DOING IT.

Egregious Error #10. Your Copy Is Deadly Dull.

I tell my clients and students that the best marketing copy should read like the most compelling of feature stories. Only with this difference. In such a story, you know you are reading about someone else. If you want to be in that story, you have to project yourself into it. But in marketing copy, you don't have to project — it's already about you.

The best marketing copy is an exciting dialogue (even if it takes place on a single piece of paper) between two people — and only two people — you, the seller, and the single prospect/buyer who is reading what you have to say about him, his problem, and how you will solve it.

This copy says: you've got a problem. This problem might be costly, frustrating, sad, bewildering, draining. But because it is your problem you, my worthy prospect, are interested in it, absorbed by it, fixated on solving it.

Until now not only have you found no one able to help solve this problem. But you have found no one as interested in it as you are.

NOW YOU HAVE.

I'm interested, knowledgeable, available — and as excited by the problem and its solution as you are.

Let's work together.

What a compelling approach to the prospect!

Consider that this poor prospect has bored everyone he knows with his problem. No one that he knows — not his working colleagues, his family, his increasingly exasperated friends — has the slightest conceivable interest left. *But the problem remains.*

Now, you enter the picture. Fresh, alert, breathing hope and possibilities, supported by telling facts and evidence of success, quite at the ready, willing to go to work — immediately — not merely to solve the prospect's problem (Benefit #1) but to take an interest in the prospect (the equally as important Benefit #2).

Why does this interest matter so much? Because we live in the most alienated age in the history of this planet. There are billions of eager self-seeking people and only a minuscule number of problem solvers to tend to the bulging majority. To buy a product or service that solves a problem is indeed a good thing. So many things we buy these day, don't. (As I write this, I'm looking at the windows in my office which only yesterday I paid to have cleaned, yet today give plain evidence of how inadequate the worker faced the task. It's glaring evidence that to buy is not always to solve.)

But to get simultaneously a person who clearly cares about us, who is knowledgeable about the situation we're in and who not only can get us out, but enthusiastically wants to help us solve the problem — why, man, this is the very definition of blessing. And beside such a blessing, what matters the cost? For we have acquired not merely a solution, but a willing ear and an interested friend. And isn't this just what we want?

Cash copy is neither dull nor stiff nor brittle. It is not the congealed language of "per yours of the 9th", "Please find enclosed." and "I will be contacting your office by telephone to arrange a meeting." And a million other wet-blanket phrases that say, "I am a business. You are a prospect. I want to sell you something. If you know what's good for you, you'll buy this something, because I said so."

No, no, no!

The prospect, *each* prospect, is the Damsel in Distress. This winsome demoiselle needs you, her White Knight, to deliver what she really cares about:

- more money
- more widgets each hour
- a thinner body
- a more obedient pet.

In short, some comparative advantage to the situation she is now in.

Of course, at some level, prospects know that what they want may actually be dull, prosaic, insipid, pedestrian. But they don't want *you* — their deliverer — to give evidence of this. They want you to be enthusiastic about what they want, not just getting it for them, but getting it in a way that excites the interest of the prospect.

Enthusiasm, you see, is a natural ingredient of successful marketing. Even a single page of copy must make the prospect feel as if:

- you are there;
- your eyes are fixed on his;
- your total concentration is on him, his problem, his desire;
- nothing matters so much as helping this single prospect — this one person — achieve his objective and reach his goal;
- you are knowledgeable, not just about the technical considerations of solving the problems, but the psychic and social situation of the prospect, for this is a real person in need of a real person's technical assistance. Yes but more than that, a real person's sustained interest and concern.

Remember that your prospect wants, really wants, to believe in you. For we Americans are a credulous people, and if the results of this credulity are often scandalous, the impulse itself is a noble and generous one. But this same prospect, having been an unwise believer in the past, is also afraid to take action. He needs to be told, over and over again, and shown, in as much detail as you can muster, that:

- NOW is the moment to act;
- you are the right person to help solve his problem, and
- waiting is not sensible.

And that you are a person of honor, probity, and enthusiastic client-centered concern.

Oh, reader, will you let your prospect see this? Or will you confirm him in his cynicism and let him continue in his despair by feeding him that paltry professional diet? A thin gruel that comes without the zesty seasoning of enthusiasm and the nutrients of empathy and your clear human concern.

It's up to you. For now, you are boring your prospects. You are sending them, or putting in their hand, or filling up the pages of their favorite magazines with evidence of your professional stodginess and your preening unwillingness to bend, to reach out, to care, to help. We know you *can* solve the prospect's problem, but it is clear you still exude the futile feeling that it is somehow beneath your dignity to work with your prospect as one human being to another; that your professional standing precludes it.

And so you write one dull sentence about yourself after another. And demand that the prospect figure out what you can really do for him. You give him one somniferous feature after another and demand that your prospect deduce the benefit for you. Either because you are too lazy to tell him for yourself, or, again, feel it beneath you to do so. Or really don't know what the benefit to the prospect really is.

STOP THIS MADNESS!!!

Before you write another piece of marketing copy — be it nothing more than a classified ad — psych yourself up. Remember:

- you are about to connect with a real person;
- this real person is in pain, either because he has a problem that must be solved, or because, like a true human, he yearns to have something more;
- this person cannot find anyone as interested as he is in solving his problem, and he is therefore isolated and alone;
- he needs your technical expertise to get what he wants, but he is less interested in your expertise than the benefit he gets from it;
- while having a problem and needing you, he is yet anxious — fearful even — that you will take advantage of him, waste his money and his time, just like a legion of others have before you. And he is right to feel this way, because you, too, have the capacity to let this person down.
- you must recognize his anxiety — and convince him that it is entirely unwarranted, that you will work to give him what he wants.

Present yourself to this individual-in-need armed with facts but sustained with empathetic enthusiasm, with a commitment to help, and a willingness to place yourself on the line.

To be sure, even if you do all this — and do it surpassingly well — some people will disdain you, dismiss you, and snap their fingers in your face. That the world is full of a multitude of the damned, I need hardly tell you! But as you successfully use these methods, more and still more people will respond to you. Will feel the force not only of your technical abilities but the power of the empathetic soul within you. They will not only be grateful that you can solve their problem with your product or service, but rejoice in connecting with a decent, humane individual who realizes that marketing is not about products or services. But is about humanity and love.

And that there is nothing, absolutely nothing, wrong with letting this humanity and this love shine out in all you do.

Are you offering your prospects a desiccated, if technically correct, solution, or are you giving them the benefit of your love and humanity, too? For I can tell you this: if you give them just the former, you will never succeed in realizing the furthest extent of your aspirations, because you will deprive yourself of the most potent fuel for your aspirations: the consequences of your own client-centered love.

How now, when did you realize you were getting not just a book in CASH COPY, but a ticket to a capitalist love-in?

Egregious Error #11. You Don't Give Your Prospect A Reason For Acting NOW!

Did you ever buy anything on sale? Of course you have. And an important reason you bought — perhaps the only reason you bought — was because the item was on sale.

When you took advantage of the sale, you used a reason for acting NOW.

Reader, you should learn from your own actions, and give your prospects a reason for acting NOW as well.

Face it. Your prospects:

- have lots of things on their mind
- get distracted
- have many responsibilities
- have limited money
- are slow moving (and more than occasionally slow-witted)
- doubt you
- mistrust themselves.

In short, they are perfectly normal — and as such, likely to need a good swift kick (as my daddy used to say) — or at the very least a quick electric shock to spur them to respond. That kick, that shock, is what you give them when providing the prospect with a reason for acting NOW.

Just what these action-generating items may be, you'll soon find out; (there's a whole chapter on formulating offers). What I want you to understand now is how much is working against you when you set out to market. You are not only competing with your competitors. Marketing is by no means a race against people doing similar things. *That* would be a piece of cake.

No, unfortunately, you are competing against:

- prospect sloth
- human ineptitude
- sufficient immediate comfort and insufficient pain
- the miracle mentality (feeling sure "something will turn up")

And everything else we humans exhibit that militates against taking action NOW.

Thus, the trick for the marketer — and the compelling cash copy he must write — is not just getting the prospect to take action at some perhaps distant point. But to get that prospect to take action NOW.

Introducing the NOW, using the NOW, profiting from the NOW, is what differentiates the advanced marketer from the merely competent marketer. And on this scale, most marketers fail. Which is why a marketing specialist like Hershall Gordon Lewis suggests that all marketers should have experience in direct mail marketing — because the objective of all direct mail marketing is to get the reader, the prospect, to do something NOW. Either to send in a check or to request more information. But to do it RIGHT THIS MINUTE.

I think Lewis is right. When I see a picture of another ruggedly handsome Marlboro man on a billboard lighting up, surmounted by some motto or other, I wonder what idiot wrote the copy and conceived the campaign for such wastefulness. This is a perfect illustration of advertising gone amuck, of marketing that has no point. The ad doesn't ask us to *do* anything. It just says, "Here's a cowboy. Here's his horse. Here's his cigarette. Here's its name." A primer of idiocy and lost opportunities that we suppose succeeds because it is repeated so often. Instead of writing smart copy, the advertiser is counting on us getting his message (whatever that may be) and taking action after we see his product over and over and over again. Frequency here takes the place of a client-centered call for action.

First, then, get this point: you must not only provide benefit after benefit to your prospects; you must give them a reason for taking immediate action. Something that will justify them in getting out of a comfortable chair, in overcoming their hesitation to call a stranger and ask for something, in superseding their fear of again being ripped off by an unscrupulous provider (like they were the last time). In short, you must motivate your prospect.

But I ask you, do you think a single mention of the motivating item will suffice to motivate your prospects?

Does it suffice to motivate you when you need the magic elixir of a kick to your posterior?

I doubt it.

Thus, you must state and repeat and repeat and repeat your offer again and again and again. In different words, of course. In different places in your marketing materials, of course. But repeated nonetheless.

Count on it. Your prospects will wallow in their current, sufficiently comfortable, thoroughly familiar (if hardly idyllic) situation as long as possible. Unless pushed and compellingly motivated, they will choose sloth over progress more times than not. *Unless you give them a reason to act today, they will not act today.* And they will go on in their unsatisfactory situation longer and longer still, with what little impression you have made upon them quickly fading, all too soon gone forever. Thus they stay relatively worse off. And so will you.

Your ability cogently to answer the question "Why should I act NOW?" is a substantial part of what determines your aptitude for successful marketing. For if people do not do it NOW, they will not do it. Until, at some later time, with some more urgent marketing piece, you apply the necessary (if uncongenial) electric jolt to their sleep-walking state and let them know — with the utmost persuasiveness — that you really did mean NOW.

Egregious Error #12. You Don't Know What You Want The Prospect To Do, (And Are Not Prepared For The Prospect When He Takes Action).

When you write cash copy you need to be the prospect's generalissimo. You are the person who knows all, sees all, is prepared for every eventuality, in whose hands every one of your prospects can feel safe. *People afraid to give directions and take responsibility do not do well in marketing.*

In everything you write all this must be present:

- facts indicating your clear understanding of the prospect's problem;
- substantial evidence (and not just your assertion) that you can solve this problem;
- benefits the prospect will get when he solves his problem, and
- exactly what the prospect must do to solve his problem now.

Dear reader, for all our talk about America being the land of pioneers, I think you should probably face the fact that most Americans are followers, not leaders. Indeed, what irks so many of us, including the followers, is that even our purported leaders are ordinarily followers. Hence, the sting our politicians feel when we label them "wimps." We certainly do not want leaders who mirror the sheeplike qualities that most of us possess, and like avenging electoral furies, we regularly destroy those who most exhibit the traits we despise in ourselves.

But I digress.

When you are writing cash copy, you must clearly lay down the law to your prospects. They don't want to have to guess at:

- the benefits you're offering;
- the consequences if they don't take action, or
- precisely what they must do to take advantage of your offer.

The most remunerative marketing is Leadership Marketing mounted by an individual (you) who fully understands the situation of the prospect and knows what that prospect must do to solve his problem. And who then straightforwardly, honestly, honorably tells the prospect in the simplest and most compelling language what that prospect must do to solve his problem. Even down to telling him that, yes, NOW is the moment to send in a check. That here's how that check should be made out. That here's the place to which that check should be sent; and so on through every single one of the details which careless marketers overlook, or somehow regard as too obvious for their consideration.

The aim of this book is to teach you how to write masterful copy, to select the right words and to use them properly so that your prospects spend more of their money on what you are selling than they do on what other people are selling. But you will only achieve this desirable result if you act like a leader, not an obsequious cringer. If you recognize that leadership — and the plain speaking that all great leaders perfect — gets you more sales than timidity and circumlocution. Which now have no place whatsoever in whatever marketing materials you create.

Know in advance why you are connecting with a prospect. It it not just to sell your prospect or service. But to sell a specific product or service by a specific time in a specific amount by a specific time. In short, whether you are mailing a million catalogs or sending a single letter to a single prospect, the aim is the same: to realize a specific objective.

The prospect needs to know what that objective is and needs to have clear guidelines from you on what he must do to have your assistance in helping him reach *his* objective.

When I ask the participants in my workshops, business people all, to tell me specifically what they aimed to accomplish with any single marketing piece, they usually have no ready answer, or they think that saying, "To sell my product" is somehow sufficient. It is not.

As a marketer, *each* day you are trying to get a single individual with a problem to make a commitment to you and your product so that he uses that product to solve his problem. Now, the fact that the number of individuals you are approaching may run into the millions, is utterly irrelevant. The fact remains that marketing is always a relationship between one seller and one specific buyer.

This individual buyer needs to:

* be perfectly clear that you understand his problem;
* know that you know what will happen to him if he doesn't solve it;
* see that there are many substantial benefits of acting to solve his problem;
* understand these benefits are more powerful if he acts NOW;
* have his anxieties about taking action recognized and assuaged;
* be motivated to solve his problem NOW and so take the necessary steps NOW to make sure it will be.

Checking the run of marketing materials against just these points, you can easily see why most of them fail and are left to be used as waste paper.

But I say this to you, once you have established a relationship of trust with your buyer or motivated prospect (for this individual must trust you before he does anything, whether it is sending in a check or requesting further information), don't undermine it by your own ineptitude, unconcern, or foolishness.

Which means telling your prospect/buyer exactly what will happen when he contacts you. Specify each thing that will happen, when it will happen, how it will happen, and who will do it. In short, develop your relationship with the prospect.

It is amazing to me how many marketing documents ask people to take action, but never suggest what will happen then. Without this information, they are asking their prospect to take a leap into a black hole, without guidance, without information on what will happen.

How can anyone think that this builds confidence in the prospect?

Remember, prospects need constant guidance. They don't expect you to perform miracles (well, actually some do), but they do expect to know precisely what will happen and in what way.

Thus, Generalissimo, your job is clear: it is not only to persuade and motivate your prospect to take action, but to let the prospect know what will happen when he takes that action.

Again, I beg you: STOP BEING SO ANXIOUS TO SELL. SOLVE — AND DEVELOP A CONGENIAL RELATIONSHIP. FOR IT IS THIS AMI-CABLE RELATIONSHIP OF TRUST THAT BEGETS BOTH PRESENT AND FUTURE SALES.

Real communication, the keystone of successful marketing, means constantly showing your prospects what you can do for them — and always letting them know what is expected of them, what you will do and when, and — a most important point — what happens when you cannot perform your part of the bargain as initially outlined.

The relationship of trust you are building with your buyers will be destroyed, perhaps irrevocably, if you do not always act like a leader.

A leader:

- seeks to understand what is wrong with his prospect;
- finds out what will happen if the prospect fails to take beneficial action on his own behalf;
- offers a sensible solution to the prospect's problems;
- lets the prospect know exactly why this solution is beneficial for him;
- tells the prospect what he must do — in excruciating detail — to get this solution;
- informs the prospect what he, the leader, does so that the prospect will have the solution, and
- keeps the prospect informed about what is happening during the delivery of the solution — both for good and for ill.

For remember, you will not always be able to do what you say you can do. But you *will always* be able to tell the prospect what you are doing to accomplish your promises — and what compensation you will give him, if you fail to deliver in the exact way you said you would.

This process of communication is, of course, the essence of a civilized society. But it also has a very practical *raison d'être*: it helps cement and develop the relationship between you the seller and your friend, the buyer.

And it is this relationship, this genuine developing friendship, that is the key. After all, how many times have our friends and loved ones disappointed us? Yet if they have not maliciously deceived us, lied and intentionally hurt us, don't we usually forgive them? And love them the better for a courageous and open admission of weakness? So long — never forgetting this — as they seek our forgiveness.

Yes, by admitting the truth when we cannot accomplish our objectives, and frankly saying so to our buyers, we still can come out ahead, with a stronger client relationship. And because this relationship is the essence of a successful business, it is worth while doing all we can to preserve and strengthen it.

Egregious Error #13. You Don't Give The Moderately Interested Prospect An Invitation to Stay In Touch (So You Can Do What It Takes To Sell Him).

Every day my mail is flooded with marketing offers from people. Most are single offers. "Buy this!", they say. Now I may have the problem the marketer says he's able to solve. I may be interested in the product or service. But — like all people — I have an enormous number of days when I feel comfortable enough that I don't want to make any changes (despite my need to do so), when I have lots of other things on my mind, or when I don't really have the money for this worthy objective, or want to spend it this way.

But the offer doesn't allow for this. It simply says "Buy." And if I am not in the mood, or not able, there's nothing I can do but "Not buy." And so the offer goes out with the trash.

The result? The marketer doesn't know that I'm interested (how can he?). And if he doesn't recontact me, he'll fail to motivate me sufficiently to buy what he's selling. Thus, he's wasted his money — and I'm still left with the problem his product or service could have solved.

This is what I call "Either/Or" marketing. It's usually a mistake, because it doesn't allow the vast numbers of people who need extra time and further persuasion to make up their minds.

Marketing, you see, must offer your prospects a spectrum of opportunities from those who are VERY EXCITED AND WILL DO ANYTHING TO ACQUIRE YOUR PRODUCT OR SERVICE NOW to those who WOULD NEVER BUY SUCH A PRODUCT OR SERVICE IF THEIR VERY LIVES DEPENDED ON IT (despite the fact that they could profitably use it).

Most buyers fall along the middle run of this spectrum, people who have in varying degree the problem that you can solve, and who need varying degrees of persuasion to take action to acquire what you're selling to solve it.

Why neglect this enormous number of people in the marketing you do? Your success in marketing is directly related to how many of these not-yet-ready-to-act people you can get to buy your product or service.

The fact that they are reluctant or relatively unable to *buy* now doesn't preclude their being able to take some action on their own behalf — action to request further information, to stay on your mailing list, to be able to derive the benefit you are offering at some later date.

Make it one of your prime marketing rules that you will ALWAYS strive to persuade what I call the Soft Prospect to take SOME ACTION now, an action that will enable you to capture this person's name, address, and telephone number so that you can carry on with what is necessary to build a relationship.

You must understand that only a tiny fraction of the people who have the problem your product or service can solve will take action right now to solve it, especially if that action involves spending money today.

Many prospects — despite the extent of their problem — need further persuasion from you, further information about you and how you can help, the impetus of more offers and continual reminding. But to be able to accomplish these objectives, you must have and maintain the information about them so that you are not entirely at the mercy of rented mailing lists, advertisements, and the like, which may or may not be read by the same people.

Thus, resolve right now to begin to assemble a mailing list for yourself.

But assemble this mailing list by selling benefits, not a mailing list.

Which brings us to how to use cash copy to build such a list.

If you read most marketing documents that do attempt to capture the soft prospect, you'll find that they promote a mailing list. But that's absurd. No one is interested in being on a mailing list for the sake of being on a mailing list. Instead, people — your prospects — want to be on a mailing list to acquire a benefit. And this benefit should be the exact thing that your product or service offers.

Thus, never say, "Check here and return this coupon to stay on our mailing list." Instead, after your hard offer (the offer that confirms the prospect in buying what you're selling) add a box with words like these: "Jeffrey, I'm not ready to take action now to start getting a 20% yearly return on my investments. But I would like to hear from you again when you've got the facts on another investment like this. I know this is a good return. Keep me in mind the next time you can get it for me."

See the difference?

The first (more common) alternative simply invites the prospect to sign up for a mailing list — to get information. The second asks the soft prospect, the prospect who is not ready to make a firm commitment today to spend money, to get in touch with you so that you can bring to his attention a specific benefit he here confirms that he wants and regards as valuable: in this case a 20% annual return on an investment. Note, in the benefit illustration, nothing whatever is said about a mailing list, because this marketer realizes that the mailing list is not a benefit to the prospect (however much it is a benefit to him) and that he must therefore lead with a prospect benefit and not a marketer benefit.

Makes sense, doesn't it, when you see it this way in black and white? Why, then, do you so rarely see marketers attempting to capture the Soft Prospect? Why don't they motivate them with prospect benefits and stop offering the pale alternative of being on a mailing list, of being inundated with more mail that they haven't time to read, and telephone calls that they really don't want?

I often wonder about this.

But I know that you'll now work hard through the wonderful copy you'll write, not just to sell to the immediately motivated but to connect with the progressively less motivated. So that through your further marketing — with your continuing persuasive copy — you will bring to even these sluggards the benefits of what you are selling. In so doing, you will have the satisfaction of helping ever greater numbers of people — and of getting filthy rich in the process. Tra la!

Egregious Error #14. You Don't Give Your Prospect A Reason To Buy More Now.

There are two kinds of sellers operating in the marketing universe. There are those who sell you a product or service and deliver it. And there are those who discover your problem and seek to solve it by delivering every conceivable product or service they've got to correct it.

Consider this illustration. When I had the track lighting installed in my office, the surly owner of the electrical company came to inspect the situation. He limited his conversation and assessment exclusively to the current situation. AT NO TIME DID HE EVER MENTION MY OTHER ELECTRICAL NEEDS NOR INDICATE THAT HE COULD SOLVE THEM.

Absurb, ladies and gentlemen, surpassingly absurd.

Did the man think that time and space and profit possibilities ended with this job? Apparently, astonishingly so.

In short, he was a lowly order-taker. He delivered (with a god-awful mess and some scratched floors to be sure) the service he said he'd deliver. But at no time did he ever seek to solve my continuing problem: how to have a safe, stylish, guaranteed and healthful source of certain light, economically available.

Here's a festive footnote to this tale: at Christmas I received a card in the mail signed with the company name (nary an individual's name to be found) and a pen with the company's name and telephone number. I had to laugh: when will this kind of cretinous marketing be outlawed by government fiat? How much better would it have been for the owner of the company to have spent 15 congenial minutes with me ascertaining the kind of electrical needs I might have.

Oh, yes, it goes without saying that my next electrical job will be done elsewhere.

The copy you write should not be about products and services but about solutions. And, unless an individual is buying all the solution that you have available (if he is, your line probably needs expanding), your job is not merely to deliver what he wants — but to find out what he needs and sell him more of what you've got that will produce the benefit he wants.

Your copy must embody the Upgrade Principle. Everything you sell must be available in individual units, to be sure. But these individual units must be grouped into larger units that are available for an overall unit price. You must make clear to the buyer his benefits — in terms of price and problem-solving potential — by acquiring the entire unit. Convincing the prospect that acquiring the unit solves his problems must be a prime marketing objective for you.

But, also, you must be prepared to continue your marketing to the individual if he fails — on the first pass — to accept your offer and acquire the entire unit. If he only gets a part, you must, in sending him this part, renew your persuasive campaign. You must reinforce the benefits the prospect will get by acquiring the entire unit and what he'll lose by not acquiring it. And move him further towards closure by telling him this offer is available for only a limited, specific time.

In short, you must continue to persuade this prospect, so long as he has problems you can solve and you have products and services that will benefit him. Do you do this?

Or are you like my lackadaisical electrician who feels he has done a good day's work by installing light bulbs, oblivious to the fact that he is not in the light bulb business but, God-like, in the business of ensuring that there is light?

*Egregious Error #15. You Don't Understand And Haven't Addressed
The Anxieties Of The Prospect, Assuring And Reassuring Him That
Connecting With You Is The Only Sensible Thing To Do.*

Successful marketers are empathetic marketers. They understand they are
involved in a dialogue with another single individual, an individual who (if they
have done their homework adequately) really has the problem they can solve
and who really will be better off by acquiring what the marketer is selling.

But they know (in part because they know their own anxieties as buyers) that the
person they're trying to help has reservations about them, fears, and anxieties.
Despite the fact these are inaccurate and erroneous, they are nonetheless entirely
real and must be dealt with by the seller before he can persuade the buyer to act.

Which is, of course, why word of mouth marketing is so powerful. The prospect
buys because of the trust and belief he has in his friend. This trust and belief —
as much as the product or service itself — is what produces the sale, which is
why contented buyers are such a potent marketing force for further sales.

Self-centered marketers don't spare a thought to the anxieties of their prospect,
because they are consumed by their own anxieties. After all they are:

- taking the risk in determining (and perhaps developing) the
  product or service to sell;
- gambling their money and time in producing the marketing
  materials;
- risking more in bringing what they are selling to the attention
  of their market through all the ways in which this is possible;
- burdened with the expense of maintaining the business organization that makes these products and services.

And on and on through all the levels of entrepreneurial neurosis.

But I ask you, does your prospect care about all this? Not a whit.

He has his own troubling concerns about you to worry about:

- Are you reputable?
- Am I certain of getting a quality product or service?
- Will I get this quality product or service delivered promptly?

- Will I be guaranteed my satisfaction?
- What can I do if my satisfaction is not assured?

These are the anxieties that prey on your prospect's mind. And he is right to be concerned about them because time after time in his checkered past he has fallen victim to his native enthusiasm (and the plausible claims of some snake-oil charmer) and — again! — come up disappointed and poorer in the bargain.

Regularly stumbling in this fashion, he is the more reluctant to risk again.

This is why you must confront the prospect's anxieties — and allay them.

There is no use trying to pretend that each of your prospects exists in an ivory-tower world where there is no doubt, no confusion, no fear of being humbled and taken advantage of. You will scarcely encounter such a phenomenal buyer in your life, unless you happen upon a play-pen millionaire with free-spending ways and no parental guidance.

No, your buyers are tainted by their history, regrets, and disappointments — and they are going to take out on you all they have learned and suffered through, unfair though that may be.

So, anticipate this. And turn it in your favor.

Give your prospect reason to trust you. Tell him how long you've been in business and the kinds of professional credentials you've got. Tell him who you've helped and what those helped say about you.

Provide precise information on when he'll get what he wants, from where it will be sent, how, in what fashion. And what will happen if he doesn't get it.

Don't blame others when things don't work out. Explain the situation and accept the responsibility. Then make it up in some beneficial, if inexpensive, way to the customer. Just do this. Don't tell him in advance that you will. But prepare for the need before it arises.

If you're offering what seems to be an unbelievable price, tell the customer how you're able to do so.

If you're offering some special inducement to get the prospect to buy now, say why.

In short, speak plainly to the prospect and buyer about what's bothering them (or even what they may be curious about) and make your best case. Only you expect perfection from yourself, but you are not the only person hamstrung by your need to achieve it.

Your prospects want you to deliver a good, solid, believable, eminently useful product and service. They are right to doubt your ability to do so, given their certain experience from those who have made similar promises in the past and failed to live up to them. All they want from you is not some demonstration of demi-godlike infallability but a solid indication that you know how they're feeling and can reassure them, while delivering the product or service that will help.

Truly powerful marketers are also willing to admit their human foibles and vulnerabilities — while making it quite clear that these are not the sum total of their being. Only the insecure and self-deluded need to keep pounding their own drums, and the more they pound the less believable they are.

By all means make your strongest possible case for what you are selling and the benefits the prospect will acquire by using it. But also take time to understand and address the anxieties of the prospect to reassure this person that he is getting at least what you promise and probably more, and that if he is unhappy he has some tangible recourse beyond rage.

In presenting yourself this way, remember the Great Puritan Autocrat, Oliver Cromwell, the most powerful man in England. *He* had no fear of being painted with warts and all. For he was a man who was comfortable with himself, the select of God and the choice of his countryman, admirably equipped to solve their problems. What needed he with pretense?

If you learn nothing else from this resource, I hope you learn the powerful marketing potential of simple human empathy and plain speaking. How many marketing documents seem to you to evidence either?

Egregious Error #16. You Don't Tell Your Prospects What Will Happen To Them If They Don't Take Action.

It stands to reason that if your prospect gets a benefit by using what you're selling, then he loses a benefit by not using it. Why then in virtually all marketing documents is there no hint of what will happen to the prospect in question if he fails to take advantage of this offer?

The slothful marketers who predominate nowadays seem to say in effect, "Hey, you. Here's a service I've got. I'm too lazy to try to persuade you about its benefits. Frankly, I don't know you, and don't really know what it will do for you anyway. But when you buy it, I'll certainly be better off! And, no, I can't say what your condition will be if you fail to use what I'm selling. Like I said, I don't know you."

Now, with an attitude and approach like this, how do these simpletons expect to sell anything?

Selling essentially revolves around these two axes:

- specific benefit after specific benefit the prospect will get if he uses the product or service;
- lost opportunities and problems the prospect will continue to have if he doesn't use the product or service.

Both are key components of successful marketing. Think of them as a two-pronged motivational attack on your prospect:

"Hey, bub, I've got this specific benefit and this specific benefit and this specific benefit for you if you take action NOW to acquire this product and service and put it to your own use."

The prospect may or may not respond. If he does fine; if he doesn't, hit him with this:

"Hey, bub, you'll have this specific problem and this specific problem and this specific problem — or you'll lose this opportunity and this opportunity and this opportunity — if you don't take action NOW to acquire this product and service and put it to your own use."

The Double Whammy.

But you can't profit from this double whammy if you lead with features and talk about yourself. And you can't profit from it unless you put yourself into the shoes of the prospect and talk honestly, candidly, straightforwardly to him about how he'll benefit by taking action. *And* what he'll lose — and have to continue to suffer — by not taking action.

Remember, the marketer is a master conjurer. From a piece of paper covered with a succession of symbols and a few graphics he reaches out to seize control of an individual's mind. To take that individual's deepest aspirations, fears, dreams and private horrors and make them work in the service of the marketer — to get that person, because of these aspirations, fears, dreams and private horrors — to take action and acquire what the marketer offers.

The marketer conjures for the prospect both future benefits for taking action NOW and future unhappiness and discontent for failing to take this action.

He makes the benefits palpable, real, rich and substantial; and makes the prospect feel the unhappiness and discontent that must result from his failure to act.

The master marketer is a Svengali, who, unlike his celluloid counterpart, is the more remarkable because he so often acts on people who are not physically present and are responding to mere language and graphics alone, not some charismatic presence.

This marketer — you! — must not only enthuse with benefits but must ignite action with the threat of an uncomfortable, unhappy, incomplete, disappointing future if the prospect doesn't act NOW.

Is this what you do? Or are you engaged in the genteel presentation of bloodless objects and sanitized services that do not connect to the achievement of the prospect's aspirations and the eradication of his anxieties?

Marketing is not a sport for those who have distaste for the messy, unpredictable, altogether rather disappointing human animal. No, indeed. When you are marketing — and writing the cash copy that is such an important part of successful marketing — you are in the business of exciting people with the realization that they can have the benefits they desire. If only they take action. And that they can avoid the demons that afflict them. If only they take action. But you must be willing to help them soar. And you must be willing to conjure up the demons — so that your prospects know how badly they are afflicted by them.

For if you are not willing to do this, you are not willing to do what it takes to market. You had better sign on for the next Challenger flight. Then you can begin to find a more perfect universe that suits what you want to do, rather than what you must do to succeed.

Egregious Error #17. You're Not Telling Your Prospect What Specific Benefits He Gets By Using Your Product Or Service.

The best marketing is laden with specific benefit after specific benefit. Most marketing, by contrast, is composed of features — facts about what you're selling — or of benefits that are so vague they could be lifted from this marketing material and set down, exactly as written, into anybody else's. This is wrong.

Whatever you write must be *specific* to the individual market you are targeting. You must stop writing copy that is generic and general, capable of being used to sell any product or any service in any situation.

Here's an illustration of what to avoid, unconsciously provided by Situation Management Systems, Inc., of Hanover, MA.

"Dear Colleague:

On (two dates), Situation Management Systems, Inc. will present a complimentary 'Showcase' Presentation in Boston, Massachusetts to provide an overview of certain programs which we offer to professionals and managers. We hope that you will be able to attend. The overview will cover the programs which are described further in the enclosed brochure. . . ."

This kind of copy is execrable, a text-book perfect illustration of what not to write. Here one meaningless, bloated word follows another until you want to howl with rage.

A perfect illustration of the "We Think We're Swell" School of Marketing, there's nothing here of any immediate interest or value to the reader. There's no attempt to:

- tell the reader that this is a letter meant explicitly for him;
- show that Situation Management Systems understands his problems and can help solve them;
- both empathize with the reader and enthuse him about the benefits that are available to him by taking action NOW.

No, indeed.

Just one pompous, self-centered phrase after another.

Nary a benefit to be seen.

Okay, then, let's move into the brochure. This leads with the heading "Program Description." "Program Description", you should now be able to tell me, is another selfish phrase. It's about the writer, not about the reader. The reader, Situation Management System's prospect, doesn't care about the program. He cares only about the benefit. Where's the benefit in the headline "Program Description"? Don't look too long. There isn't any!

Then follows the headline for the first of their programs: "Positive Power And Influence."

Again, I ask you where's the benefit? Who is the writer talking to? Is there any reason for the reader to pay attention when what he is looking at is obviously not directed to him and obviously promises no benefit. As far as the reader is concerned, this is merely a string of words without a single clearly stated benefit for him.

(Need I say that by now the discerning reader sees that Situation Management Systems, a company that no doubt considers itself a hard-working and client-centered entity, instead appears to be supremely selfish, interested only in its concerns and oblivious to serving its prospects?)

Now to the opening paragraph. "This Program helps participants to develop or refine the skills required to influence others in a positive or constructive manner. Having mastery over several influence styles is the key to achieving effective results in different types of situations. Individuals who attend the Positive Power and Influence Program learn to make effective use of their personal power, regardless of the position they may hold. This is particularly relevant in today's business world, in which managers often must rely on and influence people over whom they have no direct authority. Participants learn to analyze situations and to select and use appropriate tactics to achieve their influence objectives."

This paragraph is a perfect illustration of selfish marketing, of marketing that has nothing to do with the prospect. Directed at no one, touching no nerve, offering no precise benefit, it could be used exactly as is by almost any marketer selling almost anything. It is about as bad an illustration of marketing as you will ever see — but the sad thing is, you will see it often.

Let's review this paragraph in detail to show where the writer failed and why the benefits this writer thinks are here are either not benefits at all or benefits so watered down and unspecific as to be valueless.

To begin with, the copy is weakened by the fact that it is written in the third person. ALL COPY — remember this! — should be written in the second person, from an individual (you) to an individual (the prospect), from the individual who has the solution, to the individual who has the problem and wants it solved by you. Thus, never, never, never say "participants". It's a bloated, foolish word. Say instead, "When you participate, here's what you'll get/how you'll be better off . . ."

Next, the writer undoubtedly feels that developing or refining "the skills required to influence others in a positive and constructive manner" is a benefit. It isn't. It's something that could be written about anything, to sell anything to anyone. And as such is meaningless.

Cash copy is specific copy. It is written by a specific person to a specific person. It says "You wish to achieve a certain objective, solve a certain problem, be specifically better. I can help you."

That isn't what this copy says. What's missing here is:

* who this program is for
* what kinds of problems they have
* how not solving these problems is affecting them
* why they need to solve these problems.

In short, every substantial and specific benefit that should be there, isn't there. What we get instead is "a positive and constructive manner." Well, man, is there anyone in the world that isn't interested in this?

Ah, says the marketer of this pabulum, that's the point: "I've cast my net to capture all the world because we've got a solution to everyman's problem. We want everyone to attend. And so we can't limit the copy." That's bosh.

To write for everyone is to write for no one. To invite everyone is to invite no one. Remember: the distinct, single individual reading your copy must say, "This person understands the problem I have and can help me solve it. He's knowledgeable about me. He's interested in me. He can help me solve my problem and get what I want. I must do what it takes to participate."

Is this what you feel upon reading this insipid copy? Certainly not!

Let's go on. The line "having mastery over several influence styles . . ." is nothing more than an unsupported assertion on the part of the marketer. Why should we believe him? Where's the evidence?

The writer has offered no reasons why we should believe him. So, we don't. How many times a day do you hear unsubstantiated assertions? Probably a couple of dozen times. And you learn to screen them right out. That's what happens when you read a line like: "Having mastery over several influence styles is the key to achieving effective results in different types of situations." Your unconscious response:

- Who says so?
- Where's the evidence?
- What's this got to do with me?

What you really want to know is:

- how can acquiring many different influence styles help me solve my problems? With my employees? With my boss? With my spouse? Or children?

In short, you want to know what's in it for you.

As you see, the promised benefit (influencing "others in a positive and constructive manner") is really no benefit whatsoever. It's just words. Because this sentence (and everything that follows it, for that matter) doesn't answer the question "What's in it for me?"

How about one more illustration from this failed brochure? "Individuals who attend . . . will learn to make effective use of their personal power regardless of the position they hold." Let's overlook the obvious problems of the poor diction and failure to speak to anyone in particular. Does this sentence offer you a specific benefit, and as such a reason for attending the program?

Is there anyone in the world who isn't interested in more effective use of their personal power? Of course, there isn't. But do you feel upon reading this sentence that there is a real benefit there for you, the real prospect? Of course, there isn't!

You want to know:

- how many ways of increasing your personal power you'll learn;
- how to master the ways of using this power and what you'll get when you do;
- how to access situations so that you can use it — and specific situations when you can.

In short, you want this tired, exhausted, third-party prose to come alive by having the discussion focused on you and your wants, not on the marketer and his.

And to think that Situation Management Systems, Inc., spent hundreds, perhaps thousands of dollars, sending this drivel to so many people. No wonder it's called "junk mail."

Here's another illustration of flaccid, mindless, "benefitless" benefit copy, this time in a postcard mailing from SMI International of Waco, TX, a company that (ironically) specializes in motivating people. In this mailing they are offering a free cassette, "The Power of Goal Setting", if you respond by a certain date. Such an offer is obviously designed to increase their mailing list so they can send material about other products.

Here's the copy they used:

"Yes, you can have THE POWER OF GOAL SETTING in your career! The cassette tape 'The Power of Goal Setting' — a $14.95 value — is yours for the asking. It will show you that you can use the techniques used by winners to reach the career and personal goals you desire. It's yours FREE!"

Now, this copy isn't all bad. But it falls far short of being good. SMI would tell you that there is a benefit to you here — getting a free tape that contains "the techniques used by winners."

My contrary contention is that one is not interested even in something free unless he is very clear on the benefits he gets from taking the time to acquire it. FREE *per se* isn't the most powerful of motivators; it's FREE linked with hard-hitting, intensely personal prospect benefits. Judged by these standards this SMI copy fails miserably.

The questions the prospect has (either explicitly or subconsciously) upon reading this offer are:

- What are the techniques?
- How many techniques are there?
- Why do I need these techniques?
- What kinds of winners benefit from these techniques?
- How many winners benefit from them?
- What did they get from using these techniques?
- What happens to me if I don't use these techniques?

In short, this copy leaves unanswered e*very* major question the prospect has, and, therefore, clearly demonstrates that there isn't *any* real benefit in taking action — beyond acquiring a perhaps meaningless cassette which may or may not (you can't tell from the copy) have any real benefit in your life.

This is weak, boring copy for all that it comes festooned on red, white and blue stock parading the word FREE like Old Glory itself. But even the powerful word "free" is only a truly compelling benefit when inextricably linked with real prospect benefit, something the individual prospect must have to achieve his desires, overcome pain, and relieve his anxieties. These benefits aren't apparent in the SMI copy, and therefore this copy isn't persuasive.

Despite the fact that SMI offered me a free $14.95 tape, I didn't bother to accept their offer. Because I had no real idea what that offer was beyond a tape that may or may not be useful to me. For I certainly don't need another piece of useless junk about the place taking up space. If only SMI had considered this, they wouldn't have wasted so much money putting together this weak-kneed benefitless offer.

Every benefit you create for your prospect must be specific. If you read a line of your "benefit copy" and find that anyone could say that about anything else, then what you have written is wrong, vague, imprecise, not worth the paper it's printed on. You write this copy because you don't know enough about the prospect; don't understand what he's trying to achieve and haven't yet spent the time to find out precisely how you can help. When you know this information — and are willing to use it in your copy — your copy must improve. And as it improves, I guarantee that more of your prospects will respond to it, because they'll know that you know what you're talking about and really can help them.

Egregious Error #18. You're Using Too Many General, Non-Specific Adverbs And Adjectives In Your Copy.

I like to say that good marketing copy is carried on its nouns and verbs, just like all good writing. These nouns and verbs are the bone and muscle of marketing copy, and you can tell if your copy is good because it will still be persuasive if you delete all adjectives and adverbs. By the same token, the glaring weaknesses of unpersuasive copy are manifestly apparent when you delete the adjectives and adverbs, as you'll see by reviewing with me a piece of promotional literature sent by the National Composition Association of Arlington, VA. This flyer is their attempt to get you to sign up for a two-day publishing workshop. Here's a section of it:

"Plotting your move into *computer-based book* publishing

This *new two-day* seminar from NCA will cover:

- All the *latest* equipment and software for publishing
- A *new* strategy for automating that focuses on *editorial*, not *production*, activities
- Where the *"desktop publishing"* packages fit
- How to deal with the author's *electronic* manuscript"

I've highlighted the adjectives.

Now, my problem with this copy is that the benefits are slack, at best; and that the marketer disguises the lack of good, solid, believable benefits by throwing in meaningless words that delude the reader. In other words, this is "junk food" copywriting, because it seems to be offering value but really has nothing significant whatsoever.

Let's look more closely at a couple of these "benefit" sentences.

First, where's the benefit in the sentence "Plotting your move into computer-based book publishing"? Don't look too long, because there isn't one. Specific, benefit rich copy tells you:

- why you should consider computer-based book publishing;
- how many benefits there are;
- why now is a good time;

- what you specifically get by using (please, not "plotting your move", an idiotic phrase) this kind of publishing;
- what you'll lose if you don't use it.

In short, good, solid, eminently believable benefits. The kind of benefits that just aren't there now.

Now, delete the underlined portion and see if the line makes any sense. "Plotting your move into publishing." Aha! It's flat, indeed. Flat because there's no muscle and no bone in this sentence. No benefit for the prospect. Leaving aside the inappropriate diction (do we need to plot? Does getting into publishing need some kind of conspiratorial effort?), the real problem with this sentence — with and without its modifiers — is that there is no benefit here for the prospect. No reason for the prospect to take action NOW to acquire what the marketer is selling.

It's the same in the next sentence: "This new two-day seminar from NCA will cover . . ." There's no need to put the words "two-day" here. That's a feature. And an utterly unimportant feature unless and until the prospect is convinced that the marketer is offering real, substantial benefits.

Remember what I said before, lead with benefits, follow with features. Here's a feature that may actually put people off ("You mean, I have to spend two whole days of my incredibly busy life. I can't possibly do that!!!") before you've had the chance to give them every conceivable benefit for attending. The marketer includes this information here, I suspect, because he wants the prospect to see the program as thorough; the prospect, however, may read this fact as burdensome, making it impossible to attend and just stop reading right there.

- "All the latest equipment and software for publishing."

What's the benefit here? Is anyone interested in knowing about equipment and software for publishing? Beyond, that is, the people who create and manufacture it? No, publishers are not interested in equipment and software. They want to know how to select the best equipment and software to produce more books for a lower cost in less time.

In other words, there's no benefit here. The lack of benefit is exascerbated by deleting the word "latest", the nonnutrient adjective. It's a word that stands in place of hard, factual data. See how much stronger the sentence would be if it read, "Come and learn why you should be using the Z-104 laser printer, the machine that has cut the cost of a 500-page 8" by 10" paperback book by $1 a copy in print runs of only 2000 copies."

Now, you're talking. The copy isn't flaccid anymore. It's dealing with a real problem and a real benefit for the prospect, because there isn't a publisher in his right mind who doesn't want to produce more books for less money. And if you can tell him how to do just that, most will jump at the chance to find out how. Most, remember, but not all. Remember, there are always people who have the problem but nonetheless, for whatever reason, won't make the slightest effort to solve it. These are the flatworms, and they are always with us.

Let's go on. I feel like the Great White Shark in pursuit of prey. "Where the 'desktop publishing' packages fit".

First delete the modifying phrase, "desktop publishing". It's jargon and as such is meaningless. Deleting this empty phrase the sentence stands exposed as futile. "Where the . . . packages fit."

Again, the marketer's word choice is weak. Does the prospect care where "packages fit"? I think not. The prospect cares, as the prospect always cares, about what's in this for him. This sentence, however, doesn't give him a clue.

- What packages?
- What do they do?
- Why should he care?
- What specific benefits does he get by using them?
- What happens if he doesn't use them?

The marketer doesn't deign to say.

Instead, he obscures the fact that the sentence is vapid by throwing in the prevailing (meaningless) buzz word, "desktop publishing." Desktop publishing, of course, means nothing; most jargon doesn't. It is a word that seems to suggest a benefit, but what that benefit is is by no means apparent.

This copywriter is just writing words. He has forgotten his craft:

- Who is he writing for?
- What does this person want to accomplish?
- What is this person afraid of?
- What happens to this person if he fails to act?

Is this person, the marketer's prospect, really interested in how packages fit? Or is he interested, as all publishers must be, in creating more books for less money? You tell me. But if you accept the fact (and I think you must) that this is indeed the benefit the marketer should be stressing, where, pray, where can you find this benefit in this — or any other sentence — offered by the National Composition Association in its attempt to excite me into spending $495 and two days of my life? Dear friend, it is not there.

Stop using sugary adjectives and adverbs to obscure the fact that your benefits are thin and anemic. Make sure each verb you use is an action verb that is about the prospect getting, feeling, experiencing and profiting from a benefit he wants. Make sure that each noun is about that benefit, too. Make sure that each adverb and adjective adds specific information and detail about the prospect benefit.

In short, make each word specific and packed with prospect benefits.

Each word must be about the prospect and either his problem or the solution he gets from you.

With each of your words the prospect must say: "This is about me. This is about my problem. This is about how I can solve this problem."

Nothing you write can be solely and only about you, the seller. Everything you write must be fully and completely about the propect, your buyer. And the bone, sinew and muscle of what you write for your prospects must never, ever be obscured by soft, vapid, vague, bloated, weak words — words that are nothing more than assertions by you and which lack the persuasiveness of hard, compelling fact. Or you'll be throwing your money away and exhibiting yourself as selfish and uninterested in your prospects and the problem they are willing to pay you to solve. If only you'd focus on that — and not on yourself.

Egregious Error #19. You Don't Have Satisfied People Willing To Stand Up For You To Tell Others Who Have The Same Problem That You've Got What They Need To Solve It.

I've told you before (and you already know) that mouth marketing is powerful; your friends telling you to get something they like that they think you'll benefit from, too.

But we marketers can't live by these kinds of referrals. And that's why we need to use testimonials.

Now I'm not talking about celebrity endorsements; actresses and hulking sports figures pitching wares. Frankly, I've never liked celebrity endorsements. Any fool can figure out that the only reason these people are crooning the honied words is for the pay-check they get. Personally, I always get the impression the advertiser must be short on prospect benefits if he has to resort to, say, Madonna or Martha Ray; (does anybody care what Martha Ray thinks about anything?). No, this isn't at all what I'm talking about.

I'm talking about real people who used you and your product or service to get a benefit that they wanted to achieve and who are willing to stand up, be counted, and say so in no uncertain terms, fully attributed.

Later in this book, we'll get into the detailed ins and outs of these testimonials. For now, I simply want you to be aware of the power of testimonials and your need to use them.

Attributed testimonials from real people say in effect:

- I am like you.
- I had a problem like you and wanted to achieve the same benefit you do.
- Like you, I was anxious about what I should do, wondering if anyone could really help.
- Well, now I know. (Your product or service) provided (the benefit I desired). Just like it will do for you, the deliberating prospect.

This simple formulation is irresistible and must be used.

I am a testimonial fanatic. I like to open my documents with testimonials; interject them right into the heart of the copy, start pages with them, reinforce every benefit with a specific individual saying that, yes, this is the benefit he wanted and that, yes, this is the benefit he got thanks to using the product or service.

Using testimonials this way is a superb technique to get real people to take action NOW.

Why, then, as I look at the marketing documents strewn around me as I write, do I look in vain through one after another to find any semblance of an attributed testimonial? Has no one used these marketers' products or services successfully? Do they really think that their own words (unproven assertions, more often than not) are more powerful than the substantial reports of real users who have solved their problems with the help of what is being offered? Can anyone actually believe this?

Or is it just a failure from one marketer after another to put themselves into the shoes of the often (justly) nervous and anxious people they are trying to persuade to take action and to do what is necessary to calm these people, answer their objections and let them know in no uncertain — but completely factual — terms that they can help?

Whatever the reason, these documents — and indeed a majority of marketing documents — have no indication whatsoever that anyone has ever successfully used what the prospect is being offered. That no one is willing to say in specific detail what benefit they derived from using the product or service. And to say unequivocally that the new prospect is foolish indeed to pass up this kind of benefit because of a nagging fear of risk.

Don't simply base your sales case on what you think about what you're selling. Bring in the support troops, your legions of contented and happy users, to clinch the deal.

Egregious Error #20. You Are Too Tentative, Weak, And Insecure In Your Marketing, Wanting Too Much To Be Liked, And Afraid Of What Will Happen If You Tell Your Prospect The Truth.

There is a curious phenomenon that predominates among particularly middle-class marketers. Each of us wants to be liked; too often more than anything else.

This fatuous desire is endemic in our society, deeply rooted in our childhood (and now childish) fear that we won't be selected (fill in the blank) 5th grade Valentine King, Prom Queen, or Student Body President. Rather than say what we know to be true, we say what we know will make us liked.

Don't tell me this isn't you, because scarcely a day now passes in my life when I don't see what might have been a profitable marketing effort being systematically destroyed because the marketer is unwilling to tell the truth to his prospects for fear that they won't like him — and that if they don't like him they won't buy from him.

Well, have I got news for you.

Being liked isn't the objective of marketing. Selling is the objective of marketing; selling to be able to solve the prospect's problem with your product or service.

Now I am not saying go out of your way to be disagreeable and argumentative to your prospect. Not at all. But I am saying, learn the benefits of plain speaking and candor.

- Do you believe your prospects have a problem?
- Do you believe that your product or service is the best thing they can acquire to solve this problem?
- Do you believe that your prospects will be demonstrably better off using what you're selling?
- Do you believe that they'll be worse off if they don't use what you're selling?

If you can answer yes to each of these questions, then you are a candidate for plain speaking and can expect to reap the benefits that come from mastering it.

You must care enough about your clients and what happens to them to level with them, to be straight with them, even blunt. Not abrasive, mind. But straightforward.

In your cover letters.

In your ads.

In your brochures and flyers.

And in everything else.

As I write I see by my side another seminar announcement from Boston University's Metropolitan College, an institution that wastes an enormous amount of money producing grossly second-rate marketing. Here's the headline for one of their courses: "Getting Started with Lotus 1-2-3."

There's no benefit here. No indication of who should take the course. No indication that this course solves a problem. It's just words. No hint of plain-speaking. Of why you need Lotus 1-2-3; of what it can do for you, and of what happens if you fail to master its possibilities.

Just mediocre words.

You'll have a better chance of not writing such useless verbiage if you consider yourself the doctor and your prospect the patient. You cannot succeed in marketing unless you realize that the patient is sick. That is to say, the patient's current state is distinctly inferior to the state the patient should be in and wants to have.

You are the person who can bring about the remarkable transformation that will produce the patient's superior state. What you have to do is to speak candidly and forthrightly to the patient, to make sure the patient understands the true extent of his current problem and what will happen if he doesn't take the recommended steps to cure it.

Some patients, the eminently rational ones, don't need much prodding to take action. They are the ones who really do see their dentist every six months; get a physical once a year, and can tell you with admirable precision how much cholesterol they ingest. But tell me, dear reader, what minuscule percentage of the population is this? A fraction's fraction.

Your task is to talk to the remainder of your prospects and to talk to them directly, earnestly, laying on benefit after benefit, and reason after reason for taking action now. Is this what Metropolitan College does with headlines like these?

- "Using 1-2-3 As A Time-Saving Professional Business Tool"
- "Introducing The Spreadsheet"
- "Financial Modeling With 1-2-3"

Certainly not!

There's not a word here that promises a specific benefit, not a word that suggests a precise advantage. These are just words tossed out by the marketer. Not one of them involves the marketer speaking plainly and directly to the prospect.

If you want to succeed in marketing, not merely to sell products and services, but to develop a customer relationship with an individual who will return to you again and again to get your help solving his problems, then you must develop the facility of plain speaking.

You must learn to be plain, sensible, believable, substantive. The kind of approach we wish that all our friends would take to us, but so few actually do. These are the powerful tools of the master marketer. But you can only use them if you are:

- confident what you are selling will actually better the prospect's life;
- willing to stand behind what you are selling 100%, and
- dedicated to helping people, not merely selling them something.

It's my hunch that so many marketing gambits fail because the people who are launching them really don't believe in what they're talking about. Yes, they may also be technically ill-equipped as copywriters and hamstrung by their foolish notions about what they can and cannot do as professionals, but, at root, the problem is a more basic one than these. It is a lack of belief in what is being marketed, a feeling that people really will not be better off because of it.

If this were not the case, so much mediocre marketing would be transformed by a new spirit. For make no mistake about it, even the best copywriting and marketing cannot for long sell an inferior product, while a superior product or service will be sold by solid, substantial, client-centered marketing, even if this marketing is not technically perfect. The marketer's honest and fully factually supported position that the prospect will better off using the product or service will sell that product or service. So long as every attempt is made to show the prospect just how much better off he'll be if he takes action now. Don't just take my word for it, either. Ask the folks at L.L. Bean.

Egregious Error #21. You Don't Guarantee Your Buyer's Satisfaction

Recently I had a problem with a printer. He printed a book of ours with crooked pages and irregular ink application. The final result was appalling. Because the printer didn't want to take a substantial loss on the job, however, he was slow to take action to solve the problem. Worse, when he discussed the problem he never said, "I'll solve it so that you'll have a quality product you and your customers can be proud of." No, he never said that! Nor did he ever say, "We'll settle this problem to your satisfaction." Not that, either.

His total concentration was on how he could get out of delivering the quality product our contract said I would have as a result of using his services. He gave no indication — none whatsoever — of caring about my feelings about the shoddy work he had delivered or how my customers would feel about it if they had to use such an inferior production to achieve their objectives. His entire approach to problem solving was the antithesis of client-centered marketing.

You can imagine how I feel about this particular firm and what I say about it to people who regularly seek me out for a recommendation on which company they should use to manufacture their books!

My printer had forgotten that to succeed in business, you must first produce a quality product or service. Secondly, you must be willing to guarantee that this product or service will meet the objectives you promised it would, so solving the prospect's problem and producing the result he desires.

Is this what you do?

Do you believe that you are delivering a product or service that you are proud of, each time you deliver it? Or are you merely going through the paces, trying to earn a living, uncaring about what happens to your prospect?

If you really do care (and I hope you really do), do your marketing documents say your prospect will be satisfied, that he will be able to achieve his objectives by using what you're offering? As I write, I'm looking in vain through a stack of marketing documents sent from companies around America, seeking for a word, a single word, in which they say that I'll be better off, that I'll be able to reach my objectives, if I use what they're selling.

And do you guarantee your prospects' satisfaction with what you are sending them or doing for them? Except for many (but not all) of the mail-order offers I'm reviewing, I see nothing with such a guarantee.

No wonder most prospects are skeptical about what most marketers are doing!

The prevailing marketing attitude these days (despite all the talk about being service-oriented) is this:

- I need money. I can get the money I need by selling you something.
- I haven't got the slightest idea if what I'm selling you will do you any good or not. And I'm not going to make any effort to

find out. I need money now. You're my best chance of
getting it.

- So I'll throw together a marketing piece stuffed with resound-
  ing assertions and grand claims, with some feature details
  about what I'm selling and with as little information as
  possible about what specific benefits you get, why you should
  pay attention to me, and about others who have successfully
  used what I'm offering.
- I'll certainly give you no indication that I'm going to do what
  is necessary to guarantee your satisfaction.
- Or that I'll solve the problem if you happen to be dissatisfied
  about something.
- Because, I'm not in business to guarantee your satisfaction,
  but to see to my own.

And we wonder why most of us are profoundly skeptical about the marketing materials we see and slow to take action in responding to them!

If you want your prospects to trust you sufficiently even to ask for more information, much less to entrust you with their hard-earned money, then you have got to give them the clear feeling you are totally, entirely, completely and profoundly dedicated to their achieving their objectives and that you will do what is necessary — *whatever is necessary* — to guarantee their satisfaction.

But merely writing these words on a page is insufficient. Your business and its practices must exemplify these words. For if they are just words . . . and not your constant business practices . . . you will fail. Oh, some smart copywriter can make mere words work for you for some period of time. But as the truth comes out that you don't mean them, your prospects and customers will dismiss them — and everything else you say — as lies and humbug, nothing but words. Instead of the constructive client-centered practices on which a successful business must be based.

You see, then, this isn't just a book about words. It's a book, first and foremost, about how to run your business successfully and then how to promote your solid operating methods and problem-solving products and services to the people who need them through the magic words and marketing configurations which compel your prospects to take action. This is why in the next chapter, I am addressing a key problem that prevents so many marketers from writing client-centered marketing copy: they are not running client-centered businesses.

Marketing copy, you see, is not in itself a panacea. It can most assuredly help a solid client-centered company offering solid benefits to a defined market spurt ahead and be more profitable. It can even help for a time to obscure the problems of an enterprise that is not client-centered, but, at root, if you fail to run a client-centered company you cannot for long produce client-centered copy and will not succeed merely in not getting a prospect to buy once but in getting your customers to buy again, the acid-test of the successful enterprise.

And so before again addressing how to bolster your copy, we must review the operations of the successful client-centered company. For if these exist, the raw material is present to create the most persuasive copy imaginable.

Chapter 2

Don't Let The Way You Do Business Handicap Your Ability To Write Cash Copy, Or What You Must Do To Become And Run A Client-Centered Operation.

It was just before Christmas when I called a Texas client of mine. The telephone rang and a tape offered this message, "We're having our Christmas party right now and can't take your call. Call back after 2 p.m. when we're finished."

That was all.

It was a marketing slap in the face, for it said as clearly as you could, "We're having a wildly good time. You're not invited. Wait until after we've finished our revels. Then try again."

I was astonished at the foolishness of the message which screamed, "We are not a client-centered business. Whatever you need will always be secondary to whatever we want — and what we want you — to do."

A most infuriating attitude, indeed.

For make no mistake about it, how you approach every aspect of your business — including the announcement of your annual Christmas party — gives your prospects an indication of what kind of company you are and how you approach the real business of making them happy.

On this basis, most companies stand indicted as falling far short of any acceptable level of client-centered behavior. Which is one significant reason why their marketing documents are so self-centered and futile.

Adopt A Client-Centered Attitude

Nowadays there's much talk about providing customers with service. It is the buzzword of the decade. Yet for most people service remains nothing more than a word. They have no idea that service must be exemplified in *every* prospect and customer contact, including:

- how the prospect is handled on the telephone and in person, and
- how quickly he receives requested information and attention.

Not to mention getting the quality product or service he expects.

Service does not merely mean delivering a quality product or service; it also means the way in which the customer is treated through each of the necessary steps that must precede and perhaps follow delivery.

Thus, each person who comes in contact with the prospect or customer is a key link in the service chain and can, through poor work habits and insufficient humanity, destroy the business' purported desire to appear (and, I hope, be) client-centered.

Each person. Which is why *each* must be tutored in the essentials of client-centered marketing and understand what his role is in achieving the desired objective of a satisfied customer.

Each individual in your enterprise must be specifically informed that yours is a client-centered entity. That their job is not merely to deliver a quality product or service (however important that is), but to:

- find out what problem the prospect is trying to solve;
- connect the prospect with the person who can solve it;
- ensure that that person can assist now . . . or find out when he can assist the prospect so that the prospect knows when his problem will be taken care of;

- guarantee that the prospect doesn't "fall between the cracks", unsure of where to go, who to talk to, and
- in conclusion, take personal responsibility for helping to solve the prospect's problem.

The job of the client-centered employee is to become a "What next?" thinker, trained in not just palming off the prospect but providing a solid, reasonable direction for that prospect, substantially answering the "What next?" question.

Whether your company consists of you alone (as mine does) or is a giant entity with thousands of employees worldwide, you must make it your responsibility to see to it that each individual customer you deal with is happy, that you have either solved his problem personally, or have seen to it that this customer has been connected to the individual who can solve it. Not just mindlessly passed on but substantially connected to the problem solver.

If this is not the publicly announced objective of your company, however small you are, this is the first — and arguably most important — reason why you cannot write client-centered marketing copy.

If you do not believe and have not committed yourself to the solution of each individual customer's problem, you project an attitude that is inimical to the creation of client-centered cash copy. No amount of client-centered language can ever succeed in overcoming the lack of client-centered commitment in each employee, no matter how junior, much less the lack of this commitment from senior operating officers. *No amount whatsoever.*

Thus, if you carry away nothing more from this book, realize that unless you are prepared to commit yourself to a resolutely client-centered policy, for yourself and each of your employees, and are prepared, not merely to announce but to exemplify this policy, all the cash copy in the world cannot save you. Because it is your operating procedures — and attitude — which are at fault. Making this commitment, then, is where your marketing renaissance begins.

Implementing Client-Centered Behavior

Client-centered behavior, as by now must be perfectly clear, is behavior focused on your prospect, the buyer; not on yourself, the seller. Thus, each aspect of your business life must be redirected so that the concentration is where it must always remain: on the buyer — past, present, and future. To achieve this result, a transformation must take place from "Us" thinking to "You" thinking.

Consider the illustration of the poorly announced Christmas party. That announcement says, "We're having our Christmas party. Call back when we're finished with it." The reason this is quite, quite wrong is because the emphasis is on the seller, on their good time and on *their* convenience. It is this emphasis which clearly marks the company — whatever they may say to the contrary and whatever they believe — to be self-centered, uncaring about the prospect and client.

No self-respecting "You-centered" business would ever allow itself to appear like this. It's anathema to everything it stands for.

Thus, the first thing you must do to institute client-centered procedures is to review all that you are doing now. Review:

- the way secretaries answer the phone. Do they talk about themselves, about the company, or are they rigorously focused on the prospect and his business?
- how long it takes for a prospect's phone call to be taken care of and how the call is dealt with. If you claim to be a client-centered company but leave prospects on hold for long periods of time without attending to them; if you pass them along to the wrong people, merely to get rid of them. If, in short, you — or your employees — are merely processing information and not solving prospect problems, then you are exemplifying habits deleterious to client-centered marketing.
- the documents you send out. Are they about you (like most foolish marketing documents are)? Or are they rightly focused on the prospect and what he wishes to achieve?
- how long it takes for these documents to be sent out.

In short, go through *each* operation of your business that involves contact with a prospect or client. Each. To see if you are just talking about client-centered behavior or if your employees and operating practices exemplify it.

And remember, even the smallest things count — both for, and more likely, against you.

Recently, for instance, I answered a newspaper ad from a company that offered information about its service. I called the day the ad came out; indeed, given the way the call was handled, I felt sure I had to be the first person to respond to it. I was told the information would be sent out "shortly". Given that the company is in Gloucester, Massachusetts, not so far away from me, I expected the information I requested to be here in a couple of days, a week at the most; (one must, after all, allow for the vagaries of the post). But it was *three* weeks later that the pre-packaged information arrived — without any indication of what had taken so long. As far as I was concerned, this was about as clear an indication as I needed that the company was:

- disorganized;
- not client-centered; (they should have explained what took so long), and
- definitely not worth doing business with.

Their slack habits were responsible not only for my loss of interest but for my very definite feelings of pique. End result? I had wasted my time. They had wasted their time and money. All to produce a feeling in me which will not profit them and which may further hurt them if I find myself in a situation where this company and its activities are being discussed. Multiply this all-too-common situation by the millions of times it occurs daily, and you see why instituting client-centered marketing procedures is not merely sensible but imperative.

Here are some more suggestions to make you that resolutely client-centered business.

- Be prepared to deal with your customers and clients around the clock.

A company that does business during regular business hours only is a company clearly indicating that it is selfish. Instead, you must indicate that you are client-centered, interested in solving the prospect's problem when he has a problem that needs to be solved.

Now, I hasten to add, you need not be actually present at all times (in a one-person operation like mine that's physically impossible), but you must have the means available to:

- let the prospect or client know you are interested in helping them;

- take their message, and
- get back to them at the earliest possible opportunity and so start solving their problem.

A simple telephone answering machine, the right marketing message, and a client-centered attitude provide what you need.

It staggers me that so few would-be marketers see their telephone answering machine as anything other than a way for people to leave information for them. It is also, and equally importantly, a way for you to disseminate a client-centered message about you, a message that says, "I want to and can help you. Leave me the information I need."

Remember what I said: *each* aspect of your business, *each* of your business practices, must be a client-centered practice. And that includes how you use your telephone answering machine. This must feature a cash-copy message. Call mine some day ((617) 547-6372) and see for yourself. Here's one of the several client-centered messages I use:

"Hello, this is Jeffrey Lant, the cash-copy writer. I can't speak to you right now because I'm helping another marketer produce copy that'll sell more of his products and services, the kind of profit-making copy I can also produce for you. Leave me a message about your copy needs — or anything else — after the beep, and I'll get right back to you to improve your marketing."

Isn't this better than the usual pallid message that the run of the world leaves on its machine? Of course it is! It's a cash-copy message that says as clearly as possible: you have a problem. You need a solution. I am that solution. And I'll be getting back to you as quickly as possible to find out how I can help you achieve what you want.

Let me tell you something, people are both impressed by and remember this message. Why? Because they've never heard a message on a telephone answering machine before that's so clearly about them, rather than about the person they're calling.

What impresses them at least as much is the fact that their call is returned the same day, often the same hour, in which they make it. You know yourself how infrequently anyone even bothers to return your calls, despite the fact that you've indicated that doing so is important. These days, in order to impress us with their high standing in the world and profound importance, people do not return calls. In fact, all they do is confirm us in our opinion that they're selfish and insensitive to anyone's needs but their own.

But this pervasive — and aggravating — failure to return calls gives the client-centered marketer a wonderful opening to impress people with his care and concern for them and willingness to help them solve their problems. The telephone message that says, "I'm out helping someone achieve the objective you want, and if you leave a message I shall help you achieve it, too" is undoubtedly impressive.

The fact that you actually do return the call and do begin to gather the information you need to solve the prospect's problem will both impress and even astonish them.

And I'll tell you a little secret, the fact that you call in the evening or on a weekend, or some "non-business" time will impress them even more. Rarely, oh so rarely in their lives, has someone taken this efficient and intensive interest in solving their problem. You are, therefore, already well on the way to convincing them that you are a client-centered business with only one interest — *theirs!*

Learn To Talk About Providing Your Prospects With The Benefit They Desire, Not The Information You're Actually Sending.

How many times have you called or written for information and been told, "I'll make sure that you get the information"? I bet it happens all the time.

Well, from the standpoint of client-centered marketing, when you hear this line, it's an indication that the seller doesn't know his business sufficiently well, and has missed an opportunity to focus on you and your wants.

For remember, the seller is not in the business of sending you free information. The seller is in the business of making a sale by convincing you that his product or service will solve your problem.

Try this instead:

Prospect: "Hello, my name is Sandra Smith. I'm calling to request the free information about how to improve my marketing documents."

Client-Centered Marketer: "Thanks for calling. Yes, I can send you the information on how Jeffrey Lant can improve the drawing power of every marketing document you'll ever use. Please give me your name, address and telephone number. I'll be sending you this afternoon the facts on how to improve every marketing document you'll ever use."

See the difference?

In the first illustration, the feeble seller is simply sending free information. There's no attempt to differentiate this information from all the other free information that Sandra Smith is undoubtedly receiving; for if she's like other people, she's inundated with information.

In the first illustration, the seller is perfectly polite, of course, but undoubtedly stupid and has missed an opportunity to get the prospect excited about the benefit that's coming to her.

Your job as a client-centered marketer is *not* to dispense information. It's to persuade the prospect that you are both knowledgeable about solving the prospect's problem with your product or service and interested in having the opportunity to work with the client to bring about the objective he desires.

In the second example, you have told the prospect you can solve her problem (her real objective) and have named the benefit she'll receive. The prospect is now not waiting to receive mere information in the mail, but a solution to an important problem. You are now using anticipation — and the prospect's own desire for a solution — on your behalf. The marketer who fails to make use of these is in a much weaker position than he should be.

At all times the client-centered marketer remembers these key facts:

- He is not in the business of dispensing free information. He's in the business of solving problems.
- It is perfectly acceptable — and indeed foolish not— to inform the prospect that you can solve his problem, and that the material you are sending can help him achieve this objective.

A note about names: Notice that I didn't immediately jump in and call Sandra Smith "Sandra." Much foolishness has been written about names and how to establish immediate intimacy with the prospect. But watch out! The subject is fraught with perils. As I've written before, I detest the name "Jeff" and punish people who presume to call me this name by making sure they don't get my business.

The kinds of people who automatically assume that my name should be shortened to a name *they* like are guilty of what I call the "Rechristening Syndrome." They want to give me a name they think I should have, rather than the name I want to be called. In their rush to a false intimacy, they make a grave error and end up insulting me. They deserve whatever nastiness they get from me in return.

Rather than make this mistake myself when someone contacts me, I wait for a cue from them. If they call me "Jeffrey" (or "Jeff", poor buggers) I call them by their first name as well. They have set the level of intimacy, and it is only good manners for me to follow their lead. (Of course, if they make the mistake of calling me "Jeff" I hasten, in as genteel a fashion as I can muster right then, to correct them).

If they use no direct address with me, I either follow their lead or use "Mr." and "Ms." (Never, never, never "Miss".) If they are older, or in a superior position, I always dignify their names with an honorific.

Here the most sensible rule is: Don't presume. The person you're talking or writing to will show you in his own good time how he'd like to be addressed. So be patient. And if you have the slightest hesitation, ask. That's perfectly allowable and eminently sensible.

P.S. If after reading this book, you call me "Jeff", I shall despair of your ever becoming client-centered and shall (perhaps not so secretly) regard you as a selfish, irredeemably stupid flatworm.

Provide The Prospect With Guidelines About What Will Happen, When It Will Happen, And How It Will Happen.

Structure is what makes people happy, for with structure they know what's expected of them, when they should be concerned, and when concern is unnecessary. It is your responsibility, as a client-centered marketer, to give your prospects and customers the structure they need.

Thus, whenever you communicate with your prospects and customers — in person, by letter or by telephone — give them the precise information they need. Tell them:

- when the information they've requested is going out ("today" is the correct word);
- how the information is being sent;
- when they can expect to receive the information they need;
- what to do if they don't get it;
- whom to call for further information, and
- when that person will be available to assist.

In short, give the prospect all the information he needs to feel comfortable that his problem is being taken care of in a reasonable fashion and what he should do if he fails to get what he wants when he wants it.

Providing this kind of specific information immediately establishes you as empathetic and client-centered. See for youself.

- "I'll send you some information."
- "I'll send you the facts today about how you can produce at least thirteen more widgets every hour. You should have it in a couple of days, and I'll follow up then."

Which is better?

I'm sure you know.

The first is a statement from a person who thinks he's doing what he's supposed to by indicating that you'll get information. All perfectly polite, of course, but lamentable from a client-centered perspective.

As you now know, your job is not to send out free information. It's to indicate that you can solve problems. So tell the prospect you're able to give him what he wants. And in my illustration, the prospect wants more widgets every hour, not more information.

Then, too, let the prospect know when he can expect to get what you're sending. Put his mind to work for you. Get him anticipating: "Tomorrow I'll find out how I can produce more widgets." What's working in your favor is increased widget production (and hence more money) — which he wants. And already, he's seeing your material as a means of getting it. How much stronger this is than the thought of receiving another piece of paper in the mail.

Needless to say, you should allow yourself sufficient time to get the prospect what he wants. Usually, instead of saying "You'll receive your material tomorrow . . .", I say, "I'm sending your material today . . ." That way they can blame the post office if it's not there just when they want it.

See how important this all is from the standpoint of client-centered marketing and, ultimately, the production of cash copy?

Remember, wherever you are in the process of delivering the problem-solving product or service, you must still be a client-centered problem solver resolutely focusing on what the prospect wants (more widgets, mind, not more information) and what you are doing to ensure he gets it.

The prospect's confidence in your ability to solve his problem grows in direct proportion to how you solve all the minor problems that precede your mutual focus on his major objective. In this way, the prospect is right to judge your ability to help him increase his widget production by the way you handle his telephone call, provide the material he requires, and follow it up. If you fail to be client-centered in these relatively minor activities, he is right to deduce that you will not be client-centered in whatever else you attempt to do for him. And he will rightly take his business elsewhere. This is why *everything* counts in the way you run your business.

Since everything counts, you must think of everything. Use things like these to cut the cost of the client contacting you:

- toll-free numbers;
- telephone calls the prospect can charge to you, and
- business reply mail and inserted stamped envelopes.

Your prospects are more likely to regard you as client-centered if you make it easy for them to contact you than if you don't. And they'll certainly order more from you if you cut the cost of their response.

Here are a few thoughts about each of these response-building alternatives.

Profiting From A Toll-Free Number

If you are selling either a line of items or items (including services) with a hefty price tag or items that the client will regularly need to reorder, you should consider using a toll-free "800" number. All a customer needs to take advantage of this number is your marketing information, telephone number, and a valid credit card. Each is a key part of this selling scenario.

It is undoubtedly true that such a number will boost both your inquiries and sales. But you must be certain you are providing a convenience to buyers and not a means for window shoppers to waste your time and money.

Personally, I do not use an 800 number, despite the fact that I meet the first two criteria above: namely selling a line of items or items (including services) with a hefty price tag. And there is a good reason why.

I invite people through my nationally-syndicated column, books, and work-shops to call me if they have a brief question relating to what I've written or to developing their business. I am as yet unconvinced that providing 800 service to all these people would not overwhelm me with an avalanche of calls (some regrettably frivolous) while producing insufficient revenue in return. And I know for a fact that since these individuals have to spend their own money to call me, they give their question more attention than if they could connect with me on my money. Even so there is an incredible number of these calls every day!

If, however, I were only selling products and services — and not making myself available for questioners — then I would *certainly* install an 800-number or rent usage from someone else.

The important consideration is that you use such a number solely to sell — and not merely dispense information. And that you do not fail to market this number to your prospects as a service to them.

Before taking the step of using expensive 800 service, try an intermediate step: let buyers placing an order make their calls collect. Just, note, their order calls.

This system will only work:

- if it increases the number of people who order from you, and
- if (because of your personal marketing once the prospect is on

the line) the unit of sale increases sufficiently to cover the cost of the call and the additional time you must spend with the prospect.

Once you decide that these two essential conditions have been met, then you must market the availability of this service to your clients in the most enthusiastic way, as yet another illustration of your client-centered behavior.

Finally, consider using either business reply mail or stamped response envelopes. The same two considerations apply as above: namely that you must keep close track of what happens both before and after using these response-increasing devices, so you know if they really are increasing the number of people who order from you and if they are favorably influencing the buyer's dollar commitment.

The only way you'll really know is by testing them.

Remember, becoming and remaining a client-centered business, means:

- staying on the alert for devices that make it easier for your prospects to respond;
- wanting to find which response techniques work best for what you're selling;
- testing until you're sure you've found the most sensible for your prospects; and
- promoting the existence of each and every one of the devices you do decide to use as fresh evidence of your resolutely client-centered operations.

Providing Many Payment Options

Americans, as I need hardly tell you, are head over heels in debt; indeed we are having a love affair with debt such as the world has hardly ever witnessed. Which means that if you want to be seen as being client-centered (as well as taking advantage of people's manifest inclination to buy everything conceivable on credit) you have got to consider the various payment options available and adopt all the ones that seem sensible to you. This means considering the use of both credit cards and credit. For make no mistake about it, these days if you are in business, you are in the debtor business.

Using Credit Cards

Whatever you're selling, you'll probably be better off selling it with credit cards. There are two chief reasons for offering sales with credit cards: the buyer's and yours.

The buyer is happy.

When you make credit card service available, the buyer can get whatever he wants whenever he wants it. He should be able to place his order — from anywhere in the world — twenty-four hours a day and can therefore expect you to deal with it promptly.

To make this scenario work from a client-centered perspective, you must have:

- a twenty-four hour order center;
- sales literature that clearly indicates you can assist the client twenty-four hours a day (and which indicates you place a premium on assisting the buyer promptly), and
- of course, the ability to take orders with a credit card.

The seller is happy.

You get payment from your buyers immediately — whether you are selling a product or service. As soon as you get an authorization code on the transaction and deposit the money at your bank, you've got it. This means no messing around with an invoice and the old problem of getting the buyer to pay up. After you've got the authorization code, if the buyer defaults, it's the bank's problem — not yours!

Note: many individuals come to me for a single hour of consultation or they purchase an hour of my time to be used by telephone. Nowadays, I let them know when the time is booked that they can either pay with a check or give me a credit card number at the end of the consultation. If the consultation has been by telephone, they may either send a check in advance or give me their credit card information; if they select the latter option (most do), as soon as the consultation is over I simply send them the credit confirmation slip; (along, I might add, with additional sales literature about other ways I can help them!).

This system has significantly cut the amount of time I have to wait for my money and the occasional hassles I had to go through to collect it. I heartily recommend it to you.

Drawbacks

Aside from the unavoidably increased paperwork of credit card sales, the major drawback is the monthly bank fees on credit card transactions. These average about 5% of the gross amount you deposit. Should you absorb these fees — or pass them on to the buyer? That, I think, depends on what your competitors do.

Thus, in my mail-order book business, I have absorbed the cost of the credit card transaction, because that's what the prevailing practice is in both bookstores and other mail-order book vendors. However, where I am charging for a service I pass the credit card charge to the client, feeling that 5% is too great an amount to give up.

Here are some guidelines of how to use your credit-card policy from a marketing standpoint:

- If you are not passing on the cost of your credit card charges to the buyer, tell him so. Don't expect the buyer to know what a great and generous person you are and that you are giving him a benefit. Tell him. Remember: there is no client-centered benefit until you announce it. Merely *doing* the right thing isn't good enough. You must tell people you are doing it and use it as a way to get them to do business with you.

- If you are not paying the credit card charges yourself but are passing them on to your buyer, give the buyer the chance to decide what he wants to do. Client-centered marketing is choice-centered marketing. You don't have to decide if your buyer should pay by cash, check, or charge. Just make all these alternatives available, and let your buyer decide. Provide your buyer with the facts ("Your credit card purchase is billed at 5% over the total to account for our bank's fees."). Then herald the fact that the buyer decides what to do. "Tell me which payment plan you prefer . . ."

The client-centered company doesn't dictate to its buyers; it presents facts, explains why certain actions are necessary, and lets the buyer decide what to do based on his own interests. ("Pay now. Save an extra 5% in credit card charges."

"Use your MasterCard or VISA and get your problem-solving products and services NOW.")

A Few Words On Billing

Frankly, I am not a big advocate of billing. From a seller's standpoint, billing is both expensive, and, as people "forget" to pay you, frustrating as all get out. But, again, there are instances where you'll need to be able to bill people. If you do so, decide to get the credit you should — as a client-centered marketer — for doing so.

When should you bill? Invoice major institutions using purchase orders. This includes colleges and schools, libraries, hospitals, trade and professional associations, and, of course, government agencies. While more and more of even these businesses have a company credit card, many (foolishly) don't. To these — and to these alone — may you safely extend credit and take marketing benefit for doing so. "Send no money now! Just give us your institutional purchase order number. You get the (benefit you seek) immediately!"

But I earnestly advise you not to extend similar credit to individuals, because here's where your downfall begins. They must pay cash — and be given inducements to do so.

If you feel badly about instituting a two-tier system where some people are billed and where others must pay immediately (personally, I don't), you can give individual buyers an incentive for paying cash. Create an information-packed (but inexpensive to produce) Special Report on a subject of interest to your buyers; (to get an idea what you might write about see my catalog at the back of this book). Offer it to your *cash* buyers only — not to those whom you have to invoice or who charge their purchases.

If adding this premium (which after all does cost money to produce and to mail) doesn't succeed in cutting monthly invoicing or credit card orders in favor of immediate cash, drop the program. These kinds of premiums — like everything else you do — should make business sense and not just be an extra expense. In other words, even things that are client-centered must not adversely affect the bottom line, or they become part of the problem, instead of part of the solution.

Final Thoughts About Becoming And Running The Client-Centered Enterprise

I know from my ongoing research that the marketing information produced by most companies — large and small — is not client-centered. As you'll see from the illustrations that punctuate this book, size is not the determining factor in producing client-centered marketing materials. What truly differentiates the client-centered company producing rigorously prospect-focused marketing from those which are not is attitude: the attitude that says, "Prospect, here you are most important. We exist solely for your benefit."

Client-centered enterprises believe this, are committed to this, and work to show each prospect and every customer that they mean this — every day. These kinds of companies rarely produce selfish marketing materials. And if by chance they do, a client-centered marketer and copywriter like me can solve their problem in a very short time, for they have a very solvable technical problem.

But what of the others? (And I hope you are not one of them.) They have a very serious problem which cannot be so easily remedied. For they are more interested in themselves and what they can get from their business than they are in what service they can give their buyers. And this is a far more serious problem to correct.

Such marketers say in effect:

- "Here are the features of what we've got. You figure out the benefits for yourself."
- "Our ease and convenience are more important than yours. Do business with us when we say you can, in the way we say you can; not when you want and how you want to."
- "If you're anxious about whether what we're selling will really work for you, we don't care. Just buy it because we tell you to."
- "You're lucky anybody here gives you any service whatso-ever. Be glad you're getting literature (even if it's weeks late). Be grateful for the fact that a secretary pays any attention to you at all (instead of leaving you on hold forever). In short, you need us, so put up with whatever we give you and be glad."

While no company ever has published these jarring statements as their operational guidelines, both you and I can name dozens that exemplify them. For such enterprises, even the best marketing copy in the world will not solve their real problem: a distaste for and even detestation of the burdensome creatures called customers.

Keep this in mind as you use this book. Is your problem really one of taking your client-centered company and presenting it to your prospects in such a way that they'll want to do business with you? If so, you've come to the right place. The answers you need are right here. Or it is transforming your operation into a client-centered business, really focusing — perhaps for the first time — on the buyer and on what you can do for him? For make no mistake about it, unless you are running a client-centered business, any cash copy you produce will be nothing more than a stopgap, an attempt to shore up a rotten foundation with cosmetic repairs. It just won't work.

So, now, be honest. Examine your heart and soul. Do you have a profound commitment to a generally announced, thoroughly understood and daily implemented client-centered program that is continually searching for new ways to help your buyers profit from the benefits of what you are selling? Or are you just going through the motions, spitting out words like "service" and "convenience" when you just don't mean them? Be honest. And remember, whether you are or not, your customers still vote with their feet — and pocket books — every single day. And *their* votes are final.

Chapter 3

The Attitude And Skills You Need To Produce Cash Copy

Here is a short but pivotal chapter, because if you don't master the attitude and skills necessary to write successful cash copy, you won't be able to produce it.

It's obvious to me, reviewing so many marketing documents for so many kinds of products and services, that many — even most — of the people producing them either didn't have the right attitude or were, in some fashion, technically ill-equipped for the job.

Don't let this happen to you.

Adopting The Right Attitude — The Cash Copy Attitude

What I'm about to say should come as no surprise to you. Indeed, by now, you should be able to tell *me* the proper attitude of the cash copy specialist. In a single word, you must be empathetic.

Empathy is defined as "the mental identification of the ego with the character and experiences of another person." And this is precisely what you need to write successful cash copy and to be a successful marketer generally. You must project yourself into the character and experiences of each individual you wish to help with your product or service. Each one!

This empathy cannot be episodic; cannot ebb and flow. It must be continual, never ending. You must have it every day with each person you deal with. It is the absolutely crucial *sine qua non* of marketing success. It is exhilarating. It is inspiring. It will exhaust you.

Not surprisingly in a society which is the very embodiment of the "me first" principle, empathy is in severely short supply. This is why so many marketing documents are selfish and self-defeating. How could they be otherwise, when most people go into business solely to realize their own objectives without a care for what may happen to the people they are ostensibly attempting to help?

You be different.

You care.

Care to understand what your prospects are trying to accomplish.

Care to let them know you can help.

Care to tell them (sometimes with the utmost candor) how your product or service can help them realize their objectives.

Care to inform them what will happen to them if they don't take action to solve their problem.

Care to understand their worries and anxieties both about what you are selling and about you.

Care to make sure that you address these worries and anxieties — and not treat them as inconsequential.

Care to be flexible in how you do business and when you do business so that your client understands that you are truly interested in his comfort and ease.

Care to guarantee your customer's satisfaction.

In short, empathize. Put yourself in your client's shoes and run your marketing — and write your cash copy — from his perspective, not from yours.

I like to think this is how I run my business and that it is one of the reasons for my success. While writing this chapter, this letter from Tom Lucier, an author from Florida and one of my clients, arrived: "Jeffrey, I sincerely appreciate your creative abilities, but more importantly, I appreciate your giving me my dollar's worth whether it's from your copywriting or from purchasing your books. In a world of shortchangers, you're a full dollar's worth!"

What Tom is saying (and I'm grateful to him for doing so) is simply this: "You cared enough to truly pay attention to me and for that I am sincerely grateful." This is *precisely* what you want every single one of your customers to say about you and what you're doing. And if you hear it from them, you know you are running the empathetic enterprise and cannot help but be successful.

This may all seem obvious to you. But before you dismiss this chapter out of hand as material you know all too well, ask yourself this: Do you merely know it? Or are you living it? If you are to succeed in marketing, if you are truly to create cash copy that causes your prospects to be excited about what you can do for them and buy what you're selling, you must exhibit client-centered empathy. Each client must feel that you are here for him and for him alone. Not as part of a mass, a group, a sector, or a niche. But for him individually. This is what empathetic marketing is all about.

More Traits Of The Empathetic Marketer

The empathetic marketer is both helpful and accommodating, eager to please, anxious to be of service.

The other day I called a company to place an order. The secretary left me on hold forever. I was told the person I wanted to speak to was at lunch. That afteroon I received no phone call back. I had to start the whole process over the next day. Do you think anyone at that company had any understanding of empathetic marketing? I doubt it.

But to find out, I decided to review their catalog and see how they represented themselves. This particular catalog, a handsome four-color production, was written in the third person, as if to no one in particular. Certainly not written for me and my needs.

It figured.

The lack of empathy and client-centered directness in their catalog was mirrored in the way they run their office operation.

What a shame!

Not helpful.

Not accommodating.

Not client-centered.

Not focused on the prospect.

Not interested in knowing my problem. And seemingly unconcerned about solving it.

In short, not empathetic.

Imagine conceiving such a selfish entity.

Imagine working for such a selfish entity.

And imagine trying to get service from such a selfish entity.

No wonder so much of human life so often seems so futile and unpromising!

Regularly ask yourself with each customer you encounter:

- Was I as friendly as I could have been? (Friendly, mind, not supine.)
- Was I as helpful and candid as I could have been about what the prospect should be doing to solve his problem and what would happen to him if he didn't solve it?
- Was I interested in helping this prospect — this individual — find a solution to his problem?
- Did I follow through and do all that I said I would do when I said I would do it?
- If my standard operating procedures didn't fit this case, did I attempt to be flexible and so meet the prospect's objectives (and my own need to make the sale)?

In short, was I empathetic?

We already know that failure to run a client-centered operation severely reduces the chance of successful marketing, no matter how successfully you produce cash copy.

If you have the wrong attitude, a selfish attitude, you cannot run a client-centered enterprise and cannot, therefore, produce the cash copy you need.

I think, for instance, of someone I know quite well, another marketing consultant. He is gruff, unmannerly, often crude, for all that he has two college degrees. He has no sense of how to relate to people or, I think, of how people see him. I know he means well, but this isn't nearly enough. Not nearly enough.

His attitude is unhelpful and self-defeating. And as a result he produces the stiffest marketing documents imaginable, totally focused on himself and far removed from the real concerns of his prospects. The result? His business languishes, marooned in selfishness, quite unable to progress. The further result? He is an unhappy, embittered, caustic man whose problems compound daily like some sort of poisoned interest.

Don't let this be you.

Resolve now to romance every prospect you encounter, to make that single individual feel that he — and only he — is the true object of your affections and that nothing else matters so much to you as that he succeeds in getting what he wants, thanks to your kindly and knowledgeable ministrations.

Make sure that this is how you feel. That this is how others working with you feel. That it is the announced and understood policy of your firm. And that every document you turn out — be it a business card or a full-page ad — resonates with this feeling of thoughtful affection and concern. For if you do not care for your prospects, why should they care for you? Why should they put any trust in you? Why should they listen to what you say or read what you write? Why should they bother to seek you out for your assistance? You see, if you do not show concern about him, your prospect is perfectly correct to show no concern about you.

The result of this idiocy? Wasteful, draining, pointless stalemate. Is this what you want? Of course not!

So care. And make sure that everything you do shows it. This is the attitude of the client-centered marketer and the master of cash copy.

Skills You Need To Produce Cash Copy

Adopting and living the right client-centered attitude is the key constituent of marketing success. But listen! It is a necessary but not a sufficient condition of success. You must also have certain skills, the skills that will translate your concern and the products and services and business operating procedures which are tangible evidence of your concern into sales. Without these skills, the most rigorously client-centered attitude in the world must fail to succeed in the ultimate objective: helping yourself while helping others. Here, then, are the skills you must cultivate.

Good Research Skills

Research always precedes the writing of compelling cash copy. You must know:

- who else is offering similar products and services;
- how they are doing so;
- how effectively they are doing so.

You cannot write cash copy in a vacuum. You must know what others are doing, including:

- what offers they are making;
- anxieties they are addressing — and how;
- their chief selling points;
- mode of business; (Do they take credit cards, accept around-the-clock orders, or use an 800-number?);
- marketing media they are using;
- how much space and time they have purchased;
- even what colors and lay-out they have adopted.

This is why you must collect all the materials that relate to your competitors, including:

- ads
- brochures
- flyers
- business cards

- cover letters
- newsletters
- books
- cassette tapes.

You need everything that enables you to find out precisely what your competitors are doing, precisely whom they are doing it for, precisely how they have decided to position themselves, and precisely how they have decided to address their prospects and deal with them.

I insist that my new clients (who all too often know little if anything about their competitors) start collecting all such materials and keep both a set for themselves and give one to me. In doing so, I remember what Sir Isaac Newton once said, "If I have seen farther, it is because I have stood upon the shoulders of giants." Well, our competitors are not giants, but at least they have often considered (and possibly even solved at least some of) the problems we must face. And I see no reason not to profit from whatever good ideas they have come up with.

Good Analytic Skills

In reviewing the marketing materials produced by competitors and in being able to analyze the possible effectiveness of those you produce, one single skill predominates: the ability to deduce whether what has been produced is in fact client-centered or not. Do the marketing documents under consideration rigorously focus on the client and his needs? Or are they yet another instance of the selfish marketing that dominates nowadays?

You must develop the skill of determining what is client-centered marketing as produced by others and developing such client-centered marketing for yourself. A single word will assist you: "You"!

As I've already said and reemphasized, "you" is probably the most important marketing word. So, use a "you" analysis to determine whether what others have produced — and what you are thinking of using — is effective.

Look at the teaser copy on your envelope. Is it about your prospect and his problem — or is it about you?

Review:

- the headline
- the opening line in the copy
- the testimonial
- benefits you have offered.

Are these about you — and hence quite inadequate. Or are they about the prospect — the "you" you must always be addressing and whose interests are paramount?

You do not need a Ph.D. to do this analysis, either. All you need to do is be certain that what you are producing — or reviewing (for it always pays to see what others are doing) — is indeed about the buyer. And not about you. This is the key analytic skill you need. But you *must* have it to succeed.

Ability To Go For The Jugular

Most marketing documents beat around the bush — a fatal problem. The best marketing goes for the jugular. Hits the prospect's supreme aspiration or anxiety. Hits it hard. And hits it immediately. And the key word here is *immediately.*

Here's a flyer that just came in the mail. It begins: "Business writing services for industry, finance, & government." These selfish words are followed by more selfish words: the seller's name and "communications consultant, advertising, public relations documentation."

This is the antithesis of client-centered cash copy. These words are:

- about the seller, not the buyer;
- features, not benefits;
- bland, not compelling.

In short, they are just words, not motivators.

What the seller is really saying here is this: "I think I'm important. I think you should spend as much of your precious time as possible trying to figure out what I can do for you. I wish to maintain a professional distance between your problem — which frightens me — and my solution. I want things to be clean and neat and detached."

This is all wrong.

Remember the jugular.

Cash copy says, "You have a pain. Let me show you how badly it hurts you." Or, "you have an aspiration. Let me remind you how badly you want to achieve it." Either way, the cash copy writer hits a nerve. And then says, oh so smoothly, "I'm here to help. Here's what I can do for you. Here are the benefits you get when you do business with me!".

Why does the cash copy writer go for the jugular? Not because he's badly bred or because he enjoys jolting people (although God knows, there are moments when that is fun), but because he knows people would rather take no action than a beneficial action. That people are looking for a reason not to act, instead of a reason for taking action. Even if that action will help them. And that people — presented with so many possibilities for their limited time and money — don't know which way to go. So, all too often they fail to do anything.

Which is why the consummate copywriter is the master of the motivational jolt. The jolt which makes the prospect take action NOW. And unless you can make your prospect take action NOW, what you've written — no matter how glib, how fluent, how graceful and charming — is futile, pointless, and wrong. That's why you must go for the jugular. To make your prospect take action NOW.

Ability To Inspire Trust

Going for the jugular alone, however, will not solve your problem — the problem of getting the prospect to take action. No, you must also develop the skill of inspiring trust. You've got to convince the prospect — to whom you've just applied the electric shock of anxiety or aspiration — to trust you, rely on you, and feel comfortable that you can do more than jolt. You must develop the skill of instilling trust.

Now I'm going to share a secret with you that you'll use profitably in all the marketing materials you'll ever use and which, to my horror and dismay, I rarely see used. To start the process of inspiring prospect trust, tell the prospect that by using your services he'll get the benefit, the advantage, the solution he wants.

What do I mean?

Well, I continue to look at the brochure I mentioned above, the brochure produced by a fellow copywriter and specialist in marketing. I'm using this as an illustration because it's a textbook perfect illustration of what not to produce and to warn you: yes, even a professional copywriter can produce shockingly inadequate work.

Nowhere in his standard six-sided brochure, does the seller once — not even once — guarantee either the quality of his work or that he will work until the prospect is satisfied. Nowhere, in short, does he say the prospect will get what he is paying for. Amazing, isn't it?

What your prospects want to know is that you know what you're doing (and they'd like some evidence of it). But more importantly, they want to know that you'll do what is necessary to give them what they want.

If your prospect feels that you are both competent (a necessary condition) and focused on his achieving his desire (another necessary condition), then you have gone a long way towards establishing a relationship of trust. And what could be better for helping this process than telling the prospect — directly, simply, candidly — that, yes, you mean to give him what he wants. And have others ready, willing, and able to stand up for you, confirming that you can do so.

Other things help, too, to establish the prospect's trust in you:

- licenses and professional qualifications;
- testimonials;
- years in business;
- membership in accrediting and professional bodies.

Yes, all these help. But what helps even more, I think, is your statement — supported by those who have benefitted from what you do — that you will work to the prospect's satisfaction. This is a very potent agent in the necessary development of the prospect's trust in you. And without that trust the relationship cannot prosper.

Ability To Motivate Immediate Action

Strangely, a great percentage of the marketing documents I read seem to suggest that it doesn't matter to the seller if you (his prospect) use his services now or not, that it is all the same to him.

This, of course, is ridiculous. It does matter whether the prospect acts now or not. It obviously matters to you. The more prospects who use your products or services now, the better off you are now. This matters.

And it should matter to the prospect, too. If you are really in the business of solving the prospect's problem and of making his life better *and* you feel that this is what your product or service will do for him, then it does matter if he takes action now. Because if he does not, his current limited, unsatisfactory, painful and even debilitating condition will continue. Is this what you want?

Not if you're a client-centered marketer, it isn't.

You want that prospect to take action NOW.

By this measure, a brochure in my hand from the Bureau of Business Practice (a division of Prentice-Hall) in Waterford, CT, fails miserably. It starts with this inane headline: "Everybody's Talking About It!" (a palpable lie). "It" is a video cassette entitled "How Supervisors Should Appraise Employee Performance."

The inducement to act? Well, I suppose it's the fact that I can get this cassette for a free 15-day trial viewing.

This is the offer. But what's the inducement to accept it? Does the offer expire? Or does it roll on forever like Old Man River? In fact, there's no expiration date, no termination — and hence, no reason to act today. Which is precisely what cash copy must inspire.

Ladies and gentlemen, the folks at Prentice Hall forgot what you must always remember: namely that there must always be a reason for acting NOW. That unless you have provided the prospect with a reason for acting NOW — a good, convincing, self-interested, compelling reason — which actually does cause him to act NOW, you have failed. Your marketing piece has failed. And you should be ashamed of yourself!

Therefore, you must develop the skill of getting your prospects to act NOW. You must have the skill of convincing them that it is in their interest to act NOW. That they will be worse off if they don't act NOW. That they can only get what they want by acting NOW.

And let there be no mistake about it: this is a skill indeed.

Each marketing document you produce must have as its *raison d' être* getting the prospect to act NOW. Not tomorrow. Not next week. But NOW. Now look at the marketing documents you are currently using, at the last ad you ran, at your brochure: do they give the prospect a reason for acting NOW? Or is he perfectly correct in assuming that procrastination makes good sense since you'll always be there, and it just doesn't matter what he does or when he does it? I hope this is not the deleterious signal you are sending your prospects!

Ability To Translate Features Into Benefits

For countless hours now, I have sat with decent, humane, educated and caring people as they've struggled with one of the chief problems of producing cash copy: turning features into benefits. Without a doubt, this is a skill that most product and service sellers don't have, but which is crucial to their success.

I cannot overstress the importance of this skill — or the difficulty most copywriters (yes, even professionals) have in acquiring it.

Recently a very bright client came to me with an investment guide covering nearly 90 international investments and how they've performed for the past quarter century. During our discussions he kept bringing up the fact that the book was studded with charts and graphs. He obviously was extremely proud of this work, but it was more difficult for him to tell me what difference they made.

All right, let's use this as an illustration. A chart, as you certainly now know, is a feature. And features *per se* are utterly irrelevant. When you hear or read about a feature, the correct response is "So what?" Because a feature is a "me" aspect; the benefit is the "you" aspect.

So my problem with this client was to figure out what benefit these charts and graphs offered to the buyer.

One of the charts shows how the nearly 90 investments have performed since 1960. This chart enables one to see which investments did well during recession and which did well during boom times. The results were amazingly similar for each of the recessions we've had since 1960. Immediately I discerned our benefit.

This wasn't just a chart, a lot of dull historic data. No indeed, it was a strictly factual guide to which investment groups performed well (and how well) and which investment groups performed badly (and how badly) during different economic cycles. Once the investment professionals (the prospects) had projected how certain key variables would perform in the next six months or year (variables like the Prime Rate, inflation rate, *etc.*), they could check the chart for when they had performed similarly and what the nearly 90 investment groups had done. And make their investment decisions accordingly. With an 89.5% chance of being right!

Now we were on the benefit track. For we didn't just have data. We had a precise, factual means for knowing when to move money from weakening investments into investments which had a nearly 9 in 10 chance of making money. Astonishing!

And a very powerful benefit indeed for people whose job it is to predict trends and move their own and their client's money accordingly.

See how you transform a feature into a benefit? In a word, it's moving from "me" to "you". It's a skill you must have, or you will fail in marketing generally, not just in the production of cash copy.

Ability To Break Free From Standard English Usage

Before moving into this section, I want to remind you that in marketing one thing and only one thing matters: making the sale. Not being perceived as professional. Not winning prizes for your work. Not being thought a nice little boy or girl. Only making the sale — and so being able to assist your prospect in reaching his objective. *Nothing else matters.*

Which is why you must develop new writing skills and move away from the thrall of standard English and its approach to writing.

This is why in copywriting you must feel at liberty to use all these means of accentuating your message and getting an immediate response — whether or not they are the standard approach.

- Short sentences. Short sentences are more action-oriented than long sentences. They take less time to read, they increase the likelihood they will be read, and they impart a sense of urgency — and the need to take action. All copy should be composed of short, active sentences.

- Sentences or sentence fragments beginning with action verbs. The objective of all marketing documents is to move the prospect from where he is now to a place where (using your product or service), he'll be better. Sentences beginning with action verbs give a sense of movement and help achieve this objective.

- Reinforcers. The best copywriting concentrates on one major point, one chief advantage the prospect gets by taking action. Everything in the document reinforces this single point, whether that point is looking more youthful, making money, or losing weight. Remember: you need one major message and many, many reaffirmations and reinforcements of it using capitalization, underlinings, bold, italics, bullets, arrows, boxes, and indentations. If the point is important, emphasize it.

- Subtlety-smashers. Copywriting is obvious writing. Clear, concise, bold and detailed. Don't expect your prospect to spend even five minutes trying to figure out what you may mean about what you think is important for him. Tell him! Make it so obvious that no one can misunderstand the benefit or fail to grasp your meaning. Note: even so, some people will.

Now unless you've had practice writing this kind of copy, you may well find it difficult. And may even feel that it's beneath your dignity. Well, get over it!

What you are doing — all that you are doing — has a single purpose: to get one single person to take action and buy what you're selling. Or take the next logical step which will, in due course, result in his buying what you're selling. Nothing else matters. If the prospect takes the action you wish him to take, your marketing material and your copy work. If he doesn't, they don't. It's really all that simple.

The Empathetic Skill

We end this short chapter where we began: with empathy. For empathy is both an attitude that informs all that you do and a skill that enables you to do it more successfully.

To write cash copy means having two empathetic skills:

- finding out what your prospects want to achieve — and expressing it in a way that moves them to take action NOW to get it, and
- discovering what's bothering your prospects now — and letting them know in the clearest possible way that what you're offering (your product or service) will solve their problem and make them better off.

You don't develop these skills overnight. It takes a lifetime of caring and consideration of others. Younger people, more self-absorbed by their own captivating development, find it harder to write this kind of copy than most older people, who have discovered, from often painful experience, that success comes only from getting out of yourself and focusing on others. This is a lesson of life, and it is the foundation of cash copy.

Let me end this chapter with one final exhortation: It is never wrong to put the prospect first. It is never wrong to make him feel that he — this single individual — is the focus of your total concern. And it is always right for him to feel your deep concern for his welfare. When he feels this concern — your empathy — he will be deeply grateful for what you do, for your candor and perhaps oversharp honesty. And he will reward you with words like these which came unsolicited just the other day from one of my clients: "It looks like I've finally found a person who would actually try to see what I'm trying to get done. I am grateful for that."

What does this sentiment lead to? Not just general gratitude but profound business consequences. For with his gratitude comes continuing trust and both his ongoing business and regular referrals. No wonder. After all, how rare it is — and how gratifying — to find in this world of profound indifference a competent person who is not only willing to help but who also wishes to help us achieve our objectives. And if it takes mere money to continue this significant connection which will enable us to get what we wish (or to avoid what we fear), why then you will find, as I have, that that money will always be available to you. Moreover, that it will be given to you with the utmost happiness by your clients, who will be profoundly grateful to have found you.

Chapter 4

Learning What You Need To Know About Your Prospects — So You Can Write The Cash Copy That Compels Them To Contact You.

What do you think of this? An entrepreneur comes up with an idea, some product or service. She knows she's always wanted to work for herself and make big bucks. Now, thanks to her amazing new business, this is exactly what she can do! Nothing else matters but scoring big. Certainly not understanding the prospect and his problem, much less preparing the marketing documents that will get this prospect to take action.

Sound farfetched?

It isn't. Day after day, I encounter these entrepreneurs, whose names are legion. These are the people who are captivated with what they've produced and ecstatic that they produced it at all. They are so mesmerized by their future prosperity that they forget one simple little fact: that this prosperity is dependent on helping thousands, perhaps millions, of others achieve their objectives. And that unless these others — their prospects — are convinced that the entrepreneur can help them do so, the entrepreneur's aspirations become pipe dreams.

Thus, let me say this as strongly as I can: you cannot write cash copy, compelling copy that motivates prospects to take action on their own behalf, unless you:

- understand the prospect;
- know his anxieties, and

95

- comprehend his aspirations, knowing what he wants to achieve and when he wants to achieve it.

Does this sound easy? It isn't. Not in a society where the emphasis is on the entrepreneur and what he gets from making the big score (the "Lifestyles of the Rich and Famous" syndrome) and not what his prospects get from his offer.

But let me tell you something: unless you understand your prospect as well as (if not better!) than you understand yourself, you'll never have the lifestyle of the rich and famous. You'll have only the regrets of the might-have-beens.

Profiling Your Prospect — Each Different Kind Of Prospect

You must understand that a single product or service may have dozens of different kinds of prospects. Each of these prospects (being different in sex, age, and circumstances) may buy what you're selling for different reasons. It is important that·you know the reasons why *each* different kind of prospect is buying — and the benefits that each different kind of prospect gets from using what you're selling.

Unseasoned entrepreneurs try to find a magic key, a few compelling words, that will excite everyone to buy what they're selling. This is a crucial error. A single product or service may have dozens, if not hundreds, of separate markets. Each market may be composed of hundreds, even millions, of different people who respond to different motivators.

You have to know who's in each market and what motivators they respond to. Only then can you produce the appropriate marketing materials — the right cash copy — for each separate market.

Thus, the first thing you must do is determine each separate market, each particular market for each product and service you are selling. Then begin to create a prospect profile for each of these markets.

This profile may consist of the following kinds of information:

- prospect age
- sex

- education
- income
- business type
- business title/function
- residence
- marital status
- children.

You'll find it helpful, I think, to create a composite profile of a single typical buyer within any given market. Make this person as real as possible. Give him a name. An identify. Begin to understand him as an individual, what bothers him, and what he hopes to achieve. The more you understand about this typical prospect within an individual buying sector, the more easily you can write the cash copy he'll respond to.

Beyond basic factual information, what exactly do you need to know about this prospect so you can position your product or service so that he'll want to buy it? Essentially two things: what is he anxious about and what does he want to achieve?

Understanding Your Prospect's Anxieties

Remember: most people are set in their habits. While people like movement (an American fetish), they dislike constructive change. Thus, even though they have problems, fears and anxieties, they are unlikely to take action to solve them. That's the American way.

Your task as a marketer is to jolt your prospect out of sloth and lethargy, to ask him to deviate from his accustomed habits (where he takes no action) and do what you've motivated him to do to better his lot. Using the prospect's anxieties is a superb way of achieving this crucial result.

Thus, to be able to motivate your prospects, to get them to take action, you must discover as many prospect anxieties as you can.

The prospect's most powerful anxieties concern losing something. Something like:

- sex appeal
- attractiveness

- friends
- status
- his home
- youthfulness
- money
- security
- health
- his job
- comfortable retirement
- a better life for her children.

Something, in short, he has had, fears he is losing, and is frightened of being without.

The real question is: how do you find out about the prospect's anxieties so you're sure about what's bothering him? You open an Anxiety File and pack it with information from many sources.

You join a professional association. Don't think you're the only one interested in finding out what's bothering your prospect or dedicated to helping him solve his problem. You aren't. Thus, join an association of others ministering to your prospect and his wants. There are over 60,000 professional associations in the United States. There's sure to be one for what you're interested in. To find out, review the three volumes of the *Encyclopedia of Associations*. Available in most libraries, it's published by Gale Research Co., Book Tower, Detroit, MI 48226.

You research publications produced by professional associations and experts interested in your prospects, their problems, and how to solve them. These publications are a gold mine of anxiety information. And, what's more to the point, *specific* anxiety information. For make no mistake about it: your objective is not just to assert that your prospects have or will have a problem. But to *prove* that they have or will have that problem.

Note: don't forget newsletters, which I regard as a key source of anxiety information. Oxbridge Publications prints some of the most detailed directories of these newsletters, including the *Standard Periodical Directory* of about 80,000 publications of all kinds, and the *Oxbridge Directory of Newsletters*. Contact them at 150 Fifth Ave., Rm. 301, New York, NY 10011.

You use government documents. It is your job to stay on top of what the government is producing in your field. Do you know the relevant government agencies that gather data relating to what you do? At the local, state and federal level? The federal government is the largest data collector in the world and is a prime source of anxiety information that, properly promoted by you, can be used to turn your prospects into buyers.

You question people who have the problem you can solve. Ask them about their problems. Find out what they are doing to solve them. Find out how badly they want to solve the one you can solve. Find out how long it took them to decide to solve it — and why they waited so long.

Every single day the kind of valuable information you need walks right in your door and is there, ready, willing and able to talk to you about what's bothering him. And remember: your prospects will be delighted to talk to you about what ails them — and what they want to achieve — because so few people in their lives take this kind of intelligent interest in their affairs. You can. So ask.

Then write everything down!

Be Active About Your Information Gathering, Not Passive

Most entrepreneurs, so consumed with what they are producing and their volume of business, do not have a systematic program to keep abreast of their prospects' anxieties and aspirations. This is a mistake. These anxieties and aspirations change — just like everything else in the world. And unless you want your product or service to lose its relevance, you've got to adapt your marketing accordingly. In other words, as circumstances change, successful marketing approaches lose their bite. As a result you lose your profit, unless you're prepared to reposition what you're selling in response to the differing circumstances of your prospect and what causes him to take action.

Remember this: there is always money to be made, whatever the economic situation. What differentiates the people who make money regularly — as opposed to those who benefit from a single trend — is that the former are always on the alert for what constitutes prospect *current* anxiety and aspiration and to admit that what makes people anxious tomorrow is not what makes them anxious today. This means you need to constantly gather prospect information and use it to keep yourself continually relevant.

Here are some specific steps about how to be active in your information gathering, and not passive.

- When you join a professional association, seek out the experts in your field, the people who are on the cutting edge of research and development, the people who have the most direct contact with the people who have the problem you can solve. Don't just chat with them generally. Ask:

  - what problems the prospects are having now;
  - how bad these problems are;
  - what's being done to solve them;
  - what's working — and what isn't;
  - what other experts are working with these people;
  - how you can get in touch with them.

When you're with an expert, take notes, or ask if you can tape what he's saying. You're not going to remember all these data, so prepare accordingly. Besides, you want to get quotations from the expert that you can use in your marketing materials.

Don't be afraid to push. Don't just ask general questions. Ask specific questions. And look for specific answers. Why? Because cash copy has teeth. What sets it apart from the general run of lacklustre copy is its specificity. You want to be able to tell (or remind) your prospects:

- what their problem is;
- how bad it is;
- how bad it's going to be;
- what's happening to them as a result of their problem: what they've got and what they're missing as a result.

Morever, you want everything you're using to be fully substantiated by the experts.

- When you read a professional publication, remember: you're gathering data about pain and what's specifically happening to — and bothering — your prospects. Look for:

  - the names of specialists in your field. These are the people you need to get to know, because they're the people who are

close to the source — your prospects — and hence gathering the anxiety information you need;
* articles about what's happening to your prospects. Note the specifics. Your task is to remind people what's bothering them (and how badly) and to position what you're selling so that it's seen as a solution;
* projections about what will happen. What do specialists say may happen to your prospects? When will it happen. And how badly will it happen? The more specific — and indeed dramatic — the information, the better for your marketing efforts.

* When you gather data from the government, help yourself by:

  * getting on a mailing list so that you are sent information about new data sources that are relevant to you and your prospects;
  * reviewing the material and the sources whence it came. Remember: you want to be in touch with the specialists who found it.

* And don't forget your prospects themselves. Develop a questionnaire that goes out with every product you ship or service you deliver. Also use it at trade shows, at your workshops and seminars, and as a stuffer in your prospect mailings. Ask the prospect to help you with information so that you can serve him better. Find out:

  * what problems he has in your area of specialization;
  * how badly he wants to solve them;
  * what other means he's used to solve them;
  * how much he'd spend for a solution;
  * what he thinks of competitors who are offering similar solutions.

Remember: people don't have a lot of time to fill out questionnaires, so keep them short, with no more than about five multiple choice questions and five short answer questions. Always allow space for comments. And give your prospect a reason to return the questionnaire to you. I use my 2000-word (five page) Special Reports as an inducement. "Tell me what's ailing you, and I'll send you information which you can use to your (specific) advantage." This works.

Specificity Is Crucial;
Unauthenticated Assertion Fatal

And what, pray, is the purpose of all this work?

To gather specific information about how anxious your prospects are about any given problem, what is happening to them now, and what will happen to them if they fail to take action to correct their situation.

One of the key problems of the marketing materials I review is that they are composed of seller assertions — unauthenticated statements made by the seller about the problem of the prospect and what their product or service can do to solve it. This is self-defeating.

Everything you say — and particularly what you say about future prospect conditions — must be fully supported by relevant experts and hard data, not simply asserted by you, unless the audience you are addressing knows you to be the relevant expert, He-Who-Must-Be-Listened-To.

As I write, I am looking at a letter one of my clients (a financial planner) sent me to improve. His second paragraph starts off: "NOW, MORE THAN EVER BEFORE, THE NEED FOR PERSONAL FINANCIAL PLANNING IS CRITICALLY IMPORTANT."

No facts follow this statement, no support for it whatsoever. Thus, it is nothing more than an unauthenticated seller assertion. The prospect thinks: Why now? What's different? Who says so? You? Who are you?

But to not a single one of these questions does the seller offer any answer. What he implicitly says instead is: "I'm the expert. Take my word for it. Trust me. Don't ask any questions. Just do what I tell you." Would you trust a man like this? Certainly, I wouldn't. At the very least, I'd find him arrogant and condescending (as this person in actuality most certainly was).

I think it's instructive that my client called this his "greed letter." He meant, of course, that it was designed to attract prospects because of their greed. In fact, I think his description tells us much more about the seller and his avarice than about what motivates prospects. And what motivates prospects is hard information — not self-interested seller hot air.

Every assertion you make must be backed by hard evidence. By the data you have gathered from:

- relevant experts in your field;
- economic forecasts from reputable authorities;
- government documents, and
- your prospects themselves.

You must consider each bit of specific information — the name of the source, the date the source spoke, the conditions under which the source spoke, the reasons the source spoke now — as motivational levers that inch the prospect towards doing what you want him to do and what he really ought to do — taking action NOW. Without this support, it's simply your word. And why should anyone listen to you? Merely because you are who you are. " 'But who,' said the Caterpillar to Alice 'are you?'" From a marketing standpoint, nothing at all!

Remember: the most persuasive anxiety information is specific information.

Thus, you must resolve to find out:

- what the prospect's problem is;
- how long he's had it;
- what it costs him to have this problem;
- what will happen if he doesn't solve this problem;
- what he's done to try and solve his problem (that hasn't worked).

Of course, getting this information takes time and a continuing commitment to getting it. But without these data, the copy you produce lacks teeth, has no major impact on the prospect, and certainly does not compel him to take action NOW — the only reason for producing a marketing document.

Is this what you want? Of course not!

Stop expecting people to listen and act merely because you say so. Support everything you say (every anxiety scenario you use to induce prospect action) with hard data from a variety of reputable sources — by name.

The Sad Reality: Even Cash Copy With Incisors Doesn't Always Cut It

Even with these facts, expect that many people who have the now validated problem won't avail themselves of your solution — even though it is the sensible thing to do. Because, as you must know, only a fraction of your prospects will act sensibly. This is one of the reasons for the Rule of Seven I put forward in MONEY MAKING MARKETING; the need, that is, to hit your prospects again and again and again — at least 7 times in 18 months.

But each time you hit them, make sure your marketing approach bites — with real facts that directly pertain to the client's situation. Remember the boy who cried "Wolf!".

He got attention the first time he cried "Wolf!" merely because he delivered his message, even though he had no facts. And he got attention, too, (although less of it) the second time he voiced his unauthenticated cry of anxiety. But then his situation seriously deteriorated as the faith of his audience in what he said plummeted. No wonder! He had no facts to back up his self-generated assertion.

Oh, yes, I nearly forgot. Finally, there *was* a wolf. And it ate him. And then there were plenty of facts. Too late, however, to help him. Don't let yourself come to such an inglorious (and messy) end. Motivate with facts . . . not assertion.

Fuel Your Profit Machine With Your Prospect's Aspirations

Aspiration is defined as "exalted desire" or "high ambition." Now look closely at these dictionary definitions. Even here, there is nothing flat or dull about what is being discussed. The desire must be "exalted", the ambition "high." In short, aspiration is the heady stuff of dreams, romance, color, and excitement — something men and women live, breathe and die for.

Not surprisingly, putting aspiration to work for you can easily persuade your prospect to acquire what you're selling. Sadly, however, you don't know what they want to achieve and therefore cannot use it to your advantage.

There are several reasons for this appalling and self-destructive situation:

- You're more interested in achieving your own aspirations than in helping others achieve theirs.
- Your own aspirations are general, not specific.
- And what you know about your prospects' aspirations is far too general, too.

When you solve these three problems, you'll be able to harness the power of aspiration.

I've said it before, and now I'll say it again. Your *total* focus must be on your prospect and customer. Your own aspirations are, of course, important; they are, after all, a crucial part of what motivates you. But focusing on them is detrimental to the success of your marketing. To achieve *your* aspirations you must focus on your *prospect's* aspirations. It's that simple.

But, like so much of what we're talking about, this focus must be specific. The reason you have trouble using your prospect's specific aspirations on your behalf is because you don't know what they are . . . and certainly haven't written them down. This is where the problem begins.

Do you doubt me? Answer these two questions honestly:

- Do you have specific, written personal objectives for this year?
- Do you have specific, written objectives for your business this year?

Case closed.

Understanding And Using Goals And Objectives

Part of the problem is the general confusion that exists between goals and objectives. A goal is a general statement of intent: "My goal is to be rich while I'm still young enough to enjoy it." An objective is the specific end to which you are working: what you wish to achieve and when you wish to achieve it. "I want to have an annual income of $100,000 a year by age 45."

Good marketing documents must use both goals *and* objectives, and one of the key reasons why they fail is because most marketers only use goals, which are of course general and nonspecific.

Consider the following marketing headlines:

"Make money in real estate."

"Make up to $20,000 in sixty days by converting a "handy-man special" into a sure-sell showplace."

Both headlines are about making money in real estate; that, after all, is your prospect's aspiration. But a goal is too general to be effective marketing. You need teeth. And here, as elsewhere, it is the objective that gives the headline its teeth — and its effectiveness.

You must be able to translate your prospect's goal into a specific objective that can only be achieved through what you're selling. The prospect buys what you're selling in order to reach the defined objective and so achieve his desired goal.

Let's review a specific marketing illustration to show you what I mean. I've randomly selected an ad from *Small Computers In Libraries* magazine, a place where many smaller software developers advertise. These are the kinds of people who do not have massive advertising budgets and must make every dollar count. See for yourself if this advertiser met that objective.

Here's the beginning of an ad published by Eloquent Searchware of North Vancouver, British Columbia.

"THE ELOQUENT LIBRARIAN leads the way.

A fully integrated library software package emphasizing a superior cataloguing and public access search module. It has features that surpass older products. This is leading-edge software that takes full advantage of the latest Personal Computer and Local Area Network Technology."

If what I am about to say sets back U.S.-Canadian relations a·decade or so, I apologize in advance. But I am the harbinger of the marketplace, and the marketplace is profoundly uncaring.

Remember what I said above: "You're more interested in your own aspirations than in the aspirations of your prospects." This headline — this entire ad — is a good illustration of this terrible problem, for its copy is about the seller, not about the buyer. It says, in effect, "We think we're swell." As a prospect my response to that is, "So what? What's in this for me?"

Leading with your company, your name, and your aspiration (for this copy screams "Buy me! Buy me!") is fatal. The prospect's defenses go up immediately — and probably never come down. Certainly not in this ad.

Now, however dimly, the seller does seem to know what the prospect's goal is: "superior cataloguing." It's not a great goal , but at least it is a goal.

If this is, indeed, what the buyer wants to achieve (and the seller will know this from his ongoing research), then it must be hit and hit again with specific buyer objectives: superior cataloguing realized by comparative advantages in speed, price, flexibility, staff, *etc.* — all specifically enumerated by the seller and which the buyer can *only* achieve by accepting the seller's offer.

Is this what this ad does?

Not at all.

Instead of offering some enticing objectives ("Now, you can catalog four more books each hour thanks to The Eloquent Librarian") that support the overall goal ("superior cataloguing"), the seller falls back on unauthenticated assertion: "It has features that surpass older products."

Rather than give the prospect facts and so induce him to take action that will (with the product or service) enable him to reach his objective and so achieve his larger goal, this oh-so-typical seller instead says, "Trust me."

But why should we?

What is Eloquent Searchware?

Who are the people behind it?

What have they done to earn our trust?

Whom have they helped?

Why should we believe them?

What can they do for me?

"Trust-Me Marketing" just doesn't cut it.

And when you see it — as you clearly do in this textbook perfect illustration — you have good reason to think:

- the seller is more interested in himself than in me;
- his aspiration is to sell *his* product, not solve *my* problem;
- he doesn't know anything about what I am attempting to do, and
- hasn't made (or won't make) the effort to find out.

Is this a company you really want to patronize?

A Footnote On Eloquent Searchware

A further look at this excruciatingly poor ad indicates that Eloquent Searchware doesn't even care if you respond to what they are saying or not. The ad ends with their name, address and telephone number. But the seller leaves you to figure out what to do with them.

Does he try to stimulate you with an offer? Give some reason for acting NOW? Not at all. He doesn't invite you to call. Doesn't say what you get when you do call. And certainly doesn't make any effort at all to get you to respond NOW. His purpose seems to have been met by placing the ad.

Is it?

You know better.

A marketing document — be it the lowly business card or a four-color annual report — fails, and fails miserably, unless it gets the prospect or customer to take some action to connect with the marketer. And connect NOW. Not tomorrow. Not next week. Not six months from now. But NOW.

How much better it would have been if the seller had really considered his prospect — and not just himself — before writing this wasteful ad. If he had answered these crucial questions:

- Who is my prospect?
- What is his goal?
- What specific objective(s) does he wish to achieve?
- When does he want to achieve it?
- What can I say to induce him to take action NOW to move towards achieving this objective?

Failure to focus on the prospect, understand his aspirations and objectives and use *them* to motivate him to take action doomed this ad and crushed its response. It leads me to think that there is a mole at Eloquent Searchware, working for its major competitor by producing such fatuous ads.

Don't let this be you. Instead, open an Aspiration File, a file dedicated to the aspirations of each prospect group you serve.

Where do you find information for this file? The same kinds of places you look for material on your prospects' anxieties: from association meetings, trade publications, the government, and from the prospects themselves. Here are the guidelines you must follow so that the information you get is the most usable, the information that will stimulate the greatest number of prospects to respond to you the quickest:

- Research their goals. Generally speaking, what is it your prospects want to accomplish? Remember, a single prospect may have multiple goals relating to a single product or service.
- Write down each aspiration or objective.
- Translate each aspiration or objective into a single sentence beginning with "You want . . ." Thus, if prospect's aspiration is to "produce catalog cards" (you'll know from your re-search), this sentence should be: "You want to produce catalog cards."
- Now make the aspiration comparatively better than what the prospect is currently doing/getting and achievable within a specific time period. Motivate the prospect by focusing on what he wants to get. "You want to produce 7 more catalog cards every hour."

N.B. Then tell the prospect what he has to do to achieve this result: call for more information, schedule a free consultation, or send in a check to get the "7 more catalog cards every hour", not just your product or service.

Let me say something about aspirations. They are powerful indeed. That's why even my staid dictionary defines them as: "exalted desire" and "high ambition", phrases that are inspirational, almost poetic.

When you think about your prospect's anxieties, think of yourself as the White Knight, the person who is rushing in to save someone's life or virtue or fortune; noble and stirring objectives, indeed.

When you think about your prospect's aspirations, think of yourself as the Dream Spinner, the person who understands their high aspirations and who can deliver them — on a silver platter.

Either way, think of what you are doing in terms of high excitement, passion, fervor and zeal, for what you are doing is of the greatest possible importance and value to your prospects, whether you are helping soothe their anxieties or realize their aspirations.

The reason so much marketing is so dull and disspirited is because the seller has forgotten that he is on an exciting and fateful odyssey; an odyssey that will, at its conclusion, give the prospect an end to anxiety — or the satisfaction of an aspiration achieved. What could be more exciting than that?

The next time you read marketing materials that are bland, boring, tiresome and tedious you'll know that behind such disappointments is a poor soul who has lost his way; who no longer understands the excitement and fervor of this thrilling game, a game where the ability to discover the anxieties and aspirations of the prospect and to use them to excite that prospect to take immediate action is what differentiates the successful marketer from the pathetically insipid.

But this will never be you! For you now know the power of both prospect anxieties and aspirations and must use them to motivate these same prospects to contact you NOW. For you have what they must get, and you have it for them NOW.

Chapter 5

Transforming Product And Service Features Into Benefits That Get Your Prospects To Buy

You're not simply going to sit down and write cash copy off the top of your head. Sorry, but it just doesn't happen that way. You've got to plan to write it. And in the next few chapters, I'll be explaining what you must do so that you have all the information you need to write the cash copy you want. And let me tell you this, too: preparing to write cash copy is arguably the more important step when compared with writing cash copy, because if your preparation has been thorough, you stand a much better chance of writing copy that sells. So bear with me: this preparation is crucial.

Understanding The Differences Between Features And Benefits

Features, as I've already said, are the elements of what you're selling, its salient parts. Features pertain to your product or service. They are about your product or service. They define your product or service.

Now, obviously, it is important for your prospects to know what your product or service is composed of. But, taken by themselves, features will not sell a product or service. Only benefits will do that. Because benefits — the advantages to the buyer — are what cause a prospect to become a buyer. Benefits, not features, answer the prospect's "What's-in-it-for-me?" question. Benefits are about "you" (the buyer); features are about "me" (my product or service.)

111

Thus, if you want to succeed in marketing, and in writing cash copy, you must become adept at transforming features into benefits, into taking the components of everything you're selling and making them into compelling reasons for the prospect to buy. Unless you can do this, you'll never become a successful client-centered marketer.

This marketer knows one profound secret: the key to writing successful cash copy and to transforming the prospect into a buyer is contained in these simple words: "Lead with benefits, follow with features." The prospect always wants to know what's in it for him. As soon as he's convinced that you've got something that he wants, then he *may* want to know what it's composed of. Very often, he'll simply take your word for it and get what you're selling because of its powerful client-centered benefits.

Therefore, your challenge in writing cash copy is plain: you've got to scrutinize every feature of what you're selling to see what benefits it offers your prospects. Unless it offers a clear client-benefit, there's no point in even considering the feature, because a feature without such a benefit is worthless.

Doesn't this all sound obvious?

It should be . . . but it isn't.

The sad truth is that a majority of marketing materials are composed of product and service features and are decidedly thin on prospect benefits. Even where such benefits appear they follow the features, as if they were an afterthought on the part of the seller. And, worse, the benefits that are given are general, unspecific, vague and flabby.

Because of this sorry state of affairs, I beg of you, if you learn nothing else from this chapter, learn these three things:

- Like you, the prospect is primarily interested in himself. So cater to his selfishness and self-absorbedness. Cater to his self-interest, first, last, and always. *Lead with something about him — not something about you.*

- Stop listing features of what you're selling as if they were in themselves somehow meaningful. They're not. A feature is only meaningful insofar as it tells a prospect: "Here's something that will help you get rid of at least one of your anxieties. Or achieve at least one of your aspirations." Aside from these reasons, nothing about the feature is of any interest to the prospect.

- Stop writing general benefits and make what you present client specific. *The only benefits that are meaningful are specific benefits.* Everything else looks like seller hype.

A Look At Some Wasteful Reality

As I write I'm reviewing an ad from The Training Store catalog published by Training Resource Corp. of Harrisburg, PA. Here's what it says:

"Expand your versatility and flexibility even more with Session Builders — Series 200.

60 ALL NEW exercises for management and supervisory training

Put this versatile collection of new exercises to work along with Series 100. Or use Series 200 by itself as a valuable, at-your-fingertips resource. Add new life to your current sessions or create your own from scratch. Most exercises in the collection take 30 minutes or less to run. TRC produced Series 200 in 1986 when satisfied Series 100 buyers asked for more exercises. Series 200 includes the 17 topics surveyed trainers liked most. And they're all exercises contributed by professionals who've used them and gotten results. Just like the original Series 100, Series 200 includes:

- Role plays, case studies, assessments, simulations, discussion stimulators, and application exercises.
- A handy index to help you locate exercises by topic, type, group, size, or time required.
- Trainer instructions for each of the 60 exercises.
- Reproducible handout masters.
- Sturdy, flip top storage box for bookshelf or desk."

This is a perfect illustration of exactly what you *shouldn't* write.

Let's look at it more closely.

1. It opens with the feature name, not a client benefit. Now, the writer will argue that "expand your versatility and flexibility even more" are benefits.

I disagree. When the prospect reads this, he cannot perceive a clear, distinct benefit for himself. Instead, he has questions: Even more than what? How much versatility? What kind of flexibility? What's this guy talking about?

2. The subheading, "60 ALL NEW exercises. . . .", is a feature. Having perused this headline, we know that the product offers 60 new exercises. The correct response? "So what?!" What benefits will I get — that I don't have now — by using (*not having*) these exercises? The seller doesn't bother to say. Deduction? Maybe he doesn't know. Or perhaps he's so selfish he doesn't care to say. "Buy this and find out for yourself" is what this headline seems to say.

3. The opening line of the main copy exacerbates the problem with more features: "versatile collection of new exercises." Again, the prospect response is "So what?" We are now well into the copy, and we don't have a single solid buyer benefit yet. And what's happening to the prospect? He's probably already lost interest. "When's this guy going to get to the point — the point about me and what I can get from him?" When indeed!

4. The opening paragraph concludes with "a valuable, at-your-fingertips resource." The writer clearly doesn't know what the buyer wants or needs or what will motivate him to take action now. So he falls back upon a hackneyed adjective: "valuable." When we observe this word, it seems out of place, gratuitous. Why should we feel that the resource is valuable? We shouldn't, because this is nothing more than unsubstantiated seller assertion. The marketer has thrown in a word rather than proven a point.

5. In the second paragraph we learn more about the features of what's being sold: "Most exercises in the collection take 30 minutes or less to run." So what? Obviously this fact is significant to the seller. But why? Is it because other similar programs take 45 minutes, so that if you use TRC's program you can save 15 minutes? Is it because so many topics have never been covered in 30 minutes? Who knows? The selfish seller doesn't bother to say. What he says instead is, "Here's something important about what we do. We know it's important (or at least we think we do), but we'll be damned if we take the time to tell you. Trust us, it's important. That's enough for you to know."

6. More feature information. Now we get more names "TRC . . .Series 200 . . .Series 100". But names are features, not benefits. "What," the exasperated prospect now asks, "does any of this have to do with me?" The response? "Nothing!" And so the exasperated prospect becomes the escaping prospect, on to something else. End result? Profligate waste.

7. In this same paragraph we get "all exercises contributed by professonals who've used them and gotten results." Again, more questions: what kinds of professionals, what kinds of exercises, what kinds of results? The

overwhelming conclusion: this is a seller who simply doesn't care if his prospect knows anything about what he's selling — or doesn't know himself either what the prospect wants, or what he (the seller's) got. Either way, disaster.

8. We are now well into the advertising copy. The seller has offered nothing that answers the "what's in it for me?" question. But now he opens the floodgates of feature selfishness with a litany of pointlessness that includes: "role plays. . . simulations . . . index . . .trainer instructions . . . reproducible handout masters." All these are features — they are all about the product the seller is offering. *Not one of them offers a benefit to the buyer.*

With this list the seller is saying, "Here's what's in our exercise packages. One of the things you get is 'role plays'. What's the significance of these role plays? What do you get from them? What possible benefit are they to you? Well, we don't know, or won't say, or can't take the time to tell. Just get them and find out for yourself." This is arrogant marketing and nothing more, marketing where the burden of understanding is put squarely where it does not belong: on the prospect.

Yet, sadly it's the most common form of marketing, notwithstanding the fact that virtually every product or service provider thinks he is client-centered, just as I'm sure the Training Resource Corp does. But can you see why I reject such smug thinking?

Now, let's save you from this kind of idiotic thinking — and it's costly, wasteful results. Let's get you to transform every feature into a meaningful prospect benefit.

List Features First

To achieve this wholly admirable result you must first know thy features. Before you can use them to motivate your prospects to take action, you've got to know what you've got. So, list them.

Here are some typical feature categories:

For a product:
- name
- size
- parts
- packaging

- color
- weight
- age
- materials

- mode of delivery
- price
- availability
- payment options.

For a service:

- name
- person providing
- time in business
- location

- availability
- price
- hours of business
- method of operation

Now, I hasten to tell you, these lists are not definitive. And they do overlap. The objective of these lists is simply to provide you with factual information about the key points of your product or service. But even when these lists are stuffed with facts, you're not ready to use them yet. You need more facts — comparative facts about your competitors.

Gathering Key Facts About Your Competitors

A fact is virtually meaningless in and of itself. Ordinarily, what gives a fact meaning (and as such becomes a motivator for a prospect) is by comparing it to similar facts offered by others. I say "ordinarily" because sometimes you will be in a unique situation — the only game in town. Then the facts are valuable and compelling because you have no competition — either wholly or in part.

Either way, however, you must research your competitors. You need to discover the features of what they do. And to discover what they may do that you don't (and why) and (hopefully) what you do that they don't. Only in this way can you place what you do and offer in perspective and decide what is important and should be stressed. This means you need to do some very basic, profoundly important research into your competitors and the key features and facts of what they're offering — or not offering. To get this information you should:

- get on their mailing lists (if necessary use a friend's name and address);
- collect every piece of information they offer about what they're selling;

- collect their product or service reviews from professional publications;
- check out what they're offering at trade shows;
- talk to people who use what your competitors are selling.

In short, get the facts. And put them into a comparative chart so you can see for yourself how your product or service compares to theirs, feature by feature. (See Chart, page 118–119).

Note: when my clients come to me they often know at least a little about their competitors. But not as much as they should. The question keeps coming up: "Do I have to buy what my competitors are selling to find out what they've got?" The answer is, "It depends." Very often, you have to use the product or service to get a good idea of how it really works, what its features are, and its benefits. Without this information you'll find it difficult, if not impossible, to draw any comparisons that benefit you, or to know how to position yourself against a competitor. There it is. You probably won't like this bit of advice, but consider any money you spend on what your competitor produces a crucial research expense. Invest this money wisely. Make sure you really understand what your competitor is offering, what's good about it, what's not good about it, and why it is the way it is. All of this information will prove most beneficial when you start writing the cash copy that'll knock his socks off!

An Example Under The Marketing Microscope

Let's say that, like a company whose sales letter is now in front of me, you've just produced a piece of software. One of its features is the amount of code it requires. That's a fact. Is this a significant fact? You won't know until you know how much code other 4GLs (I'm taking this jargon from their letter) require. So, you gather the information that tells you. Now you have the facts about you and the comparative facts about your competitors.

Here's what your chart looks like so far:

Your Product	Their Product
Fact 1. Amount of code it requires.	Amount of code it requires.

What you find when you compare the two: either both have the same amount of code or they don't. If they do, there is then no comparative advantage to be

Look at these boxes. They "call out" benefits in the chart that might go unremarked were it not for this, or some other, kind of emphasis. Hence, their name: "call outs." Remember, your job is to direct the prospect's attention to what you think will motivate him to take immediate action . . . the superior benefits of your product/service and your irresistible offer. All words are not equal. Your job is to direct your prospects to the truly important ones.

Look how little you pay for how much you get! You get all the features of CPROPS — with more benefits than all of our competitors combined! — for less than a third of what you pay for our nearest competitor!

You get a complete thirty-day money-back guarantee — something no one else gives you. See for yourself. You get more. Pay less. And can return CPROPS if not absolutely satisfied!

CPROPS has full math coprocessor support. It uses the 8087/80287 chip that is installed in your machine. If you don't have a math coprocessor, CPROPS will emulate one!

CPROPS puts state-of-the-art programming at your fingertips. You get keyboard interaction and a two line menu system (just like 1-2-3), so that you can instantly use the program.

You get context sensitive help screens so that at any moment you can receive help to your specific problem — and continue with your design immediately. 39 individual help screens are available.

You get references to the AASHTO and Curved AASHTO Specifications inside your help screens so that you are alerted to the rules which may affect your design.

You get Rolled Beam Selection Tables so that you don't need the AISC manual on your lap while you choose your member. All bridge members from W18 up to W36 are included. 72 selections in all!

You get state-of-the-art personal computer interaction which speeds your design. This is exactly what you need to fully utilize your PC!

Mb Microbridge International Corporation 35 Preston Avenue P.O. Box 310 Auburn, MA 01501 **508-757-2346** Here's what your section properties software must give you. Make sure yours does . . . **CALL NOW**	CPROPS	GS1-C	SECTIONS	BMINERT	P-INERT	GEOPAC	Beam Sections
Price	**$99.**	$300.	$100.	$95.	$145.	$250.	$120.
Demonstration Diskette	YES	No	No	No	No	No	No
30-Day Money Back Guarantee	YES	No	No	No	No	No	No
Uses 8087/80287 if present	YES	YES	No	No	No	No	No
Keyboard and Menu's like 1-2-3	YES	No	No	No	No	No	No
Context Sensitive Help Screens	YES	No	No	No	No	No	No
References to AASHTO Specs	YES	No	No	No	No	No	No
References to Curved AASHTO	YES	No	No	No	No	No	No
Rolled Beam Selection Tables	YES	YES	No	No	No	No	No
Plate Girder Properties	YES	No	No	No	No	No	No
Rolled Beam Properties	YES	YES	No	No	No	No	No
Generic Shape Properties	YES	YES	YES	YES	YES	YES	YES
File Manager Utility	YES	YES	No	No	No	No	No
Torsional Properties	YES	YES	No	No	No	YES	No

derived *from this fact alone*. Any possible marketing advantage from this fact must be taken from comparison with other facts, like price.

What happens if both products require the same amount of code, but your product sells for a dollar less? Then you have a comparative marketing advantage that takes this hitherto neutral piece of information and transforms it into a piece of compelling information that can be used to induce prospect action. You begin to see why gathering your facts, feature by feature, competitor by competitor, is so important.

Let's look at other alternatives. What if the amounts of code vary between the two products, with more code being a negative point? If you require more code than your competitor, you must either correct this problem in the product itself, or drop this fact from your marketing materials (if it's not significant), or downgrade its significance by showing why it doesn't matter (if it's a crucial product point). On the other hand, if your competitor requires more code than you do — and you can clearly establish why this is significant — here you may have discovered a compelling motivator to be used in your marketing to get prospects to take action. Moreover, its importance can be significantly reinforced if, in other features, what you are offering is superior to what the competitor is offering. Thus, the following scenario:

- Bam! We've got this benefit for you that the competitor doesn't have!
- Bam! And this comparative benefit!
- Bam! And this comparative benefit!

You must stress — again and again and again — the benefits you've got. And again and again and again your superiority to any competitors you've got. You hit the key prospect advantages over and over again, hitting the prospect and hitting him again, never allowing the prospect to forget what you've got for him or letting the competitor off the mat.

All's fair, you see, in love, and war — and in war's domestic counterpart, marketing. Don't ever forget it!

Yes, this is where you must go for the jugular. Which is precisely what the company in the actual sales letter failed to do. Here's what they wrote about their product: "It requires less code than other 4GLs."

This isn't marketing, the factual, persistent, hard-hitting attempt to compel prospect action and demolish a competitor. It's just words. Marketing, remember, is the art and science of inducing indolent, other-occupied, slothful but problem-racked human beings with gigantic aspirations to take action NOW. By this standard, this line (in the important fifth line of their sales letter) fails miserably. A line that fails to support your crucial point of inducing prospect action NOW is simply wasted.

But this result isn't at all necesssary . . . because the facts themselves have the potential of transforming the feature into a compelling prospect benefit. How?

- By telling how much less code their product takes than the industry leader or than some precise number of other products (perhaps cited by name) they reviewed;
- By telling in no uncertain terms what difference *that* fact makes. If indeed it makes any. (And if it doesn't, there isn't any point whatsoever in mentioning it.)

Thus the sequence goes like this:

- Here's how much code we use.
- Here's how much code each of our competitors uses.
- Here are the factual comparisons between us and them.
- Here's what difference those comparisons make to you, the prospect; the reason(s) why you should use our product, not anyone else's.

The Power of Specificity

A line like "it requires less code than other 4GLs" is a weak, slothful, flabby, uninteresting, boring line. And, what's worse, it begs all the important questions. Questions like:

- how much less code?
- compared to what other systems?

And the Ultimate Question: "So what?"

You cannot expect your prospect to answer these questions. You've not only got to get the facts, you've got to tell your prospect the exact significance of the facts. *The more explicit, precise, and specific you can be, the more believable the copy you're writing.*

When I read a line like "It requires less code than other 4GLs", I make these deductions:

- the inventor of the product may or may not know (but certainly should) why this fact is important;
- the marketer of the product probably doesn't;
- the inventor hasn't talked to the marketer, or (if they have talked) hasn't explained what difference this fact makes;
- the marketer, not knowing what difference the fact makes to the user, cannot properly position the fact so that it's compelling to the user, so that it motivates him to act and acquire the product with the less code. Thus, he produces flaccid, uninteresting, uncompelling copy which explains nothing and gets no one to do anything.

The Road To Hell Is Paved
With Marketing Fluff Words

Because he doesn't have the facts, the marketer starts tossing in the telltale fluff words, words like:

- valuable
- significant
- important
- interesting
- perfect
- best
- powerful
- extensive
- superior
- revolutionary
- productive
- efficient
- decent
- famous
- acclaimed
- state-of-the-art
- full
- developed
- leading
- preeminent
- renowned
- world-class (a particularly noxious descriptor)
- conscientious
- responsible
- resourceful
- successful
- right
- acknowledged
- specialized

- quality
- informative
- advanced
- comprehensive
- cost-effective
- profitable
- improved
- innovative

- enhanced
- competitive
- economical
- reliable
- trouble-free
- potent
- expert
- insightful
- better

What's wrong with these words? Everything, from a marketing standpoint. They are just words, nothing more — *unless you prove them*. Without this proof these are simply bombast and nothing more. *Unless you prove them.*

What enables you to prove them? Your research — your knowledge of the features of what you're selling, compared with what else is available. Most people, of course, couldn't be bothered to prove these things. They indulge themselves — at exhorbitant cost — in Arrogant Marketing *par excellence* — and hope that no one notices.

Well, that's just the point. No one does notice. And no one buys, either. Hence, the seller doesn't sell (and so has a problem) and the buyer doesn't buy (and so retains the problem that the product could solve if the buyer could be induced to try it).

What a waste!

All because the seller doesn't:

- know the features of what he's selling;
- know the features of what his competitors are selling;
- compare them;
- make a strong selling point about what he can do for the prospect (as opposed to what the competitor can do), and
- ask for immediate action.

What an extraordinary system!

Do you doubt my word that this is happening?

I took the (very partial) list of fatuous words featured above (words you'd be well advised never to use — unless you can prove them) from ads in a recent issue of *Training Magazine*, Minneapolis, MN.

Here is as glaring an exhibit as you're likely to find between covers of people falling over themselves to make hideous — and expensive — marketing mistakes, for I took at least one unsupported word from *every* ad in the magazine. These mistakes prove beyond a shadow of a doubt that the marketers:

- haven't done their homework;
- don't understand how the features of what they're selling relate to the benefits of what their buyers want, and
- demonstrate consummate selfishness — and stupidity — page after page after page.

Let me say again and say so there is no fear of misunderstanding this crucial marketing message, this key constituent of cash copy: your buyers aren't interested in you and *your* power and glory and terrestrial magnificence. They are interested in both achieving and maintaining *their* power and *their* glory and *their* terrestrial magnificence. All they want to know from you, bub, is how you're going to help them get it NOW. And what they have to give up to get the something more they really want. CAN YOU GET THIS THROUGH YOUR EGOCENTRIC HEAD!!!

They're not interested in the features of what you're selling.

They're interested in the benefits those features give them.

They're not interested in how superior you are.

They're interested in how superior you're going to make them.

NOW!

A Few Words On The Belief Of Most Marketers That Their Fellow Countrymen Are Idiots

Most marketers operate as if they are graduates of P.T. Barnum University, certain "there's a sucker born every minute." And so because of their vast disregard for the consumer and their own abiding sloth and laziness, they produce marketing documents of unsurpassing contempt — and mediocrity.

They proclaim they're a leading company, a renowned company, a client-centered company. But . . . and it's the crucial but . . . they don't bother to prove this assertion; much less show how what they're selling, the features of their products or services, connects to this entirely unsupported assertion.

This marketing says in insolent terms, "We're here. We're superior (or world-class or state-of-the-art or whatever you will)". No proof. Just assertion.

But cash copy, dear reader, must rigidly follow these crucial guidelines:

- "What we're selling has these (enumerated) features."
- "What others are selling has these (enumerated) features."
- "As a result of comparing what we offer with what our competitors offer, here are the facts we've discovered."
- "Thus, we are fully entitled to say _____ (now fill in the blank and add the correct descriptive word)."

But please, please, please tell us how you arrived at this conclusion!

Reviewing Your Current Marketing Materials

Most people reading this book will already be in the soup. They will already have produced marketing documents, some costing thousands of dollars. Now I ask you to review them with a view towards improving them, specifically in transforming each feature into a benefit.

Pick up one of your marketing documents — an ad, a brochure, a cover-letter. It doesn't matter which.

Now underline the product or service features you present in this document, the things that pertain to what you're selling. Then answer these questions:

1. Where did you get these features? Off the top of your head? Or did you completely analyze your own offering to make sure you had identified every feature?
2. Have you compared your product and service features, particularly those

outlined in the marketing document in your hand, to those offered by your competitor(s)? If you know what you've got, do you know what they've got?

3. If you know your product and service features, and your competitor's product and service features, have you made any factual deductions based on a comparison of these facts?

4. If you've drawn one or more factual comparisons, have you used what you've discovered to your benefit in the marketing document in front of you to induce your prospect to take immediate action?

5. Or have you fallen back on some unsupported fluff word, like one of those on the list above? If you have, your marketing documents need major surgery. (Psst... you'll find my telephone number at the back of this book!)

A Look At A Superb Comparison

Facts give your marketing teeth — and are the basis for persuading your prospects to take action — but only if you properly position them. Take a look at the chart on pages 118–119. Produced by entrepreneur Paul Norton, it shows how his CPROPS bridge-design software compares to his six competitors.

This chart tells you this entrepreneur has done his homework. He knows where he's strong and where he's weak, for like most people he doesn't have an absolute advantage in every category.

His task is to:

- neutralize his competitors' advantages (for some do have advantages);
- present his facts in such a way that his prospect draws the inevitable (purchase) conclusion. He must persuade his prospect that any other decision than buying his product doesn't make sense.
- make sure the discussion rests both on what the prospect gets with his product — as well as what the prospect doesn't get if he chooses any competitor.

Now let's see how we can realize these three crucial objectives with cash copy, for remember: cash copy is the art and science of persuading your prospects to take immediate action.

Creating The Straight Forward Benefit Statement Where You Beat The Competitor Hands Down

Feature: The prospect can preview the product.

Cash Copy Based On This Feature

"Doubtful? See for yourself. Only CPROPS has a step-by-step demonstration diskette so you can see for yourself if we've got exactly what you need. Not one of our competitors offers you the chance to find out for yourself. With them, you have to pay full price. And not one of them gives you a complete money-back guarantee like we do! Just send $5 for your complete demonstration diskette and discover all the ways CPROPS can help you. If you're not convinced, send it back. We'll gladly refund your money. Try asking any one of our competitors for that. You can't!"

Feature: 30-day money-back guarantee

Cash Copy Benefit Based On This Feature

"No risk! Get your CPROPS program and use it for up to thirty days. Prove to yourself that it's worth more — far more — than what you invested in it. And if you're not absolutely convinced that it is, return it for a complete refund! Try doing that with any one of our competitors. *We're the only ones who give you a complete thirty-day money-back guarantee.* Why? Because we think you'll never want to part with your CPROPS once you've got it! P.S. *No one has ever returned a single copy to us. Ever.*"

Note: Look carefully at this guarantee. And particularly the two lines "No one has ever returned a single copy to us. Ever." This is a positioning statement. In truth, this company is new. It has very few of its products out on the market. Yet, it is still absolutely true that no one has ever returned a single copy to them. Use this absolute truth to reduce the prospect's anxiety about the product and induce action. Remember: cash copy isn't just about facts; it's about how these facts are positioned to induce the prospect to take immediate action.

And when someone, inevitably, does return a copy? Change the statement to: "P.S. Only one person has ever returned a copy to us. Ever. Just one. You can't please all of the people all of the time, but we're awfully close." See how this works, transforming an incident (the return) into a prospect-persuader benefit (the client-centered guarantee)? This line looks, feels and sounds authentic. And hence reinforces prospect trust in you. No wonder! It's absolutely true!

Crafting Benefits Where Both You And The Client Have The Same Thing To Offer

You will often face situations where, in some things or all, you and your competitors have the same features and (at least in theory) might offer the same benefits. You've got to differentiate yourself from your competitor so that your prospect invests in you.

As you see from the chart, both CPROPS and competitor GS1-C use 8087/80287. Result? Both let you (the prospect) spend less time designing what you want. Cash copy (and its marketing magic) is what persuades the prospect to acquire your product over your (seemingly similar) competitor's. Here, as you see, we expand the discussion — as quickly as possible — beyond features both products share — and move it into areas where the comparison is definitely in favor of CPROPS.

Cash Copy Based On This Situation

"CPROPS uses 8087-80287, so you spend less time to get the design you want. Of our competitors, only GS1-C has it — the other five don't. Does this mean CPROPS or GS1-C are a toss-up?

Sure, if you'd like to do without the demonstration diskette CPROPS gives you. Or its use of color. Or CPROPS' help windows and menu. And its Graphical Interface for easy use. And the file manager and generic props. *And a whole lot more.* (Just check out the comparison chart above!) Yes, you won't get any of this. But you will get something really big from GS1-C — a big price tag. Because GS1-C costs almost five times as much as CPROPS, yet doesn't give you so many of the advantages you want! Now, shouldn't you really be investing in CPROPS?"

Positioning Yourself When You Don't Have The Lowest Price

As you see from the chart, CPROPS doesn't have the lowest price among its competitors. BMINERT offers a lower price. The trick here, however, is to show the prospect exactly what they're losing if they go with the competitor. People buy higher priced items all the time over lower-priced items *if they can be convinced that the lower-priced item doesn't give them everything they want.* Your job is to make sure they know what they're missing and to let them know that price alone — unless all other factors are equal — is usually not a good basis on which to make a purchase decision, (*especially if you don't have that lowest price!*).

Cash Copy Based On This Situation

"If I told you CPROPS has the lowest price of the seven bridge-design software programs, would you agree? Maybe you'd first say, 'Hey, can't you see that one of your competitors has a lower price tag?' But wait! Think how much you're giving up if you buy what he's selling. You don't get:

- generic props. And if you don't have them, you can't auto-matically design generic sections. But you get them with CPROPS.
- rolled beam props. So you'll have to design your rolled beams by hand. But you get them with CPROPS.
- plate girder props. Which means more time-consuming hand design work. But you get them with CPROPS.

And if you don't use CPROPS, you also don't get references to either Curved AASHTO or AASHTO Specs. Or much, much more! Given how much more you get in CPROPS, don't you think it makes sense to invest just a little more to use it?"

Squeezing Adjectives Out Of Hard Facts

Any adjectives you use to describe your product or service must be based on facts, on comparisons with what else exists. Otherwise, what you say is just deceptive hype that means nothing and increases prospect distrust for you and all marketers. Looking at Paul Norton's admirable factual chart comparing his product to his competitors' products, here are some factual adjectives we can prove, descriptors that come right out of the facts:

- No risk. (He gives a thirty-day money-back guarantee. No one else does.)
- Complete. (He offers more design features than any of his competitors.)
- Lowest cost. (Others may have a lower price tag, but with all features taken into consideration, his price is the lowest.)
- Most up-to-date. (He offers more problem-solving features than anyone else.)
- Easiest to use. (He offers help windows and menus. No one else does.)

This gives you an idea of how to take the facts and (by reviewing them in comparison with your competitors) draw the appropriate, action-inducing adjective from the facts, not impose a hyped adjective on the situation that you don't have the facts to support.

Here we can absolutely prove that this product is what we say it is — and we can make the prospect feel our certainty (and enthusiasm) through our cash copy.

A Few Words About Transforming Every Benefit Into Action-Oriented Prospect Persuader Cash Copy

Cash copy is action-oriented copy. It's brisk, fast-moving, and has one objective only: getting the slothful prospect you're communicating with to sit up, take notice, and do what's necessary to acquire what you're selling. If your prospect doesn't act (no matter what else he does), your copy — and hence your marketing — has failed. DO YOU UNDERSTAND THIS?

You can help achieve this result by mastering the Prospect- Action Verb- Prospect Benefit Sentence.

Start this sentence with the prospect's name. If you have a real name, use it. If you don't, start the sentence with "you". In other words, capture the prospect's attention with the prospect's favorite subject: himself.

Then follow with an action verb, an involvement verb about use or possession by the prospect of the product or service. Here's a very partial list of such verbs.

- get
- keep
- have
- use
- profit from
- benefit from
- obtain
- win
- achieve

- attain
- reach
- earn
- make
- secure
- reap
- harvest
- garner

Hint: whenever you're stuck in your marketing copy, you can always write two-thirds of a compelling cash copy sentence, thus: "You get/or have/or keep. . . ." Now just fill in the blank that gives you the specific client-centered benefit (like "30-day no-risk money-back guarantee!").

Such copy will never win an award, but at least it will always be honest, client-centered copy. AND YOU DON'T NEED A COPYWRITER TO WRITE IT FOR YOU, EITHER. YOU CAN DO IT FOR YOURSELF.

This is the vanilla ice-cream of copy, plain but always acceptable.

But vanilla ice-cream is better with a topping. And the cash copy topping is the appropriate adjective or descriptor reinforcing the message of this brisk prospect-centered sentence. Let's look at Paul Norton's chart and deduce the appropriate descriptive word or phrase.

We know he gives a complete thirty-day money-back guarantee. Now let's add the appropriate descriptor. How about "NO RISK!"? This is always a good one because prospects are continually afraid of being ripped off. They want to buy, of course; but they've also made unwise buying decisions in the past. Whatever lowers the threshold of their resistance and encourages them to act is a good thing. This phrase, then, is a good one.

Note: See how I already begin (almost automatically in my case) to emphasize the key descriptor, in this case both by putting it in capital letters and by adding an exclamation point? Both attract attention. Don't treat an important descriptor the same way you treat other words; if it's more important to the prospect, something that will help induce him to take action, make sure you highlight it accordingly.

Second Note: It's always acceptable to add direct address, a "you", to your descriptor. Thus: "YOU RISK NOTHING!" is a perfectly acceptable variation here. It's hard to go wrong when you use and reiterate the key cash copy word "you."

Your compelling cash copy sentence now looks like this: NO RISK! Complete thirty-day money-back guarantee!

How about another illustration?

We know from looking at Paul's chart that CPROPS offers more problem-solving features than any of his competitors. This is a fact. Descriptors like the following come to mind:

- thorough
- total
- exhaustive
- indepth
- complete.

For this situation, I like the last one.

Write the You-Action Verb-Prospect Benefit Sentence. Here, because the programs the prospect gets are disparate, I've chosen to concentrate on the fact that they only get these benefits from CPROPS — not from anyone else.

"You get 4 programs from CPROPS you can't get from a single one of our competitors!"

Now add the descriptor or adjective you've selected. "COMPLETE. You get 4 programs from CPROPS you can't get from a single one of our competitors!"

We'll do one more, this time neutralizing a possible negative against Paul's product (the fact he doesn't have absolutely the lowest cost) and transforming it into a positive.

"You get more benefits from CPROPS for your investment than from any one of our six competitors. You could pay up to $350 for their program — and you still wouldn't get as much as you get from us for just $99 postpaid."

The right descriptor: "MOST FOR YOUR MONEY." Fact. Not assertion. And ready to be used as a compelling prospect motivator.

A Few Last Words About Features

We've now roamed a bit from the straight and narrow path of features, touching on other crucial cash-copy topics that will be far more elaborately treated in chapters yet to come. But I hope you haven't lost sight of the central point of this chapter: that a feature per se — something of the product or service — is virtually valueless. True, a list of product or service features may make a dandy summary for a marketing document, but such a summary must follow the chief marketing points you make, the client-centered benefits that emanate from the features. Features in themselves, you see, are not important. Their significance comes from the benefits that you squeeze from them and which you present in as persuasive a way as you can to the people you want to take action to acquire them.

This key point — absolutely crucial to the success of your marketing — seems entirely beyond most people. But it will now never be beyond you. For you now know one of the secrets of cash copy: that the one thing you must feature in your marketing documents — far more than anything else — is your prospect. If you can focus on him and motivate him to take immediate action, your own success is ensured. When you use benefits — and not features — the focus is just where it ought to be . . . and the results will be just what you want them to be.

Chapter 6

Getting Testimonials That Persuade
Your Prospects To Buy What You're Selling

When it comes to buying, Americans are pulled in opposite directions. On the one hand, we want to buy — really *want* to buy. In fact, the freedom to buy something is as close to a birthright as we Americans are ever likely to have.

But at the same time, we are nervous about buying. No wonder. We are a nation of stupid buyers; buyers who make one foolish buying decision after another. Who buy things we shouldn't. For too much money. Things with too little value. That leave us a legion of post-purchase regrets.

Yes, we have reason to be nervous when we contemplate the possibility of buying anything else.

Your job as a marketer is to do two things: to fuel your prospect's natural desire to acquire what you're selling *and* to understand that your prospect is anxious about his pending decision and needs you to reassure him, to take his doubts into account and answer them — in the strongest possible way.

What's great about testimonials is that they can assist you to achieve both these sales objectives: exciting your prospect and soothing his anxieties. Yes, both. For the solid testimonial restates and reinforces at least one major benefit of what you're selling. Moreover, by attributing this benefit to someone like him, it lets the prospect know that this benefit is really attainable and that he is not making a foolish decision in spending his money.

Because of their ability to excite desire and soothe prospect anxieties, testimonials are very powerful marketing modules and should ALWAYS be used. There isn't a marketing piece going that cannot be improved through the use of testimonials that reinforce prospect benefits and diminish prospect anxieties. Why, then, are they not used more often?

Why Marketers Neglect Testimonials

There are, I think, two major reasons why marketers fail to use testimonials:

1) testimonials are about prospects and most marketers focus on themselves — not their buyers;
2) it's a bother to get testimonials — particularly the kinds of testimonials we're talking about here.

The first of these points I have discussed before: Selfish Marketing, Arrogant, Self-Absorbed Marketing is what distinguishes most marketing efforts. This kind of marketing is easy — and, face it, it's gratifying, too, insofar as it focuses on the marketer and his pronounced need for ego-gratification.

For most marketers, focusing on themselves and what they're selling is infinitely more satisfying than focusing on their prospect. Focusing on themselves may not get the client, but it certainly offers the seller the opportunity to give himself a much needed pat on the back, some much needed attention. God knows, we live in an alienated age, and most people are in need of attention.

But to my way of thinking, to give yourself this attention at the cost of lost sales is perfectly ridiculous!

The second reason is equally important, arguably more so. What I'm going to tell you in this chapter about testimonials means work for you. It means making contact with your satisfied customers and talking to them, means keeping in touch and finding out what success they achieved with what you sold them. For most people (the people I call Order-Takers) the contact with the buyer ends the minute that buyer plunks down his money and walks out the door.

The Order-Taker doesn't care if he ever sees that person (you!) again or not. He's got his money and that's *all* he wants.

To secure the kinds of testimonials that are useful for marketing means to succeed in doing two things:

1) transferring the focus of your attention from yourself to your prospect, and
2) keeping up with your buyers to see what they managed to achieve using what you sold them. In other words, it means building a relationship and keeping tabs on their progress.

If you succeed in doing these two things, you can get testimonials that will sell your product or service to other people who are like the people you've already sold to.

The Kinds Of Testimonials You Don't Want

Now to be sure, many marketers are already using testimonials. And they may feel that their testimonials are what I'm talking about. But don't be too quick to make this deduction. All testimonials are not the same. In fact, there are three distinct kinds of testimonials which are probably not worth having at all:

1) the celebrity endorsement
2) the testimonial that does not reinforce a specific benefit, and
3) the unattributed testimonial.

Let's look at each in turn.

Considering The Celebrity Endorsement

A recent article in the *Boston Globe* provided information about how American film and rock stars pick up mega-bucks in Japan by endorsing products there. Rock star Madonna, for instance, can easily pick up over a million dollars for a single endorsement. Does this work?

Obviously, the answer is yes — but equally obviously, endorsements (acts of public approval by recognized names) only work if:

- the endorser's image fits the product, and
- the endorser projects sincerity about actually using and profiting from the product.

Too often this is not the case.

Recently actress Cybill Shepherd was hired by the beef industry to extol the virtues of their product. Shortly after her commercials went on the air, she was quoted in a major national interview as saying that she personally didn't eat much meat, thus throwing suspicion on the veracity of her televised message. Needless to say her employers failed to renew her contract. Net result? More public suspicion of both celebrities who endorse products and the people who hire them, I'll wager, than increased sales of beef.

Which brings me to my major point.

While it is a fine thing to be able to quote someone in your marketing pieces who's a known name, their endorsement is only meaningful if it is honest — and if the endorser can point to specific benefits he has gotten by using the product or service. In other words, it is the combination of celebrity plus believable benefit that packs the wallop — not just the name alone.

The Testimonial That Does Not Reinforce A Specific Benefit

Too many testimonials say things like this (I'm quoting from a workshop brochure I received in the mail):

"Great program! I'd certainly recommend it."

"I especially appreciated the instructor's humor."

"The day just seemed to fly by. So much good information."

What's wrong with these comments, absolutely typical of the kinds of testimonials most people use? Why, they're unspecific and do not reinforce any precise benefits of attending the program.

Good testimonials, you see, grow directly out of benefits. You will remember that every feature of what you're selling needs to be transformed into at least one benefit; (perhaps more, for a single feature may lead to many benefits). Each feature has at least one benefit and each benefit should have at least one testimonial. This testimonial should, in the words of a satisfied customer, excite a comparable prospect (the key word here is "comparable") to take action by showing him (the prospect) that someone like him has achieved a benefit worth having by using your product or service. It should comfort the prospect that this satisfied customer is willing to stand up and say so publicly by letting you, the marketer, use his name and such other information about him as will persuade any new prospect to take action to acquire what you're selling.

The comments quoted above don't do this. Not one of them has a single specific benefit to persuade a prospect to take action.

Take a look at just one of these comments, and you'll see what's wrong with it:

"Great program. I'd certainly recommend it."

Remember, the winning testimonial excites a similar prospect by using a specific benefit he (the prospect) wishes to achieve to induce him to take action. The useful testimonial closes a sale by making a strong case for what is being sold. It does not leave questions unanswered — as this testimonial most assuredly does.

Such questions as:

- Why was the program great?
- What did the happy buyer specifically get out of it?
- Why would he recommend it?

All these questions, you see, are begged — and desperately need answers. You don't want the prospect to have questions in his mind about the benefits of what you're selling. You want him to know — immediately — what kinds of specific, tangible, palpable, meaningful benefits he gets by acquiring what you're selling. Thus, this testimonial fails. Try this instead. "There are three reasons why this is a great program:

1) you learn seven ways to cut stress at home and at the office;
2) you get a 45-page directory of stress- reduction resources that you can turn to when you need some help, and
3) you get the instructor's personal recommendations on your own stress level and what you can to do keep things under control. For these three reasons I'd really recommend this program!"

Now you've got a benefit-packed testimonial that's focused exactly where it should be: on what the satisfied buyer got out of the program and on the benefits the prospect will get if he, too, signs up.

This is the kind of testimonial you want.

But even this wonderful testimonial isn't finished yet. It can't be — until a real person, a person just like those you're trying to get to take action, is willing to sign it. Sign it and be publicly recognized as someone who's received real benefits from using what you're selling.

This is the Attributed Testimonial — and it is exactly what you want.

But just a name won't do. What difference does a name make? When used alone, the answer is not much.

What you are trying to do, of course, is show a prospect that someone just like him — or someone he has reason to listen to — has received real benefits from what he is now being asked to acquire. What the endorser has to say will be more meaningful and have more impact if the name is modified with the following kinds of information:

- title
- company
- age
- location
- awards and honors
- book and publication titles

Anything, in short, that says either one of these things to the prospect, or both: "Here is someone just like you who's achieved these real benefits," or "Here's someone really worth listening to — look at his accomplishments! — who's achieved these real benefits."

Thus, a testimonial is an endorsement made by an individual like the person you are trying to attract — or respected and admired by the person you are trying to attract. It's an endorsement they make citing the benefits they've acquired and which they sign with their name and other pertinent information about them. As a result of reading this information the reader (your prospect) says, "This endorser is like me or is someone whose opinion is worth paying attention to because of his cited accomplishments. I'm going to listen to him and get this product/service, too!" That is the testimonial you must have.

The great question is: how do you find them?

Getting The Testimonials You Need

You're always going to need testimonials, so you always need to be involved in activities to acquire them.

Here's what you should be doing:

— When You're Newly In Business

You'll have the fewest testimonials (perhaps none!) when you've just gone into business. Perhaps you have the kind of product or service people have to use for awhile before they can see results. Under these circumstances, it's difficult to get testimonials right away. But, remember, you need testimonials. So here's what you've got to do to get them:

- If you've just opened a business, get testimonials about yourself. Unless you were born yesterday, you've had some experience in the business you're in — experience and client results. What's important is that you've helped people like your prospects achieve success, not that that success was achieved through your business. Go to people who know you, who've benefited from your services and experience, and ask them to stand up for you with some glorious testimonials.

- Send samples of what you're selling to selected individuals. The letter that you send should:

  - tell people you're sending them a sample to elicit their candid opinion;
  - give them areas in which to respond, both through open-ended and closed questions;
  - include a response envelope so that they can speed their comments back to you.

What kinds of people should you target? Try two kinds of people:

- known names in your field. Find them by culling through articles in professional publications, by writing to the authors of books, by contacting politicians with an interest in what you're doing, and approaching those who are known to be concerned about your topic. Think big! You have nothing to lose in contacting these kinds of people except a few moments of your time, a sample of your work, and the postage. And much to gain. Not merely an endorsement you can use again and again — but contact with a well-known and knowledgeable individual who may well turn out to be a new friend and continuing source of useful information. I know. This happens to me all the time.

- more ordinary people who have the problem your product or service can solve. Remember, your testimonial can be offered either by a knowledgeable celebrity who has actually received benefits from what you're offering or from an individual who has the problem you can solve and who is like other individuals you want to sell to.

In either case, you need to give away some of what you'll ultimately be selling. Look upon these gifts as an investment expense.

Don't expect these people to respond to you right away. Most won't. Send along your letter and questionnaire to each and make sure you are explicit about your need for precise comments about what's good about what you've sent. You know how long your customers need to use what you're selling to achieve results. So when that time has elapsed, make sure you send a follow-up letter or card along, reminding the person you're anxiously awaiting his response. This follow-up card is crucial, although if all your customers are local you might well decide to call them, too.

The important thing is that you make renewed contact and get the kinds of testimonials you can use in your marketing.

Whether you write or call, make sure you get the information you need. Ask people specific questions. Don't simply say, "What kinds of benefits did you get?" Say things like:

- "How fast did your begonias grow? How did this compare to similar bulbs you've used in the past?"
- "How many blooms did you have on your plant? Did you get more from these bulbs than you did from comparable packages?"
- "What size were they? Were they bigger than comparable plants you've grown?"

- "How easy were our directions to follow? How do they compare to other sets of directions you've had to follow?"

You want comments that you can use in your marketing, testimonials that reinforce the benefits of using what you're selling, not just a general, unspecific comment. Note: you'll notice that the questions above all use the word "comparable." There's a reason for this. You want people to think about your product or service in relation to similar things they've used. Only by comparing what you've got with what they know will you get the really great comments, comments like, "I've bought seeds from every major seed catalog. But yours gave me the biggest and most fragrant flowers."

To get these kinds of comments, you must lead the customer, whether he's responding in writing or orally to your questions. You'll find that if you ask your users the right questions, they'll supply you with just the testimonial information you need.

As they give it to you, write it down! Superb testimonials are lost every day because marketers don't write down what they hear. Don't be one of them. When a user tells you what specific benefit he's achieved using your product or service, he's just given you the testimonial you need. Don't be foolish enough not to write it down.

Ways To Get Testimonials
When You're In Business

As long as you're in business, you're in the business of gathering testimonials. That's why you need to institute a regular program to get testimonials all the time, testimonials you can use in your:

- cover letters
- brochures
- advertisements
- flyers
- posters
- annual reports
- upgrade letters.

Anything, in short, that can be used to induce prospects to take action to buy what you're selling.

Here's what you need to do.

Talk To Your Customers

If you are in regular touch with your buyers (and if not, why not?), start asking them questions about what happened to them when they used what you're selling. It's your responsibility to open this discussion — not theirs — and it's your responsibility to ask the questions you need to to get the testimonials you must have. Don't be shy! People love to talk about what they've done and will be happy to share their experiences with you. Just ask. Keep in mind that it's your responsibility to write down what they say and clear it with them.

When a customer says something good about you, say, "May I quote you?" And then write down the statement, send it to your customer with a short note and a stamped self-addressed envelop and your request to use it in your marketing. Remember: you don't just want the testimonial and don't just want it attributed by name. You also need information about the person offering the remark: their age, area of residence, business title, *etc.* This information adds weight and substance to the testimonial.

Note: give people who've spent time with you answering your questions a small thank-you gift. Don't tell them you're going to give it, just do. Personally, I like to give a copy of one of my Special Reports, those oh-so-versatile and information-packed premiums that contain valuable information your customers will profit from. As I've said before these Special Reports make superb premiums for three reasons:

- they are inexpensive to produce;
- they are packed with information customers will use and hold on to, and
- they can be personalized, right at the top, with the customer's name and a distinguishing phrase like "Special for (customer name)".

Solicit Your Customers' Opinions

Whatever you're selling, product or service, you are in a position to get testimonials on a regular basis — but only if you ask for them. Send a questionnaire (remember, both open and closed questions, please!) to all the people you serve. You'll get a better result, if you put your questionnaire in the form of a letter. Your computer enables you to do this quite easily. Either enclose your letter-questionnaire with each outgoing piece of mail or (if the high price of what you're selling warrants it) send it separately.

If you don't have many testimonials, I suggest enclosing a stamped self-addressed envelop. This will help your response. Or, use a small premium (remember those wonderful Special Reports) to induce people to respond. Here I suggest telling people what they'll get from you so they'll be more likely to take the time to give you the information you want.

"I want to hear how you benefitted from using (name of product or service). Would you please take just a few moments to tell me? For your trouble, I'll be happy to send you — with my compliments — my 2000-word Special Report 'Testimonials For Your Product Or Service: Why You Need Them, How To Get Them, How To Use Them'. It has a $5 retail value and is something you can use to improve the persuasiveness of every marketing document you ever create. My thanks for your help!"

Notice how this paragraph reads: you're asking people for a favor. I find this tact works remarkably well. Americans love doing favors for people — especially when it doesn't take too long and when they get both the intangible reward of feeling good about themselves and the quite tangible reward which you're offering for their assistance. And I'll tell you a little secret: no one is going to send you a bad review when requesting your free gift. The words that they'll get will be enthusiastic and warm — and eminently useful for your marketing.

Note: I'm constantly asked about whether you must secure permission from people before quoting them. Yes, it helps to do so. And you can by:

- sending people two copies of their testimonial. Ask them to keep one for their files and sign the other indicating that they give you their permission to use it.
- Or by sending a note along with your premium advising the individual that you may use their comment and that if you

don't hear from them within, say, thirty days you will take it that you have their permission to use what they've sent in your marketing.

Obviously, the first of these suggestions is better, but in our terribly rushed world, I think the second probably works just as well. The truth of the matter is, people are tickled pink about seeing their names in print, and I can scarcely imagine anyone objecting so long as you've quoted them accurately and given them the opportunity to block your use if they want to.

How Many Testimonials Do You Need?

According to my rule of thumb, you need about two testimonials *per* page in each of your marketing documents. Given the fact that you have many of these documents, this means you're going to need a good many testimonials. Moreover, like everything else, testimonials age and need to be replenished. A testimonial that was just the thing a year ago, may seem — and be — distinctly stale today.

My second rule of thumb says you need a testimonial for every benefit you're offering, a testimonial made by someone willing to stand up and be counted and say, "I got this distinct benefit by using this product/service." You can make your life easier and organize this task by creating a simple little chart:

	Feature	Benefit Based on Feature	Confirming Testimonial About Benefit
1.	_____	_____	_____
2.	_____	_____	_____
3.	_____	_____	_____

When you have at least one testimonial for each benefit and at least two testimonials for each page of your marketing materials, you probably have what you need. What you need, remember, to:

- excite your prospects about the real, tangible, substantial and meaningful benefits you've got for them, and

- to lower their anxieties about purchasing what you're selling, because they know that people just like them — or people they have reason to respect and admire — have achieved benefits they themselves now want.

Just how you use these testimonials in your marketing, just where you put them, must await another chapter of this book. For now it's enough to know how to get them. Why not start collecting them right away, so that when we get to the section of the book that tells you how to use them you'll be able to do so — immediately!

Chapter 7

Creating Offers Your Prospects Find Irresistible — And Get Them To Act NOW!

When a marketer has something for sale — be it product or service — he wants to sell it NOW. That makes sense, doesn't it?

A sale now is worth two in the future, isn't it?

But if this is true, why do most marketers write marketing materials that offer no inducement for acting NOW?

To demonstrate my point, I've selected at random a mailing from my marketing compost heap, the huge stack of marketing documents I keep in my office and which supply me with an indication of what people are using to sell their products and services — or at least attempt to.

This one comes from the Commonwealth Medical Laboratories of Vienna, VA. What they want to sell is allergy testing.

Now these people have their foot on the right road, but only their foot. In the last paragraph of their opening page they say, "We will screen one of your patients absolutely free. No phony discount, hidden handling charge, or future obligation . . . FREE! Mail the enclosed prepaid reply card and we will send you the necessary supplies."

Let's take a good close look at this paragraph.

This marketer knows that offers help induce immediate action. In other words, he understands a basic fact of marketing life, namely that all prospects are inundated with ways to spend their money. In major urban areas, you can easily get hit with up to 8000 marketing messages each week from people who want you to spend your money on what they're selling.

The marketer knows he must somehow differentiate himself from the pack, from all the other 7,999 people who want to sell to his prospect. And he's heard that using something free will induce action.

He therefore creates a free patient testing program.

So far, so good.

But now things begin to deteriorate rapidly.

The marketer is speculating that this free offer will stop his prospect in his tracks and be of such value to him (the prospect) that he'll drop everything to take advantage of it.

But think a minute. Think about the situation of the prospect when he gets this offer. It's sent to his office. Consider what that means:

- It's mixed with lots of other mail. Mail that contains checks and messages of cosmic import. These get considered first.
- Then the phone is ringing.
- And throughout, our prospect is being asked to put out brush fires.

Other demands — demands for immediate action — are made upon his time.

End result? The message which is so important to Commonwealth Medical Laboratories — which will cost them money if you respond to it — gets lost in the shuffle.

And the fact that the marketer is offering something free is insufficient to induce immediate action when the recipient has so many other demands on his time.

So what happens?

Nothing.

The reason for this lack of action on the part of the prospect is clear —" free" is an insufficient motivator unless linked with two other factors: a distinct time limit and at least one focused benefit for the prospect.

This offer can be considerably improved by limiting it — and by clearly driving home the benefit the prospect will get by taking advantage of the free screening. One of these benefits is perfectly obvious: ordinarily the screening costs money. With this offer, it's free.

But look closely at the paragraph above. There's not a single indication from Commonwealth Medical that what they are offering has a real value — a real cash value.

And beyond a real cash value, there are other benefits, too — like accurate information that might help save a patient's life and will certainly help lead to a precise diagnosis. Accurate information supplied by expert staff and shipped expeditiously. Yes, these are benefits, indeed.

Now you certainly see how this offer could be strengthened to generate an immediate response from the prospect:

The formula that makes FREE work:

free + limited time + at least one prospect benefit to be derived by using what is free = meaningful offer that induces immediate prospect response.

Using this formula, let's restate the Commonwealth Medical Laboratories offer, thus:

"Free $40 allergy screening for you or any or your patients. Find out what you're allergic to so you can do something about it. Stop letting your allergies put you out of commission. This limited time offer expires (45 days from mailing date). So act NOW!"

This isn't Nobel Prize winning copy. I'd have to know more about the benefits of the actual screening, what the prospect gets by using it, to make it more incisive. But this is on the right track.

Let me ask you something. If this offer is so important, where do you think it should be placed on the marketing page? In the final paragraph, like this marketer has done?

CERTAINLY NOT!

If you want your prospect to regard your offer as important — treat it like it's important. Lead with it. Remember this: if the offer doesn't interest the prospect, it's unlikely anything else in the marketing piece will interest him. So lead from strength.

I'll be talking more about how to use offers in a bit, but for now remember this: LEAD WITH AN OFFER THAT INDUCES YOUR PROSPECT TO TAKE IMMEDIATE ACTION. Follow with details. And remember: "free" by itself is almost never the strongest possible offer you can make.

Considering Offers

As you now see, an offer is your attempt to get your prospect to stop in his tracks, pay close attention to your product or service, and to take immediate action to acquire it, (or do the first thing he must do to acquire it, *e.g.*, contact you).

The key word here is "immediate." Sadly, I have come to the conclusion that if a prospect doesn't take action NOW! (I always think of this crucial word in capital letters with an exclamation point), he'll probably never do it — notwithstanding the fact that you have something which really helps him solve a crucial problem and enables him to live better.

What you must do is get the prospect to take immediate action and either pay you NOW or take action NOW that will lead in due course to his buying what you're selling. Either way, the key word is NOW.

The trick is finding the formula that enables you to spend the least possible amount of your money to induce the greatest conceivable prospect response. You can achieve this desirable result by making an offer that costs you relatively little but which convinces the prospect to act to acquire it because of the benefits it will bring him.

Beyond this, the best offers are those which the prospect can benefit from over and over again so that he won't dispose of what you've given. They should also be offers which enable you to send key facts about your business, its name, products and services, address and telephone number; facts which the prospect must retain because he values what they're a part of.

Businesses have tried many ways to meet these conditions. Pens, keychains and similar merchandise have been used. My personal feeling, however, is that these are inadequate to spur prospect interest. Moreover, they are insufficiently valuable for the prospect to keep tabs on them.

Enter The Special Report

You've heard me speak of Special Reports before. Indeed, I've asked you to refer to the catalog in the back of this book and get a glimpse of some of Special Reports which I've produced. Now I'm going to make the case as to why you should use them as offers for inducing immediate prospect response.

What Is A Special Report?

A Special Report is a step-by-step list of guidelines produced by a specialist for the benefit of someone who wishes to achieve a specific result or objective. Special Reports are prescriptive; their function is to advise an individual on what to do either to achieve a specified objective — or to avoid a certain problem.

To be effective, a Special Report must:

- be based on what the reader (your prospect) wishes to achieve;
- take into account why he wishes to achieve it;
- consider the difficulties that stand in the way of the reader's achieving this result;
- provide clear, accurate, factual and up-to-date information on achieving this objective;
- offer valuable information that's immediately useful, as well as names, addresses, telephone numbers and other crucial support data.

Special Reports must not be dry and academic. They must be personal and conversational, not just offering the findings of a problem-solving specialist but giving that specialist the opportunity to talk directly to his reader. This feature of "talking directly" is crucial to what makes a Special Report special. The person reading the report must not feel he is just getting helpful information to enable him to solve his problem or reach his objective but that the specialist/ writer actually cares that he (the reader) achieves this result; that the specialist is committed to the reader's success.

In short, there is more in a Special Report than just valuable information (though this information is obviously of the utmost importance). There is an attempt to create a bond between specialist and reader as between two people who are working together to achieve a mutually important goal.

The reader keeps the Special Report on hand for two separate and important reasons:

- it's packed with guidelines, steps, techniques, procedures, "tricks of the trade", tips, and information of proven helpfulness that will enable him to achieve his objective as soon as possible, and
- because of its personal tone and direct style. He feels it's written directly for him, feels it's the considered wisdom of a personal friend who really cares what happens to him.

Crucial Facts About The Special Report

Remember above all else that a Special Report is itself a marketing document. All marketing documents must have objectives, must move the reader to do something as a result of reading them. A Special Report has these objectives, to:

- establish a bond between writer and reader, marketer and prospect;
- get the prospect to heed the advice of the marketer and so develop a habit that will result in future contacts between them;
- put the prospect/recipient in the debt of the writer/marketer;
  - give the prospect something of value that he will not throw away — and that thus insures that information about your

business and its products and services will not be disposed of, but retained.

To achieve these objectives, the Special Report must:

- address the reader directly using "you" and "I" language;
- remind the prospect right from the start what he wants to achieve and lead him through a series of information-packed paragraphs to this objective.
- be complete and thorough. The specialist loses his credibility if he fails to provide crucial information that will benefit the reader/prospect.

Length Of The Special Report

Special Reports can, of course, be virtually any length. But when used as a premium (or as an additional profit center, for that matter), I have found their best length to be about 2000 words, that is, 5 pages single-spaced. Actually, the report itself should be about 4 1/4 – 4 1/2 pages long. The additional space should be devoted to two essential components:

- a Resource Box offering follow-up information. Special Reports are by their very nature brief. While they can and certainly should offer important problem-solving information and key facts, they ordinarily are insufficiently long and detailed to tell the prospect/reader everything he needs to know about the subject under discussion. This is where the Resource Box comes in.

In the Resource Box, you add detailed follow-up information about other information sources, including books, cassettes, specialists, workshops, anything that will help the reader interested in a fuller grasp of the subject to do what's necessary to get it.

- secondly, details about your own products and services and how to acquire them. The last third to half of the final page should be devoted to you, to your own products and services and their benefits (note I say benefits, not merely features). Information, in short, about what you can help people achieve when they use them.

This is your opportunity to fashion a winning advertisement about what you do and the benefits your reader (a prospect) will get from you. Including this advertisement is one of the key reasons for writing the Special Report in the first place. Without it, you have begun to establish a bond of trust with your prospect without giving him a way of developing your relationship. The prospect must always know what you want him to do next and what benefits he'll achieve by taking further action.

Here's what a Resource Box and product and service details should look like. I've taken this information from my Special Report "Copy Flaws That Doom Your Expensive Marketing Documents To Line Birdcages in Saint Louis."

Resource Box

Two superb books by author Robert Bly will help you to write better, more compelling copy, the kind of copy that will sell your product or service. Use CREATE THE PERFECT SALES PIECE: A DO-IT-YOURSELF GUIDE TO PRODUCING BROCHURES, CATALOGS, FLIERS, AND PAM-PHLETS (242 pages, soft cover. $16.45) and THE COPYWRITER'S HAND-BOOK: A STEP-BY-STEP GUIDE TO WRITING COPY THAT SELLS. (368 pages, soft cover $14.45). Both are available from the Sure-Fire Business Success Catalog, 50 Follen St., Suite 507, Cambridge, MA 02138 or (with your MasterCard or Visa) by calling (617) 547-6372. Don't forget to ask for your FREE year's subscription to this quarterly 16-page business-solutions guide!

If you're running a small business, nonprofit organization or independent professional practice, Dr. Jeffrey Lant, a Cambridge, Massachusetts consult-ant, can help you create marketing documents that get more of your prospects to respond faster. Work with him directly or follow the guidelines in his books, including his latest **MONEY MAKING MARKETING: FINDING THE PEOPLE WHO NEED WHAT YOU'RE SELLING AND MAKING SURE THEY BUY IT** (285 pages). Also, **THE UNABASHED SELF-PROMOTER'S GUIDE: WHAT EVERY MAN, WOMAN, CHILD AND ORGANIZATION IN AMERICA NEEDS TO KNOW ABOUT GET-TING AHEAD BY EXPLOITING THE MEDIA.** (366 pages). Each is $34 postpaid from the **Sure-Fire Business Success Catalog**, 50 Follen St., Suite 507, Cambridge, MA 02138. Ask Jeffrey for details about how he can help improve the quality and persuasiveness of *every* marketing document you use!

Note: I hope you noticed that these boxes are composed of two kinds of offers, called "hard" and "soft" in the trade. Hard offers ask the prospect to send a check NOW. Soft offers ask the prospect to get in touch with the marketer NOW to acquire further information, but do not ask the prospect for any money. Make sure you use both. And, if you are able, mix offers for products and services, too. There's no reason why you shouldn't. The key is that at all times you are perceived as client-centered. If you succeed in achieving this objective, there's no reason why you can't mix hard and soft offers in your Resources Boxes along with offers for products and services.

Writing And Producing Your Special Report

Having worked with many individuals creating Special Reports — and having written many myself — I assure you there's a knack to creating them, a knack you can learn if you are willing to follow these simple rules:

- Tell your prospect *exactly* what he needs to do to achieve the objective of the Special Report. Don't leave anything to his imagination. If he must do it, it is your obligation to provide the detailed information he needs to be able to do it. To succeed, Special Reports must be densely written, must explain everything to the reader and must assume nothing. Most Special Reports fail because their information is too unspecific, hence unusable. And if the information isn't used, you cannot hope to build the bond you wish with your prospect.

- Use "What Next?" Thinking. To achieve the objective covered in the Special Report (like "What You Need To Know About Selecting A Nursing Home Before You — Or Someone You Love — Is In One: 10 Steps For Finding A Place You Want To Be In."), write down each thing that must be done in logical order to achieve the objective. This is "What Next?" Thinking, an approach to problem-solving that succeeds in getting you where you want to go by continually asking — and specifically answering — the question, "What next?"

- Don't leave your prospect hanging. It's better to take a small — though important subject — and treat it thoroughly and completely than to tackle a topic you can't finish and where you beg too many questions. The Special Report is valuable to the extent that you *precisely* tell your reader/prospect what to do to achieve his objective, and what to avoid.

The Compelling Special Report
Starts With A Problem-Solving Title

There isn't a business in America which wouldn't be better off producing a Special Report packed with information its clients would find helpful. Such Special Reports begin with the apt selection of client-centered, problem-solving titles.

Now, as you will already have discovered, I like long titles, titles that leave nothing to the imagination, that tell the reader precisely what he's getting and the benefits he can expect to derive by reading the Special Report. Such titles, of course, have a marketing slant; they are intended to induce the prospect to take action (either to acquire or to read them) because of the benefits he gets from having and using the information in the report.

The best titles are composed of two parts: the Grabber and the Descriptor. The function of the Grabber is to catch the prospect's eye, to stop him in mid-step and get his attention. Frankly, grabbers can and should be as direct and pungent (even outrageous) as you like and as is necessary to capture the prospect's attention.

Grabbers should be followed by Descriptors, a secondary title which describes the benefits the prospect will get by reading the Special Report. In the example above, "What You Need To Know About Selecting A Nursing Home Before You — Or Someone You Love — Is In One" is the Grabber. "10 Steps For Finding A Place You Want To Be In" is the descriptor.

I like to include specific numbers in my Descriptors. For one thing, they make it easy to organize a Special Report; they also make it easy for the prospect to read and follow the data. Moreover, they give the report an aura of authenticity, because only a specialist like you knows that there are ten things the reader needs to know.

What Should You Write About; Hints For
Gathering Information For Your Special Report

I have found in practice there could be millions of Special Reports. The trick is producing reports that are of immediate interest to your prospects, the people you want to take action NOW and that you wish to build a relationship with.

Thus, if I were a nursing home administrator interested in filling my beds, I'd write a Special Report like the one above. An audiologist might write one on how to select a hearing aid, while a copywriter (like me) could do one on how to effectively create marketing documents that sell more products and services. In short, Special Reports address key subjects and are directed to key groups of your prospects.

Where does the information for these reports come from? Everwhere. From the professional publications you read. From workshops and conferences you attend. From the daily newspaper. And, importantly, directly from the real life situations of the people you serve. I find, now that I'm a Special Report fanatic, that ideas for these reports come easily and at any time.

Moreover, the writing of them is easy — once you've got the facts and detailed directives you need. But that's the trick. Thus, you must develop a system to store your information and have it readily at hand. Thus, when you're writing a Special Report on, say, hearing aids, you need the latest figures at your fingertips for the number of hearing-impaired individuals who could benefit from hearing aids. Knowing where to get that information and organizing it once you have it, seem to me to be the greatest problems once you've developed the direct, conversational, personal, and prescriptive style that distinguishes the Special Report as a marketing form and communications device.

Calling On Experts To Write Your Special Reports

While I certainly advocate that you write at least some of your Special Reports yourself (you are, after all, the expert in your field, right?, whether you know how the secrets to waxing floors or constructing, à la Maoist China, a backyard blast furnace), I certainly don't think it necessary for you to write all the Special Reports you'll ever need. Indeed, I think that part of what distingushes a successful marketer who wants to use Special Reports to induce immediate action (or further sales) is his ability to find experts with knowledge of interest to his (the marketer's) prospects and persuade this expert either to provide the information, or, better yet, to write the whole Special Report himself.

Is this really possible?

Most assuredly, it is.

I am thinking, for instance, of a Denver-based company I often work with that sells a variety of sports furniture and fixtures to camps, playgrounds, and other young adult facilities. The owner of the company is not a great writer. But he does think like a marketer, and he accepted my reasoning that offering a Special Report on how to have a winning games season written by a renowned sports psychologist might well induce additional sales.

But could this sports psychologist be induced to write that Special Report without a stipend?

Certainly. The reason? The sports psychologist had just authored a new book on the subject. My client could promote this book (with complete order information) at the end of every Special Report and could give the author natiowide publicity through the marketer's catalog mailing, since each catalog could mention the name of the book and the availability of the Special Report to all customers doing what the marketer wanted. In short, a win-win situation whereby the author got to the people he needed to get to and the marketer got a sales inducement he needed.

All very neat.

Of course, I do the same thing. Through my catalog I sell many products, books mostly. The authors of some of these books have contributed Special Reports to my series as a means of publicizing these books and helping me sell them. Such sales, of course, are very much to the author's benefit — and that of their publisher, who often helps persuade the author that it would be a good idea to be part of this series.

By the way, if you'd like me to promote your book (whether you are an author or publisher), contact me for details on how you can participate in this unique marketing venture that will get your name to the attention of hundreds of thousands of prospects nationwide.

Once You've Got Your Special Report

Once you've got your Special Report, put it into your personal computer — and keep it updated. There are several benefits to having your Special Report on computer:

- It's easy to print;
- Each can be personalized with the name of the individual you're sending it to. I start the report with a line like "Special for (prospect name)."
- It's easy to update when new information becomes available;
- It's easy to edit when you want to base an article on the information in your Special Report and have it printed in a trade or business publication in your field (as you most assuredly will.)

Additional Uses For Special Reports

I'm talking about Special Reports here in this chapter as the basis for offers that induce your prospects to take immediate action. "Act by (date) and you'll receive a free five-page Special Report on (benefit). A $20 retail value, yours if you call (phone number) now. Offer absolutely expires (date)."

Note, that even here when the Special Report is being given away as a free offer, it has a retail price. That price is crucial because it firmly establishes perceived value. What would you rather have: something that's free or something you can get for free that costs the rest of the world $20. It's obvious, isn't it? So make sure your Special Report — even if it will only be given away free — has a price tag, and hence additional value. Its perceived value is one of the reasons why your prospects will act to acquire it.

Giving it a price, of course, should suggest to you that your Special Report is capable of being sold. And, indeed, you may find, as I have, that Special Reports are, in themselves, a wonderful source of profit as well as a marketing tool. Special reports can be:

- used as inducements for prospects to take action;
- given away as thank-you gifts to people who have helped you;
- the basis of articles in trade and business publications, and
- may constitute the basis for speeches and workshops.

And, of course, they can also be sold separately. These additional uses are largely beyond the terms of this book, but they do pertain to Special Reports and are part of why this extraordinarily sensible and inexpensive device is so useful from a marketing standpoint.

By all means, create and use them to get your prospects to take action. You'll rarely find a more useful, less expensive inducement for getting your prospects to take immediate action than with a Special Report. Take my word for it!

Other Offers

Special Reports, of course, are only one thing you can use to excite immediate action. In a minute, I'll be listing lots of others. What I'd like to say first, however, is this: don't get so interested in the inducement for action that you forget that it's just a tool to connect with your prospects.

I have seen marketers over and over again get so interested in the offer they are making that they have forgotten that, while important, the offer is secondary to the need to make a connection with the buyer. It isn't the Special Report that's ultimately important; it's inducing your prospect to take action — and then moving to close the sale. Never forget this. Whatever works to induce immediate action is right; whatever fails to work — no matter how intrinsically valuable — is wrong. It's as simple as that. That's why you have to be aware of the various types of offers — admittedly some overlapping — and learn to use all that are appropriate.

Free Offers

We all know the power of the word FREE, but now you know that this word only becomes irresistible when it's linked to a direct prospect benefit and made available for a limited time. *Never just rely on "free."* Essentially, the notion you're communicating is "free to you, this price to others; this benefit to you, but only if you act by (date)." With this caveat in mind, here are some things you should consider making available free:

- free brochure. But remember, don't push the brochure, push the benefit of having (or better, using) the brochure.
- free booklet
- free catalog (though I prefer the words "resource guide". Catalog is now a word that's far too commonly used. It's lost its punch. I like the phrase "resource guide" because it has a greater perceived value and because it's easier to assign an actual retail value to a resource guide (which sounds as if it

should have a price) than to a catalog (which is generally offered free). But suit yourself.

- free newsletter. (Again, don't push the newsletter, push the value of the information in the newsletter — what the prospect gets from it — and the value of the subscription. Things may be offered free, but they should never be without a price, which is evidence of value.)
- free information kit
- invitation to a free talk program
- free information
- free trial
- free use of product
- free product sample
- free gift certificate
- free coupon
- free consultation
- free survey
- free phone call (toll-free number)
- free analysis
- free estimate
- free problem evaluation
- free product demonstration
- free audio cassette
- free video cassette or film
- free gift (for providing names of others who may be interested in your product or service)
- free sample issue
- free information if requested on your corporate letterhead
- free information to qualified buyers (all others pay X dollars)
- free postage-paid response envelope.

Before moving on to the next category, I would again like to stress a few things about this list. What you see on the list above is features. To work, each of these must be tranformed into a client-centered benefit. In each case the individual must see this thing as something of value, something which:

- only he can have;
- others can't have or will have to pay for;
- has a retail value — but which he gets without cost;
- offers him some defined, explicit, persuasive benefit — if (and only if) he acts by a particular time.

In short, don't just rely on the power of the phrase itself. Remember "sell the sizzle, not the steak." In this case, the lines above are the steak; you've got to make the prospect want them. That's the magic of marketing!

To show you what I mean, let me tell you about my free document review service. As you know, I am in the business of improving the quality of marketing documents, of getting more people to respond so you can sell more of your products and services. Like you, I have the problem of connecting with people, first of letting them know I exist, second of getting them to identify themselves to me so I can persuade them to take advantage of my service. We all have this problem, and each of us must solve it or go out of business.

When I'm especially anxious to get more clients, I sometimes offer a free evaluation of any two of their marketing documents. The trick, of course, is creating a premium (for that's what the review is) which is perceived as valuable, so that the prospect will treat it with respect, but that doesn't take vast amounts of my time.

To achieve this result, I have created a four-page document which is based on two essential parts:

- Part I is a list of key components of any successful marketing document. By reviewing a prospect's existing (or draft) marketing document against the features of an optimum document, I can advise him on the quality of what he is currently using, or plans to use.

- If he is not happy with what he hears (and I am brutally candid in my evaluations, as I always am in my consulting practice), he can refer to Part II of the document, a guideline on how I can work with him to improve the quality of what he's got.

The existence of Part I (which is exclusively focused on the prospect and his situation) is what ensures that Part II will be read and considered by many more people than would consider, say, a direct mail letter they had received.

Key Points About This Free Offer

It's important to point out that this offer is:

- only available to people who have already bought one of my books, that is to say, made an investment. I limit the people who can get this free offer to those I see as qualified prospects.

- available for $45 to all others. This is useful both as an independent revenue source *and* because it shows the recipient that he is getting something with an actual value, an important point.

- available to book buyers (my prospects in this case) for a limited time only. They must send me their two marketing documents for review within thirty days of the time they buy their book, or the offer expires. In other words, you've been given something valuable, but you must act within a specified period or its value is gone.

It is important to point out that this offer is promoted not on the basis of what it is (its features) but what it does for the prospect. The prospect gets a professional review of his marketing materials for free instead of paying the usual cost, and he gets ideas how to improve his investment so they can get more customers. These facts are what give this offer its real weight and substance. In other words, as I've continually been saying, you can't simply say "Free marketing document review"; you've got to sell the benefits of this review. It is these benefits coupled to a limited time offer coupled with the now-magic word FREE that makes this offer truly unbeatable.

P.S. Just in case you're wondering how many people avail themselves of this offer, I'll be happy to tell you. When I'm especially interested in getting new copywriting clients, all the people who buy my books directly from me get this offer. About half of them send me their marketing documents to review (which can mean that I am often a couple weeks behind in reviewing them). As a result of their free review, many become my clients. Indeed, these days I draw almost all my clients from this pool. Oh, yes, I believe in this offer and this way of doing business, because it's cheap, easy to administer, aimed directly at my prospects, focused exclusively on them and how to make their lives better, and gets results!

Take advantage of this offer for yourself. Within thirty days of the time you've bought this book, send me any two of your marketing documents, and I'll happily send you a detailed written critique of what you've sent and tell you what's wrong with what you're using and how to improve them. Stop using marketing documents that don't get your prospects to buy what you're selling. If you didn't buy this book from me, please send $45, and I'll be happy to give you the same expert critique, too, so you can get more people to buy what you're selling.

Offers That Lower Anxieties

Remember, Americans want to buy. Buying things is a way of life for us. At the same time we are afraid that what we're considering buying is the next foolish buying decision we'll make. And no wonder. We've already made so many foolish buying decisions!

Our job as marketers, of course, is to reduce people's anxeties, to get them to make a limited commitment, and to show them they are not risking very much. Offers help do this.

Here are some offers that lower your prospect's anxieties:

- money-back guarantee
- money-back guarantee plus extra 10% if you don't like what you bought
- double-your-money-back guarantee
- Call our satisfied customers and see for yourself if we can do what we say we can do.
- special price on small trial orders.

What your prospects are really worried about is:

- do I get from you what I think I'm going to get; do you deliver what you say you're going to deliver, and
- if I don't get what I want, can I get my money back?

Both these anxieties can be significantly lowered through your offers.

No-Money-Now Offers

As I need hardly tell any *bona fide* American, we live in a world where we want and must have things NOW — even though we don't have the money to pay for them. That's why "No Money Now" offers work. Here are a few of them:

- Send no money now. We will bill you.
- Order now. We won't bill you until (date).
- Send no money now. Pay in easy monthly installments.
- Order by credit card.

I am putting credit card orders in this category for one simple reason: many people don't feel that using a credit card is actually spending money. This is one of the insidious reasons why credit cards work and why, whenever possible, you should be selling your product and, yes, your service, too, by credit card.

Save-Money-Now Offers

We all like to save money, don't we? That's why you should consider using these save-money-now offers:

- discount for new customers
- discount for past customers
- free price-off coupon when you request catalog
- extra discount for large volume purchases
- extra discount for payment with order
- discount with trade-in of your old equipment
- seasonal sale
- warehouse inventory reduction sale
- remnant sale
- buy at low prices now — before prices go up

Get-More-If-You-Act-Now Offers

To induce people to buy more of what you're selling, offer them something additional if they act NOW!, by a certain date. Here are some of the things you can offer them:

- free gift in return for your order
- free gift in return for your order of a certain amount
- free gift for your paid-in-advance order
- surprise gift with your order
- extra quantity if you pay with your order
- order product X — get product Y free
- order now — before price goes up
- discount if coupon or certificate returned with order

Easy-(And Inexpensive)-For-You-To-Do Offers

People like things that are easy. Your job is to make it as easy as possible for your prospects to connect with you without committing yourself to vast expense. Here are some of the offers you can use:

- call toll-free number
- order whenever you want, we're always available to help you, twenty-four hours a day, 365 days a year. (Obviously this offer relies on an answering machine with order message!)
- mail postage-paid business reply card
- complete and mail questionnaire in your postage-paid envelope
- our representative will call on you, you don't have to come to us

Win Something Offers

- Enter our drawing and win prizes
- Enter our contest and win prizes

Lose Something Offer

- If you don't buy something by (date), your name will be removed from the mailing list. (As always, tell the about-to-be-zapped-from-the-mailing-list person what he'll lose. Remember, being on a mailing list is a feature; what you get from being on the mailing list is the benefit.

It'll-Be-Gone-If-You-Don't-Act-Now Offer

In this case, don't just talk about the fact that supplies are limited and will soon be gone. Talk about the benefit the prospect won't have if he fails to act, or acts after supplies are exhausted. Don't build your case on features; clinch it with benefits.

- Order today. Supplies are limited.

Exclusivity Offers

In a world where the theory is that everyone is as important as everyone else, people are dying to be more important than anyone else. Absolute equality fuels the flames for devices that conclusively prove relative worth. Hence the need for exclusive offers.

- Become a member and get things other people can't get.
- Buy a certain amount and receive things others won't get.

Not-Ready-Now Offers

The marketing spectrum is a long one, made up of people of various degrees of readiness to act. On the one end of the spectrum is "Mom", the person who says, "I'll buy anything you ever produce. I just think you're the bees' knees." At the other end is the Rooted Disagreeable, the person who says, "I'll never buy what you're selling. I don't care what it is and how it can help me." Most people obviously fall somewhere in between, the "I'm-from-Missouri-show-me" people who have the problem you can solve, but may not be ready right away to do anything about it. This is the Moderate Middle.

Your essential marketing job is to:

- get those who have just bought to buy again;
- get those who haven't yet bought to buy;
- get those who haven't yet identified themselves as prospects
  to do so.

The Not-Ready-Now Offers category is designed for this third group. DO WHAT IS NECESSARY TO GET THEM TO IDENTIFY THEMSELVES SO YOU CAN CONVERT THEM FROM VERY SOFT PROSPECTS INTO ACTUAL BUYERS. (Who, I need hardly say, should then be upgraded into better buyers.)

Your offer in this case?

- not interested now — try me again in the future. (Ask him to
  provide his address or return his mailing label.)

And a related offer:

- Not interested, here's why.

The clear objective of these offers is to:

- get the prospect to identify himself
- get him to tell you why he's not buying.

In either case you can continue dangling benefits in front of your prospect that induce him to act NOW!

What is important in either case is that you:

- tell the prospect what he gets for acting NOW, and
- remind him of what he's failing to get by not buying now.
  You always want people to know they'll be better off by following your directions, that identifying themselves to you is only the first step towards the solution of their problem!

Near-Final Words About Offers

Later in this book, I shall be discussing how to use offers, where they go in your marketing materials, how many you need, and how to present them for best effect. But I cannot leave this chapter without a few near-final words on the subject.

As I've said throughout this book, you must work to make your prospects act NOW! If you haven't given them a reason to act NOW, you have diminished the chances they'll ever act. Your job is to conjure up the field of clover and its benefits and to do whatever is necessary to induce your prospect to act immediately to get there. WHATEVER IS NECESSARY.

To do this means selling the offer. Yes, successful marketing is about selling offers, not just products and services. And I say this to you: if you cannot persuade your prospect that the offer is valuable, then you can't persuade him to buy what you're selling either. Your job, therefore, is to make an attractive offer and to promote it to your prospects so they'll have a superb idea what they'll have when they take advantage of the offer. Not something free, for example, but something that is only free to them but costs a certain amount for others; something that gives them a benefit they want, but which they must act by a defined date to get. Anyone can offer something free; the trick is making what you're offering your prospect persuasive and valuable (and so be the inducement that gets him to take action).

That's marketing!

Before we go to the next chapter, do me a favor. Take a minute — right now! — and review just one of your current marketing documents to see if you've made an offer that will get your prospects to act NOW. Have you? Have you lead with it? Because you now know you're in the business of selling the offer as much as, if not more, than selling the product or service itself.

And if you haven't created such a compelling offer, or haven't lead with it, what then? Well, until you correct this problem, you're giving your prospects a reason to put off taking advantage of what you're selling, to put off acting to acquire it. And as a result, their lives stay relatively disadvantaged, because they don't have the advantage of your product or service. I hope this is no longer satisfactory to you. I pray you're ready to fashion an exciting, benefit-rich offer for your prospects and do what it takes to motivate them to take immediate action so they'll be better off as soon as possible.

Because if you don't make these changes, and don't do what it takes to make your prospects respond through your compelling offers, I'll tell you something: you're a certifiable flatworm. I guarantee it!

A Word Of Gratitude

I am grateful to my friend and fellow copywriter Robert Bly, and quite specifically to his book *Direct Mail Profits: How To Get More Leads And Sales By Mail*, for ideas which helped me write this chapter. Bly is a protean source of marketing information, some of which you'll find in my catalog. To get a copy of *Direct Mail Profits* contact Asher-Gallant Press, 131 Heartland Blvd., Brentwood, NY 11717. (800) 523-8060

Chapter 8

Finding Out What You Need To Know About Your Competitors — So You Can Blast Them Out Of The Water!

Let's be blunt: a competitor is a person who's getting your prospects to buy what *he's* selling and so lowering *your* profit. Is this something you like? Something you want to keep happening?

OF COURSE NOT!

You know that. But the real question is, what are you going to do about it? Before you can definitively answer this crucial question, you've got to know — really know — who your competitor is and how he works. Hence, the need for research.

The point of this research is simple:

- you're looking for information to assist you in reaching your primary objective; getting your prospect to contact you first, before he contacts your competition.
- information to persuade your prospect to buy what you're selling, instead of buying what your prospect is selling.

This wooing process is complicated by the fact that you are not making your case to the prospect in a vacuum. Your competition may well be doing the same thing, presenting counter-arguments to get your prospect to take action to buy what *he's* selling.

In addition, each prospect may suffer from a number of constraints which may make it difficult for him to acquire what you're selling:

- he has limited resources to take action;
- he may have a prior relationship with the competitor;
- he may have heard more about the competitor than about you;
- he may have heard something negative about you, which, while factually inaccurate, still disinclines him from acting on your offer.

Two things will help you deal with this situation: factual information about your competition and how you present this information so that you get your prospects to take action NOW. In this chapter, I'm simply going to deal with how you get the information you need. Later, I'll be telling you how to use it to your advantage.

Getting The Goods On Your Competitors

How you deal with your competitors is a direct function of what you discover about them. Thus, you've first got to gather the key facts. This breaks down into two questions: what do you want to know and how are you going to find it?

What You Want To Know About Your Competitors

Essentially, you've got to discover five key kinds of information about your competitor.

1. What are the features of what he's selling? That is, what is his product or service composed of?
2. What are its benefits? What do people get from using it?
3. What is the best case the competitor is making to get people to buy what he's selling? That is, what is he saying about his strong points and how is he handling his weak points?
4. Where is your competitor making this case? What markets is he attempting to connect with and how is he attempting to connect with them?
5. Where is he not making his case? What markets is he *not* connecting with, what means is he *not* using to present his best arguments for buying what he's selling?

Let's look at each of these points in turn so that you understand why you need this information.

What Are The Features Of The Product Or Service Your Competitor Is Selling?

If you want your prospect to buy what you're selling, as opposed to what your competitor is selling, you've got to demonstrate to the prospect's satisfaction that what you're selling is better. This necessarily means comparing what you've got to what your competitor has got — either implicitly or explicitly. And this comparison starts by developing a complete listing of the features of your competitor's product or service and comparing it to the features of your own.

To accomplish this, you've got to list all the features of what you're selling and all the features of what the competitor is selling.

To get the information you need, you must either buy what your competitor is selling or convince him to provide this information to you free of charge. Now, no competitor is going to turn over crucial information to you if he knows you are a competitor. If you don't want to buy the information you need by acquiring your competitor's product or using your competitor's service, then you're going to have to pose — or perhaps have a friend pose — as a prospective buyer of what your competitor is selling.

Since you probably don't want to spend the money buying what your competitor is selling, I suspect the latter is the route you'll use first. If you do this, make sure you ask all the questions you need answers to. Remember, your pointed questions are likely to arouse your competitor's suspicions, so disarm them right from the start. Tell the competitor that you are a careful shopper, the kind of shopper who wants to have specific, comparative information before making a buy decision. Then act like a shopper, not a researcher. Ask only questions that a prospective buyer would ask, not those that might interest a competitor.

This procedure is not ethical, of course; you're misusing a valid sales argument to get information that not only will not lead to the competitor making a sale, but will (when used in connection with your marketing program) actually hurt his interests. Still, I'm mentioning this to you because (let's be frank) this sort of thing goes on all the time, and you're probably thinking about doing it anyway!

To make sure you're getting the information you need, start by developing a list of the features of your own product or service. Write down every conceivable component, part, aspect, process, procedure or technique that applies to what you're selling; the things, that is, that are the basis for the benefits you deliver to your buyers. Now begin to gather similar feature information on what your competitor is selling.

Before talking directly to your competitor (or buying what he's selling), find out how much information you can get free and easily. Get your competitor's:

- brochures
- information kits
- direct mail letters
- annual reports
- ads, and
- publicity articles.

Have a friend call to get on the mailing list for:

- publicity releases
- workshops and seminars
- new product information
- catalogs
- flyers, and
- trade shows and exhibits your competitor is participating in.

As you read and receive things about your competitors, call up the spokesperson or individual featured in the article or release and ask for additional details and clarification. People are especially primed to talk after they've sent out material — so gather ye (informational) rose buds while ye may.

Your objective is clear: you've got to get information on your competitor's product and service features comparable to what you've got on your own. Remember: you cannot make the strongest possible case for the features (and ultimately the benefits) of what you're selling unless you know the features of what your competitor is selling. And this means systematically gathering information and filling in a chart that lists information about you — and about your competitor. For an example of such a chart, refer to pages 118–119.

As you can see, this chart is just a table of facts, facts about CPROPS and facts about its competitors. Nothing is being done so far to position these facts to induce the prospect to take action to acquire CPROPS and forego acquiring one of its competitors. That positioning comes later. For now, the facts are all that matter. (Of course, just looking at these facts begins to suggest how you will position the product to achieve what you want, an immediate sale.)

NOTE: Your facts must be accurate. Using incomplete or inaccurate facts to bolster your sales argument can boomerang, destroying your credibility and enhancing your competitor's. Make sure that all the facts you gather are checked and double-checked for accuracy.

What Are The Benefits Of What Your Competitor Is Selling?

To be able to make the strongest possible case to your prospect for buying what you're selling, you must know the reasons why someone might buy what your competitor is selling. Then you must make a case as to why these reasons are not compelling.

If you want to succeed in selling your product or service, you've got to understand why someone might buy what your competitor is selling — and either answer these reasons explicitly or implicitly, letting your prospect know why, in the final analysis, they are not so very convincing after all.

To easily handle this part of your competitor analysis, review each feature of what your competitor is offering. *Each* feature must have a benefit — just as each of yours does. The best way of rendering a feature into a benefit is in the following way:

- write down the feature
- now transform this feature into a benefit by imagining yourself as your competitor talking directly to your prospect. Imagine yourself in a situation where the prospect says, "What's in this feature for me?" (as well he might). You wouldn't respond by merely restating the feature, would you? Of course not! You'd try to transform that feature into a selling point, a lever which helps induce your prospect to buy. Which is exactly what you're going to do here by using this formula:

You + get + specific benefit based on and deriving from the feature = sales point helping to induce your prospect to buy now.

Now let's use an example based on Paul Norton's CPROPS chart from pages 118–119.

Feature

rolled beam selection tables

(This is something CPROPS and GS1-C share in common, an aspect of these programs. It's still a fact, however, and not yet a selling point. Both companies want to use it to induce people to buy; each wishes to neutralize this as a sales point for its competitor, while preserving it as a buying point for itself. That's the game.)

Okay, now let's use the formula, transforming the competitor's feature into a benefit for the competitor's prospect (who is also, of course, your prospect).

"You get specific benefit" formula.

"You get part of the AISC manual inside your program. You don't have to spend time flipping pages and inputting the beam properties. Simply point to the rolled beam you want, and its properties are entered automatically."

Once you have stated your competitor's benefit deriving from this particular feature in the strongest possible terms, you now have the competitor's selling point. In the marketing documents you create, you must either refute, neutralize or ignore this point. What you decide to do is a tactical matter we'll discuss later. But remember this: you cannot possibly make the strongest argument for what you're selling until you know the strongest possible argument for what your competitor is selling — and deal with it.

Note: if you are thorough in your competitive analysis and write honest benefit statements about what your competitor is producing, you'll find yourself writing copy about your competitor that's ordinarily stronger than he's writing for himself!

The reason for this curious situation is not hard to find: most marketers, as you now well know, focus on features, not on benefits. The minute you start writing benefit copy, albeit about your competitors, you produce stronger, more compelling copy than they're currently using. Ironic, isn't it, that you should be able to make their case so much better than they are? Which is why you must never tell anyone the process that produced your marketing copy or even share your notes with anyone. Remember, the process you're now beginning to use successfully can as easily be used by your competitors — against you!

What If Your Competitor Doesn't Have The Feature That You Do?

First, celebrate! You are in a position to gather truly crucial information that will be of the utmost benefit to you. Then follow these steps so you get the most benefit from this significant discovery.

A quick look at Paul Norton's chart shows you he is the only entrepreneur in the group offering a complete thirty-day money-back guarantee for his product. The guarantee, of course, is a feature. It is something that pertains to the product. No one else has it. In a case where only your product or service offers a particular feature and its corresponding benefit, start by writing down the feature. Then transform it into a benefit using the formula above: "You get (specific benefit of the feature)."

Write down the feature.

unconditional thirty-day money-back guarantee

Write down the benefit(s) you offer your prospect that derive from this feature.

"You get up to thirty days to try the product for yourself and see if it does what you need and want it to do.

If you don't like it, don't feel it meets your needs, return it for a complete refund — no questions asked. You risk nothing."

Now focus on your competitors and write down what they don't have and the benefit(s) the prospect doesn't get because the competitors lack this feature.

"You don't get an unconditional thirty-day money-back guarantee. You don't get to try the product and return it if it doesn't meet your needs."

Now write down what happens to the prospect because he doesn't get this benefit.

"You have to buy the product and if you don't like it because it doesn't meet your needs, you're stuck with it because you can't return it. That's very risky because you can never be sure that what you buy by mail will absolutely meet your needs."

Now put this fact into perspective.

"There are 7 bridge-building software programs, but only CPROPS offers you a complete unconditional thirty-day money-back guarantee."

See what's happened?

1) You've identified a fact of significance — namely that no one else offers a money-back guarantee.
2) You've put this fact into perspective, both writing the benefit the prospect gets from having this feature and pointing out the benefit he lacks when he doesn't get it.
3) You're ready to make a case, an argument composed of reasons why your prospects should buy what you're selling and reasons why they should avoid what you're competitors are selling.

This is positioning, and we'll talk more about this later. But what I must stress now is that you go through each feature of the product and service offered by your competitor to derive the corresponding benefit. And, where your competitor has no corresponding feature to what you're offering, tell the prospect what he gets from you, what he doesn't get from your competitor and what he should do as a result.

What Is The Best Case Your Competitor Is Making To Get People To Buy What He's Selling?

A case is composed of two kinds of information: strong points compelling immediate prospect action that you stress. And weak points militating against immediate prospect action that you defend (or ignore).

Speaking generally, you are trying to convince your prospects (who, remember, are also your competitor's prospects) that your competitor's strong points are not so compelling and that his weak points constitute sufficient reason for not buying his offer. Simultaneously, of course, you must stress your own strong points and defend (or ignore) your weak ones. As I've already said, what complicates this game is that your competitors may well be doing the exact same thing; coming up, of course, with a dramatically different argument than you're using and a conclusion the complete reverse of yours. But that's the fun of this game, isn't it?

Before you can make the strongest case, you've got to look very carefully at the case your competitor is making. You must do the following:

- Write down every positive thing the competitor has said to get you to buy what he's selling NOW.
- Write down anything beyond the fact itself that the competitor has said about this positive thing.
- Write down any weak point that the competitor may be defending about what he's selling.
- Write down the argument the competitor has advanced to answer this (implicit or explicit) weakness.

Now you have the basis of your competitor's case. You know why he thinks you should buy what he's selling NOW. And, either explicitly or implicitly, you know what he feels is weak about his case — and the points he's raised to answer that perceived weakness.

You now know what his case is — or should know. Because this process is not always as easy as you might assume from reading my last few paragraphs. No, indeed. And there are very good reasons why this is all rather complicated.

Your competitors may not understand that they are making a case for persuading an individual to do something, for getting their prospect to take immediate action. As should now be clear, too many marketers simply produce documents, a hodge-podge of facts, features, testimonials, offers, benefits, and — most often — just words that are meaningless because they don't compel an immediate response.

We know that to produce a document is not necessarily to produce a compelling marketing document, a document that gets your prospects to respond NOW! We know that to produce a document is not necessarily to make a case for immediate

action. But our competitors (praise be!) don't know that — and so it takes time
to find out what they think their best case really is.

As I write, for instance, I'm reviewing a brochure sent by Keye Productivity
Center of Kansas City, MO. Keye is a constant mailer, but not always a
persuasive one. I'm reviewing their brochure for "The Secretarial Seminar." On
the first page of this 8-page 8 1/2" x 11" brochure (a length which demands a
real commitment from the prospect) there is this information:

- the name of the presenter
- the name of the seminar
- information that this is a one-day seminar and its price
- the fact that your satisfaction is guaranteed
- a list of the cities where the seminar is offered
- a toll-free number for registration, and
- the address of the presenter.

Now, if I were putting on a rival secretarial seminar, I'd want to screen this
information for Keye's case. But this wouldn't be easy because the first page
(with the exception of the weak phrase "Satisfaction Guaranteed") is entirely
composed of features; facts, not selling points.

Keye has forgotten the prime reason for sending a marketing document; that
such a document is intended to make a case, to present the strongest possible
reasons for taking immediate action; to present them as early and as strongly as
possible, while either defending or ignoring weak points.

Just from my review of this opening page of my (supposed) competitor's
material, I can deduce the following:

- Keye is insufficiently client-centered. Except for the words
  "satisfaction guaranteed", there isn't a benefit on this crucial
  opening page.
- Keye fails to lead with an enticing offer that can get me to take
  immediate action. In fact, there isn't *any* offer — any reason
  for taking immediate action — stated *anywhere* in this brochure!
- There seems to be no prime benefit for taking this seminar
  now. Instead of a benefit, Keye leads with the seminar name,
  which is, of course, a feature. The prospect needs to know

right away what benefit she gets from attending this program. Keye makes you dig for it.

* Keye hasn't bothered to do a feature-benefit analysis, to transform every feature into a benefit and to sell the benefit, not the feature. Keye lists facts, to be sure, but doesn't tell you what benefit they are to you.

All this makes it difficult to find out what Keye's case for attending this seminar really is. But while establishing that case is undoubtedly difficult, by reviewing how Keye does present its information, we get a very good idea of how we could present ours to aptly differentiate ourselves from this unfocused competitor.

As this example demonstrates, it won't always be easy for you to find out what your competitor thinks is his strongest possible case. Nor will the competitor always defend his weaknesses. Sometimes he'll make his case clearly, and you can easily write down both what he thinks his strongest arguments are and how he answers any criticism against what he's selling.

Sometimes, however, — more often, in fact — you'll have to dig through the murky depths of his marketing documents, deducing, rather than discovering, his case. Either way, persist. Your job is to know your competitor better than he knows himself, to glean his case — and, in due course — to outmaneuver him on every point he thinks compelling and expose every little weakness he doesn't really want the world to know about. This all takes time, time you may not want to invest. Because, of course, it's easier simply to dash off a marketing document, to write it off the top of your head, and suppose that you've done what I'm recommending. Resist this temptation! To be able to rout your competitor, you must understand his argument. It's the only way you'll be able to decide how to deal with it.

Where Is Your Competitor Making His Case?

Here I want to discuss just where your competitor is making his case — the markets he is trying to tap into and how he is attempting to do so.

I hear a lot of wild talk nowadays about markets. And frankly much of it leaves me puzzled. Many people discuss the idea of a market the way Christopher Columbus discussed the idea of the Indies — as something "out there" that has only to be discovered to be exploited.

Nothing could be further from the truth. No market exists without the means of connecting with it. Thus, the means of connecting with a market are (at least initially) more important than the market itself. For without the means of connection, there can be no market. You see, a market is not a mass of people who have a want or need. A market is a mass of people with a want or need who have been given by the marketer a means of solving their problem. And that's why I say, the medium — the means the marketer uses to connect with his prospects — is the market.

Thus, rather than focusing on the abstract markets that your competitor is selling to, you need to focus instead on how he is connecting with these markets, the forms of communication he is using to get his prospects to take immediate action.

These forms may include, but are certainly not limited to:

- paid ads
- free publicity
- direct mail and mail-related techniques.

Your job is to find out those which your competitors are using and to attempt to find out which ones are working — and which are not.

Having analyzed your competitor's case, you must now seek answers to the following questions:

- Which general ways is my competitor using to connect with his markets?
- Which specific media is my competitor using to connect with his markets?
- What can I deduce from his choices about the markets he feels have the problem his product or service can solve?
- Which markets — as evidenced by his continuing use of the means connecting with them — appear to my competitor to be meeting his objectives of both identifying people who have the problem he can solve and getting them to buy what he's selling?
- Which markets — as evidenced by the fact my competitor is no longer using certain means to connect with them — appear to my competitor to have failed to meet his objectives of both identifying people who have the problem he can solve and getting them to buy what he's selling?

And, on the basis of all this information, what do I now know about where I should be spending my time and limited resources in my own attempt to identify people who have the problem I can solve with my product or service and get them to buy what I'm selling?

As you consider these questions, remember: to successfully answer them you must be both researcher and sleuth. Getting this information demands care, commitment, and deductive intelligence. Having it, however, will spare you much future aggravation and assist you in your own marketing. Let's, then, look at each question in turn.

What General Ways Is Your Competitor Using To Connect With His Markets?

You want to know which forms of marketing communication your competitor is using to connect with his prospects. You need to find out which of these apply and which variations within each category he is using:

- paid ads, including newspapers, magazines, newsletters, radio, television, electronic data bases, and billboards and signs;
- free publicity through all of the above (with the exception of billboards and signs), and
- direct mail and mail-related techniques.

What you need here is alertness. You must start thinking like your competitor, understanding that he, like you, has limited resources.

Which Specific Media Is My Competitor Using To Connect With His Markets?

Your job is to figure out where your competitor is using his money successfully to connect with his markets and where he has failed to connect successfully with his markets using certain specific media. But to discover this information you must first find out what specific media he is using and in what way he's using them. Thus, you want to know where your prospect is:

- placing his ads. Be specific. Where is he advertising, how often, with what size ads? And, since you're always alert to what he's saying, with what message?

- getting free publicity. People send releases and information to media that connect with their markets. If your competitor's name and information about what he's selling keep popping up in certain publications and on certain electronic media, you can be certain he regards this as an important market, one that justifies the investment of his time and limited resources because of the response he gets from his prospects in that market.

- sending mail. It would be nice to know which mailing lists your competitor is using, wouldn't it? Unfortunately, this is difficult to find out. Mail, by its very nature, is a much more private medium than advertising or publicity. While list vendors will certainly be happy to share with you what lists they have, they don't tell you who rents them. And the people receiving the information may not even know how they got on the list that results in their receiving information.

Still, you're not entirely helpless. There are basically two kinds of mailing lists: compiled lists and lists of buyers, often periodical subscribers. You can get your name on lists your competitor is likely to use by buying comparable products (including his own, of course) which generate mailing lists. Never use your exact name. Always vary it slightly and keep accurate records of the name you used. (A changed middle initial is the easiest). Then you'll know how your competitor came by that name. And if he uses the list again — that's a sure sign his initial use has been profitable.

Once you have this information, there are several questions that need answers:

- Do you agree that the media your competitor are using also make sense for you?
- If you do, how will you position yourself against your competitor in these media? (This is where outmaneuvering his message comes in.)
- Whether or not you use the media your competitor is using, what additional media will you use based on your deductions about what is working for your competitor (along, of course, with your deductions about what is working for you already)?

What Can I Deduce From My Competitor's Marketing Choices About The Markets He Thinks He Is Serving?

What you are trying to find out here is this: who is my competitor selling to — and what can I find out about them?

Knowing which media your competitor is using enables you — by discovering certain basic demographic information — to find out who he thinks his market is. Continuing use by your competitor of these means allows you to deduce that, yes, indeed, that market is a profitable one for him — and may well be so for you, too.

To get the information you need:

- write down the name of the media sources your competitor is using;
- get their addresses (your local library can help);
- write a letter and ask for information on whom they're selling to (their demographics) and their rates.

Gather all this information regularly and regularly study it. But make your decisions based on this information all at once. That's because in deciding where to place your scarce resources, it's easier to look at all the alternatives and make your choices at one time than attempting to recall crucial facts through several meetings. Your key marketing rules are:

- Review your competitor's marketing decisions on an ongoing basis.
- Gather the specific information you need about the media he's using and what you can find out about the markets they represent.
- Review all your marketing choices at one meeting.
- Make your decisions for the next 90 or 180 days for all media at this single meeting.
- Then monitor results (while continuing to monitor your competition).

If you handle matters in this way, you'll make the most intelligent decisions.

Which Markets Appear To My Competitor To Be Meeting His Objectives Of Identifying People Who Have The Problem He Can Solve And Getting Them To Buy What He's Selling?

Your research — if it's thorough! — will definitely uncover information about where your competitor keeps marketing, that is where he keeps making an effort to connect with his prospects through:

- paid ads;
- free publicity;
- direct mail and other mail-related activities.

As a result of your research, you may notice that your competitor is using a particular medium more than 6 times to attempt to get new prospects and get them to respond. If so, this is a place that is particularly worthy of your attention, since you may now deduce:

- either that your competitor is a damned fool, interested in throwing his money away recklessly on a gambit that isn't paying, or
- that he's getting a sufficient response to justify his continuing investment of scarce resources in this marketing alternative.

While there's no doubt that some of your competitors — and hence their decisions — fall into the first category, I think I'm safe in saying that if you see a competitor's marketing message more than six times in a single medium within a year that is sufficiently lucrative to justify the expense. Let's proceed on this basis.

Here you must answer these crucial questions:

- Who is my competitor attempting to reach?
- Is this who I am attempting to reach?
- What is he attempting to achieve from his initial contact with the prospect? To simply gather a name? To break even? Or to make an immediate profit?
- If he doesn't at least break even on this initial contact, does he

have additional products or services he can sell to this prospect so that the expense of acquiring the name pays off?
- Do I have such additional profit centers, or must I make this
initial contact pay off immediately? (A much more difficult
proposition, of course!)
- Can my competitor make additional money (and thus cut the
expense of acquiring the name) by renting out his mailing list,
thus justifying a lesser profit (or even a loss) on the initial
contact?
- Can I do this? Or must I make this initial contact profitable
immediately to justify placing the ad?

Finally, do I have a product or service that is demonstrably superior to what my
competitor is selling and can I present it in such a way that in this marketing
medium my competitor is outmaneuvered and prospects compelled to respond
to my offer, not his?

What you are trying to do, of course, by answering these questions is discover
what makes this marketing medium a sensible choice for your competitor and,
by the same token, what would make it a sensible choice for you.

Let's say that your competitor has been in business for a while longer than
you've been. He sells not a single product or service, but a line of them. And he
rents his mailing list through a list broker for additional revenue. (You have
checked with your broker, haven't you, to find out?)

You have created a demonstrably superior product to the one that your
competitor markets but:

- you have only this single product (thus precluding any upgrade sales), and
- you have too few buyers to put your mailing list on the market
and so generate additional "back-end" revenue.

This, of course, is a very tricky situation, one that all too many entrepreneurs
encounter — disastrously.

Let me warn you: in considering where — and how — your competitor markets,
you must also consider all the factors that help create revenues — and ultimately
profit — for him. Otherwise, you cannot evaluate whether using the same
marketing medium will make as much sense for you as it does for him.

If you are in a situation like the one I've described above and do not have the additional profit centers that your competitor has, then you have to factor in the expense of at least two follow-up mailings to the name you have acquired and a positive response factor of no more than 5% (a conservative estimate) of those who have responded to your initial marketing effort.

Thus, to determine if any particular marketing investment makes sense, draft a budget along the following lines:

- Cost of initial marketing activity (say an ad), repeated twice. Three insertions.
- Cost of your initial response to those responding to the ad, repeated twice. Three prospect contacts.
- Cost of the product or service plus shipping, *etc.*, based on 5% of respondents actually buying.

Add these costs. They will be considerable.

And your revenues? Figure that 5% of those responding to your offer will actually buy.

On this basis, even if the marketing medium makes sense, even if it does put you in touch, for a reasonable price, with the people who want what you're selling, should you invest your money in it?

Be coldblooded as you consider this situation. Too many marketers aren't. And the result — which I see daily — is that they've thrown their money away. This is the consequence of an imperfect understanding of how their competitors are profiting from any given marketing medium as well as out-of-control entrepreneurial optimism, which often can be so fatally incorrect.

And if the analysis proves that this is not a place where you should spend your money (even if it may make sense for your competitor to do so), what then? Find an alternative means of reaching your prospects that cuts your costs. Where are they? You'll find them in my book MONEY MAKING MARKETING: FINDING THE PEOPLE WHO NEED WHAT YOU'RE SELLING AND MAKING SURE THEY BUY IT.

But what if you decide that, yes, indeed, this is a place to invest? Well, two things actually:

1) Don't even consider using the same marketing medium as your competitor unless you take the time to understand his message and reasons for buying what he's selling and work to outmaneuver him. In other words, if you are successfully to use the same medium, you must fashion a more compelling argument than your competitor — an argument that offers the prospect more benefits and gets him to take action NOW!

2) Make a tentative decision about whether to use this source. Make it tentative until you've reviewed all your marketing alternatives, both those which your competitor is using, and those he isn't. Until you've reviewed all your alternatives — and your limited resources — you won't really know if this is the place for you to invest. That's why it's so helpful to have all your marketing information available to you at one time.

Reprise

As you consider the media your competitor is using, ask yourself these questions:

1) Using this medium, who is my competitor connecting with? (The marketing source itself has the demographic information you need to answer this question.)

2) Does this group make sense for him? Is he profiting from this market simply by selling the single product or service he may be leading with in connecting with them? Does he have a line of products or services that he can sell (thus minimizing the expense of acquiring the name)? And can he make additional money by renting his list?

3) Given what we know about our competitor, does this medium make sense for us? Or are the dollars invested in this market dollars that are not sensibly spent? Should we, in short, invest some of our resources here, or should we seek another medium that makes more sense, either because it's less expensive or because it connects us with our prospects, and is not currently being used by our competitor?

4) If this medium makes sense for investing our scarce marketing dollars, can we outmaneuver our competitor by presenting a sharper, bolder, more client-centered, action-NOW message? Or will our message be weaker than our competitor's? (Remember: if you cannot present this kind of message, though the medium may be correct, you still shouldn't be using it since your competitor will then have outmaneuvered you!)

Which Markets Appear To My Competitor To Have Failed To Meet His Objectives Of Both Identifying People Who Have The Problem He Can Solve And Getting Them To Buy What He's Selling?

Is there more that we can learn from our competitors that influences what we may do? Emphatically, yes! We can review media our competitors have once utilized but utilize no longer, and see if it makes sense for us to use them.

To do this, of course, means being particularly alert. Alert both to when your competitor uses a marketing medium to connect with his market, and alert to when he stops doing so. Now, we can assume that a competitor stops using a marketing medium because the cost of acquiring the name becomes too expensive relative to the profit he makes from that name. Your competitor reaches this decision when he:

- discovers an alternative marketing medium where the cost of acquiring the name is less (and the resulting profit greater);
- sells only a single product or service and thus cannot make additional profit from the name;
- doesn't rent his names and thus fails to realize any additional income from this source, or
- goes out of business altogether.

The question is: Should you use a marketing medium a competitor no longer uses? Your answer depends on whether:

- the demographics of the medium are suitable. Will you reach people who have the problem you can solve for less cost than if you used another medium?
- you can fashion a client-centered message that resolutely makes a strong case for what you're selling and gets people to respond NOW;
- your profit margin for what you're selling is such that you can justify additional follow-up letters and reminders to the prospect about why he should buy what you're selling imme-diately;
- you can make additional money from the respondent, not just

by selling him the initial offering, but by transforming him into a customer who will buy other things you're selling;
* you can make additional profit by renting his name as part of your mailing list, and
* you can (following the Rule of Seven) use other devices (some less expensive, like free publicity) to connect with the same prospect and so increase the chance that he'll respond to your offer.

If you can do these things, then you should add this marketing medium — even though abandoned by your competitor — to your list of possibilities and consider it along with the others in which you may be investing.

On The Value Of Competitors

Many people see only the negative side of having a competitor, of having to deal with someone who sells something comparable to what they're offering. They'll tell you that having a competitor means having to be unendingly vigilant; of always having to look over their shoulder, never being able to rest, always wondering what their fellow marathon runner will do in the race for the prospect and his patronage — and having to make unending changes in their own way of doing business as a result of this pesky opponent. And, of course, they are right.

Having a competitor means never being able to say, "This is the price. This is the way we do business. And we don't make any changes. For anyone. Ever." Competitors, you see, can very well force you to make fundamental and wide-reaching changes in the way you do business. Because that's what having a competitor is about.

At least, partly.

Because the good news is that your competitor (whether he knows it or not) is running a research department for you. He's:

* doing research to determine new markets which you can exploit;
* investing his scarce marketing dollars in media which might work for you;
* finding media for you that work, and work very well;
* finding media that won't work at all for you.

He is, in short, accumulating an avalanche of information that's literally worth its weight in gold to you.

But only if you spend the time to get it. And to scrutinize it. Because remember, a competitor is not merely a competitor; a competitor is a gamester, just like you. Someone trying to find out where there's gold and where there's fool's gold.

And just because he knows, doesn't always mean he profits.

Recently, in reading a biography of Commodore Vanderbilt, one of America's earliest millionaires, I found that he had made an interesting point. He said he didn't want to be the first into a new venture. That he wanted other people to spend their time and money finding the source of profit (and, so often losing their stake attempting to do so.) *Then*, having analyzed what worked for them, he'd move in and outposition them. In short, he regarded his competitors as pioneers, people who were in charge, not so much of finding a new market, but of handing the enterprising Commodore the information he needed so he could create a winning strategy and adopt the right tactics to achieve his objective.

Oh, yes, the Commodore was a marketing man!

This is not, of course, a book that's simply about competitors. I fear you may feel I have already gone on quite long enough about them, though, I think, the importance of the topic justifies this length. Still, I cannot leave without giving you some final research guidelines that'll help you get the crucial information you need so you can benefit from your competitors as you are supposed to.

Gather Everything In Which
The Competitor Makes His Case

This sounds obvious, but isn't. Most of us are not aware of all the documents that a competitor must complete that may contain information about him and what he's doing. Some of these documents include:

- ads
- brochures
- direct mailing pieces
- signs and billboards
- articles by competitor

- articles about competitor
- annual reports
- government mandated documents
- yellow pages listing.

To know where your competitor has made his case, you have to understand something about his operations. Sometimes (as in a paid advertisement) he makes his case voluntarily; sometimes (as in the case of a filing to a particular government department), he doesn't. Have you done everything you can to get ahold of all the information that exists? Remember: if a document exists, there is usually a way for you to get it!

Have you:

- gotten yourself on relevant mailing lists;
- subscribed to periodicals carrying your competitor's ads;
- joined trade associations where your competitors make presentations;
- found out if your competitor's mailing list is for rent;
- bought a share in his company so you'll receive stockholder information;
- found out which government agencies regulate your competitor's business and found out what kinds of information they put out?

Have you, in short, attempted to understand what your competitor makes available and how you can easily get access to it?

Ask People Questions About Your Competitor

All sorts of people have some of the information you want about your competitors — secretaries, sales representatives, people who work in the shipping department. And all these people talk.

What's amazing about getting information on your competitors is how really easy it is. During World War II, there was a slogan, "The slip of a lip can sink a ship." Now, very few people are actually told what's important, and what's not. So, if you want to find something out, ask someone either in the company itself or someone familiar with the industry. You'd be amazed to find how much people tell you if only you ask! This means getting to know the following kinds of people:

- editors of trade publications
- executives of industry associations
- employees of your competitors
- recognized specialists and experts in the industry
- employees of government agencies regulating the industry
- suppliers of products to your competitors.

Get Your Friends To Give You The Information They Get

For years, I've had reciprocal relationships with a number of people who supply me with anything they see about my competitors, in return for my supplying them with anything I see about theirs.

Such a relationship need not be haphazard either. You can organize things so that you actively seek information for your friends and they actively seek information for you. This works so long as both parties regularly get information they can use from the operation.

The trick here is to:

- identify people who are well informed and well organized;
- start clipping information of interest to them, and
- ask them to clip and send comparable information of interest to you.

Tell them precisely what you want. And ask them precisely what they're looking for. I've been given a good deal of useful information this way. So will you!

It's Just Common Sense

The trick to all this is:

- knowing where to find the information you need;

- making sure you have done what it takes to get it, and
- sensibly evaluating it when you have it.

Remember: being anxious about your competitors doesn't make sense. Learning from them does. Four books will help you achieve this desirable result.

Finding Facts Fast by Alden Todd (published by Ten Speed Press) tells you how to find the information you need. It's a nifty little book chock full of ways to find information. There are two especially admirable things about it: it's short, and packed with tips. When you want to find information, use it.

Then use, *Competitor Intelligence* by Leonard Fuld and Fuld's new follow-up volume, *Monitoring The Competition: Find Out What's Really Going On Over There.* Finally, use *How To Check Out Your Competition: A Complete Plan For Investigating Your Market* by John M. Kelly. Fuld's books are the more rigorous (and demanding) about gathering information. He's a Cambridge, Massachusetts, consultant specializing in helping corporations learn about their competitors. Kelly's book is lighter reading but offers a plan, with lots of forms you can use, for getting the most information in the least painful way. These three resources are published by John Wiley & Sons.

Last Words About Your Competitors

This chapter has been about gathering information about your competitor. About knowing what he's doing, and about discovering — both directly and indirectly — what's working (and not working) for him so that you can act accordingly.

Frankly, now that I understand that my competitor is really a part of *my* organization — gathering crucial information for me — I rather enjoy finding out what he's up to. Not least because he often saves me a lot of time and money. Perhaps you'll allow me just one anecdote in this regard.

As you may know, I do seminars around the nation. One of my perennial profit-makers is my workshop on "Establishing And Operating Your Successful Consulting Business."

A year or so ago a competitor launched a series of these workshops around America, all taught by surrogates. They were promoted through *USA Today* and major local newspapers and featured phone-in registration on a toll-free number. It looked like my market would be savaged. But rather than panic, I resolved to monitor the situation.

I sent people to some of the workshops to check both content and registration numbers. I started checking my own information sources in the industry. I called some of the newspapers and checked the cost of comparable ads. And checked with the 800 service to find out what that cost. As a result of a few very elementary steps, I soon had the cheerful information I wanted: the expenses were far outstripping the income. I knew the business was doomed — as indeed it was.

That company is now bankrupt. My operation survives nicely, built on selected target markets and my own "slow but sure" marketing philosophy. And what did I learn from all this?

1) Information about your competitor is not difficult to get if you use common sense and work at it regularly. As even the U.S. Navy knows (which supposedly gets about 95% of its peacetime intelligence from generally available sources of information), what you want is available — if only you'll take the time to find it.
2) Having the information enables you to discover whether you'll compete with your competitor for a lucrative market, or, as this case demonstrates, wait until he's put himself out of business through a series of devastating miscalculations.
3) It isn't always necessary for you to test markets yourself. Your competitor will act (if all unknowing) as your pioneer. You've simply got to make the effort to determine what he's doing and how well he's succeeding.
4) Using the information you get from your competitor enables you to make the most intelligent decisions — even (or sometimes especially) if your competitor has failed to do so!

Remember, you are at war with your competitors. Your prospects have only so much money to invest. When it's gone, it's gone. Marketing is a zero-sum game. When you get more, someone else gets less — and the reverse! Your job is to:

- discover who your competitors are;
- constantly monitor what they're doing;
- find out what their strongest case is for getting their prospects (also, your prospects, of course) to buy;

- deduce their weakest case, the things which if known by their prospects would cause them not to buy;
- outmaneuver their strengths and emphasize their weaknesses in media where you decide head-to-head competition makes sense;
- while finding additional cost-effective media where you can have the show all to yourself, because your competitor isn't using them — yet!

If you succeed in doing these things, you will outfox your competitor and have the satisfaction not only of making money — a dandy thing in its own right — but the thrill of beating someone else, the quintessential American experience!

Chapter 9

Understanding The Anxieties Of
Your Prospects And Answering Them —
So They Buy What You're Selling Faster

Every American, as I've said often enough, is made up of two equal and opposite tendencies: the raging desire to buy now and the nagging fear that what they want to buy is a terrible mistake (as evidenced by all the foolish buying decisions they have made in the past).

Now, if all Americans had unlimited resources (as so many of my benighted fellow countrymen seem to think they do), the first (I might say primal) tendency would overwhelm the second. For an individual of such inexhaustible means, it wouldn't matter if he made a stupid buying decision. Such an individual could keep on buying until he got the exact thing he wanted, or until he had exhausted his compulsion to buy. With the advent of credit cards, of course, this is precisely how many people actually behave!

But I think it safe to say that most of us — and most assuredly you! — don't behave that way. You are sobered by the incontestable fact not only that your resources are limited, but your *realization* that they are limited. What also inhibits you is the fact you've made any number of foolish purchase decisions in the past . . . and your fear you'll make more of them in the future. You want to buy as much as the next fellow. You wouldn't be American if you didn't. But (most of the time) you need to be convinced that your purchase is sensible and necessary.

This makes you part of the marketing majority, the people you need to consider as you create the copy and the materials that will get them to buy.

Working With The Marketing Majority

In general terms, your strategy is clear: you must spur the natural desire of the prospect to buy NOW while simultaneously taking on and knocking out the reasons which make him cautious about buying. You must undercut his fears and anxieties about you and your product and destroy their ability to influence his behavior and sabotage his natural desire to buy. In short, you must leave your prospect with only one course of action: doing what he loves most, experiencing the thrill of buying NOW, that sublime American experience.

What Your Prospect Needs From You

To achieve this objective means understanding what your prospect needs from you. Your prospect needs you to understand that:

- He wants to buy. If you are approaching the right prospect, the prospect who has the problem your product or service can solve, and if this prospect has the means to buy what you're selling (either through an immediate cash payment or through credit), then that person will want to buy what you're selling — if you make the compelling case it is your job to do. If we have done our homework and we know we are connecting with the right prospect — the prospect whose life we can improve with what we're selling — then we marketers must realize it is up to us to motivate our prospect to take the action he strongly desires to take — but has both reasonable and unreasonable anxieties about taking.

If the prospect doesn't buy (or take the appropriate action leading to a buy decision), it's because we have failed to make the strongest conceivable case to answer his implicit or explicit objections and so get him to take action. For remember: each of our prospects wants to BUY NOW. And if he doesn't buy what we're selling, he will not stop buying. He will simply buy something else as soon as he can. This is what being an American consumer is all about.

- The total responsibility for the prospect's acting is on you, not him. The consummate marketer understands that it is his responsibility to create the conditions that result in the buyer doing the only thing that only the buyer can do, namely to complete the marketing circuit with payment (or take the next logical step that leads to this ultimate buyer act). *It is the marketer's job to do everything else.*

If the prospect fails to take action, and he is the right prospect and has the resources to buy what you're selling, it is because you have failed to show him it is in his best interest to act NOW. This means, you always have both to excite your prospect's natural desire to buy and to answer his natural fears and anxieties about buying from you. If a real prospect with resources fails to act, it is your fault. Not his.

- It's your responsibility to know what fears and anxieties he has about buying from you. It continually staggers me just how little most marketers know about their buyers, how they think, and why they act. Most seem to have no recognition of the fact that their prospects have both legitimate and (it's true) unreasonable anxieties about them, the marketers. The stance of the average marketer to his prospect is this: "Me Tarzan. You Jane." In other words, these marketers say, "I'm valuable to you because I'm here. I don't need to understand you. You need to understand me. You're lucky I'm here, and if you know what's good for you, you'll do what I tell you, because I'm telling you. And I'm telling you to buy what I'm selling. Which is all you need to know."

Don't tell me machismo is dead. It's alive and well in marketing, although with this discouraging new twist: both men and women exhibit its traits with equal abandon — and disastrous results.

It is not your prospect's responsibility to tell you what's bothering him about you and what you're selling. It's your responsibility to find out — and to answer these anxieties with your best argument.

This means you must ascertain from your prospects what's bothering them, and respond to these anxieties. And you must realize this process is never ending. Your prospects will always have some reservation about you. Your prospects will always need reassurance. This means you must dedicate yourself to the ongoing task of discovering what is bothering them and the equally continuous task of responding to these anxieties. Even if you think these anxieties are boring, obvious, unbelievably beside the point and childish. What *you* think is unimportant. What does your *prospect* think? And have you made your best case to lay his anxiety to rest and get him to act NOW? Which means, of course, that you'll be using your marketing documents to do two essential things:

- excite the prospect's natural desire to buy NOW, and
- overcome his objections and anxieties about you so that acting NOW is the only alternative he has.

If you succeed in achieving these twin objectives, you will get the client to buy.

Thinking Through The Anxieties Your Prospects Have About You And What You're Selling — And Coming Up With The Strongest Conceivable Response

Marketing, remember, is a game of positioning. It is not a moral exercise. It is an activity that is gauged by one simple, compelling criterion: did what you do get the prospect to buy? If it did, and if the number of buyers made the exercise profitable, what you are doing is right. If it didn't, and there were too few buyers to make what you did profitable, what you are doing is wrong. Get it?

The point of understanding your prospect's anxieties is equally simple. These anxieties keep him from buying. Answering them, laying them to rest, gives you a better chance of making the sale. But before you can answer them, you've got to know them. So, let's get started discovering the characteristic anxieties of your buyers, while understanding that the list that follows is necessarily incomplete. There are as many reasons for not buying what you're selling as there are people who consider buying from you at all. But here, at least, are many of the leading things your prospects think about you, even if they don't say them, and what you need to say back to them to neutralize this response, or turn it into a distinct advantage.

- "I don't know you. Never heard of you. And have no reason to trust you."

Why do people pay more for brand name merchandise every day of the week, despite the fact that they can almost always find the same thing for less, often in the same store, but under a generic name? The reason, of course, is that they trust the brand name. And they trust the brand name, because it's been around a while and, most importantly, because they've heard of it before.

The trick is to neutralize this objection. Or, better yet, to turn this situation into a distinct advantage for you. Is it possible? You better believe that it is!

Either this objection is valid, or it's not. Either way, once you decide this is a reason why your prospects are not buying what you're selling, you must answer it. If the objection is valid (namely that they haven't heard of you and have no reason to trust you), you must work to turn this to your advantage. Here's what you do:

- First, don't fight the objection. Admit it. Say, "You're probably wondering if a company you never heard of can do anything for you." Obviously, this is a major objection prospects have with companies they haven't heard of. Bringing up the prime prospect objection early makes good sense. It defuses the issue and allows you to get beyond it.

- Now begin to turn the objection into an asset by calling on basic American fairness, a very strong national trait. "No, you've never heard of us before, but we hope you give us a hearing." We all want to be fair. So use fairness on your behalf.

- Continue the transformation of the negative into a positive by calling on your prospect to give the little guy a hearing and by making a reasonable case for why he should. "Yes, we're new and you haven't heard of us before. But because we're new we're going to work harder than anyone to win your trust and get your business. I guarantee it!" Of course, you'll recognize that Avis built a very profitable business using a variation on this theme.

What's going on here is this:

- Your prospect has either unarticulated or explicit anxieties about you and what you're selling.
- Your job is to find out what they are.
- Your job is not to fight them, but to admit these may be grounds for not purchasing what you're selling

At all times, your job is to make the strongest possible case for why these anxieties shouldn't get in the way of the prospect buying — and, indeed, to transform them into motivators that induce the prospect to buy. (As in, "No, you don't know us and have no reason to believe what we say. But we'll work harder to show you, because we want you to trust us and develop a relationship. Why not give us a chance?")

By following these steps, you are now understanding your prospect, empathizing with him, and talking to him. His negative feelings have been answered and even turned into positive reasons for taking action now. Which, if there is sufficient motivation and he is not a flatworm, he now does. This is positioning.

- "I'm afraid I'll be stuck with something I can't use."

Most people are uncertain about their judgment — and for very good reason. Most make terrible buying mistakes. They get carried away with the impulse to buy, only to discover later they can't really use what they've purchased. Over time, this makes people more and more cautious.

Your job is to make sure that remaining cautious is not the decision they make. But that you take their caution into account and use it to help you impel the buying decision. You must work to neutralize their caution by:

- providing a money-back guarantee
- giving a free-use period
- providing a demonstration in their office or home
- giving back-up support, *etc.*

Neutralizing this caution in this fashion is crucial whether you are aiming to build an on-going relationship with the individual, or whether you are selling a one-time-only purchase. Either way, people are fearful they'll be stuck with a white elephant, just like all the others they've already purchased.

Now, take this negative and turn it into a selling point. "We don't want you to be stuck with something you can't use. So, take this home for a month. Use it for thirty days. And see for yourself if you don't get all the benefits we've promised. If not, return it and get your money back. Guaranteed!" In this way, your prospect knows he's not going to be stuck with something he can't use, because either what he buys benefits him or it doesn't. If it does, fine. And if it doesn't, he reasons, I can return it and get my money back, or whatever you've promised. Thus, his decision doesn't come down on the side of a cautious "don't buy".

Note: when you offer a money-back guarantee or other caution-lowering device, there will be people who'll take advantage of it. That's for sure. But my experience has been that not even one in one hundred will. Credit sloth, disorganization, and inefficiency.

Most products that ought to be returned (because the buyer really doesn't have any need for them), aren't. It's as simple as that. This is why you mustn't worry about doing what you can to lower your prospect's anxiety about getting stuck with something he can't use. Your job is to provide the soothing guarantee that meets the prospect's need and to develop your reputation for being a client-centered marketer. Remember, knowing he can return what he's bought is usually more important to the prospect than actually doing so. Which is all to the good for you.

- "I don't know the people behind the enterprise and have no reason to believe or trust them."

Assertion marketing, which I've roundly condemned in this book, says, in effect, "Buy because I'm telling you to buy." If you review the marketing communications you receive or see, you'll find that most of them fall into this mindless and selfish category. But, think for a minute! How many times have you decided not to buy something because you didn't know the people behind the enterprise, didn't know if you could trust them, had no reason to believe them? I bet I know the answer: plenty! The answer to this problem is plain: understand that your prospects are unsure, and provide them the reasons they need to overcome this feeling and do what they want to do: buy.

Now, to be sure, you're not going to need to do this with all products and services. There are, it seems to me, some where prospects are more likely to be cautious about buying than others. In general, prospects want to know more about the people providing a service than they do about the people providing a product. They are more likely to ask questions about a dentist and his credentials (though a dentist can rarely kill you, thank God!) than about an aircraft designer and his; and far more likely to look into the track record of a financial planner, than an automotive engineer. This is perhaps unfair, but it is a reality. Thus, if you are selling a service and not a product, this section is more likely to be for you.

Gather the name of the individual creating the product or service and his formal credentials. Write down such information as:

- his professional training
- years in the business
- prizes and awards
- professional recognition.

These are facts, features. They are about that individual. Now, put them in perspective for the prospect; in short, transform these features into client-centered benefits, reasons that inspire a prospect's confidence and reduce his natural anxiety about who you are and the fact he knows nothing about you.

In this connection, I think of a woman who took a workshop from me recently at the University of Maine, Augusta. She is a massage therapist. Among her credentials is the fact that she offers a program on the subject through the University. That's what it says in her brochure. This is a fact.

This marketer no doubt thinks the fact that she offers this course is significant; to be sure, it is certainly better to include it as a credential than say nothing at all. But it is grievously incomplete. Indeed, this marketer is losing the potency of the fact by failing to transform it into a client-centered benefit that answers the prospect's cautious query, "Why should I entrust myself to you for help?"

Here's where the magic of marketing comes in. Having written down the fact, you must now ask the pivotal question, "So what?" As a result of asking this crucial question of this marketer, we learn:

- the University of Maine, Augusta, has never hired any other massage therapist to do a course on this subject;
- it is the only course offered through a university in the state of Maine;
- the marketer had to go through a rigorous selection process against a dozen other therapists in the area before being selected.

In short, we now have context, significance — and hence the means to lower the prospect's implicit or explicit anxiety about using this marketer's service. We can now go to work to lower the prospect's anxiety and move him closer to taking immediate action:

"You may not know Anne Anderson, but experts in her field do. She was selected to offer the first massage therapy course in the history of the University of Maine, Augusta. Her credentials were pitted against 12 other therapists, and she was selected because of her ability to provide (client-centered benefit). Anne's is the only university-level massage therapy program in the State of Maine. No, you may not know her. But her credentials have been certified by these experts. You can feel safe with Anne."

See the difference? And see how it positions Anne against her competitors? She emerges as *la prima*, very much in a class by herself. (Once this differentiation from competitors has been established, by the way, she must maintain it in everything, including price.)

Let's look more closely at what's happening here:

- the prospect's fears are not being dismissed as groundless or inappropriate. Indeed, whether they are groundless or inappropriate is irrelevant. If the prospect feels them (and we know in this case that they do, because I asked the therapist what inhibited her prospects from taking immediate action), they are germane and must be effectively dealt with.

- the marketer knows that these anxieties must be answered. She knows that mere facts *per se* won't allay them. Telling a prospect that she teaches at the University isn't sufficiently weighty either to lay the prospect's caution to rest or to differentiate her from her competition. She needs context.

- the marketer now asks and answers the "so what?" question, producing significance — and reducing the prospect's caution about taking action. "Aha," the prospect now says, "this isn't just a therapist. This is a therapist whose credentials have been confirmed by reputable authorities, authorities I can believe in and follow. I can't do all this homework myself. But they have. And as a result of their homework, I now know I can trust this person." And so, if you have given sufficient reason for this prospect to take action NOW, he will take action.

Before leaving this topic, let's look into my intellectual compost heap and pull a flyer at random. This one comes from National Career Workshops of Shawnee Mission, KS, and promotes their "Powerful One-Day Workshop 'How To Work With People'." Six trainers provide this program and their biographies are enclosed. Here's that of trainer John Mattone:

"John Mattone knows that an informative, dynamic workshop can be an invaluable experience. In his 10 years as a seminar leader he has trained thousands of people, including representatives from Boston Edison, DuPont, and the Federal Aviation Admnistration. He relays insightful information drawn from his experience as a corporate manager, human resources development consultant, staff coordinator and from his private practice as a management consultant for the U.S. Navy. Seminar participants will find his workshops to be a creative mixture of facts, discussion and interaction."

Now, dear reader, you have been with me long enough on this journey towards marketing communications perfection to know that what you've just read is text book perfect — dross, the kind of selfish marketing that sabotages every effort of a firm to be seen as client-centered. There are facts in this paragraph, to be sure, but the correct response to this droning rendition is "So what?" What does any of this have to do with the prospect? What does this have to do with recognizing that the prospect has limited funds and unlimited appetites? That the prospect cannot do everything that is brought to his attention (up to 8000 opportunities weekly to spend his slender resources, mind!) That the prospect is trying to decide what to do, what's in his best interest to do?

I think you know.

A paragraph like this, which is utterly characteristic of the mailing piece as a whole, doesn't help the prospect overcome his caution about buying and help him buy. Because this is a perfect illustration of selfish Assertion Marketing.

These facts, all features about the no doubt admirable Mr. Mattone, need context, need significance, need to be redirected towards the prospect and his concerns. First look at the assertions:

- This workshop is "informative and dynamic." This leader is "insightful." Is there any proof? No!
- This leader has trained thousands. So what?
- This leader has certain credentials as a corporate manager, *etc.* What does this have to do with the prospect?

In short, has this marketer, or anyone connected with National Career Workshops, considered the circumstances of the prospect and his legitimate need, not for hard-sell, but for legitimate information about what difference these facts make?

What this paragraph shows us is that the marketer is not client-centered, has spent insufficient time understanding the prospect, and not troubled to put the facts — about this trainer and everything else — into a meaningful perspective for the prospect. Let's just take one fact in particular: Mr. Mattone's involvement as a management consultant to the U.S. Navy. There's nothing in the fact itself, its mere statement, to inspire a prospect to sign up for the workshop. Thus, the fact fails in its essential purpose.

Instead, here's what will help the prospect make up his mind and lower his resistance to spending his scarce resources on this program, from among so many other alternatives:

- How did Mattone get to be a consultant?
- What's significant about his credentials?
- Did he have to go through a competition (or did his brother-in-law, the admiral, appoint him on a no-bid contract?)?
- What has he achieved while being a consultant?
- Who's benefitted from his being a consultant (besides himself)?
- What will the prospect get from the fact that Mattone has served in this consulting capacity?

In short, what difference does this fact make and how can we position this fact, this feature about Mattone, so that it induces a prospect who has no reason to trust him and knows nothing about him or the marketing company to take action and spend his money? Which, I assert, he will do — will be glad to do — if you can show him what's really in it for him and what sizable benefits you can deliver *to him*. Because, remember, he's an American. And nothing's as American as buying, not even apple pie.

Dear reader, you think you're swell. You know why (or at least you have reason for feeling this way). But no one — except perhaps your dear old mother — knows these reasons as well as you do. Even these facts must be positioned. And the reason for positioning them is plain: it's to minimize the doubts your prospects have about you and what you can do for them. And if you don't reduce these doubts, then they have a very good reason for doing nothing. Which is, of course, what most of them do — even though they have the problem that you can solve. Is this really what you want?

- "I have to do too much to get it."

If anything is true about my lazy countrymen, it's that they want (or should I say we all want?) things to be as easy as possible. This trend waxes, indeed. Myself a son of pioneers, I regrettably see inexorable sloth eating away my moral fiber. Sadly, I must admit that like everyone else, I want things to be easier, no matter how easy they are already.

Your prospect, of course, declines to buy what you're selling because he's afraid he's going to have to exert himself too much to acquire it. Even though he wants what you have, he dislikes the effort he must engage in to get it. Indeed, even if you are selling a fitness center membership (where the end result is presumably concerted exertion) the process through which that membership is sold must be as easy as possible. Why don't people understand this?

The other day I called the Kerstein Branch of the Boston Public Library and asked for the address of the Panasonic Corporation; I wanted to file a complaint. The bored voice on the other end of the receiver said, "You can have the telephone number, but I can't give you the address." I said, "But surely you have the address right in front of you right now." He was forced to admit that he did. But he cited their "policy" (another word for bureaucratic obstructionism) on not providing addresses over the telephone, and said I had to come in for the information. Damn the fact that I was miles — and a tormenting subway ride away. Damn the foolishness, given the fact that he had the information right in front of him. And yet he thinks he's in a service business and bewails the fact that his raises are sporadic. If I had my way, this bibliographic flatworm would never get another!

Don't let this happen to you.

Understand that the people you want to buy from you will buy less often, perhaps not buy at all, if you don't make it as easy as possible for them. But remember, *how* you make it easy for a prospect to take action is a feature. This feature must be sold to the prospect, just like any other feature. Here are some of the ways of making things easy for your prospect:

- providing a toll-free number
- taking credit cards
- accepting collect calls
- taking orders twenty-four hours a day with an answering service or machine
- providing free pick-up and delivery
- sending paid business reply mail
- including a stamped addressed envelope.

This is a very partial list. The point is, these are features. They must be transformed into benefits that overcome the prospect's sloth and compel him to take action NOW.

- Feature: providing a toll-free number. Benefit: Don't spend your own money.
- Feature: taking credit cards. Benefit: No waiting for a check to be processed and clear. Immediate shipment of your order. You can call in your order anytime — 24 hours a day. You get what you want FAST.
- Feature: accepting collect calls. Benefit: Don't spend your own money.
- Feature: taking orders twenty-four hours a day. Benefit: Whenever you're ready to order, we're ready for you. Call at 3 a.m. and, with credit card purchase, your order will go out first thing in the morning. Nothing's faster.
- Feature: providing free pick-up and delivery. Benefit: You don't have to go through the bother of leaving home and trying to find a parking space. Save your gas money and spend it on something else!
- Feature: sending paid business reply mail. Benefit: Don't spend your money. Super-convenient. Just put your order in the envelope and drop it in any post box. Your order will be shipped within twenty-four hours!
- Feature: including stamped addressed envelope. Benefit: Don't spend your money.

What's happening here is this:

You've recognized that your prospects are slothful. Recently, I've been reading a lot about how people are spending more and more time at home and the implications this holds for marketing. This trend doesn't surprise me. As you know, I work at home myself and can tell you the substantial benefits of both living and working in one place. Anyone who's ever attempted to compete with rush-hour traffic knows and appreciates the new movement towards comfy, convenient home-centered living. If you're to benefit from this trend, you have to make things as easy for your prospects as possible.

But don't just say what you provide (a toll-free number), tell your prospect its significance, too. Don't make the incredible mistake that so many marketers do; namely forcing the prospect to deduce the significance of the fact, if he can. I have a very basic marketing rule that is daily broken by the marketers whose sterling (and expensive) efforts cram my compost heap: nothing in marketing is obvious. The significance of no fact is obvious. The benefit of no feature is obvious. Each point, in short, must be transformed into a lever that induces immediate prospect action.

Some of you will dislike hearing this. You may regard this recommendation as somehow condescending. "Surely," you think, "I don't have to tell my incredibly sophisticated, incredibly rich, incredibly well-educated audience what THIS fact means." Perhaps not. *Maybe* they know.

But maybe they don't. And if even *one* person in your audience doesn't know and if you have failed to use the power of the benefit because you've assumed that that benefit is self-evident in the fact, then you have diminished the impact of your marketing. We all use shorthand, of course; we all are under deadlines. None of us ever squeezes as much benefit from *every* fact as we could. Debilitating reality does intrude and inhibit us.

But the truth is, it is always the sizzle that sells and almost never merely the steak. And you cannot assume that seeing the word "steak" will conjure up the flavorful meal that gets the prospect to buy. In other words, you can't leave it to the prospect to deduce the benefit. More than anything else, it's your responsibility to make that benefit lucidly clear and irresistibly tempting so that the prospect takes action *as soon as possible.*

While writing this section, I think of several helpful things that establishments in my neighborhood provide their clientele, like the grocery store and stationery shop that both deliver. Yet checking their advertisements (including their listings in the yellow pages), neither cites these facts or uses them to induce prospects to become customers.

These marketers probably think that everyone knows they provide these services; thus, there's no point saying so. Or that, perhaps, because so many other places do the same, there's no benefit in saying so.

What idiocy!

Ladies and gentlemen, I have this to tell you and heed me well: everybody doesn't have these facts at their fingertips. And even if everyone else in the world does the same thing, why that's of no significance whatsoever unless someone uses it as a positioning statement, and uses this fact to induce immediate prospect action, thus: "We deliver, so you can stay home in comfort. All you do is pick up the phone and call in your order. Rain or shine." Now there's a benefit, indeed, and one which even the most slothful (perhaps mainly the most slothful) can respond to with unaccustomed vigor. Which is why you should be using it and not leaving it to your prospect to deduce the benefit.

* "You don't care about me. You're impersonal. You're only out for yourself, and I'll be damned if I'm going to help you, even though I do need what you're selling."

I have a friend who is a competent public relations consultant. He is thorough, knowledgeable, and profoundly reputable. But his business flounders, stumbling along despite his manifold virtues. Unfortunately, he hasn't read his Shakespeare, and he doesn't know the troubles of Coriolanus, who preferred unbending virtue to the success attending suppleness. Coriolanus, of course, could afford this stance; if he lost high office, he at least had the solace of an inherited income and assured social position. If you don't, pay close attention to what I'm about to say. . . .

I am weary pointing out the alienation of our age and the need for true human care and concern. So hungry are the creatures of our time for the consolation of touch and the communion of empathy that we regularly abandon our powers of discrimination in yet another outburst of belief in yet another cloven-toed evangelical deceiver. Despite the always inevitable and invariably sordid scandal, the hope for compassion and unconditional acceptance remains; indeed, it is unquenchable.

And you need to take this into account when planning your marketing.

What your prospects want from you is not a slogan about caring, they want care.

Hertz, for example, expends an enormous amount of money extolling the virtues of its company as a client-centered entity. But the other day when I had occasion to rent a car from its Harvard Square office, I watched that image dissolve, crushed between the unyielding (and unknowledgeable) office operator and the blind fury of a rightfully-aggrieved consumer. (Yes, I do evesdrop, particularly in marketing encounters and especially when I am next in line!)

Your prospects fail to take action to buy what you're selling, because they fear the way you'll treat them. They fear they'll get a run-around. They are anxious about all the time they'll waste and how profitless — and infuriating — their encounter will be.

Recognize this.

And let them know this won't happen with you.

I've long advocated that every company have at least one ombudsman, one true customer service representative. This must be an individual who doesn't just hold a hollow title, but who understands what the prospect needs from him. This individual must not merely refer people, but take the responsibility to solve a customer's problem. This, of course, is precisely what most inaptly named "customer service representatives" do not do. They regard their title as sufficient proof of their function; I see it as what it almost always is, a howling irony.

You must — and shall — be different. Here's how:

- First, plan to be personal. This means making sure that you and your employees know the answers to questions, both the usual and the unexpected. All people who deal with prospects need to understand how to handle questions so they are solved, not shelved. Your prospects want to feel confident about you and what you're selling. And the only way they can is if you know what you're doing.

Note: To help you solve this problem, use Marian Woodall's helpful little book *Thinking On Your Feet: Answering Questions Well Whether You Know The Answer — Or Not*. It's published by Professional Business Communicators, 11830 S.W. Kerr Parkway, Suite 350, Lake Oswego, OR 97034. The sad fact is, most people can't think quickly, and as a result they end up looking foolish and disillusioning prospect after prospect. Don't let this happen to you!

A Challenge From Your Author

Before passing on to the next point, take a moment — right now! — to order one of your products or services from your company. Call up your office and request information. Send in your coupon. Use your 800 number. Or try ordering from one of your distributors. From a bookstore carrying your book. . . . or a university promoting one of your workshops. And see what happens. I think you'll be appalled.

I'm amazed at how few of my clients — all professing to be client-centered and service-oriented — have ever attempted to buy what they're selling from their own organization. Perhaps they've made the biggest mistake of all: believing their own marketing, rather than seeing for themselves. Don't you make it, too.

Remember, it's far worse to say you're service-centered and fail to deliver than it is to muddle through without any promises, abhorrent though this situation is.

- Once you've ensured that your organization can deliver on any promises you make, start using service- and client-centered behavior as a draw. Tell your prospects exactly what kind of service you give them. Do you:

  - open an extra cash register when the line reaches a certain point?
  - give them some premium if you fail to deliver on time?
  - have a customer service representative or ombudsman who really answers questions and gets results?

In short, do you say you are in the service business (which is nothing more than a hollow claim), or have you thought through what it means to provide service, training your people to ensure that prospects get the attention they want, and not the run-around and snubbing all of us have so often experienced?

Now, if you do provide service, say so — in all the marketing documents you create. And say, too, what your credo of business is, the goal for which you strive. Remind people that:

- you are in business to serve them;
- that service with you is not a word, but a way of operating with the customer in mind;
- that all your employees are trained to adhere to this standard, and that
- you work hard to ensure that it is maintained and that new ways of serving the customer are constantly researched and enthusiastically adopted.

Before leaving this section, short though important, let me reiterate my key points:

- First, you must decide that you are running a truly client-centered service business, whether you are providing a product or service. It is my experience that all businesses mirror the beliefs of their founders and managers. If these managers are selfish, rapacious and egotistical, then no amount of service education will result in the business being truly customer-centered. "The fault, dear Brutus, is not in our stars but in ourselves . . ." as Shakespeare says. If you are not selling a product or service for which there is a certain need, one good possibility is because the company does not have a service culture. My first question to entrepreneurs, then, is this: "Why are you in business." If the answer, their first instinctive response comes back, "To make big bucks" or something else that's selfish, I know that here is a marketing problem just waiting to happen. A quick look at their marketing materials usually confirms my suspicions.

• Now institute truly client-centered procedures. Train yourself and your staff to think through what the prospect wants and needs from you and train yourself to deliver it — as quickly, inexpensively, and courteously as possible.

• When you're sure you have mastered the art of client-centered service, then tell the world. Proclaim it far and wide, for whatever you say about service and your commitment to it isn't hype or bombast. It's an operating philosophy, quite a different thing, daily apparent in everything you do, a bond between you and the perhaps as yet unseen prospect.

One last word. When you know you deliver service, you need not be tentative or cautious about saying that you deliver service. Remember the words of Mama Rose in "Gypsy" — "Sing out, Louise!" Sing out, indeed! Put some passion into your words — and don't forget the context.

If you open up another register when the line reaches a certain number — say so. And tell people why: so they don't have to wait, and get frustrated. Don't just rely on the feature to carry your message. Remember to sell the context! If you're the only store in the neighborhood that provides this service, say so. "You can only get this benefit from us!" It's okay. It's better than okay. It's marketing . . . not hype.

"Hype" is the abominated abbreviation for the word "hyperbole", or exaggerated. Many people, misinformed people, think that hype and marketing are synonymous. Nothing could be further from the truth. Proper marketing is not about making exaggerated claims to delude the unwary into parting with their money. No, indeed. Real marketing is about identifying wants in a designated group of people and letting them know precisely what you can do for them and precisely what benefits they get from you. It is maximizing the positive to induce immediate action. Not exaggerating to commit fraud and create quick disappointment.

This, then, is marketing, to:

- found a business on a service credo
- make sure that all aspects of the business exemplify and reinforce this credo, and
- let people who can benefit from this way of doing business know that you are available to assist them.

The fact that others offer similar services is irrelevant — so long as they are not promoting the fact that they do. It is the business of the marketer, after all, to take what may well be a common fact and turn it into a compelling benefit, a lever that induces the prospect to take immediate action because he knows that the marketer gives him something he feels he must have and can only get from this source . . . notwithstanding the fact that the landscape is littered with others doing the same thing, who haven't the brains, forethought and expertise to use it comparably.

What you must avoid, then, is saying you are running a service business, when you aren't. And running a service business — with all the expense, personal commitment and, yes, aggravation that entails — which you are not marketing as such. The one is fraud. The other foolishness. Both quite wrong. Make sure you do neither.

- "What you're selling is too expensive, not worth the money."

Money to an American is an ambiguous commodity. On the one hand, most Americans spend their days in relentless pursuit of it. On the other, they cannot wait to dispose of it the minute they get it, or, indeed, even before they get it (ah, the Age of Credit) in exchange for something else. Unless one is a miser (one does occasionally meet one) or numismatist, money as a physical object is of no particular interest. It is ordinarily soiled, crumpled, cold, and altogether unappealing. No wonder we rush to exchange it.

Knowing this, if you cannot get an American to exchange his money, which he doesn't really want and which is totally unappealing in its own right, for the thing you have, which he ought to want and should make his life better, then the fault is yours. *You* have failed to convince your prospect that the money is less valuable than the product or service (with all its benefits) that you have for him. For shame!

Many people ask me about price. Ask me whether their price is too high, too low. My answer is simple: do the benefits to the prospect outweigh the price he must pay to get them; is the money more valuable to the prospect, or the benefits resulting from the thing you are selling? Can he get these benefits from someone else for less? And does he know who this person is and that this competitor actually has the same, or similar, benefits?

Price is the result of these questions and their answers.

Now let's look further at the expressed or implicit objection centered on expense. I am not going to talk here about a person who cavils at price because he doesn't have the resources to buy. Such people may well want the item but simply can't afford it. These people are legion, but are, for marketing purposes, insignificant. If I sell Rolls Royces and people who have not the money to buy them find them expensive, what matters that to me?

I am only concerned if people with means find what I make available expensive and hence less valuable than the money they must expend to acquire it. *This* is a marketing problem, and one that must be solved.

You will not, perhaps, be surprised at what I have to say about how to solve this worrisome problem. Price, dear reader, is a feature. Consequently it must be translated into a benefit. Now, how can price, which involves expense, be construed as a benefit? Here's where we need the magic of marketing.

For a prospect, the inhibition of price can be diminished or removed altogether because:

- of the benefits he gets when he makes this investment. You must lead with benefits and, as you'll recall, follow with features, including price. Price is irrelevant where the benefits are sufficiently convincing to those with the means of acquisition.

- what the prospect pays you for the benefits is less than what he must pay another. This gives you yet another, crucial and differentiating benefit: price savings. In many instances, this is what finally induces the prospect to take action, especially if the period for saving is of limited duration.

- you remind the prospect he will stay in his present unhappy circumstances (or in circumstances which must worsen) until he acquires what you're selling. It is your job to remind the prospect — in the most specific possible way —that he is relatively unhappy now and that only by investing in what you're selling will he be happier. The prospect must be vividly reminded that retaining his money does not solve his problem, that the money is not a solution, and that, therefore, his problem remains to bedevil him, and to fester.

While I was writing this section, I received a call from a Massachusetts-based software developer, deeply dismayed because his last mailing (designed at vast expense by an advertising firm) had failed to draw even a one percent response. Was it the price, perhaps, of what he was selling, he asked me? Could the $25,000 he charged for each system be the culprit?

Before answering, I asked him what the benefits were of using (not buying!) his system. Note his answer. "The company will get its money back within twelve months."

IS THIS A PRIME BENEFIT?

Certainly not!

And if this is the benefit that the exalted firm of Boston advertisers created for him. And if, I say, this is the benefit he himself thinks he's delivering, then it is amazing to me that this firm received a response as high as they did. But then, P.T. Barnum's notable maxim on American suckers certainly remains valid today!

Without knowing any of the merits of this software, I can tell you this: its prospect isn't primarily interested in recovering the money he's invested in this product. He's interested in what precise benefits he will acquire with it, either because it helps him cut expenses (to some specific figure) or increase sales (to some specific figure) within some specific period of time. Note the key word "specific".

If you have these numbers, the marketing equation changes. Let's say that the software helps an entrepreneur save $50,000 a year and that you can prove this. The real question then becomes, "Mr. Entrepreneur, how much can you be induced to pay for certain savings of $50,000?" And that, my friends, is the open question, the answer depending on how clearly you've presented your benefits and how well you've made your case for immediate action *and* how much this prospect would have to pay your competitor (assuming there is one) for comparable results.

Price, you see, is a feature. And like all features, must be transformed into a benefit, set in a context, and used to motivate a prospect to take immediate action, just like every other feature.

Finding Out Why Your Prospects Don't Buy From You

To counter the reasons why your prospects don't buy from you, you must know the reasons. You cannot answer, after all, what you do not know. You must first research these reasons. Here's how:

- Listen. Your prospects will tell you why they don't buy. Pay attention to what your prospects say to you during the sales process.

- Ask. If prospects who fail to buy what you're selling don't tell you why, ask them. I find that people are only too willing to talk to you, if you have the courtesy and good sense to ask. When you get this information, of course, you may well be able to respond to it immediately. But even if you make this individual sale, you should not dismiss the importance of the objection and the need to answer it in your marketing materials.

- Deduce. Sit down and deduce the objections to what you're selling. You can figure out yourself most — if not all — of your prospects' objections. Be logical! Think! If you are asking your prospects to drive to an out of the way spot to purchase your product, you can be sure this is going to be an objection in our sloth-ridden society. And you can deduce this yourself. Of course, you'll want to confirm it later.

- Survey. Some of your prospects you'll never see. You'll talk to a prospect, for instance, over the phone and present your reasons why he should act now. He fails to act. You need to find out why. If you deal with large numbers of callers, you don't need to contact all; a continuing fraction will do nicely. Send them a multiple choice or true/false survey questionnaire (not more than 10 questions, please) to find out why they didn't respond. Don't forget to include this crucial possibility: "no money for this investment this time." Perhaps, you see, this individual, lacking the necessary resources, wasn't a real prospect after all.

Note: the prospect who fills out this questionnaire and returns it is on the road to becoming one of your buyers. Prospect involvement, even this kind of prospect involvement, is a crucial step to the sale you want to make! You can foster this relationship by sending this prospect a premium, perhaps one of your Special Reports, as thanks for his taking time to help you. For this individual has told you something valuable, something you can use to both break down his reservations about buying and help you more effectively get others to buy sooner.

Writing Down What You're Hearing

As you hear the reservations of your prospects, write them down. This sounds obvious, but isn't. Most people think they'll remember the reservations, and in a general way, they may. But you don't want things to be general, you want them to be specific. Thus, instead of thinking that prospects have reservations about price, you need to write down the exact reservations as stated by particular prospects.

Beyond remembering what you hear, there are other good reasons for this:

- If you want your marketing materials to sound authentic, you'll use real reservations, perhaps in the exact words of the prospects making them.

Real reservations help you formulate the strongest possible responses *and* make the strongest conceivable case for buying what you're selling. All you have to do is transform the "I"-centered objection to a "you"-centered response that induces immediate action. But you cannot write the latter, until you know the former.

This is why I always advocate listening closely and writing down exactly what you hear. Inelegant, graceless, grammatically provoking though it may be, it is the true voice of your market — and as such profoundly important to you.

Last Words About Buyer Reservations And Your Rampant Enthusiasm

When you are an entrepreneur, fueled by your peculiar and abundant enthusiasm, it is easy to forget that the rest of the world does not share in your interests and aspirations. That's why I so often wince when I come into contact (as I so regularly do) with entrepreneurial enthusiasts. On the one hand, I know that their enthusiasm is absolutely necessary, for what great thing has ever been accomplished without it?

On the other, I fear that their enthusiasm may well be premature, the result of too much concentration on their inevitable and oh-so-sweet success and too little on the market which must be motivated to act before that success is even remotely possible. This enthusiasm makes me unhappy, because it is the result of selfishness, not of profound knowledge of one's market, including the reasons which may make that market reluctant to act.

This is why I must urge you to hold back your enthusiasm (your certainty of impending triumph) until such time as you really understand the reservations of your prospects, the reasons why they might not buy from you, and until you have formulated the strongest conceivable case in response, the case that will overcome these objections and get these prospects to take immediate action.

Once you have this case, *then* you may — indeed should — use your enthusiasm to propel you towards meaningful prospect contact. Sadly, you will have much need of this enthusiasm, not least because even those who most need you take so long to admit it and to act. Before you have your case, however, rein in your enthusiasm until you discover what may inhibit your prospect. Once you understand and can overcome those inhibitions, then your enthusiasm is a *sine qua non* of success. But not before.

Resource

In this chapter, I have only dealt with some of the major reasons your prospects might not buy from you. You will encounter others, which is why you should know about my friend Joel Martin and his helpful booklet *Closing The Sale*. Joel has systematically researched all the prospect objections and come up with superb responses to them. I strongly recommend his book to you. Contact him at Bristol-Hunter Publishers, 90 Keswick Rd., Amherst, NY 14226.

Chapter 10

How To Transform What You've Done — Your Resumé — Into Compelling Reasons For Your Prospect To Buy What You're Selling

This chapter is dedicated to the legion of specialists — be they doctors, lawyers, accountants, financial planners, advisors and consultants of whatever kind — who continually cite their credentials as a reason for prospects to trust them and buy what they're selling. These specialists need to learn how to transform these credentials into compelling reasons that get their prospects to act NOW.

This chapter follows naturally from what has gone before and is based on a few key principles:

- People buy what you're selling, not because of where you've been (your formal credentials), but because of what you've done (the results you've achieved for others that you may be able to achieve again for your prospects).

- Formal credentials are not synonymous with results. Results are always more important than credentials.

- Credentials are features. And all features, as you now know, must be transformed into benefits. The results you achieved for others are the benefits your prospects want you to achieve for them.

- To merely state your credentials and to leave the prospect to infer what this means to him is to abdicate as a marketer, and to force the prospect

225

into the illogical position of having to deduce the reasons for his taking action himself.

The Absurdity Of The Professional Syndrome

Perhaps because we are in theory a classless society (though in fact far from it), Americans go to outrageous lengths to differentiate themselves from each other, to convince each other (and, of course, themselves) that they are better, superior, today's aristocrats.

The whole exercise is pathetic, of course, but important, since millions of people engage in it. Why, just this morning I read about a Rand Corporation study ("The Evolution of Teacher Policy" by Linda Darling-Hammond and Barnett Barry) that deals in part with whether teachers are full-fledged professionals or merely "semi-skilled workers."

As our schools become advanced merchandising centers for drugs and soulless detention colonies for hapless minorities, this question strikes me as breathtakingly beside the point, rather like Mexico's Emperor Maximilian working on his Court hierarchy and titles while Benito Juarez inexorably ate up that fantastic *imperium*. Still, as I say, millions of people engage in this dedicated search for worth, this need to call — and believe — themselves professionals. It is a subject as much a part of our epoch as that of the Victorians who were consumed with whether one was — or, more importantly, was not — a gentleman. Is one, or is one not, a professional? And if one is, what should one do, or, better, not do? These are the questions.

What Is A Professional?

- A professional is the trained repository of a body of arcane knowledge, knowledge which can only be acquired after long and arduous study, the longer and more arduous (so as to weed out the unsuitable) the better.

- A professional is an acknowledged member of a defined group. This group may either be self-regulating in its requirements for admission and good standing, or it may be regulated by government authorities. Or both. The more complicated the admissions standards, the better.

- A professional adheres to certain (often quite loose) standards of ethical conduct and contemporary morality. No one can say what these standards are until they are broken and brought to the attention of the public, ordinarily through the prying and overzealous media. At that time these standards, which are ordinarily quite lax, become terribly important.

- A professional must remain up to date in his field. In fact, he cannot qualify as a professional unless he remains at least a half-step ahead of the people who rely upon him for assistance, for if ever they were to know as much as he, his very reason for existence would cease.

These rules of what constitutes a professional, though admittedly I've written them rather cynically, remain current. Until recently, there was a fifth rule that the old fogies would still like to enforce, but which the shock waves of the market place have battered into rubble: a professional, as today's true aristocrat, is sought. He does not seek. Working with a professional must always be perceived as an honor by the client, unrelated to common mercantile transactions.

So strong was this fifth regulation that professional groups like dentists, lawyers, and doctors were until recently actually barred from seeking business. Unbending pillars of the establishment, they had to wait in isolated (if all too often shabby) splendor for business which all too often didn't materialize.

I'm happy to tell you, however, that changes in society have rendered this fatuous position obsolete (though you'll find plenty of dinosaurs about who still believe it). Fertile professional parents (and those who aspired to this comfortable plateau) have produced since World War II too many professional children.

Today, therefore, we have too many doctors, too many dentists, too many lawyers, too many financial planners — and too many, I suspect, of every other professional category. Add to this the ravages of rising costs, particularly in the urban areas where so many of these professionals reside, and you have the basis for an astonishing transformation. The result? Those who were supposed to wait to be sought must now seek — with a vengeance — or give up the professional title and lifestyle they crave. *Voilà*, the age of professional marketing.

Now, I am scarcely the only person to notice this phenomenon. Indeed, a host of people have arrived on the scene to dish out advice on how to handle this situation. Sad to say, most of what they say, while perhaps assuaging the immediate anxieties of their clients, doesn't make ultimate sense. Because professional marketing is pointless unless it gets you the business, unless, that is, dollars change hand.

Here's a sample of the kind of advice others dispense:

- Write an article in a professional publication, all the books say. This will establish your professional credibility and get you clients.

Doubtful, I respond. In fact, while writing this chapter, a woman called me from New York (it's significant, I think, that she was referred by a friend who had read one of my books) and told me this sad story. She's a public relations professional (her exact words) who recently had an article published about her practice (they spelled her name wrong) in a very good magazine (her emphasis). But no one called after the article was published. And she got no business from this superb spread. What had gone wrong?

"Was the article about you," I said. "Or was it about what you can do for the people you are in business to help?" "Did the article ask people to track you down, or did it provide the prospects with the information they needed to get to you easily?" You can guess her responses!

As a professional, she assumed it was her obligation to have the article be about herself. She never thought (a public relations professional, no less!) it was her responsibility to make it easy for her prospects to get in touch with her. In short, she was the dupe of the prevailing Professional Syndrome, the debilitating disease that makes it difficult for you to connect with your prospects.

- Give a workshop, all the books say. A workshop will get you to the attention of clients and will establish you as a leader.

Recently, I met with a client in Austin, TX, a financial planner; a very bright and sensible man. He had just given a workshop at an upscale senior citizens' home; (look for far more of these as my Baby Boom Generation ages into spoiled senility). The entire audience was women (of course), women of a certain age, as the French say; women who were trained to make much of a man. And they did. They petted him. Complimented him on his talk. Gave him plate after plate of homemade cookies. Until, of course, he had quite lost his head — and the reason why he was there.

He never bothered to ask for their names and addresses (though three gave him their cards; as a professional, he quite expected that). He never troubled to distribute any kind of survey questionnaire trying to discover what kinds of financial problems they wanted to solve. He didn't even bother to take his business cards or brochures! He never tried, in short, to turn this event into a prospecting session, to make real and lasting contact with the people who had gathered to hear him. "If they want me," his entire attitude seemed to say, "they'll somehow figure out how to find me."

And this is a bright and sensible, I might even say sensitive, man. Who came away feeling good because his audience had lavished attention on him. Rather than business. How appalling!

- Wear a blue power suit and a red tie and loafers with tassles, all the image brokers say, be ye a man or woman. This will surely establish you as a reputable professional.

Recently, in Charlotte, NC, I addressed a large gathering of financial service professionals. As I looked across into my audience, I had to congratulate John Malloy, that preening haberdasher, for the superb job he has done reviving the sumptuary laws I once thought had died with the Stuart Kings. Everybody, whichever its sex, was dressed alike. Colors alike. Fabrics alike. Accessories alike. How Hans Christian Anderson would have loved that scene! And yet, how abjectly beside the point it was. For when I read to these assembled worthies lines from their own marketing documents, the result was all the same:

- We have this feature and this feature and this feature.
- What the benefits of these features are, we cannot say, perhaps do not know.
- We have given you no reason to act NOW, and so you probably won't.
- We don't know why you are anxious or what you wish to accomplish. So we must concentrate on how anxious we are and what we want to accomplish.
- We must stay cool, impersonal, impassive, impervious — whatever your pressing need for what we do.
- We must dazzle and overawe you with our credentials, convincing you not that we can help, but that we are better. And if we condescend to help you, consider it nothing more than a favor, for you surely are unworthy of being aided by the likes of us.

Oh, God, forgive them, for they know not what they do!

This entire book takes direct aim at this cascading idiocy, at such unrelieved destructiveness, destructiveness that leaves both prospect and provider in need — in need of connecting with each other. For without this connection, there can be neither transaction nor mutual betterment. And so we are generally diminished.

Here I take up another piece of the puzzle, how professionals — service providers mainly — need to present themselves so that the following things happen:

- the professional is seen as warm and welcome, helpful and interested, not self-absorbed and detached;
- the professional's credentials do not oppress the prospect and make him feel insecure, unworthy, but reassure him about the professional, convince him that here is a person who can indeed help him solve his problem;
- each feature of the professional's resumé is transformed into a lever that helps convince the prospect that this is the person he should be working with to achieve his objectives.
- all levels of prospect interest are dealt with. That the people who are ready to buy NOW are given what they need to do so — while the people who need further information are not neglected, but given what they need. In short, that the marketer is ready to meet every level of interest.

Before I show you how to do this, ladies and gentlemen, I wish to remind you of these crucial points:

- Your standing as a professional is not dependent on how you appear. It is dependent on what you achieve with others.
- It is not a function of your feeling good about yourself. It is a function of others feeling good about you.
- It is not a measure of how you have overawed your prospects with who you are, but of how you, a great problem solver, have made it easy for them to connect with you and so reach their objectives.

It is, in short, the exact reverse of what today passes for so-called professional behavior, where the professional is the center of the universe and the client prospect the periphery.

Selections From Randomly Selected Professional Brochures. Is This How You're Presenting Yourself?

If you doubt what I'm saying, take a moment to review your current brochures and any marketing communications that feature information about you. As you now know, the first task is to change the focus of what you're disseminating from you to your prospects. The real problem is that most biographical information used by professionals is of the "aren't I terrific?" variety. This may be personally satisfying, of course, but it is marketing suicide. For the key to success in marketing is making others feel terrific about themselves and want to work with you. The more of this that takes place, the more successful your marketing will be. On this basis, how do these actual sections from marketing materials stack up?

From a brochure sent by Dun & Bradstreet, New York, NY, for a workshop entitled "Controlling Your Day."

"Meet Liz Kearney. The Seminar Leader Who Knows First-Hand The Problems You Face And Can Help You Handle Them!

Liz Kearney is a dynamic, sought-after D & B speaker who draws on her own work experience to show you how to get ahead... and stay there. You'll discover unique time management techniques that will make your job easier the very next day....

Liz knows that the secretary or administrative assistant's job is difficult and is anxious to help make it easier for you."

From a brochure sent by Patton Consultant Services, South Hamilton, MA, for a workshop entitled "Efficient Board Service: Improving Skills To Meet Responsibilities."

"About Our Trainers:

John Paul Dalsimer, CPA, Founder, Accountants for the Public Interest, Pennsylvania. Trainer and consultant in accounting for not-for-profit organizations.

Barbara Nesbitt, Associate, Aisworth & Associates, Inc., South Carolina. Facilitator for non-profit organizations specializing in training for leadership development and boardsmanship.

Jane Pratt, Registered National Parliamentarian, Florida. Specialist in making parliamentary procedures comfortable for board members and chairs."

From the envelope for materials sent by Alan Shawn Feinstein, Cranston, RI, for his "Wealth Maker Program."

Under his photograph:

"Alan Shawn Feinstein

- 20 years Best Selling Author
- International Financial Columnist
- Listed in Who's Who In America."

Shall I go on or do you already know what's happening?

These people want to be marketing successes, each and every one of them. They — like you — want to sell more of their products and services. But they are sunk by the Professional Syndrome, their overweening need (born of ignorance and ego) to appear professional, to overawe you and make sure you see them as contemporary titans who bestride the world.

Remember, *each* section of *every* marketing document you create must help you get the client, make the sale. If a section of a marketing document doesn't help, it hurts, not least because of the considerable expense of bringing this useless information to your public.

You must ask of every paragraph in every document, does this section help (or hinder) me in getting the business? Does this paragraph, this section make it more (or less) likely that the prospect, the person who must take action, will take action NOW?

If you don't know, if the section isn't entirely clear (as the best marketing always is), then the section is wrong and must be rewritten, no matter how flattering it is to your fragile ego. The sad truth is, however, too many supposed marketers are more interested in their egos than in the sale. What madness!

Now let's take this efficient yardstick and apply it to the examples I have chosen at random from my intellectual compost heap, the examples that flood in daily.

• **"Meet Liz Kearney."**

Liz Kearney teachs one of Dun & Bradstreet's secretarial workshops, this one about "Controlling Your Day," for secretaries. Remember, this section, while ostensibly about the presenter, should actually be a lever, something that must help induce a prospect to sign up for this program NOW.

Here's why Kearney's write-up fails:

• It's straight Assertion Marketing, right from the opening line, "The Seminar Leader Who Knows First-Hand the Problems You Face And Can Help You Handle Them!" The marketer is saying, in effect "Trust me." Trust me that I know what the problems are you face. Trust me that I know how to handle them. Trust Liz Kearney that she is what I say she is.

But why should anyone, anyone at all, believe this in a world as rife with hype and corruption as ours is? Dun & Bradstreet, of course, is relying on its well-known name to convince you, rather than on proof about what it says. In so many words, this is Dun & Bradstreet's marketing argument, "We're well known. You know who we are. So you have every reason to trust us, even though we haven't bothered to think through what you get from this speaker." Is this a comforting case, a convincing case? I think not.

Go deeper into the text. "Liz Kearney is a dynamic, sought-after D & B speaker...." Who says so? This is more Assertion Marketing. Just hype. Meaningless words that foster neither confidence nor trust.

The marketer has forgotten that we have never heard of Liz Kearney. That we have no reason to trust her. That we're not coming to the workshop because of her, or to swell her ego, but because we have a problem, an objective, that we want this specialist to help us with. But there is nothing, nothing whatsoever, in this marketing section that helps us make the decision to attend. It's just one bloated word after another. "Blah, blah, blah." Too bad Clara Peller isn't around anymore to utter that immortal line, "Where's the beef?" Where, indeed?

Remember, *each* part of *every* marketing communication must move the prospect to take *immediate* action. This means:

- focusing on the prospect's problem
- letting him know you have the solution he needs
- understanding his reluctance to act and helping overcome it
- giving him an incentive to act NOW

Here's what I think people want to know about Liz Kearney:

- How does she know about the problems a secretary faces in controlling his day? Has she been one herself? Studied them? Worked with dozens? No one bothers to say. All we know is that she "draws on her own work experience", whatever that means. How does this slackness impact on our need for reassurance? Liz needs to be knowledgeable about secretarial problems. Where does it say in this copy that she is? And where does the marketer bother to convince us, show us, not just tell us?

- Instead, the copy *asserts* that she's "dynamic." A meaningless word. What does that mean? We want to know that she can do two things: make us a better secretary and give us a good program. And we want to know that D & B isn't just saying that she can deliver on both, but that she *can* deliver. We want proof. Here there isn't any.

- We want to know that Liz has helped real secretaries to improve, which means in this context, to better please their bosses, get more done, and get higher paying jobs. Instead of this reassurance, we learn that Liz is "sought after." By whom? For what? So what!

Dun & Bradstreet, rather than get the facts, is trying to sell this workshop by hyping the instructor as a celebrity. But does anyone care that Liz is a celebrity, beyond Liz and, of course, her mother? Dubious. The people who attend don't care that Liz is sought-after; they care that she can help them solve their problems. Which is just what this section fails to reassure them about.

This is painful, painful, but I must continue. I writhe in discontent at what I see before me. I consider the trees that have been killed off so needlessly. I contemplate the wasted hours spent concocting this inept production. I think of the stress the marketer endured to create it, and its lasting effects. I think of the high hopes Ms. Kearney entertained when she heard how many of these brochures would be sent; hopes which cannot conceivably have been fulfilled. I consider how many minutes in how many lives were spent in even the barest consideration of this piece and how futile this consideration must have been. In short, I grow tired and despairing as I look upon all the waste associated with this single piece of marketing. And consider how many other wasted pieces were produced on that single day!

And for what? So that Liz Kearney could be regarded— however momentarily — as "dynamic, sought-after."

In this brochure, the marketer is making another elementary error, by asking the prospect to make either a thumbs up or down decision, nothing else. Either enroll he says, or don't enroll. This is a mistake.

What of all the people who — besieged with other offers, uncertain of what to do and unsure of the benefits they will get by attending — want further information? The marketer's job is first to approach them, to get them to self-select and identify themselves, and then convert them into customers.

If the marketer (and Liz, his surrogate) were truly concerned about helping you (by getting you to their workshop), they'd pull out the stops; they'd recognize your doubts and invite you to call and have them put to rest. They'd provide access to Liz, saying, "Ask Liz directly about what's going to be covered. Liz is warm and approachable. Call her to get the information you need about what's taking place."

Lines like this do several things: they *prove* that you're warm and approachable, not a god to salute on bended knee with veiled eyes. They also smoke out prospects who aren't sure about wanting to attend, who aren't sure about what they'll get from you. Make it easy for these people, the softer prospects, to identify themselves to you so you can do what you must do: sell them on their need for your product or service. Don't pass up the chance — as Dun & Bradstreet did — to give them access to you by forcing them into a foolish "all-or-nothing" position.

• "About Our Trainers"

The problems here start, as they usually do, with the headline. From a headline you know if the marketer is focused on himself, or on you. In this case — with the focus on the trainers — it's clear what he's thinking about: himself, not you. For this headline is about the trainers, not about the people being trained who'll get the benefit from the program. Remember, *everything* in a marketing document must relate to the prospect. *He* is the important person, not you; certainly not "the trainers".

What Patton Consultant Services has produced is standard substandard marketing. IT HAS NOTHING TO DO WITH THE PEOPLE THEY WANT TO ATTEND and precious little to do about the trainer either, for that matter.

Take a look at the write-up for John Paul Dalsimer. Now, Patton Consultant Services hired him for a reason, presumably because he has essential information to assist participants achieve a crucial objective, in this case being an effective nonprofit board member. Sadly, the title of this program ("Efficient Board Service: Improving Skills To Meet Responsibilities") is weak; it's not clear what the benefits are or who should attend. It is, in short, a title with neither clear audience definition nor defined prospect benefits. Useless.

If the sponsors of this program were interested in writing marketing material that got people to attend, they'd ask themselves these simple questions: "What does Dalsimer have that will get people to attend this program? What problem can he help solve that's of compelling interest to our prospects; that literally forces them to drop everything, ignore every other offer, and do whatever it takes to come to this program because of the benefit they get from it?"

I'll bet my bottom dollar that the program sponsors never asked trainer Dalsimer these questions; never thought they should. Because what they got is about Dalsimer, not about the people who they want to get to the program.

Let's go through each of his credentials and find out if it matters, or how it might have mattered.

He's a CPA. So what? What does this mean to a prospect who's paying good money to get defined benefits? The fact that he's a CPA is irrelevant, unless it is positioned to get a prospect to respond to this marketing piece. Remember, everything counts!

He's Founder of the Pennsylvania Chapter of Accountants for the Public Interest. So what? What does this mean to a prospect who's paying good money to get defined benefits?

He's a trainer and consultant in accounting for not-for-profit organizations. So what? What does this mean to a prospect who's paying good money to get defined benefits?

We don't know. I can't say. And the prospect certainly isn't told. Instead, this is Patton Consultant Services' argument: "Trust us. You never heard of us before. You never heard of John Paul Dalsimer. But we want you to invest some of your limited resources coming to hear him. We either don't know or can't tell you what benefits you'll get from him. We either don't know or can't tell you how he'll help you solve your problem. But even so, trust us with your money."

Do you find this argument sufficiently convincing to invest your hard-earned dollars in the company making it? I certainly don't! And yet I feel certain this organization regards itself as truly devoted to the welfare of its clients. Why, then, do they produce such insipid marketing materials?

The kind of "trust-me" marketing copy displayed here by Patton Consultant Services is very, very common. And very, very wrong. In presenting information about people whom your prospects must trust and work with to get defined benefits, you must transform the biographical credentials of the service-provider into levers. These levers must move your prospect to pay attention to this provider and what he can expect to get from him, the benefit that induces him to invest his limited resources.

In short, biographical features must be transformed into client-centered benefits.

- **"Alan Shawn Feinstein"**

Here's another example of "trust-me" marketing. Trust me, not because I have given you reasons for trusting me, but because I am who I am, a demigod whom you ought to trust.

- "20 years Best Selling Author."

What conceivable benefit is this to the prospect who's being asked to invest in this "Wealth Discovery Top Secret"? None that I can see.

This presentation, under a photograph of the marketing culprit, no less!, has nothing to do with the prospect and what he wants — and everything to do with the marketer and his ego.

Remember, all marketing — everything you use, however you use it — must answer one insistent prospect question: "What's in it for me?" By this standard, Feinstein's marketing falls ludicrously short. The real question, the question that must be answered for the prospect, but is here ignored, is "What's in this man that I can use?" What, indeed?

Instead of answering this sensible, must-answer question, the marketer shows himself as self-centered and insensitive to the needs of his prospects.

Note: I cannot let this particular mailing piece, from a well-known mailer, go by without telling you about another particularly egregious flaw on his mailing envelope, where his copy begins. At the top there is this line: "I paid a Financial Wizard $125,000 for his services and his promise to keep this Wealth Discovery Top Secret. Now YOU can get it free."

In other words, the marketer, by his own words, looks like either a promise-breaker or a liar, since if he promised someone to keep the secret, what does it say about him that he is now making it available?

When will people learn to see their own copy as their prospects will see it?

What You Have To Do To Transform Your Credentials Into Marketing Levers That Get Your Prospects To Respond NOW

What I am about to say may seem obvious. It isn't. It's certainly something I've said before. And you may find it redundant. It isn't. I can assure you, as I glance through the gigantic heap of marketing communications in my intellectual compost heap, that it isn't.

The object of a marketing communication — be it delivered by the Goodyear blimp or on a simple post card — is either to make an immediate sale, or to move the prospect closer to that sale. The sale matters. Nothing else does.

Thus, in seeking to transform your credentials into a marketing lever that leads to this sale, do the following:

- Make the decision to approach the issue of your credentials dispassionately. What is important is that your prospects buy, not that you get presented as a star. For most of us, celebrity status is entirely unimportant to selling our product or service.
- Write down all the credentials you have.
- Now put these credentials into context. Tell us what difference they make to the prospect.

- Write down the kind of prospect you want to take action.
- Now select the elaborated credentials that relate specifically to the prospect you want to transform into a buyer.

How about an example to make this clearer?

To succeed at marketing means rethinking what constitutes your credentials. Your prospects don't want to know where you've been or what degrees and honors you have. They want to know what you've done. Resumé "credentials" are not marketing credentials. For marketing purposes, you need to tell people what you've done that they can have reasonable assurance you can do for them.

Stop thinking, "I was here; I got this." Start thinking, "I accomplished this specific thing. Here's who benefitted."

In this connection, here are a few of my credentials:

- internationally-syndicated columnist with articles regularly appearing in about 100 publications and electronic databases
- helped Saunders Hospital, Boston, achieve 50% return on selected mailings promoting its Healthline Data Base.
- assisted Wyndham Home Care Corporation raise nearly $100,000 for its Free Care Fund.*

   *These are actually things I've recently accomplished with my clients. But because they are clients, they deserve their privacy, so I've changed the two names.

Put credentials into context. Tell your prospects what difference they make.

All facts need to be interpreted so that people who have never heard them before can understand their significance. A fact is generally meaningless — certainly for marketing purposes — until you show its significance.

Now let's look at the credentials I listed above and transform them into client-centered marketing information:

Columnist. Unlike any other syndicated column, this one is sent free to any publication that wants it and will run information about products and services discussed in it, including mine.

Marketing consultant. Used my marketing techniques to improve the response rate of selected mailings from under 3% to over 50%, with a proportional increase in profits.

Fund-raising consultant. Helped Wyndham Home Care Corporation go from $7000 in annual fund-raising receipts to over 14 times that amount at the same time that other local home care corporations were going bankrupt because of their inability to raise money.

What's happening here?

As I just said, a fact by itself has no significance. Therefore, you must provide a context which sets off the fact, enabling the prospect to get its full meaning — and to motivate him to do what it takes to get a comparable result.

Let's say you were selling a marketing communications consulting service, as I do. Would you want to deal with a marketing consultant (feature) or with a consultant who had assisted a major urban hospital improve its return from around 3% to over 50% on selected mailings? Admit it, isn't the latter statement (so long as it can be proven) far more attractive, far more likely to get you to act? Of course it is!

All facts need context, that is an indication of why they are significant to the prospect. No fact stands alone. It must always be related to the thing you want to accomplish — the person you want to motivate — because of it.

Now select the prospect you want to take action as a result of the fact. If I wanted to motivate a community health agency that was interested in raising money to retain me as their fund-raising consultant, the fact that I had an internationally-syndicated column (while certainly something the budding star in me likes to have known) would be of no importance. In other words, this fact — with or without its context — wouldn't help me get the business. What would help, of course, was the fund-raising result achieved with a comparable organization. Thus, lead not just with the credential that's persuasive to your prospect, but with the compelling context for that credential. That's what's truly meaningful. And stop leading — now and forever — with the feature information about *you* ("fund-raising consultant") which is of interest to nobody but you.

What, then, have you learned?

- Everything in a marketing communication must reinforce the major message of that communication, the single thing you want your prospect to know when he reads your document: "Here's another benefit you get, prospect, if you acquire this product or service." In short, everything in every marketing communication — even the biographical information about the service-provider — must be prospect-centered. For only the prospect is significant.

- Biographical facts are features; features that are no doubt interesting and compelling to the service-provider, but which do nothing in themselves to persuade the prospect to take action.

- All features must be transformed into benefits. If you are promoting a training session with a Florida parliamentarian, you must transform that information into a lever that induces the prospect to sign up for it. The mere fact alone is insufficient.

- Each fact in every marketing document — including biographical information — must answer the prospect's key question: "What's in it for me?". Don't provide a fact; give another reason for the prospect to take immediate action.

Taking Yourself Out Of The Picture

You probably think that the biographical facts you include in your marketing communications are about you. Well, don't you? But think again. They are useful and can be justified only if they move the prospect closer to completing the sale. If they don't, they're wrong . . . and worse than wrong . . . they're a stupid waste.

Here is your single standard of utility for anything appearing in any marketing communication: does this help get the prospect to act NOW. Or does it not? If it doesn't help get the prospect to act NOW, then it must be ruthlessly weeded out, no matter how satisfying to your ego.

You see, the objective of marketing communications is not to make you feel better, is not to make you a star, is not to get people to think you're swell, is not to establish superiority to them. No, indeed.

The purpose of marketing communications is profoundly simple: it's to get your prospect to buy what you're selling.

My work area is littered with the marketing materials of people who have forgotten this crucial truth.

People like Ed Sawicki, who teaches a workshop entitled "Networking" for the Accelerated Learning Center of Lake Oswego, OR. Ed's "been involved with data communications and networking for 16 years." So what? How does this help persuade the prospect to take immediate action? Why should the prospect invest in Ed? What tangible benefits will he get from him?

Or Dr. George Lundberg, who helped present a program called "The Future Of Health Care: Public Concerns And Policy Trends" for Mass. Health Data Consortium of Waltham, MA. Dr. Lundberg "has been the Editor of the Journal of the American Medical Association for six years." So what? How does this help persuade the prospect to take immediate action? What's in it for this all-important prospect to connect with the good doctor?

Or Marte Kernodle, presenter of the "Powerful Presentation Skills" program for The Business Women's Training Institute, Shawnee Mission, KS. Her profile begins with her "Business Experience: Over 20 years in business with well-known national and international corporations; positions held in marketing, management and sales." So what? How does this help persuade the prospect to take immediate action?

My Plea

What all these people are doing — and the millions like them across this country who daily make this marketing mistake — is plain: they are asking the prospect to do all the work. They are asking the prospect to deduce the significance in the fact that Marte Kernodle has had over 20 years experience. This means something, no doubt. Ms. Kernodle accomplished something, no doubt. But what? Sadly, either she doesn't know, or won't say, because she leaves it to the prospect to figure it out and transform this fact (of which she is obviously proud) into a marketing lever that gets the prospect to take immediate action.

Of course, this is wrong, dead wrong. And the end result is shocking, if predictable:

- the prospect doesn't take the time to figure out what you mean
- the prospect doesn't buy
- the prospect's time has been wasted
- your money is wasted.

No wonder there's trouble in River City with this prodigal process!

Stop it now! NOW!!!

From this moment on, resolve:

- you will do the work in your marketing piece;
- you will ask the prospect to do nothing but the one single thing he must do to complete the marketing circle: act NOW;
- that you will transform every fact, including every biographical fact about you, into an immediate benefit that induces the prospect to take action, and
- that everything that doesn't talk of prospect benefits will be removed from all your marketing communications.

Leave your ego out of the marketing process. You are not its focus. Your supremely important prospect is. The extent to which you succeed in removing the focus from the prospect and put it on yourself is the extent to which you — yes you! — are sabotaging your own marketing.

Hear and obey — for the good of your bottom line and the improved lives of all the prospects who are not now buying what you're selling because you are making it unnecessarily difficult attemping, as you are, to get them to focus on you, when all they want to do is benefit themselves.

Chapter 11

Your Prospect In Pain? Then Sell Your Solution And You Both Must Gain!

You've probably heard the Nautilus exercise equipment motto "No pain, no gain." Well, I've adapted it for marketing purposes to the title of this chapter.

To succeed in writing cash copy you've got to:

- identify your prospect's pain
- make him *really* feel it
- let him know you can take it away, and
- remind him that if he doesn't act to remove his pain he'll continue to have it.

And so, "Your Prospect In Pain? Then Sell Your Solution And You Both Must Gain!"

What must you do to make this formula work for you?

First Step, Overcoming Your Aversion To Using Pain And Understanding Why You Need This Painful Information

As I go around the country talking to people about what they must do to improve their marketing, many of them feel distinctly squeamish when I get to this subject, when I talk about how they must conjure up their prospect's pain to get him to take action. Somehow, they reckon, this is like hitting below the belt; it's not right, not playing the game.

HOLD IT!

Let's reprise a few key points:

The only thing that matters in marketing is making the sale, because until there is a sale, your prospect stays in a state of relative discomfort (because he isn't using your product or service), as do you with your unsold product or service.

The only way there can be any progress is for the marketing exchange to take place, for your prospect to get the benefits emanating from what you're selling and for you to have the benefits that result from having made the sale.

Never forget this!

The only question worth considering, then, is "What must I do to ensure that my prospect takes action to acquire what I'm offering?" All other questions are superfluous.

Thus, as you contemplate whether to use prospect pain as a motivator, you actually have *only one thing* to consider: will reminding prospects of their pain get them to take action faster to remove it than simply offering them some positive benefit which does not reference that pain?

What You Have To Consider
In Order To Answer This Crucial Question

Now, as you probably can guess, I think motivating with pain is often the best way to get people to take action. I am only going through this exercise because you probably don't feel that way . . . right now. Indeed, you probably feel better using *any* other approach.

But as you consider which approach to use, you must remember that your prospects are besieged with offers. That they have limited time and money. That they are, in any event, prone to put off until tomorrow what they might do for their benefit today. In other words, they don't make purely rational decisions about whether to act now or not. They need incentives.

And that's exactly what I'm talking about. For pain is an incentive to action. Getting rid of pain is an incentive to action. Reminding people that they'll still have pain if they don't act is an incentive to action. Action NOW. The only kind of action that matters.

This is something the writer of a recent ad in the real estate section of the *Boston Globe* forgot. Here is the expensive ad he ran:

"Shhhhh. The Best Kept Secret in Boston isn't in Boston.

Our secret and yours is a spectacular panoramic view of Boston and Cambridge, overlooking the Charles River on the Cambridge/Watertown line, only minutes from Boston.

Luxurious suites or townhouses are still available with private underground parking. Our little secret also includes a four seasons pool, jacuzzi, sundeck, locker rooms with steam or sauna and a health club within walking distance. With a two story atrium lobby and a 24-hour concierge our best kept secret will soon be out!"

This is an illustration of the "Positive/Passive" school of marketing, and far too many ads come from it. Its writer thinks, "If I present just a few good points about what I'm selling, people are smart enough to know what they ought to do. I certainly don't have to tell them."

Oh, but you do!

Moreover, you cannot just tell, you must sell.

Telling, in marketing, is always insufficient. Because telling is like saying "here are some factors for you to consider. You figure out why they're important." Selling is the name of the game, and motivating with explicit pain — and the possibility of its quick removal — is one way to sell.

If the writer had considered the question of prospect pain, his ad could have been dramatically improved. The writer, for instance, might have told propects about:

- the appreciation in value of this property, giving specific figures. The argument? "You've already missed out on substantial appreciation. The longer you wait, the more you pay, the longer you have to wait for your appreciation. Act NOW."

- new building regulations that mean no more of these river view units can be built. The argument? "There's only so much river view property and if you don't act to get it now, it will be gone!";

- the low turn-over in river view properties. The argument? "People who get their hands on these properties, keep them. Which means dwindling choice for everyone else — including you".

See the pain here?

If you fail to act NOW, you'll have to wait longer to get the appreciation you want. You're already losing money!!! Ouch.

If you fail to act NOW, you'll have less chance of getting a piece of a very scarce resource. If you don't act NOW, everything that's desirable will be gone!!! Ouch.

If you fail to act NOW, you'll be on the outside looking in, just as you already are in most things in life. If you want the good life, act NOW, because your chance of getting it is evaporating!!! Ouch.

Are these statements motivating, or what? You know they are!

But are they hype? Untrue? Not at all — if you've done your homework. And that's the point. If these are just words, then you are doing something immoral. But what if this is fact — hard, provable fact? Why, then, it is your *obligation* to use it to motivate your client to take immediate action. Because if he doesn't, he really is:

- losing appreciation benefits which he wants and which you want him to have;
- likely to miss out on the prime river front property, which is a very scarce commodity . . . or have to wait for it for years, until someone already in possession gives it up.

These are facts and as such should be used by you . . . to motivate your prospect to take immediate action.

This argument seems so compelling to me that I have trouble understanding why all marketers don't do this. Part of the reason lies in how different marketers approach the world. Seasoned marketers look at the world as it is, warts and all.

We know we've got to work with what we've got . . . not what we'd like to have. The unseasoned look at the world as *they* want it to be . . . not as it is.

They'd *rather* make a rational argument to people about the merit of what they're selling and have that be sufficient to persuade these people to act. So, because they'd rather do things this way, they've come to believe the world works this way. When it doesn't.

They'd *rather* be passive than active in their marketing, perhaps because their mother told them that nice people don't push. So, because they'd rather do things this way, they've come to believe the world works this way. When it doesn't.

They'd *rather* be the sought-after than the seeker, because they profoundly believe there's something superior to being run after, than having to do the running. So, because they'd rather do things this way, they've come to believe the world works this way. When it doesn't.

They'd *rather* people understood the good points of what they're selling as well as they do and therefore persuade themselves to take action to acquire it. So, because they'd rather do things this way, they've come to believe the world works this way. When it doesn't.

They'd *rather* there was more sweetness and light in the world and that sweetness and light were the prime motivators for people to take action. So, because they'd rather do things this way, they've come to believe the world works this way. When it doesn't.

Whom am I describing? The marketer who penned the real estate ad above. He'd probably deny it, but his work stands as a silent and appalling (and no doubt ineffectual) reminder of his perspective on the world. As your marketing materials probably do, too.

As you reflect on the relative lack of power in your marketing materials, I think you know this. But I also think many marketers suffer from the fatuous delusion that if they use pain to motivate, they are responsible for that pain; that they have somehow caused it and are somehow evil. Of course that's ridiculous.

Seasoned marketers reason differently. They see the pain as clearly as anyone — arguably, clearer. Indeed, through the process of empathy, they actually come to *feel* their prospects' pain. And from this felt pain (shared by prospect and marketer) comes the profound marketer resolution, the decision to do *whatever is necessary* to remove that pain and improve the quality of prospects' lives.

These marketing paladins do not see the pain or its cause as their responsibility, but they most certainly do so regard its removal. And thus they — I might say we — feel sufficiently motivated to do whatever it takes to get the prospect to respond, for only by responding can the prospect move towards the completion of the marketing process and so acquire what he needs to lessen his pain and achieve his corresponding want.

I repeat: if you don't sell your product or service, that is, if you don't do EVERYTHING YOU CAN to get people to acquire the solution that you're selling, you're guilty of leaving them in relative unhappiness, in a state of incompleteness, and even outright pain. YES, YOU!!! Because you have not done everything you possibly can to make their lives better by allowing them to benefit from what you have available.

And if it takes reminding the prospect of his pain to get that prospect to take action and to eradicate that pain, why, then, you'd be witless (not to say reprehensible) if you failed to use it.

But all this is dependent on knowing the prospect's pain.

Getting The Painful Information You Need

Like so much else in this book, it takes preparation to use pain successfully to spur sales. If you want to use pain to motivate your prospect to act, you've got to know how much pain he's in. The greater the pain (always assuming that the prospect retains the resources he needs to acquire what you're providing), the more likely he'll do what's necessary to acquire what you're selling. There is thus a direct relationship between your prospect's pain and your prospect's willingness to take immediate action.

Your task, therefore, is plain: you need to gather as much information as possible about your prospect's pain:

- how long he's had it;
- how much it costs him;
- what happens to him because he has it;

- what he cannot do because he has it;
- how he feels as a result of having it;
- what will happen to him if he continues to have it.

In short, you must look at the problem from the prospect's perspective, not from yours. Which means, of course, being empathetic, truly climbing inside your prospect's skin and considering his problem just as he does. Only with this difference. That you are approaching his problem with stark single-mindedness, with the resolution to solve it. You know — as the prospect often does not — precisely what the prospect must do to solve his problem. And you have — as the prospect certainly does not — the solution to this problem already in your hand. Thus, you are in a position to do everything necessary to motivate the prospect to do what he must to acquire what he needs.

How does this work?

I wonder if you've ever considered that because your prospect doesn't have what you're selling he exists in a state of relative pain, unhappiness, or incompleteness. Well, think of it now.

Write down exactly what you think your prospect's life is like without your product or service. What you are looking for is Prime Pain Benefits. And what are these? They are the pains you can use to motivate people to take action, to do what is necessary to remove the pain they have, for when your prospects are without your solution they are in pain. These Pain Benefits are helpful to both you and the prospect, because when you use them you get the prospect to do what is in his own best interest. He in turn does the thing that is beneficial to you. Hence, Pain Benefits.

I'll work along with you, too, using this book as my product. Without CASH COPY, my prospect continues to spend too much money to produce marketing materials that get too few responses. My prospect gets frustrated because he doesn't know how to correct the situation and either reduces his marketing (Mistake 1) or increases it without having corrected the error in his marketing copy (Mistake 2). Either way, he gets too few buyers to either sustain his business and/or justify his expense. As a result he becomes subject to bouts of rage and disappointment, making him difficult and demanding to those around him.

Doesn't this just about sum it up?

Now what about your prospect?

You can start the process of mobilizing pain on your behalf by thinking about your prospects and visualizing their situation. Remove yourself from this process. *Focus exclusively on your prospect.* Without you, what situation are they in? You'll find this process easy if you complete this sentence:

"Without my (product or service), my prospect doesn't have (fill in *benefits*, not features.)"

Remember: if you can ask the question "So what?" after writing this line and that question makes sense, you have not yet completed your assignment, have failed to discover your prospect's total pain.

Let's say you've written "Without my pancake batter, my prospect doesn't have pancakes." Have you captured the prospect's pain yet? Certainly not.

You can ask the "So what?" question, and it makes sense. So you know there's further to go. This is because pancakes are features, not benefits. Answer the "So what?" question and rewrite the original sentence.

"Without my pancake batter, my prospect doesn't have pancakes and so cannot feed her children a hot nourishing breakfast."

The correct response is "Aha!" — because now you have something you can use in your marketing. You have a Pain Benefit. It's a benefit to you, the marketer, because it clearly focuses on a pain the prospect has.

And what is this pain? Your prospect feels guilty about not being able to provide this breakfast. Why? Because serving a hot breakfast is a sign of LOVE, the Ultimate Benefit here. And it is because of love (as well as other subsidiary benefits) that your prospect can be motivated to take action. As Pillsbury knows: "Nothing says loving like something from the oven, and Pillsbury says it best."

Where do your pancakes fit into all this? Why, once you have figured out your prospect's pain, you can position your product or service as the apt solution to it. For the smart marketer, then, pancakes equal LOVE — and the end to the pain of guilt.

Another Example

Suppose you are selling home security equipment. To sell it you must stop thinking about yourself and the features of what you're selling. You must conjure up prospect pain. Start by jotting down a list of what you think of as the prospect's pain:

"Without my home safety alarms, you (the prospect) don't have (fill in the blank) _____."

Be careful!

Enter a benefit and make this benefit as specific as possible.

See if the word "home protection" works.

It doesn't, does it? It's too general, too impersonal. Remember: the best marketing is specific marketing. And the most motivating pain is personal pain.

Fill in the blank with prospect pain, that kind of pain that motivates prospects to take action NOW.

"Without my home safety alarms, you don't have any protection for your jewelry when you're at work and your house is empty. It's just sitting there at the mercy of the next thief that hits your neighborhood."

Ouch!

If the line works — if it is sufficiently motivating — it goes through the prospect like a jolt of electricity. In this instance, if the prospect doesn't feel the pain of being violated by the thief, doesn't feel the pain of losing something important, THEN SHE WON'T TAKE ACTION. Which is why we have to use the pain . . . as an efficient motivator to get her to do what's in her own best interests.

Getting The Pain Information You Need From And About Your Prospects

One of the things I always tell my clients is: "Don't assume you are your market." What this means is, you can't make the assumption you understand what your market is thinking, what motivates your market to take action . . . and what bothers your market, even if you are a member of your marketing audience.

You have to find out how your prospects feel, which means reading information produced by others about your prospects and continually talking to your prospects in an attempt to understand their pain.

It continually amazes me how few entrepreneurs really talk to their prospects, really attempt to understand their prospects. They make the fatal assumption that what they think about their prospects is what these prospects think about themselves. Nothing could be further from the truth.

So start asking pain questions. These are questions that either provide you with the information you need about your prospect's current painful state or which enable you to find out how the prospect might feel if the eventuality takes place that your product or service can prevent.

Selling CASH COPY, I want to ask my prospects about their marketing endeavors. How much money they have to spend. How much time they must invest. How difficult writing marketing materials is for them. How many responses they get back. If they get enough responses to sustain their business. What they have to do without if they don't get enough responses. See what I mean? My prospects have present pain, and it is my obligation to find out how serious it is.

But let's say I was selling that home security device. People who haven't been robbed can only speculate what their feelings would be if this happened to them. So you need to get the feelings of people who have already been robbed — and then use them to motivate people who haven't yet taken appropriate action. You need answers to painful questions like these:

- How did you feel having an intruder freely enter your house and steal your prized possessions?
- How do you feel now when you come home, knowing that your house has already been broken into?
- How do you feel about the fact that you didn't bother to get a home security device beforehand?

Are these questions intrusive? They most certainly are. Is it indelicate to ask them? Certainly not! Because if you can use what you learn to help both these people and other prospects take action that may help avoid the problem in future, then it is your obligation to do what you can to motivate them to do so.

Consider why your prospect will act. Does he really care about getting a home protection device? Of course not! He doesn't want an object. He wants to avoid the sickening feeling of violation that always comes with theft (not to mention the loss of his goods). That's pain. And you must make your prospect feel this pain to induce him to take immediate action. The more you are focused on this pain — and the less on the features of the product or service — the more likely the prospect is to take fast action to protect himself against the very pain you have used to motivate him in the first place.

And how do you get this information?

- Read professional publications.
- Attend programs in your field.
- Clip articles from the newspaper.
- Offer a premium for people to supply you with information.
- Give your prospects questionnaires to complete.
- Ask clients pertinent questions that focus them on their pain and how they feel about it.

You want both the information and statistics of experts and the painful recollections of your prospects themselves. Remember, people — particularly those who have been or are in the painful situation you can help alleviate — are most happy to tell you about their problems. Your job is to do what is necessary to connect with them and then take an intelligent interest in what they tell you. Write things down. Tape them. You can't remember all you hear, especially the pain itself. And the more painful the stories you hear, the more you need to be able to remember them. Because maximum pain (so long as your prospect has the means of action) stimulates quickest response.

When you follow these steps, you gather an amazingly powerful store of motivational information. Now you must craft it into a tool that motivates your prospect to respond. You must make it hit home.

Making Your Prospect Really *Feel* Pain

Either your prospect currently has the problem you can solve, or he doesn't. Either way you must motivate him. People being the way they are, they are usually easier to motivate if they have the problem than if they don't. If your prospect doesn't have the problem now, you have to work harder to make him feel it, to get him to experience what it would be like if he had the problem.

"You hurt" marketing is stronger than "You will hurt" marketing, and the trick of the latter is to make it sufficiently vivid that it is like the former.

Start with a series of factual sentences directed at your prospect, beginning with "you hurt because . . ." These sentences must be as specific and factual as possible.

"You hurt because your home was just burglarized."

"You hurt because the bank has just foreclosed on your mortgage."

"You hurt because 99 people out of 100 receiving your marketing materials throw them away."

These sentences are not finished. At the moment they are just facts, features, if you will. Now you must transform them into motivating sentences, sentences that get your prospects to take action. You must give them the reasons why they need to take action NOW. Do this by using the words "so that" to link the fact in the first half of the sentence with a Pain Benefit at the end. (Remember what Pain Benefit means: it's a benefit to you and your prospect because it's the pain that motivates the prospect to take action NOW.)

"You hurt because your home was just burglarized *so that* you don't feel safe in it any more."

"You hurt because the bank has just foreclosed on your mortgage *so that* you have just been tossed out of your house and have no place to live."

"You hurt because 99 people out of 100 receiving your marketing materials throw them away *so that* everytime you do any marketing you're wasting your money."

See how the "so that" clause works? You cannot just leave it to your prospects to figure out what being burglarized means to them. They might make the wrong deduction, the deduction that doesn't lead them to get what you're selling, but to take no action whatsoever.

You've got to help them by being the marketer. Reminding them of their pain . . . so that they take the necessary and immediate action to remove it. Thus the fact that "your home was just burglarized" is meaningless for marketing purposes unless you remind the prospect that "you don't feel safe in it anymore" — and had better acquire your home safety device so that you will! "Just burglarized" is a fact from the past. "don't feel safe in it anymore" is about the present. And it is the uncomfortable present — not the past (however catastrophic) — that motivates people to take action.

Are prospects bothered by the directness of this approach? Oh, yes, some certainly will be. But take my word for it, most of these people are flatworms, the creatures who are going to criticize you anyway; the people, I remind you, who won't do anything to help themselves. Real prospects will be grateful that you had the courage and good sense to call a spade a spade. That you are willing to talk to them directly, candidly, as a good friend ought.

For that's what you are. A very good friend. The kind of person who feels no need to mince words with people, falsely to soothe them with mere words. You see, the prospect who's been robbed doesn't just want soothing words. He wants a solution. And the friend who can provide it. And don't forget the person who may be robbed needs a friend, too; someone who's willing to speak directly about the prospect's risk and what he must do to avoid it — and to avoid all the pain that others, so well known to you, have already experienced.

Be the candid friend to both, even though you will very likely get some criticism. How could you not? When you discuss important matters — like the problems you are in business to solve — all people are not going to agree with you. What do you care? You can't please all the people all the time. It should be sufficient for you that you consistently please — and sell to — more of them more of the time. Selling to more more often is what distinguishes the successful marketer, not daydreaming about selling to all.

Tricks Of The Trade For Making "You Will Hurt" Have (Nearly) As Much Impact As "You Hurt"

Many of us sell products and services that help people avoid problems. Disability insurance, for example. Or financial planning for a child's college education. Or the home safety device discussed above. The objective is to get people to buy before they have the need.

If you sell such a prospective solution, I need hardly tell you it's difficult to do so. We Americans as a people are now-oriented. Which is one reason why we have the lowest savings rate of any industrialized nation. Why should we plan, today's flawed reasoning seems to run, when spending now is so much more fun? Why, indeed?

Those of us who sell a prospective solution must solve this problem, or two people suffer: our prospect, who doesn't get the solution we have available and who is thus subject to the full force of the calamity, and, of course, ourselves.

Here, then, are some helpful hints.

- You must work to make the make the future real in the present. My father is fond of saying, "Tomorrow never comes." Millions of Americans have taken these words to heart, although not at all in the spirit in which they were uttered to me as a boy. As marketers, our job is to make tomorrow real; to make tomorrow, if you will, today. You can do this by avoiding the future tense in your marketing documents. Don't say "You will need $50,000 a year to put your child in a good college." Instead, even though the event is in the future, bring the pain into the present. "In the year 2010 your children are in college — *each* costing you $50,000 annually. You can either put a little away each month now. Or hope for a miracle then. Or just tell your kids they're on their own. It's up to you." Make the future, present.

- Don't use the word "if". Change it to the word "when." Don't say, "If you're disabled, where will you get the money to live on?" Say, "When you're disabled . . . ." It's much stronger.

- Remind your prospects what's happening to people just like them NOW. Don't say, "Your home could be burglarized." Say, "Two of the homes on your street have already been broken into. Your neighbors have already experienced the sickening feeling of violation that comes from having a robber in their homes . . . and the anger of having their favorite possessions stolen . . . or destroyed. Take action so this won't happen to you."

Here you've given a vivid sense of what's happening in the present, even though the two robberies are past and what could happen to your prospect is only a possibility.

- Don't ask questions about future possibilities, make statements that suggest present realities. Don't say "How will you feel when your home gets torn apart by a robber?" Say, "When you come home after a robber has vandalized your home and stolen your prized possessions, you know what rage . . . and helplessness . . . are really like."

Take what is only a future possibility and make it vivid in the present to get the prospect to take immediate action.

- Make the prospect feel it could happen to him by reminding him that it happened to other people who said "It can't happen to me." I find that an enormous mass of people go through life believing "It can't happen to me." The fact that "it" hasn't happened so far supports their grounded belief that it won't happen at all . . . thus negating any need for action now . . . or later.

You must turn this future-oriented excuse for sloth into a reason for taking immediate action by convincing the prospect that it can, indeed, happen to him. Pictures are great for this, by the way. Under the picture of an accident victim how about these simple words? "He used to tell everyone it couldn't happen to him. Just as you do. He was wrong. . . ."

Techniques For Making
Prospect Pain Really Hurt

Americans live in a world of cartoons, fairy tales, and television where their heroes are shot weekly — and always miraculously live to love another day. In a presentist society like ours, it's hard for people to believe anything really bad can happen to them . . . although bad things are going on all around us. We have a collective tendency to bury the distasteful, as Evelyn Waugh portrayed so brilliantly in *The Loved One*.

Add to this the fact that people would rather postpone action than take action and that they are besieged with other marketing offers, and you have a very serious marketing problem to overcome.

Enter pain.

Pain the motivator.

But to stimulate action the pain you use had better be used skillfully so that it really does get the prospect to take action and doesn't scare him to death . . . and so cause him, in typically American style, to do nothing. You want your prospect to be motivated to take action, don't you know, not be scared witless and run to engage in another mindless activity that diverts him from the distasteful scenario you've frightened him with.

Here are some things to keep in mind to use pain properly:

- The pain you use must be personal. We Americans, as I need scarcely tell you, are constantly assailed with statistics. So many statistics that we are numbed by them . . . and do nothing. It's rather like all the warnings we've had about foods that cause cancer. Some people do alter their eating habits. Most others simply shrug their shoulders and say, "Everything's bad for you" and go on gourmandizing as before, changing no habit and being altered in only one particular: an enhanced disdain for supposedly motivational information.

Thus, you cannot talk about pain in general or abstract terms. Which means that just quoting statistics is out. Instead of saying, "35,000 Americans will suffer from X this year," (far too general to motivate anyone), you must say instead "You could be one of 34,987 Americans to die this year from X." By the way, you'll notice I changed the number to an odd one. That's because odd numbers are more believable than round numbers. An odd number looks like a real number; round numbers look like statistics, and thus have far less impact.

- Always include the person you are speaking to (your prospect) in the pain. Too many (admittedly unsophisticated) marketers create an artificial detachment between their pain facts and their prospects. Remember, pain means nothing unless it is connected to and focused on your prospect. All the pain information you present must be pointed at your prospect; must be made personal to him. Facts are irrelevant, and I'm talking about all facts, not just pain facts, unless they are linked to your prospect and made highly personal to him. "Robberies are going up in your community" isn't nearly as powerful and persuasive as "Every thirteen minutes in Syracuse there's another robbery. Yours could take place while you're out at the corner store buying a carton of milk. . . ."

An opening like this is powerful because:

- It takes the overall robbery statistic and makes it personal. It's hard to visualize what 1,000 robberies are like. But everyone can understand "every 13 minutes." This phrase has another important benefit, too: it suggests that the pain is continuing.

Pain in the past, as I've said, is not nearly as motivational as pain in the present. That's why you want a phrase suggesting a continuing event, an event that happens over and over again and which could well hurt your prospect.

- It uses a location the prospect knows, in this case, Syracuse.
- It projects the prospect of pain into the midst of a common event like running to the corner store. In other words, it raises the prospect of present pain and lets the prospect know he is *never* out of danger... *until* he buys what you're selling.

Going For The Jugular

The process I'm describing to you here I call "Going For The Jugular", and it has one purpose and one purpose only: to persuade the prospect to do what is necessary to acquire what you're selling . . . or to take the next logical step which will in due course result in his acquiring what you're selling.

To make this process work:

- you've got to make the prospect feel you are talking to him. He must feel that you understand his unhappy situation and hold the key to changing it.

- you must focus squarely on the prospect's pain and must never let the discussion be diverted from that pain. Your argument is a simple one: YOU HAVE PAIN. YOU HAVE PAIN. YOU HAVE PAIN. AND YOU'LL KEEP HAVING THIS PAIN. THIS PAIN. THIS PAIN. UNTIL YOU DO WHAT YOU MUST TO SOLVE YOUR PROBLEM AND ACQUIRE THE SOLUTION. THEN YOU WON'T HAVE YOUR TERRIBLE PAIN. YOUR TERRIBLE PAIN. YOUR TERRIBLE PAIN.

How different this is from most marketers who act like their clients are forever young, forever charming, immortals all who have no problems, no pain, no pressing, insistent needs, but who may, if the spirit moves them, want to acquire what you're selling. As a favor to you.

Most marketing materials seem to me to be disembodied, to have no connection to the real people with real, often horrifying, problems and the real people (us!) who have often worked heroically to understand these problems and create solutions that seem nearly miraculous.

As I write, for example, I am reviewing yet another of the ubiquitous weight-loss brochures that one finds everywhere these days. This particular company sells subliminal audio weight-loss cassettes, a popular product in a society where the popularity of sweat and personal initiative have declined together.

"Another one of our programs," the brochure says, "is becoming increasingly popular. So far, 100% of those who have listened to the Weight Loss program have lost weight. Yes, 100%. I know it sounds too good to be true, but as of this time everyone who has listened to this program regularly has lost weight."

This is poor marketing for several reasons. First, it's defensive. "I know it sounds too good to be true . . ." A doubt is raised that didn't need to be. As a result the prospect is diverted from his own situation to the seller's, wondering if the seller is honest or not, when he should be being motivated to take action to solve his obesity problem.

I look in vain through this marketing material for any indication that obesity creates pain, that obese people suffer. Yet we know they do. And we know that this suffering is a motivator to many of them. At some point the ones who aren't flatworms say, "I've had enough. I want more in my life than fat."

Why skirt the significant issue, then, when it makes so much more sense to say, "You — or someone you know — are overweight." Now bring home the pain: "You're missing out on some of the best things in life . . . you're not having a popular social life. You're not in good health. You can't experience the joy of wearing nice clothes. And you're constantly experiencing some of the worst things that life can dish out — like the rude remarks made about you behind your back . . . or right to your face . . . day after day. Isn't it about time you stopped letting fat rule your life and took control of your body... and your life? Well, now you can!"

In other words, "You know you hurt. Here's how you hurt. NOW GET MOTIVATED AND DO WHAT NEEDS TO BE DONE TO GET OUT OF YOUR UNENDINGLY PAINFUL SITUATION."

Which brings me to my next point: you must always let your prospect know that there can be an end to their pain . . . if only they DO SOMETHING.

Here are the two formulas you need to keep in mind:

YOU HURT – DO NOTHING ABOUT YOUR HURT =
CONTINUING PAIN, DAY AFTER DAY.

YOU HURT + DO SOMETHING ABOUT YOUR HURT =
FREEDOM FROM PAIN AND A BETTER LIFE FOR YOU.

The trick is, when you are using pain as a motivator, you must use BOTH THESE FORMULAS, not just one.

If other words, if you are using pain as a motivator, you must tell your prospect — in the strongest possible terms — what he needs to do NOW to remove the pain and get the benefits that come when the pain is removed. AND you must let the prospect know that if he fails to take action, to solve his problem and get the benefits you can deliver, his pain will continue... without end.

If you leave *any* part of the total formula out, you are weakening your marketing and allowing many of your prospects to do what they like best: nothing.

No Pain Without Gain

The problem with using pain as a motivator is that it can turn your prospects off. Remember, all of us each day are inundated with pain information. Because the media like pain stories — the tales of murder, rapine and general chaos — we hear a lot of such information. Media people crave the adrenalin high such stories give them. But while people in the media like them, the rest of us often run for cover and just stop paying attention.

Let me be clear about this: pain must be judiciously used in connection with solution. YOU HURT... BUT YOU DON'T HAVE TO. THERE'S A SOLUTION. DO WHAT IT TAKES AND YOU CAN HAVE IT! OH, YES, YOU HURT... BUT YOU DON'T HAVE TO. THERE'S A SOLUTION. DO WHAT IT TAKES AND YOU CAN HAVE IT. NOW!!!

You cannot use pain, unless you are prepared to tell people how they can quickly and easily acquire the antidote. Because if you don't tell your prospects about the solution they can get, and how easily they can have it, they'll do what Americans have become superb at doing: escaping reality into one of the myriad fantasy machines that abound these days. When I heard that Aaron Spelling, the producer of "Dynasty" and many other escapist classics, was building a forty-five million dollar home in the Holmby Hills section of Los Angeles, I thought to myself how unbelievably lucrative fantasy really is... and how painful life must be for most of us to warrant such sums being spent to escape from it.

You must ensure that your prospect is sufficiently motivated by pain to pay attention to you. But not overwhelmed by the pain so that he fails to take the action he must take to overcome it.

And you must, above all else, always let him know that you have the solution he needs. If only he'll act NOW . . . by doing what you've told him to do so that he can immediately acquire the solution he must have.

And What If He Doesn't Act Now?

You make it plain that if the prospect takes action NOW, he'll have (tell him how quickly!) just what he wants.

But that if he doesn't . . . he'll keep having pain, pain, pain.

- Pain that continues.
- Pain that worsens.
- Pain that has specific, invidious consequences.
- Pain that ensures he cannot be as happy as others who have wisely taken action and who are now without pain.

In short, don't make the serious mistake that all too many marketers make at this point: of failing to remind your prospects of the benefits they will not get, the pain they will continue to have, if they don't take action.

Thus: you hurt, you hurt, you hurt.

But you don't have to, you don't have to, you don't have to. Do this, do this, do this.

Fail to do this, and you will keep hurting, keep hurting, keep hurting.

Now think!

Some people reading your marketing message will take action because they hurt.

Some people reading your marketing message will take action because you make it easy for them to stop hurting.

And some people reading your marketing message will take action because you've not only made present pain vivid but have strongly brought home to them the future pain that must occur because they've failed to act.

And the rest of the people reading your marketing message — the people who didn't act. They:

- need to hurt some more before they take action. Their present pain (even as strongly driven home by you) is yet insufficient. Patience, marketer. Your day draws nearer with the more painful twinges of your prospect... so long as you keep bringing your ability to solve his problem to his attention.
- were never prospects to begin with. These are the window shoppers.
- are overwhelmed with other things in their life. These people have so many pains, they scarcely know where or how to begin addressing them.
- don't have the resources to acquire your solution. They hurt. But they cannot act. If their pain is sufficient, they will find the way. If you keep bringing yourself to their attention.

And then, of course, there are the flatworms, who, whatever their often inglorious situation, are perfectly happy with the world as it is. They will never do anything, although they'll often make you feel bad by giving you the impression they *would* have done something . . . if *only* you had approached them differently. Don't believe them. They wouldn't have. Obstruction, not change, is their preference . . . although they can't resist an opportunity to tweak you.

All these people, those who didn't act, must not distract you from your crucial audience: the people who will act, if only you remind them that they hurt . . . and that they can stop hurting if only they do one beguilingly simple thing: contact you. If they do, their lives will be immediately better. But if they do not, it is surely your obligation, you Old Testament prophet you, to tell them just what will happen to them . . . and of the pain they must continue to suffer. All because they didn't take the oh-so-simple action of connecting with you.

The prospect is your fish, marketer.

You must do all you can to hook him.

Chapter 12

The Rules You Must Follow For Writing Cash Copy, Or One Constructive Thought After Another For Writing What Gets Your Prospects To Act NOW!

I'm well aware that when you're writing your marketing documents, you don't have time to reread this entire book (which is, of course, a pity). So I've designed this *chapter* to be read *each* time you prepare a document . . . until these guidelines for getting your prospects to act immediately are in your very bones.

Some of what you read here you should already know. A reprise at this point is, however, a good idea. Some ideas are new. And some are a preview of what you'll be reading in later chapters. But here you have a check list of key ideas you can review every time you confront the crucial business problem of how to get prospects to buy and existing customers to buy again.

• Select the market you're talking to.

The mistake too many marketers make is trying to create a single document that can be used for every kind of prospect. This can't be done. All people, after all, are not alike and certainly don't have the same reasons for acting. Oh, sure, in the interests of efficiency we will always seek ways to produce the fewest number of marketing documents. But we must always remember that all marketing is essentially a conversation, a communication between just two people: the marketer and the person he wants to take action. You have to know who that person is and as much as you can about him. The best conversations,

you see, are always between people who know something about each other —
or are at least willing to learn from each other.

The magic of marketing takes place when a person you don't even know, have
never met, but certainly understand, feels that the document you have created
speaks directly to him, was designed for him, and moves him to action. This
means targeting. And targeting means different documents. The marketer who
attempts to create a marketing communication that seeks to be all things to all
people is more likely to create something that is useless to everyone.

- Talk to a specific person.

All your marketing communications will be better if you address them to a
specific individual, a person who's representative of all the people you're trying
to motivate to act and acquire the benefit you've got. Don't write for a group.
Write for this specific individual. Like all individuals, this one should have a
name, an age, a sex, a personal identify. Too many marketing materials read as
if they were addressed by Big Brother to the Nameless and Faceless. This may
be acceptable in a socialist utopia where the eradication of personality and
individuality is an objective, but it is most assuredly not acceptable here.

If it helps you, design your marketing communications in the form of a personal
letter, a letter you are sending to a friend to induce him to take immediate action
to get something he'll profit from. When you're finished, remove the salutation,
and you've got your marketing document.

- Get your perspective right: the sale should be considered
  exclusively from the standpoint of the prospect.

One of the key reasons marketing documents fail is because they are about
sellers, not about buyers. This means you've got to change your perspective as
you write marketing copy. While two people are involved in the process —
seller and buyer — the buyer is infinitely more important than the seller. It's easy
to forget this. After all:

- the seller is present when the marketing document is being
  created. The buyer isn't.
- what's being presented — product or service — is owned by
  the seller and is also immediately present.
- the seller, being egocentric, is understandably more interested

in what happens to him as a result of the sale being made than what happens to his buyer.

Net result: the buyer gets forgotten.

But you must stand this situation on its head: you must focus first, last and always on your buyer and what *he* gets from the transfer of your benefit for his consideration. Thus, as you write marketing copy you must continually ask yourself: Is this headline, this sentence, this word, this phrase, about me? Or is it about the more important person in the sales process, my prospect? If it's about you, it's wrong and needs either to be taken out altogether or reshaped so that what you've said becomes relevant and focused on your prospect. If what you're presenting is about you, it is quite incorrect. It must be about your buyer. Know what you want your prospect to do as a result of reading or hearing what you've said and make sure you've told him how to do it.

A marketing piece fails unless the individual you're addressing takes *immediate action*. But you've got to both tell your prospect what you want him to do and make it easy for him to do it.

As I write, I'm looking at a flyer promoting an exhibition that came in yesterday's mail from the Small Press Center in New York. Its headline is "Cookbooks By Small Presses." Now presumably the writer of this flyer wants you to attend this exhibition. But he never says so!

In fact, there are lots of problems with this flyer, but one of the key ones is that the writer is talking to the "public", not to an individual, as in "All Events are Free and Open to the Public."

The writer is leaving it up to the "public" to figure out what he wants them to do — and why they should want to do it. In other words, the marketer is failing to market. He's guilty, instead, of saying, in effect, "We have something going on. You figure out what's in it for you. You figure out what we want you to do. You figure out how to do it." Put like this, such an approach is pretty foolish, isn't it?

A marketer is a person who wants another person to do something. A person who wants this other person to do something NOW. A person who understands what his prospect wants and is willing to do *anything* to make sure he gets it. And who understands why his prospect may fail to take action, and who goes to any length to make sure that these reasons do not inhibit the prospect from taking action.

- Consider your tone.

When you're with a person you care for, you show it. You show it in lots of ways, but especially in your tone of voice. You can't afford to do anything less in a marketing document. And this is most difficult for most people because they don't write like they talk. Indeed, most people write in a stilted, pompous, dull, even insulting fashion that would abash them mightily if they ever heard themselves. But marketing is not some arcane process. The best marketing is a conversation, even if it takes place entirely on a written page between people who have never met and will never meet, but who still need to be in a friendly, trusting, and sincere relationship.

That's why I must advise you to carefully consider the tone of everything you write. And, when you've finished writing your marketing documents, to read them out loud to yourself and see if they really achieved your tone objective.

There are, in fact, many different tones you can take in a marketing document. You must decide which is appropriate. What is common to each, however, is that it is a tone of care and concern. The best marketing is not disembodied. It comes from a concerned person with a solution to a concerned person with a problem. I've said it before, and now I'll say it again: marketing, as communication and persuasion, is an act of humanity. And nothing says this as strongly as the tone you adopt to speak to and with your prospects. These are the tones of love, and it is up to you to consider which of them is most appropriate given the situation of your prospect and your prospect's readiness (or reluctance) for acting NOW. In other words, you must select the tone that gets the prospect to act immediately. That is the prime consideration. Thus, you can show your concern by:

- commanding
- exhorting
- reasoning
- being impassioned
- shaming
- demanding

But not just by stating or by telling. Which is, unfortunately, the style most ingenue marketers adopt.

Let's look a little more closely at these different styles and how to use them.

Commanding

Commanding is a very powerful marketing tone. People don't always know what to do or how to do it. But you do. You know what your prospect's problem is and what he should do to solve it. You're in a position to command. Only don't start by doing so; rather end by commanding. What this means is that you should first build your case for action, the reasons why the prospect should act NOW. Once you've made your most powerful case, then and only then should you shift into the command mode. "Act NOW. Yes, NOW, to get the benefits you want." To use the command style successfully, start with prospect benefits and end by commanding the prospect to do what is necessary to get them.

Exhorting

Here you urge the prospect to take action. For two reasons: to get what he wants (a scenario you sketch in brilliant colors) and to avoid what he doesn't want (depicted equally brilliantly). What you are saying, in effect, is this: "I urge you to act for this reason and this reason and this reason. Because you'll get this benefit and this benefit and this benefit. PLEASE TAKE ACTION NOW FOR YOUR OWN GOOD!!!"

Reasoning

I've put the reasoning style here, towards the middle of the styles you can adopt, for good reason. While most professionals approach people as if their prospects made all their decisions for rational reasons, most marketers know that they don't. Large numbers of people make an irrational decision and only later seek a rational explanation for what they've done. Personally, I am dubious about the efficacy of rational marketing used unadorned and on its own. And you should be, too.

The underlying theme of this style is, "Let me persuade you to do what's good for you by giving you reasons why it makes sense for you to take immediate action to acquire this product or service."

If you are using this style, your job is to discover every last reason that makes sense for your prospect to buy, to put them in order of priority, and to bring them to your prospect's attention by saying, in effect, "You're a rational person. I'm a rational person. I know what you want. And I can give it to you. Here are the reasons why you should act NOW."

Note. Don't be afraid to link the Reasoning motif with the Commanding or Exhorting one. In other words, after you've brought forward all your reasons for acting, don't wait for the prospect to mull things over (and perhaps get away). Urge him to act NOW — or command him to. "Don't wait. Take action NOW. Good things like this don't wait forever. So neither should you. Call today!"

Being Impassioned

Passion excites people, but sometimes makes them nervous. Passion can easily provide you with the most transporting experiences of your life, moments never to be forgotten. Or it can embarrass you and make you deeply uncomfortable. The keys, of course, are audience and timing and what is being sold. The real question is, how do you know when to use passion?

Use passion if a situation is critical, that is to say, if something irreversible or catastrophic is about to happen, something that will leave the prospect worse off — either directly or indirectly. You would be ill-advised to use passion in selling office supplies on a regular basis, for instance. But if you knew that a strike was about to cripple the paper supplier and leave your customers without supplies for six months, you'd be foolish not to use it. And guilty of the worst marketing sin of all, lack of concern for your prospects.

What you are saying when you use impassioned marketing is clear: "It matters, IT MATTERS VERY MUCH, that you take action NOW. Here's why it matters to you. It matters for this reason and this reason and this reason. And it is because of all these specific reasons that you MUST ACT NOW. Or you (your family, your neighborhood, your world) will be worse off in the specific ways I've told you about."

It should be obvious to you that when you're using the Impassioned voice it is easy to segue into the Commanding or Exhorting mode at your conclusion.

Shaming

You've occasionally used shame to motivate people. But the key word in this sentence is "occasionally." Shame is powerful . . . but can easily be overdone and lose its persuasiveness. Which is why you must use it carefully . . . and rarely.

Shame is the apt motivator for people who have failed to take action and as a result have caused problems . . . particularly for others. Thus, the office supplies buyer who fails to lay in a stock of constantly used products before a strike and is responsible for resulting plant lay-offs should feel ashamed. But if you approach this person in the wrong way (and too often) with a shame message, he'll certainly become defensive and stop listening. When you use shame as a motivator, you must carefully pick your shots. And must remember to make a sense of future shame a present motivator.

That's right, you don't want your prospects to have to feel actual shame before they finally take action. You must bring a sense of the shame they *will* feel (if they fail to take action) to bear on them NOW and so get them to take immediate action.

To make this work, you must open with a picture of what could happen. Only, you don't say "this could happen." You treat the situation as if it had already happened. Remember, your job as a marketer is to make the future into the present to induce immediate action. Thus:

"Every day another lay-off is announced. Another person leaves without a job, without the means to support himself and his family. Why? There are the same number of orders.

But no way to ship them.

Because you didn't order the supplies you needed before the big strike."

Sentences like this really hit home . . . really make the prospect feel ashamed. EVEN THOUGH HE DOESN'T HAVE TO FEEL ASHAMED YET. But that's the trick, you see; bringing the shame he'll feel in the future into the present and using it to ensure that he makes the right decision.

As I said, this is powerful . . . but it also must not be overused.

Demanding

I've put the Demanding Mode last, because it ought to be used last — just as it should be used last in real life. In fact, what you should be looking for in marketing is what you should be looking for in any human encounter: what it takes to get the person you're dealing with (even if you never see him!) to do what you want, the thing which is also in his own best interest. In other words, you are looking for persuasive tools.

Demanding something of someone does work. Oh, yes, it most certainly does. But to use this style too much transforms you from a concerned friend into a tyrant. And tyrants, while occasionally effective, are, in the end, unloved and even gleefully disregarded. As a marketer, this is precisely what you must avoid.

Which is why you must be very careful when you use the Demand Mode of tone and persuasion.

The time to use Demanding is when you are in a position of power over the prospect, when the prospect needs what you have available, when his options for getting it elsewhere are decidedly limited (the more limited the better), and when the use of your power is clearly in the prospect's own best interest. On this basis, then, demanding anything of our prospects for most of us just doesn't make sense, because we sell products and services that are competitively available.

But not all of us. If the situation meets these criteria then you can surely say, "You need the benefits I have available. You know you need them. You know you cannot get them elsewhere. And so I demand that you act NOW to acquire the benefits. For your own good."

As I said, this is a difficult marketing scenario to carry off, and I've placed it last on my list for very good reason. The important thing to remember is you can use even this tone and mode with a perfectly good conscience so long as you're acting in the prospect's own best interests — and not out of some vainglorious pursuit of personal aggrandizement and pride. That is the very antithesis of client-centered marketing behavior.

As you consider the tone of your document, then, what you must keep in mind is:

- how likely the client is to act now. Remember, your objective is to get the prospect to act NOW. If a "come let us reason together" approach doesn't work, it is your obligation to try another tack. It doesn't matter what you think of the approach. *It only matters that what you select stimulates immediate action from your prospect so that he's better off quicker.* If what you're using doesn't achieve this objective, then you have to change it to something stronger and more persuasive. And that's a fact.

Resolve To Make What You Write Interesting.

If most marketers actually read what they've written from the standpoint of their buyers, they'd know why they get so few responses.

Ladies and gentlemen, you can't bore anyone into buying what you're selling. What you write has got to be interesting. And what people find most interesting is what deals with their own lives. Let me ask you a question. How much thought did you give today to the food situation in Tibet. Quick answer! Truthful response? Not much, right?

And yet how much did the Tibetans themselves think about food? A lot, I'd say.

You must bring what you do right into the heart, soul, life, and spirit of your prospect. You must touch him. You must, in short, make yourself, your product or service, of crucial interest to him.

Take a moment to review your own marketing materials. Is this what you're doing now? You know you're not. One women I met recently told me that her marketing materials bore *her*, and yet, year in, year out, she goes on producing, by her own admission, materials that weary her and parch her soul.

STOP IT!!!

What happens when you encounter someone who bores you during a personal conversation? Why, you tune out, of course. Stop listening. Day dream. Long to escape. Plot your revenge. Do *anything* other than focus on what this pitiable creature is saying. But I'll tell you something, nine times out of ten what you find boring about the bore is his provoking tendency to keep the conversation away from something that really interests you — namely yourself.

Of course there are other reasons why you're bored:

- the story goes on interminably;
- the bore is trying to instruct you;
- his monotone makes you suicidal — or murderous;
- the pacing is wrong;
- the words are dull.

In short, the bore has no ability to entertain or enlighten you. Much less move you to any action more constructive than immediate escape. Which is, of course, the sad result visited upon *you* when your marketing materials bore your prospects. As they so often do.

Here, then, are some rules — many familiar to you by now — that I guarantee will enthrall your prospects and get them to take faster action to acquire what you're selling.

- Make *everything* about the prospect. If what you write, be it headline or body copy, is not about the prospect, it is wrong. Everything must be about the prospect. First, last and always. Anything that is about you must obviously relate back to what the prospect wants to achieve. "You" is the most important word there is in marketing.

- The second most important word is "get" (or as I sometimes render it in my residually midwestern way "git"). Think of yourself as a person lighting a fire under your prospect, the end result being his fast movement. A twig aflame produces heat. Add another twig, and you get more heat. More twigs. More heat. Until at last the prospect *must* take action or face posterior disfiguration. The twigs are the "you git" benefits. And your job is to pile them on, one atop another, until immediate prospect action becomes irresistible.

- Make all your sentences active. Marketing is about action, about moving a person from a place he no longer wants to be in to a place he now desires. This means MOVEMENT. Here's your marketing argument: "You're here in this uncomfortable place. You want to be there in that comfortable place. But to be there you have to do this. And you have to do it NOW."

In short, your client must act.

And you must induce him to act by making everything in what you write active.

This means deleting:

- the conditional. Don't say "You could have" or "You can have", simply say "Have" (or enjoy, experience, thrill to, profit from, *etc.*)
- the future. Don't say "You will have" say, "Have".
- the passive voice. By definition, what's passive is anathema to successful marketing.
- the word "if". Marketing isn't about "if"; it's about "when". Your job is to remove the drag of deliberation and make action seem like the only conceivable possibility.

And anything else that doesn't represent immediate action. All marketing is about action. Whatever you're selling. Stop telling people things. Start persuading them, inducing them, motivating and compelling them into taking action NOW.

- Vary your sentence lengths. Ever hear the old Edwardian music hall song "A little of what you fancy does you good?" It's true, of course. But caviar every day would become, even I admit, a tad dull. The same is true of sentence lengths. Vary them. Some should be as short as a single word (NOW!); others may go on for 20 words (but rarely, very rarely, more). And what, pray, is the objective of these sentences: to move your prospect through the piece and to get him to take action. The objective of the first sentence is to get the prospect to read the second sentence — and to respond if he's ready. The objective of the second sentence is to get the prospect to read the third sentence — and to respond if he's ready.

Remember, you're not writing an English composition. You're trying to motivate another human being to send you a check, fill out a coupon, walk through the door of your establishment — NOW — to plunk down those still-good yankee dollars. And you've failed if he doesn't. Even if every word of your marketing materials is linguistically perfect.

- Write the way people talk. This means starting sentences with conjunctions. It means using elipses (dots like these . . .) to get the reader to pause . . . but still connect two parts of the same thought. It means ending your sentences with prepositions. Or starting them with same. It means using contractions. And sentence fragments.

It also means differentiating between words — because not all words are equally important. Important words (by which I mean words that are more likely to get prospects to take action sooner) are words that need emphasis. And there are lots of ways to emphasize these important words:

- You <u>can underline them.</u>

- **You can put them in bold.**

- You can use a bullet to set them off.

- You can indent them.

*** You can set them off with asterisks ***

. . . or with ellipses . . .

- You can use color, (picture this as aquamarine).

- OR CAPITAL LETTERS.

- You can use arrows. ↔ ⇥ ↘ ↗

- And boxes.   (Or other shapes.)

- Or reverse type.

- You can use color breaks.

- Or margin notes.

- Use checklists.

- Or start your sentences with over-sized capital letters.

In short, you must use everything possible to tell the prospect — in any way you can: "HEY, LOOK!!! THIS IS IMPORTANT. I MEAN REALLY, REALLY IMPORTANT. BECAUSE IT'S GOT SOMETHING TO BENEFIT YOU!!!"

I look in vain for these kinds of "setting off" devices in the stack of marketing materials at my elbow today. What are these people thinking of? That all words are equal? No marketer thinks so. We believe, "All words are equal, but some are more equal than others." (With apologies to George Orwell.)

The Internal Message

And now I'll share a very important secret with you, the secret of the Internal Message. Most marketers, when writing a single brochure, write a single brochure. Seems to make sense, doesn't it? But it's terribly, terribly wrong. You should be writing *two* marketing documents simultaneously in every marketing communication you create, to give your message reinforcement and to make sure that it can be understood in even the briefest reading. Which is probably all you're going to get anyway. Enter the Internal Message.

The Internal Message is the crucial gist of your communication as emphasized and reinforced by the various devices cited above. With these devices you create a compact and powerful marketing message that enables your client to get the essential thrust of what you're saying, even if he scans. Which most people do these days; certainly the first time they look at something.

Here's how the internal message works. Let's take that flyer sent by the Small Press Center of New York City.

"On Exhibit

Hundreds of books from hundreds of publishers
Current cookbooks in print, rarely found in bookstores and libraries
Browse at your leisure
Order direct from publisher — catalog available."

You won't be surprised to hear me say this is execrable copy. But what is artistry for if not to render the old and forlorn into the attracting and exciting. Let's see what we can do . . . without the rewriting which this cries out for.

"On Exhibit

HUNDREDS OF BOOKS from HUNDREDS OF PUBLISHERS
Current cookbooks in print, *rarely found in bookstores and libraries*. Browse at your leisure!!!
Order **direct from publisher — catalog available!**"

Now you know as well as I do that this is *still* not good. But it IS better. And that's the point. What is more, a reader can get the (admittedly paltry) message in a fraction of the time it would take to wade through the whole. And if he's convinced by this message . . . why, then, he's more likely to really pay attention to the marketer's point. And perhaps even take action; (though in this flyer there's no reason to take any step IMMEDIATELY. Which is a sad mistake.)

Your internal message constitutes the essentials of what you're saying to your prospect, what's in it for him, and what you want him to do . . . all the key points, in fact, that motivate him to move. In fact, everything that gets the prospect to move *must* be in the internal message. Nothing of significance can be neglected. Or you just haven't done it right.

Lead With Prospect Benefits, Follow With Product And Service Features

Ingenue marketers lead up to the point. The seasoned (perhaps I could say jaded) marketers know how little time their prospects will give them. *They* make their persuasive points at once. Yes,.immediately.

In other words, you must lead with benefits and follow with features.

And your benefits should be in priority order with the most important going first. And where, pray, is subtlety in all this? Where it must remain: in the dictionary! *Not* in your marketing documents. Your job is not to be as enigmatic and secret as the wily Cleopatra but, as always, to get your prospect to take immediate action.

Where, then, do you start piling the benefits on? Where the eye of the prospect first rests, of course:

- on the outer envelope
- in the upper right hand corner
- in the headline
- in the first line of the copy
- in the first paragraph of the copy

In short, right from the very first moment. You do not so much build a case as hammer home successive reasons for immediate action. Remember, if the benefit you lead with is not of motivating interest to the buyer, the chance of his reading the remainder of what you've sent is negligible. Practically speaking, you've lost him.

Thus, lead with the sizzle (the benefit). Follow with the steak (the feature).

In each of these places, you must concentrate on your prospect:

- speak directly to him;
- offer him a benefit;
- excite him;
- scare him;
- let him know what he has to do to get the benefit;
- tell him when the deadline for getting the benefit expires.

Above all else, remember you are trying to motivate a human being. Trying to get someone with lots of other things to do, lots of other possibilities continually thrust upon him, to follow your advice and do what you want him to do — though he may know nothing about you and have no reason to trust you.

It is sheer madness to think this individual is sitting in an empty room with nothing to do waiting for you to communicate with him. The veriest folly to think he'll be so glad to hear from you that however you approach him will make him act. Yet this is how most marketers approach the task of communicating with their prospects, as if they were conferring an honor upon them by coming into their otherwise vapid lives.

You've got to fight for the right to garner even a morsel of your prospect's attention — much less his money. Neither is yours by right, whoever you are, however exalted your position in society, your degrees and intelligence. Marketers don't expect response. We compel response.

And this means getting to the point . . . immediately.

Look at your current marketing materials. Take any one at random. And read the first 50 words starting from the very *first* word. Does your prospect know what you can do for him? Do you tell him what he's getting and why it's important to do it NOW? Does he know what your offer is?

Unless the answer is yes, the documents are wrong and should be secretly burnt at midnight as an embarrassment to you.

Don't force your prospect to read your entire document to get to what interests him: what he gets. Tell him immediately!

What this means, of course, is you'll be able to cut the fat out of most of your documents and leave them shorter. So long as what you're talking about is not about the prospect, then it is mandatory they be shortened. But there is nothing wrong with long documents, even letters of four or six pages . . . so long as you're talking about the prospect and piling benefit on benefit.

As I write I am looking at a single 8 1/2" x 11" flyer produced by a local library for a program entitled "Managing your Files: A Seminar". This single line constitutes the entire description of the program and all the copy about it. For such a line, this flyer is at once too long and too short. It is too long because it fails to produce a single reason why the prospect should bother to give up his time to attend. Of course it is too short for the same reason. But length is not the problem here. It is the lack of client-centered benefits.

Address The Prospect's Anxieties

Whatever the product or service offered, a prospect is right to have anxieties about it. Even with the free seminar above, a prospect may well suspect that it could be a waste of his time. Such anxieties must be answered.

Sadly, too many marketers are resolutely self-centered. *They* know what's right for their prospects and feel no obligation to understand, much less address, their prospects' anxieties. Why should they? These marketers are experts and to be an expert in late twentieth century America is to expect subservience. When has he who commands ever felt bound to explain? The autocracy of the Tsar of All the Russias has given way to the equally unsavory adamancy of the specialist.

If you want your marketing to work, you must be different. You need to understand what your prospect's anxieties are, and you must work to reassure him. That he is not wasting his time. Or his money. Or his scarce resources. Just because you are who you are is no reason to trust you. Why should I? Why should anyone? You must earn my trust and that of all the prospects in the world. It is not yours by right.

Give The Prospect An Immediate Reason For Action

Marketing fails unless it compels immediate action. You now know this and will, I trust, never forget it. Real people do not hold onto marketing materials for vast amounts of time waiting for the moment they need them. Most are tossed out the very day they're received. So why do you suppose that yours will be treated any differently? And yet you do, you do! You hope against hope your own patterns of destruction will not be replicated by your prospects. But they will be.

What you send will be quickly destroyed by your prospects unless you give them an immediate reason to act. And as we sadly know, even that is no proof against mass destruction. Merely a pivotal help.

Confirm The Benefits Your Prospect Receives By Providing Testimonials From Satisfied Customers

Though you're a pillar of the community, no one who has not previously used your services has any necessary reason to trust you. Why should they? Which is why you need to confirm that others — who are willing to stand forth publicly — have, indeed, received benefits by using your methods.

Such statements, as you well know, must not be general, but specific. They must breathe authenticity and reality. Real numbers are as important as real names.

We live in a skeptical age; you in your own dealings are sufficiently skeptical that you should not be surprised that others are equally so. And yet you write your marketing documents as if your merest word were sufficient to cause others to ante up their resources. It isn't and won't be, until *all* the people you want to sell to actually know you and have substantial reason to trust you.

Make It Easy For Your Prospects To Do
What You Want Them To Do

Once you've persuaded your prospect to act, make sure you can easily accommodate him. If you cannot, all you have done is convince him that the words that should have motivated him are hype, not truth, and you have made him more skeptical than ever, certainly disbelieving about you and what you can do for him.

Your total focus — and that of everyone in your organization — must be on making the prospect's life easier. Of getting him what he wants faster. Of promoting his benefit. By this standard, most of the enterprises in this so-called entrepreneurial nation fail. It grieved me in my nationalistic spirit when I recently saw a program on service in Japan and realized how hollow the word is here by comparison. By this crucial standard alone, we are a nation in need of empathetic revival. And I'll tell you where this revival must start: with you! In fact, through what you do. And in the way you present yourself to your prospects as able to provide for his advantage.

Don't Rely On A Single Rendition
Of Your Important Message.
Say It Again And Again And Again.

Marketing is simple. It involves targeting a precise kind of person. With a precise kind of problem. That can be precisely solved by your product or service. And bringing the fact that you can solve his problem to his attention over and over and over again — until even the dimmest prospect cannot fail to get the message. This is marketing. And it means reiterating — rephrasing — restating — reprising the same basic client-centered message even within a single marketing document.

You don't always get a thing the first time it's said, even if this thing is of direct interest to you. "I'm bad with names," you say. "What did you say yours was?" And so the name, just a few syllables, is repeated — for your benefit . . . and is as likely forgotten again. That's why within a single document you must repeat your basic message over and over again. The objective of marketing is not creativity, it is the exchange of your benefit for the prospect's consideration: commonly called the sale.

Give your prospect your benefit-rich message on the envelope.

Give it to him in the upper right hand corner of the first page.

Restate it in a client-centered headline.

Start your body copy with it.

Repeat it in a box halfway down the first page.

Restate it on the top of page 2.

Put it in a postscript at the end of the text.

State it again on the response coupon.

In short, be a terrier. Fight for your prospect's attention and fight for the right to have him benefit from what you've got available. Whatever you're selling. Even a free library seminar . . .

Will this offend someone? Oh, yes, it most certainty will. It will offend those who say "We don't do that sort of thing around here." It will offend those who feel it's nobler to have the prospects discover them, rather than their doing every conceivable thing to connect with the prospects. It will offend those for whom such vigorous client-centered outreach is "unprofessional." They will call this the "hard sell", and they will condemn it . . . thoughtlessly . . . as they condemn so much else that is necessary.

Well, you tell me something. Are you interested in being a "professional", or do you want to do all you can to make someone's life better by ensuring that they know about and use your product or service . . . prospering yourself as a result? Unfortunately, I know plenty of people who would rather be threadbare professionals, secure in their exclusivity, than "soil" themselves by reaching out to anyone. These are sad, selfish creatures, despicable in their habits and pitiable in their limited influence, all too often flatworms of the most irremediable type. Often, too, they work for organizations that don't judge them by their results, by the number of people they have sold to, by the number of people they have helped. They get their trivial paycheck whatever they do.

These creatures must not be your models. For at root, they hate our human kind as flawed, stupid, loathsome withal. A position no marketer — interested in transforming something less good into something better — can abide or approve.

Before I leave this chapter with its check list of imperatives for marketing success, I must remind you that you will be communicating with your prospects many, many times in your career. Each time entails a cost of both time and money, and, yes, of hope and expectation. These are very limited resources. Which means that no marketing communication is a throw-away (that hateful phrase). Every one counts. For with *every* marketing communication a unique opportunity for loss or gain is established . . . for both you and your prospect.

As a result of what you do, either you will be measurably poorer in resources because you have failed to connect with prospects who trust you to transform their lives and make them better. And your prospects will be poorer, too, because they are not benefitting from what you have to help them.

Or, you will have convinced these prospects to act . . . and act NOW . . . to get what you have for them. And so improve their lives. And also yours.

No marketing communication is, therefore, routine. No marketing communication is negligible. None is insignificant. All count. Because all hold within themselves the prospect for gain . . . or loss. Which is why you must know what to do . . . and must do it. Every time you create every kind of marketing document.

If you fail to master these rules, and fail to review them and work them into the very marrow of your bones, you must continue to produce marketing communications that are not only a titanic waste of resources, but also an embarrassment to you. Such communications leave the people who need you without the benefit of your ministrations. This, of course, is the greatest sadness of all . . . because it is entirely avoidable.

Chapter 13

Looking At Some Crucial Pieces Of Your Marketing Communications: Envelope Messages, Headlines, Opening Paragraphs, And More.

Marketing, as I've been saying, is really quite a simple thing with a very simple, explicit purpose. As a result of marketing, you either get someone to buy what you're selling (or move them a logical step closer to buying), or you don't. Trying to "build an image" isn't marketing. Attempting to "show the flag" isn't marketing. And using the means of marketing for self-aggrandizement isn't marketing, either.

By my rigorous standard, it's easy to construct marketing communications, for *each* part of *each* thing you do either helps get the prospect to act NOW . . . or it doesn't.

The only way the overall communication can conceivably succeed in getting the prospect to act NOW is if all its parts move the prospect to act NOW. Sounds reasonable, doesn't it?

But if this is so sensible, why don't most marketers (who presumably do want their prospects to act NOW) do what they can to stimulate this necessary action?

To illustrate my point I've selected a flyer that's just arrived, a self-mailer. Produced by the National Community Education Association for its 1988 National Educational Institute, its purpose is to sign people up as exhibitors. Fair enough. Now let's examine the first page and a half of its copy to see if *each* word, *each* sentence, *each* paragraph gets you to do what the marketer wants you to do and what is presumably in your own best interests. In short, is NCEA presenting words, or spurring action? You be the judge.

(panel 1) "Exhibit And Advertising Information

1988 National Educational Institute
June 1-3, 1988
Hyatt Regency, Ohio Center
Columbus, OH

Cosponsored by:

National Community Education Association
American Association for Adult and Continuing Education (three other organizations)

Critical Issues
for Educators
and Trainers

Successful Job Transitions

(panel 2) An Invitation

You are cordially invited to display and advertise at the 1988 National Educational Institute on SUCCESSFUL JOB TRANSITIONS: CRITICAL ISSUES FOR EDUCATORS AND TRAINERS, June 1-3, 1988 in Columbus, Ohio. This is your opportunity to participate in a major national effort to improve the skills of educators and trainers who work with adults in job transition."

It goes on, but I think you get the drift.

As you consider this material, ask yourself these questions:

- Does the marketer give you one benefit after another that gets you excited about investing your money in this service?
- Does he talk about himself, or talk about you?
- Is there an incentive for acting NOW?

- Is the marketer using words to motivate you or is he just droning on? Is he telling? Or selling?
- Is the marketer using headlines to bring home the benefits to you? Or are the headlines dull?
- Is the marketer using emphasizing devices to drive home key client-centered points?

By now, you know the answers to these questions, don't you? And when you do, you realize how far the marketer in this case has strayed from his prospect's interest, and his own.

The purpose of this chapter is to examine several other key constituents of marketing communications. To make sure that *everything* you present has but a single objective: getting the prospect to act NOW!

With this in mind, how do you feel about the opening line of the document above: "Exhibit And Advertising Information." These are just words. They come from no one and are directed to no one. They present facts but do not ask for action. Because they focus on the seller, they are selfish. And they are dull, dull, dull.

Selling, dear reader, starts from the very first word, of the very first line, on the very first page that your prospect sees. For only when the prospect is sold on the benefits of what you're selling do the facts assume any relevance whatsoever.

By this measure, the headline of NCEA's brochure is wrong. And so is EVERY WORD on its opening panel. There is not a single benefit on the first *page*, much less the first line, for the prospect. And yet the marketer is interested in having the prospect invest in exhibit space!

Your Client-Centered Sales Message Begins Where the Prospect's Eye First Alights

Whenever you first expect your prospect to look is where your benefit-rich sales message begins. Now, on the NCEA brochure (a self-mailer) there are actually two logical possibilities for the prospect to look first: on the panel with the mailing label and on the panel with the copy I've quoted above. Either is a possibility. Both, then, must have strong client-centered marketing messages. Let's start with the Mailing Panel or Envelope Message.

One of the many hot debates among people in the direct reponse field is what, if anything, you should include on the mailing panel or envelope to stimulate prospect action. I think you can imagine on which side of this raging debate I firmly plant myself. But in case you cannot, I'm going to give you hints. Let's look at real mail from real people. Again, as we discuss these examples, remember: real people spent real money sending these materials in an attempt to get me to spend my money on what they're selling. Did what they decide to do help make the sale, or did it not? That is the only question worth considering.

Here are some examples for your consideration:

1. On the mailing panel of a self-mailing brochure from Cosmoenergetics Publications, San Diego, CA:

"Announcing the pre-publication release of the new book:

SEX, PLEASURE, AND POWER: How To Emerge Spiritually Without Going Nuts."

2. On the envelope of a mailing from *Changing Times* magazine:

"The favor of a reply is requested."

3. On the envelope of a mailing from Broadcast Interview Source, Washington, DC:

"Are You Getting Enough Media Exposure?"

4. On the envelope of a mailing from GBC, Northbrook, IL:

"How to make your company
(and yourself) look good."

5. On the envelope of a mailing from *Foundation News* magazine, Washington, DC:

Nothing at all.

Let's look at each of these.

1. Cosmoenergetics at least understands that they should be using all their available space for marketing purposes. But they have failed to focus on the prospect, deciding instead to focus on themselves.

   Now, do you suppose the person getting the Cosmoenergetics mailer gives two hoots and a holler that they have a new book out? Not likely! What that prospect wants to know is, "What have you got for me?" The answer, dear reader, is not a product, not a service. But a benefit. Presumably this marketer has a benefit. Why, then, have they locked it away? For the benefit isn't there. Nor is there a benefit in the book's title, either.

   The mailing panel fails because it talks about a feature not a client-centered benefit. And doesn't answer the "What's in it for me? What do I have to do to get it?" questions. And certainly if one were promoting a product with sex, pleasure and power there ought to be something there for the prospect, no?

2. *Changing Times* is relying on human curiosity to get its envelope opened. Its marketer is gambling that you'll say "Who's writing me? Why do they want the favor of my reply? What am I supposed to be replying about?"

   Personally, I didn't think much of this opening; I let the letter sit without being opened for several months and only retained it because I was writing this book. Ordinarily, such letters get the most cursory of inspections.

   What appalled me, however, was the fact that the marketer had overlooked a much stronger offer that he decided to put at the *foot* of the first page of the copy. There I learned I could get a free trial subscription (it didn't say how long) and receive their latest Money Management Guide Book. Although the marketer didn't bother to tell me what kinds of benefits I could get from either (a significant flaw), here at least was a stronger opening than "The favor of a reply is requested."

   This marketer forgot that people get lots of subscription offers and that the trick, as always, is to sell the benefits you get with the subscription, not the subscription itself. And while people certainly buy favors all the time (don't ask me to go into too much detail about this, please), they are not greatly motivated by "the favor of a reply," the limpest of dishrags.

3. Broadcast Interview Source seems to know that an envelope message is important. It just doesn't know how to create one.

I ask you, are people interested in "media exposure" (whatever that may mean), or are they interested in selling products by using *free* time on radio and television. Put this way, the answer's obvious, isn't it? No one wants to be "exposed" on the media (a terrible choice of word, by the way). That conjures up visions of that media pitbull Dan Rather. This marketer has forgotten that many people are afraid of approaching the media for fear they will run into a character assassin like Morton Downey, Jr. This terrifies them.

What they really want is to sell more products and services by getting free time . . . that others have to pay for. And this is what Broadcast Interview Source should concentrate on, because this is what it can deliver.

Besides, a question is really dangerous. What if the prospect says, "Yes. I'm getting enough." *Then* where's the marketer? Lost. Irrevocably lost. Even turning this question into a statement helps: "You aren't getting enough media exposure!" It still isn't good, but it is better.

4. GBC knows that people are interested in how to do things and that "how to" headlines can be effective. But where's the substantial benefit in its feeble line "How to make your company (and yourself) look good"? It just isn't there.

A line like this is too general. It could apply to anyone and thus isn't sufficiently particular to the one person it must apply to and motivate: your prospect. When you see this line, you wonder "What's in this for me? Why doesn't the marketer just tell me what he's got to say? Why is he making me reach for the information? I'm busy. And this irritates me."

As with some of these other marketing communications, GBC has the basis for a *much* stronger opening, but you have to dig deep into their material to find out what it is: a free copy of a booklet entitled "How To Create A Best Selling Presentation." I don't like the title of this premium; (do you think the prospect wants to create "a best selling" presentation, or a presentation that gets his prospect to buy now?)

Be careful. These are not the same. When you say "a best", you're asking your prospect to figure out what you mean. When you supply the benefit yourself, you're telling the prospect what he can have and selling him on doing what's necessary to get it. I hope you see the crucial difference between these statements.

Your prospect may well take fast action to acquire the secrets of getting *his* prospects to buy what they're selling. This is, after all, far more attractive than merely getting a booklet, even if it's free, the benefits of which they don't know — and haven't been sold on. But I say this: even without the backbone of those client-centered benefits (which GBC doesn't bother to use to spur immediate action), the free booklet is *still* a stronger opening than the ineffectual line "How to make your company (and yourself) look good."

5. *Foundation News* decides to say nothing, like so many marketers. It gambles (for that's what it is) that the prospect will open a blank envelope saying "Foundation News" (or anything else), merely because they get it. Frankly, I don't believe this.

This marketer reckons that a blank envelope is more powerful than a client-centered, benefit-rich message. That such an envelope looks more "professional." And that its prospect will open the envelope because it doesn't have the look of "junk mail", where messages predominate.

But listen up! People know the difference between an envelope with a check, a personal letter, and a piece of direct response advertising. Why, even the texture of the paper and the way the letter is addressed are different. A blank envelope can't fool them. And if the prospect doesn't get past the envelope, whatever's inside is an utter waste.

Now, what do you think? The second paragraph of the first page of the *Foundation News* letter has the basis for a much stronger opening. It's this offer: "May we send you the very next issue — without cost or obligation?" And in the second paragraph of the letter itself (the fourth paragraph on the page) are these words, "And I'm willing to send you a $5.00 copy of FOUNDATION NEWS at our expense to show you what I mean!"

This offer, of course, is focused on the product, not the benefit the prospect gets from using it, the same problem that GBC has. But, while weak, it is *still* an offer. And a blank envelope cannot begin to compete in power and persuasiveness with the prospect of a $5.00 free copy. Yet this marketer decided to gamble that a blank envelope would be a sufficient "sell" to induce the prospect to read on. I strongly disagree. A benefit-rich, client-centered offer is always stronger than a blank piece of paper. Always.

You must remember this one significant fact: if your opening doesn't induce the prospect to read on, your opening has failed. And if your opening fails, it is considerably less likely that your prospect will continue. And if he doesn't continue, *all* you have done to get him to this point — the time you have spent, the energy, the money — is lost. Entirely lost. You must keep the prospect interested! You must keep him stimulated! You must keep him persuaded that it is very much in his interest to stay communicating with you and to keep paying attention to what you have to say! Nothing else matters. Because once the prospect breaks the thread that keeps you together, you have both lost!!!

Let me conclude this section on Mailing Panel and Envelope Copy thus:

- Keep this copy brief. One or two lines is sufficient.
- Don't present the product or service. Present the reason the prospect should act NOW!
- Don't write copy that could be used to sell any product or service. Use copy that is relevant only to what you are selling . . . and to whom you are selling it.
- Don't try to be humorous or clever. Save that for your friends. The immediate objective is to convince a prospect you've got something for him, something that's worth acting immediately to get.
- Make the benefit believable. If it appears too good to be true, most prospects know it isn't.

Using Headlines To Move The Prospect Towards Immediate Action

Not surprisingly the rules I've just written for envelope and mailing panel copy also apply to headlines. For what is this other copy, after all, but a version of a headline, a line that will be read first?

Think for a minute. What do you think a headline should do?

- Your headline must draw attention. A headline fails unless it captures the attention of your prospect.

- Your headline must scream to your prospect, "Hey, bub, I'm talking to you." Headlines let the prospect know you've got something for him, that you are talking to him.

- Your headline must deliver a complete, immediately understandable message. Headlines are part of the Internal Message. They let the prospect know in no uncertain terms what you've got is for him . . . and leave him in no doubt that it's important.

- Your headline must pull the prospect into the copy, must compel him to read on, getting more fillips for action with every word he sees.

These are the purposes of headlines. Do yours match up?

Or are you using headlines like these from Coronet/MTI Film & Video, Deerfield, IL? Here's one: "Sexual Harassment." Here's another: "Ethics." And a third: "Service." Surely you must now see that these are just words, passive, unfulfilling words, not client-centered benefits. They're dull, pointless, undescriptive and hang in the air like a verbal blob. Certainly they motivate no one to do anything and place the full burden on the prospect. "Here," the marketer says, "you figure out what we mean by these words, and you figure out what we want you to do with them."

Eight Different Kinds Of Headlines You Can Use To Motivate Your Prospects

There are at least eight different kinds of headlines you can use to motivate your prospects to respond. They include:

- Direct
- Indirect
- Command
- Question
- Reason-why
- Testimonial
- News
- How-to

Let's look at each, always remembering the job of the headline is to show people you have something for them, induce them to read on, and, if possible, take immediate action to acquire what you're selling.

• **Direct Headlines**

Here you put your proposition squarely to your prospect in blunt, client-centered language. There's nothing subtle about this kind of headline. "Save $5 on designer shirts through Thursday only." This is an ideal format for announcing limited-time-only specials where the duration is as important a motivator as the price.

• **Indirect**

This kind of headline arouses your curiosity. It intrigues you so that you read the remainder of the copy to find out what's really going on, what's really in it for you. Here's such a headline from an ad in *Online*, the CompuServe magazine. "It's healthy to stay up all night." This ad is promoting the Medline database and new lower prices if you use it after 6 p.m. Why is it healthy to stay up all night? Read on, the headline tempts, and find out for yourself.

• **Command**

Command headlines tell the prospect what to do.

Here's one that summarizes the genre: "Join", the headline of an ad from The Condominium Association, Framingham, MA.

The imperative verb is the essence of command headlines. Another famous one is Zola's immortal headline "*J'Acuse.*"

Here you leave nothing to the imagination. You are the generalissimo; the prospects are your troops. You command them to do what is in their own best interests.

• **Question**

Question headlines are very popular. But they can easily be misused. To make this format work, you've got to focus on the prospect by asking a question that interests him sufficiently to read the answer. Boring question = a failed marketing piece.

The best kinds of question headlines are involvement-headlines. By answering them the prospect gets involved with your marketing and is well on his way to becoming your next customer. A famous illustration of this kind of headline is: "Do you make these mistakes in English?" It was designed to sell a language improvement program.

Beware of self-centered questions: "Do you know what we're up to these days?" Who cares? As you surely now know, the prospect is always self-centered. Which means the question headline must be focused on him, too. Always.

• Reason-Why

Here you tell the prospect there are specific reasons why he should act NOW to acquire what you're selling:

- "Three reasons why you should invest in municipal bonds before April 15th."

Reason-why headlines — which do not have to use the words "reason why" by the way — are effective because they are packed with facts: specific numbers and dates. They suggest you know what you're talking about and should be listened to. That you are the expert and want to help your prospect achieve his objective. "Listen up," you're saying, "to the facts. With them you can achieve your desire."

• Testimonial

Here you get your customers to sell for you by exciting prospects about the benefits they've received. And which they can get, too, if only they do something. The best testimonial headlines focus on both the benefits the prospect can acquire — and answer the reluctance the prospect may have about taking action to get them.

"I never thought I'd win the sweepstakes either. But I have 50,000 good reasons I'm glad I entered!"

• News

These headlines present the prospect with something new — something that makes his life better than other things he can get.

Sadly, too many news headlines focus on the new things themselves, the actual products and services. This is a mistake. Remember: lead with the benefit, follow with the feature. Your prospects are more interested that they can get something better (more of a benefit for them) than they are in the new thing that will give it to them.

Thus don't say, "Mileage Plus Adds Royal Viking Line". Remember, the prospect isn't interested in either Mileage Plus or the Royal Viking Line *per se*, but in the benefits he gets by using the former and experiencing the latter. That's why United Airlines was (nearly) right to headline a recent promotion "Mileage Plus and Royal Viking Line Bring You Exciting, All-Luxury Cruise Awards." Note: I say "nearly" because the marketer forgot that people want luxury cruises, not "cruise awards". It's a phrase that sounds pompous and official.

There's a lesson here whose importance cannot be overstated. All the words you select must work together. Most people go on cruises to relax, not for excitement. Hence a diction mismatch. Same with "exciting" and "luxury". I can think of lots of things that luxury is, but exciting isn't one of them. And while a cruise may be luxurious, a "cruise award" certainly isn't.

Let's rewrite the United headline, then, like this: "Our luxury Caribbean cruises for you and someone you love come faster than ever with the new Mileage Plus-Royal Viking Line plan." Remember: lead with benefits (the luxurious cruise), follow with features (the plan).

- **How-To**

Last, but not least, we come to the perennial favorite, how-to. These headlines engage the prospect's interest by promising to reveal important information he can use to achieve his objective. "How to lose weight and still eat what you like!". "How to get free time on radio and television to sell products and services." Or like the Center for Entrepreneurial Management, New York City: "How to Write a Winning Business Plan to Raise Debt and Equity Capital in Hard Times."

If your prospect wants to achieve what the headline presents, then he'll read the copy that follows. And if he doesnt, he won't. It's as simple as that.

Most Marketing Pieces Don't Use Any Headlines At All — For Shame!

Marketing specialists will argue about whether one kind of headline is preferable to another. About whether I've improved the Mileage Plus headline above, or not. It is, after all, in the nature of experts to quibble. We get enormous pleasure out of doing so; out of deciding the relative merits of one kind of headline over another. So be it. On one thing, however, we are all agreed: there must be a headline, whatever its sort. And by headline, I mean words that induce the prospect to stop in his tracks and start reading what we have presented to lure him into the text that follows.

What is sad is that most marketing communications have no headlines of any variety whatsoever. They merely start. And then, after awhile, they stop. They do not grab the prospect's attention and systematically do what they can to hold it. They do not, in short, sell.

The following were presented as headlines. But are they?

- "Small Press & Magazine Expo '88. The 2nd Annual Conference and Exposition for Small Book and Magazine Publishers", Meckler Corporation, Westport, CT.

- "Circulation Supplies", Steel City Corporation, Youngstown, OH.

- "Sunburst 1988 Career Education. Videocassettes and Filmstrips," Sunburst Communications, Pleasantville, NY.

Headlines? Bah, humbug! These are just words. And marketer-centered words, at that. They have *nothing* to do with the prospect. And certainly do nothing to draw us into the copy that follows. They offer no benefits and no inducements to read on. They are passive and dull, the products of arid imaginations . . . and of a failure to recognize that these documents are supposed to persuade real people to do things.

Lamentably, this is the way most marketing communications are nowadays. Unfocused. Pointless. Selfish. Telling facts. Not selling prospects. Examples like these — and sadly I say these are now the norm — say as clearly as anything can that the marketer places the burden of marketing on the prospect, either because that marketer is lazy and uninformed, or just plain incompetent.

Don't do this. Don't just write words. *Use* words. When you face the matter of writing your headline, ask yourself:

- What do I want to communicate to my prospect?
- What benefit have I got for him?
- What do I have to induce him to respond now?
- Have I written a headline that will motivate him to act?
- Am I talking about myself, my products or services, or am I talking to my prospect about himself, and what he wants to achieve?
- Am I really talking to my prospect, or am I talking to everyone in general?
- Have I made the headline interesting?
- Is my headline about action, or is it passive, an inert lump of words that has nothing to do with movement?
- Do the words I'm using in my headline match up with the other words I'm using. Or do I have mismatched, incongruous language?

In short, have I thought about the headline, what I want it to say, and what I wish it to accomplish, or have I just written something because I had to? Because if that's what you're doing, don't do anything at all. That result is woeful, indeed, and lets the prospect know you care nothing for him, and everything for yourself.

Opening Your Marketing Documents

Too many marketers write copy as if they had gone to the Robert Browning School of Marketing. "Grow old along with me," they seem to say to their prospects. "The best is yet to be." Instead of presenting the strongest possible reasons for immediate action immediately, they withhold them, expecting their prospects to read every word of every marketing communication to find, at the end, the gold they should have had from the first. As poetry, of course, Browning's sentiments are inspirational; as marketing, they are repellent.

Which is why you must give your very considerable attention to just how you begin all your marketing communications.

To energize you, let's walk through a marketing cover letter, the kind of letter you're almost certain to be creating to sell your products and services. You already know how to create mailing panel and envelope copy and headlines. Now it's time to look at the copy itself.

A Helpful Prospect-Centered Diagram

Start by putting your strongest benefit and reason for acting at the top, in a place the prospect will look first. Since biblical times, and beyond, the right has always been the most important side. So use it to connect with your prospect. Thus:

> *In the upper right hand corner, place your strongest prospect benefit and reason for immediate action. Put this copy in bold, or in italics, or put it in a box. Or otherwise set it off so the prospect cannot fail to pay attention to it. Remember, if this copy is unconvincing, it gives the prospect a very good reason not to dig deeper into the copy. That is why what you do here is so important.*

In real life, we all know the crucial significance of first impressions, of those critical few seconds when we encounter something — or someone — new. Do we really give the benefit of the doubt? Do we search for reasons to like? Or do we judge, often finally and irrevocably? Of course you know. And if you do this day-in, day-out, why should your prospects be any different? That's why you must make this opening brilliantly client-centered. Because if you don't, you will not have the chance to sell anything at all.

Is this what Buying Office Products, Austin, TX, has done in a self-mailer flyer?

"Buying Office Products Premiers!

The office products market has a dynamic new arrival with the Premier Issue of Buying Office Products. Your copy of the February 1988 issue should be reaching your desk within the next few days, introducing you to the magazine that makes buying (and selling!) office products easy."

This copy constitutes their crucial opening. But that's just the point: it doesn't open. It just starts. Do not mistake a client-centered opening with just the

beginning of a document. They are not the same. The former begins —
immediately! — to hammer home benefits. Reasons for acting. Offers. Things
that are important to the prospect. The latter . . . well, you can see what the latter
does when you review this uninteresting effort. What do I care if they are
premiering a publication unless I am clear what the substantial benefits are for
me . . . including the free copy stuffed with advantageous information?

Once you've presented this information, DON'T STOP!

Create A Salutation That Isn't A Cliché

Marketing communications shouldn't start with the salutation. Lovers thoughout
the ages have known this, hence "SWAK". (Remember this from days gone by,
letters "sealed with a kiss"?) And when you get to the salutation, it should be
interesting, not another mindless cliché.

"Dear Friend:"; "Dear Colleague:"; "Dear Collector:". Must we always use
openings like this? Openings that can't possibly convince the person we're
trying to persuade that we are, indeed, a friend, a colleague, or even a collector?
Besides, look at the punctuation (taken right from several examples at my
fingertips.) How many friends do you know who write you using a colon, that
quintessentially official punctuation? Personally, I don't know any. I've never
received a truly friendly letter with that kind of punctuation, and I warrant you
haven't either. Yes, even your punctuation must be client-centered, and that
means (in this instance) commas, and not colons. Hear and obey!

As I've said before, don't use words merely because you have to. Use words in
ways that get your prospects' attention and *compel* them to read deeper into what
you've sent them. Hence:

"Dear Fellow Consultant In Search Of New Clients," or

"Dear Newsletter Editor Who Needs Quality Articles . . . And Wants To Spend
As Little As Possible To Get Them".

Are these salutations long? Yes, they are longer than the garden variety "dear
friend" that bores us silly. But the length is no problem . . . so long as the prospect
pays attention. And pay attention he will, so long as you focus on the objective
he wants to achieve. Again, I'm talking about benefit. Now put that benefit right
in the salutation.

Don't be afraid that you've never seen anyone else do this. Most people are sheepish and follow the leader. Which is why they turn out copy of unrelieved dullness . . . and selfishness. You must be different. You must focus on the prospect in whatever you're writing. Including the salutation. Cut through the conventions. Let the prospect know, in every way you can, that you can give him what he wants: new clients, quality articles without cost, whatever he wants. Thrust home a consistent, simple, client-centered message. And don't let the worn-out epistolary conventions (which surely have nothing to do with marketing) get in the way.

Now, Into Your Client-Centered Opening Paragraph

See how much client-centered copy has already been written, even before we get to the opening line of your letter? It appears on the mailing panel, in headlines (yes, a letter can indeed have a headline), and in the upper right hand corner. Even in the salutation. Oh, yes, long before the opening line of the "official" copy, your prospect knows what's in all this for him.

Indeed, he may already have skipped ahead to the response coupon . . . or called your 800-number . . . or placed his order. For you see, if your offer is a strong one and your benefits have been well presented, your prospect doesn't need to read everything. The right moment for the prospect to act is when the prospect is ready to act . . . anytime, that is, when he's been persuaded that what you've told him is in his best interest. AND THAT MAY BE FROM THE VERY FIRST SENTENCE HE'S READ. So give him what he needs . . . as early as possible.

And certainly do so in your opening line and paragraph.

When you write your opening line (and the paragraph that contains it) think of these two words: BENEFIT and ANXIETY. One or the other of them is your motif, that idea that provides the essential structure for your opening. Do you want to motivate your prospect by piling on one benefit after another, by motivating him (as some vulgar marketers say) by greed? By all that he'll get from you and what you're selling? Or do you wish to motivate him (for you see, this prospect must always be motivated to take action) by anxiety (or, as others say, fear)?

Of course, you can decide to use both in your copy . . . but you must open with one, just one. But why these? Because the acquisition of benefit or the avoidance and quelling of fear are the two major reasons why prospects act. Always have been. Always will be.

And since action is what you want — motivating the prospect to do something that will result in his having a benefit or avoiding fear — you must use them.

Now let's take a look at one or two openings of documents that real people (I must continually stress this, for occasionally skeptical readers think I invent these illustrations) have wasted real money on. Why? Because they forgot the basics of client-centered marketing and the need to induce prospects to take immediate action. Take these crucial opening paragraphs from three letters sent by the following companies:

Microsoft Corporation, Redmond, WA

"Because of the tremendous enthusiasm you show when you talk about Microsoft Excel to your friends, it's become an enormously popular spreadsheet program."

Transition Nutrition, Inc., New York City

"As members of a greater network of people making this planet a better place to live, my wife and I would like to be the first to introduce you to an exciting new product, MATOL KM."

Foxworth Publications, Coraopolis, PA

"My name is Taryn Foxworth, president of Foxworth Publications. During my dealings with mail order, I have found a badly needed publication that is apparently nonexistent: a directory of mail order dealers and a description of their publications, products, or services."

Now ask yourself, do these openings:

- focus on you, or the seller?
- persuade you that the seller has a benefit for you, (or that you face a terrible fear or anxiety)?
- make you feel the seller is more interested in you than himself?

Or do these openings:

- make you feel the seller wants to sell you something?
- that the seller is interested in himself, and not you?
- that the seller has products and services, but not necessarily benefits for you?

I think you can see for yourself.

A Closer Look At Each Opening

Microsoft is saying, in effect, "We're popular and rich." Is such an opening calculated to make you want to help them more (which is what they want)?

Transition Nutrition (not a great name for a company, by the way) also leads off with self-praise: "Look, folks, we're planet savers. That's important . . . we're important. Pay attention." Not, I think, a great opening.

And Foxworth Publications? Well, I find this opening rather incoherent; it needs editing, badly ("During my dealings with mail order . . .", indeed!) Worse than all this, however, is the lack of client-centered benefits. It would have been better if Taryn (and her other colleagues above) had focused exclusively on the prospect, immediately answering the prospect's insistent question, "What's in it for me?" Reading these paragraphs you just don't know. And that is why these paragraphs don't work.

Think Benefit (or, if you've selected this route, Anxiety). And then motivate. Pile one benefit upon another; one anxiety upon another. Until you have really captivated your prospect.

Think of each line as a Benefit (or Anxiety) Line. Think of each paragraph as a Benefit (or Anxiety) paragraph. And lay on the motivational information thick and fast.

To make this work, as you should already know, you must have the benefits and anxieties, and you should have prioritized them . . . so you are ready to lead with the one that's most important, most motivating. Thus:

You get this.

And this.

And this.

And this.

And then you get this.

Or:

You fear this.

And this.

And this.

And this.

And you also fear this.

Now you are making your case. Now you are building your argument. Now you are truly motivating another human being. Whom you have grabbed because you focused on his focus: himself.

Cash copy does not meander. It thrusts. It compels. It moves. Because it has a purpose: motivating action. And if it does not succeed in so motivating the prospect, it has failed. Whatever it has said. However beautifully it has been presented. You must understand this and make this understanding the basis for every attempt you make to connect with your prospect.

Punctuating Devices

Marketers who approach the business of motivating people as if they were writing a high school English composition invariably fail to use crucial punctuating devices. Devices that break up the copy and reinforce critical marketing messages.

You already know about some of these devices, the indentations, bullets, underlinings, and all the rest. Now you must use them, just as you use seasonings in the kitchen. For that's what they are, the seasoning of good copy.

After you've written three benefit-rich paragraphs, focusing exclusively on the prospect (during which you may not even have named your product or service . . . but have certainly focused on what the prospect will get by using it), it's time to punctuate. To reinforce significant marketing messages and break up your copy.

Use a box. Run it right throught the middle of your copy. Cram this box with additional client-centered information: about your offer and its duration, or a crucial benefit the prospects gets by acting NOW.

This box need not be directly connected with what precedes or follows it. But it must be packed with at least one item of interest to your prospect.

By putting it in a box — or using another emphasizing device — you are saying to the prospect, "Hey, look. Here's something REAL IMPORTANT for you. Pay attention. Look at how much you get."

You must remember, all words are not equal. Some are more important than others. And words that describe benefits and offers and duration are some of the most significant of all. Don't forget to include your phone number in this box. Remember: give people what they need so when they're persuaded they can take immediate action. Your job is to persuade . . . and to make it easy for your prospects to take action. This box can help you achieve both objectives.

Note: try to keep this box to a single paragraph. Don't overemphasize. This box, for instance, is too long, has too many words for a real marketing situation. Keep what you emphasize short.

Don't hesitate to do the same with another punctuating device, the testimonial. Personally, I adore testimonials. I love getting them, and I love using them. They lend a very human touch to my marketing — and convince people to take action . . .so they can have what others like them have and are already benefitting from.

So, use a testimonial box . . . or insert.

Run a testimonial (**why not in bold?**) right in the middle of the
text. Don't mention it in the sentence that precedes or follows
it. Just drop it in . . . those good words that say, "Hey, look at
what I got when I used this product or service. I felt nervous
about taking the risk, too. But am I ever glad I did!" And make
sure this is signed by a real person from a real place.

Or run the testimonial in a box.

Just remember: if you've restated your offer in a box, you can't put the
testimonial in a box, or vice versa. Too many boxes . . . just like too many inserts
. . . reduce the emphasis. Which is just what you don't want to happen.

What's happening here?

You're selling. *Not telling.* You've giving your prospect reason after reason
after reason to buy NOW. If these reasons don't convince him, no rendition of
mere facts will. Ever.

And you must keep on selling throughout the whole of your marketing
document, whatever it is. Your energy must never flag. Nor the necessary
enthusiasm that gets the prospect's blood rushing and his heart beating faster
with one insistent word now . . . now . . . NOW!

Restate Your Benefits

Do you get everything that people tell you the first time, even if it's for your own
good? Of course not. And neither do your prospects. Which is why you must
restate your benefits.

You are not obliged to use a single benefit just once and never use it again. You
are obliged to get the prospect to take action. And either you have sufficient
benefits to do that . . . or you must reuse, that is restate, your benefits so that he
does.

But don't use the same words. Use different words to make the same point. Thus,
Take 1: "Don't forget. When you order 3 of my Special Reports . . . they cover
everything from what it takes to write brochures that get your customers to
respond faster . . . to getting free time on radio and tv stations to sell your
products and services. — you can select a 4th one FREE — a $4 retail value."

Take 2 — "Act now. You can profit from my Special Reports fast — they're sent First Class the day you order. And, of course, when you order any three, you can select a 4th with my compliments. And there are over 30 to choose from."

See?

The same offer, different words, and, I might say, seasoned with different benefits.

Side Two

If you have not managed to put all your sales reasons on a single side of the page that includes your offer, testimonials and one benefit after another, don't worry. I rarely can either. Just continue onto the other side of the sheet.

Here, as before, you continue to present the benefits the prospect gets by acting NOW, to restate and represent the offer, and to punctuate the main copy with emphasizing devices like testimonial boxes. As before, each line, each paragraph is about the prospect and what he gets from you.

In this way you make a very convincing case. Don't blow it now. Though the main text of your letter is finished, there is still more to do.

Sign Off Warmly

How you sign your letter is very important. Again, you want to avoid the cliché, the "sincerely" close. Everybody does it. And if everybody does anything, that thing soon loses its impact. And impact is what all marketing communications must have, even the shortest. So sign off with a difference; sign off by reminding the prospect what you can deliver. "Yours for more clients"; "yours for the free time you need to sell more of your products and services on radio and television"; "yours for the benefit you want." Yes, they are different. And being different, they are more likely to be read. How many times have you really focused on the close of a letter that read "sincerely yours"? Which is exactly the problem.

Now Don't Forget The Postscript

Marketers generally agree that the postscript is one of the most significant parts of a letter because it is heavily read. Don't waste it like Foxworth Publications did: "P.S. Any questions we haven't answered, feel free to write to me at the address above." This line is obvious, trite . . . and dull. And doesn't reinforce the thing the marketer wants the prospect do to. But that's just what a postscript is for: to make one last attempt to get the prospect to take immediate action.

So, restate your offer. Push your chief reason for taking immediate action. Cite your prime benefit. Or the fear that you're certain your prospect wishes to avoid. In short, emphasize what is important to the prospect and what will get him to take action. This is the only reason for the letter as a whole, and it is certainly the only significant reason for the postscript. Don't forget it!

And when you are finished?

Why, then, you go back and use all your other emphasizing devices to create the Internal Message. Because there isn't a marketing document going that couldn't be improved . . . and strengthened . . . through the devices that focus the prospect squarely on the essentials of what you're telling him and what he gets by taking action. So, when you're finished with Letter 1, you must immediately return to the text and, with the consummate artistry of the marketer, use it as the basis for Letter 2, your Internal Message, emphasizing all that's significant to the prospect.

And where in all this is there space for telling about your product or service? For the facts about what it's made from or how it works, how long it takes to get it, or anything else that constitutes an essential feature. If these items have not been transformed into benefits that belong here, why, then, they do not go in this letter. They go in a separate marketing piece, such as a fact sheet or brochure. Which is why many marketers rightly say, "The letter sells. The brochure tells." And while the latter is important, the former is crucial.

Last Words

I hope you now see that *every* line in *every* marketing document, however long or short, either works for you in getting the prospect to take action, or works against you as a waste of your time and money. Client-centered as you are, you must assess your marketing communications in the most calculating and cold blooded fashion. Ask of every line and every paragraph one thing and one thing only: "Does this help motivate the prospect to take immediate action?" And if the answer is no, then it must be reworked until it does, or dropped altogether as failing to reach your objectives.

If all marketers — if you! — would use this standard to review what they're about to bring to their prospects' attention, the drawing power of all marketing communications would improve dramatically. But the point is (and this is important to you when you begin to do things better), all marketers will not take the time to scrutinize, and then improve, the marketing communications they use. *They* will continue to bring forth materials that are at once selfish, boring, passive and beside the point. You won't. Because you will have learned a crucial Lant axiom: "In marketing — as in life itself — everything counts." Everything.

Understand this and you cannot fail to persuade prospects to become buyers.

Chapter 14

In Which You Discover Certain Critical Information About How To Get Your Prospects To Respond To Your Flyers, Brochures, Proposals, Ads, Postcards, Annual Reports, Media Kits, Free Client Newsletters, And Catalogs

Now let's continue by looking at the major kinds of marketing communications you'll create. This chapter is here because I wanted to give you tips about each major format to make sure that when you use it you remember you are using it for one purpose and one purpose only: to motivate a real person to take immediate action. Otherwise, I frankly see no point in your wasting time and money to create any marketing format at all.

A Cautionary Tale

Once upon a time before they retained me, one of my clients, a social service organization, went to great expense to create an annual report. Why they had created this document no one could or — later — would say. Everybody else had an annual report . . . so they must have an annual report, too. This was their first mistake.

Persuaded by a zealous printing sales representative that an agency of their eminence must have a multitude of such reports, the executive director went ahead and ordered thousands of them. A garage full, in fact. Just who was to get them . . . and why, had never been decided. But what of that? Eminent organizations have annual reports of unsurpassed beauty . . . and so being eminent (or thinking itself so) this group must do the same.

This was over two years ago. Today the bulk of these reports, several thousand of them, still sit in the garage, silently accusing the decision-maker of ineptitude and profligacy.

Multiply this illustration by the millions upon millions of people who create marketing communications without going back to basic principles, and you find as glaring an example of waste as you're likely to see outside the Pentagon. If you have brochure you can't use . . . flyers that crashed . . . reports that were outmoded upon publication . . . why, then, you are contributing to this debacle. Resolve here and now that this will never happen to you again. Ever.

What You Need To Do Before Creating Any Marketing Communication

As you will learn in this chapter, if you have not already learned, before you create any document you must return to first principles. Ask yourself these questions before putting pen to paper, or fingers to the keyboard:

- Why am I creating this document?
- Whom am I creating it for?
- What's in this document for my prospect?
- What do I want this person to do?
- When do I want him to do it?

If these questions are not properly answered, the creation of any marketing document makes no sense at all.

I am going to assume that when you approach each of the following formats you ask yourself these questions and come up with precise answers to them. If you do, you can produce persuasive marketing materials. If you don't, you won't. It's as simple as that.

Creating Flyers That Soar
(Without Excess Baggage)

A flyer is a single sheet of paper, usually 8 1/2" by 11". Usually this sheet is intended to be used unfolded; folding it ordinarily results in its being termed a brochure. In any event, such communications are used for many purposes, including:

- announcing new books;
- promoting workshops and talk programs;
- marketing virtually any product or service.

Flyers are good to use because:

- they're inexpensive;
- they can be produced quickly, and
- updated immediately.

Because of the very ease and lack of expense with which they can be produced, too many people produce them without thought. A mistake. Whatever you intend to use to get another human to take immediate action should be thought through and given the benefit of your client-centered consideration.

Thus, to start with, remember that flyers are composed of these elements:

- a clear indication of whom you are talking to (your prospect;)
- a precise indication of what he gets, with most significant benefits first (what);
- an offer that compels immediate response (when);
- easy ways for the prospect to respond (how);
- information on where the prospect should respond (where).

These components MUST be present. Anything else is additional. Thus, write the "must" copy first; then see how much space you have left to add anything else. Remember, the objective is to secure an *immediate response*; not to bury the prospect in words . . . or facts.

You'll probably find it easiest to write the easy sections of this document first: information like where the prospect should send his order, how much he should send, by what date he should send it. There's no rule in creation that says you have to write a marketing communication from the beginning to the end. And there are very good reasons, if you are a less practiced marketer, why it makes sense to write the easy parts first.

Work from the easy parts . . . to the harder (benefit) parts.

In a flyer, as in all other marketing documents, you must give your attention to what you want the prospect to see first. Put yourself in your prospect's shoes as you consider this question. How will he receive your flyer? What will he see first?

These are very important questions, and you must know the answers. That's because where the prospect's eye first alights is where your selling argument begins. This is a decision you as a marketer cannot afford to abdicate. It is your responsibility to decide where the prospect's eye falls first . . . and your responsibility to make sure that when the eye is there it is filled with compelling reasons for immediate action . . . with benefits . . . or anxieties. And certainly with an offer.

As I write I am looking at a flyer whose author didn't consider these factors and so produced a piece of work that's both dreary and pointless.

Headed by the name of the publishing company, this one-sided 8 1/2" by 11" flyer features pictures of two book covers, the first for a volume entitled *Management Of Poisonous Snakebite* and the second for *First Aid For Snakebite*. Under each cover picture there is a write-up. A few lines of what is printed under the first will give you their flavor:

"This book describes what happens to the human snakebite victim and how the layman and the physician may prepare and handle this type of emergency."

As you see, this suffers from a host of marketing problems . . . problems that must be solved even within the limited space offered by the standard sized flyer . . . or that flyer is useless.

This kind of problem cannot occur if you ask yourself — at the very start of your project — what you want this flyer to accomplish and if you have provided all the incentive and information the prospect needs so that this objective can in fact be realized.

PROVIDING INFORMATION IS NOT AT ALL THE SAME THING AS
MOTIVATING ACTION. AND UNLESS YOU HAVE COMPELLED
IMMEDIATE ACTION, YOUR MARKETING PIECE FAILS.

Let's look at each significant section of the flyer in turn:

• **Who**

Your headline should clearly tell the reader, "Hey, friend, this is for you!"
Headlines are best utilized to let your reader know he is your prospect, the person
you can help. You must never leave the prospect in doubt that you're talking to
him. And he must know immediately. Your headline enables you to do this.

• **What**

Never, never, never let the prospect deduce the benefits. In the illustration
above, I'm guessing that a person who uses the author's techniques will recover
from snakebite. It's a reasonable assumption, given one of the books titles (*First
Aid For Snakebite*), but it's just that: an assumption. At no time does this
marketer state the benefit that accrues from using his methods. Instead he says,
"This is a book describing the first aid management of the person bitten by a
snake." But who cares about that? If I'm bitten and use this book, I want to know
I'm going to get well . . . not about first aid management. "Getting well" is the
benefit; "first aid management" is the feature. And the Lant rule? Lead with the
benefit, follow with the feature. Always.

• **When**

A flyer fails, indeed all marketing documents fail, unless there is an immediate
incentive for action . . . as there isn't here. It doesn't seem to matter to this
marketer if you use his methods now. Or later. Or, indeed, ever. But, of course,
we know that it does. You cannot put aside your responsibility as the marketer.
If you want your prospect to act NOW (and, of course, you do!), then you've got
to provide the reason for that immediate action. If you don't, you've failed as
a marketer . . . and your flyer fails as a client-centered piece of action-oriented
copy. Too bad for you . . . and your prospect.

• **How**

You've got to tell people how to get in touch with you . . . and you've got to make
getting in touch with you easy. Have you? Have you provided the 800-number?
The paid-response mechanism? The twenty-four hour order-center? If you

have, say so. But don't just end with this information. It's important that people get in touch with you. It's important both for them . . . and for you. So show them. Don't conclude your marketing communications with this information. Lead with it, along with your benefits. If your prospects don't feel the importance of action, they won't act. And it'll be your fault!

• **Where**

I can't tell you how many flyers I get without complete "where" details; without the names of organizations, complete addresses and other crucial follow-up facts. Don't print marketing materials without this information . . . even if you are designing different materials to be used together. Materials get separated all the time. You don't want to frustrate your prospect by forcing him to go looking for information you should have given him in the first place. Make sure these details are on *everything* . . . and always *obvious*.

The Internal Message

You're not quite finished yet . . . not by a long shot. Because you've got the Internal Message to create. (By the way, in the snakebite example, *nothing* is emphasized. Not a single word). Now go through and make the important words — like benefits, dates, special prices and the rest — stand out and be important. Don't let your prospect deduce importance. *Show* them what's important and make them *feel* it.

This is a real flyer.

Now do a test. The next time you get a flyer in the mail, or have one thrust into your hand, review it with these key principles in mind. Does it measure up? Or does it fail like the one I've been quoting from?

Are you finished? Maybe yes, maybe no. It depends on your lay-out, the size of your type, how much white space there is, and other design factors. But never let the design become the tail that wags the dog. Design is always subsidiary to copy. Always.

Once you've made sure your key points are included, then you can decide — with an eye on design variables — if you should add anything else . . . say a testimonial. But if you're smart you've already included that testimonial, which is, after all, nothing more than benefit copy between quotation marks.

Now you have a flyer that's a marketing document.

Your Product Or Service Brochure

Three things seem to represent "being in business" to most people: having a business bank account, a card . . . and a brochure. I must admit to being a bit of an exception in this regard, since I have only the first of these. But since others esteem such things highly, I must discuss the last two. Particularly since one of the standard marketing packages nowadays is composed of a two-page cover letter and a six-sided brochure. Whether you're selling a product or service, you'll probably be using this format, too.

To begin with, remember what a brochure is: the "tell 'em" portion of the sell 'em/tell 'em duo, with the cover letter being the former.

But don't get me wrong, the brochure is also a marketing document . . . which, by definition, means it has an objective: getting the reader to take immediate action to acquire what you're selling. Just because it has a different emphasis, then, doesn't mean that the brochure is passive. Not at all. It just approaches its task in a rather different way than the benefit-upon-benefit/pain-upon-pain cover letter . . . unless there is no such letter. In that case your brochure must combine both components. Let's look at it more closely.

The First Question To Answer: Is This Brochure Working Alone Or With Something Else?

How you approach the business of writing a persuasive brochure depends on how you intend to use it. Is this the only thing your prospects will receive from you? Then it must certainly contain the immediate reasons for acting and all the benefits. Or do you intend for your brochure to act along with other marketing materials . . . like a cover letter? In this case, the immediate reasons for acting (which may change, after all) can be featured in the letter . . . allowing other facts and benefits to be featured in the brochure.

My advice? Stay flexible. If you produce a single brochure that doubles as both letter and brochure or two separate documents, write and design what you're producing so you will always appear abreast of developments in your field. This means either producing materials in smaller quantities and/or designing what you produce so you can insert new information as circumstances dictate. Nothing is more irritating than a brochure that's out of date with crossed-out information and hand-written insertions. It's better to throw these materials away and start again!

Thus, before you can even write a brochure, you need answers to these questions:

- Does what I'm writing about — product or service — change often? If so, I need a format that accommodates these changes without stress. Or, I must reconcile myself to producing only smaller quantities of my marketing materials, or quickly disposing of those I do produce.

- Does just a part of what I'm writing about change often? If so, I need a format that will retain the basic information and enable me to add the new material without jettisoning my document. This suggests a format that allows for periodic updating inserts.

- Do I anticipate that my business will stay constant for the next six months? If so, a single brochure featuring all the information about what I'm selling should do nicely.

- How many people do I expect to send or give my brochure to? Production should be limited to only about 10% more than the number of people you realistically expect to connect with within six months, or a conservative period during which you expect no significant changes in your business. Most people produce documents and then consider the matter of disposing of them . . . which is why this business is so wasteful. You should consider the question of distribution first. And then produce the number of materials you need accordingly.

When You Intend Your Brochure To Act Alone

If your prospects will consider your brochure alone . . . without anything else . . . it must function as both the sell 'em and the tell 'em document. In function, then, it is no different from a flyer. Rereading the section on flyers will help you produce it.

What's important to remember is that each word, each line, each paragraph in this brochure must relate directly to the prospect and his interests . . . and give him a reason to act NOW.

Advance Tax Representation, Inc., Irvine, CA, forgot this in the brochure it designed. This brochure, a six-sided self-mailer, has as its headline: "A New Low Cost Service For Taxpayers. Prepaid Income Tax Audit Representation." Its secondary headline is: "Most professional representation services cost hundreds — even thousands of dollars. Advance Tax Representation, Inc. (ATR) has the sensible alternative which provides the same service at a fraction of the cost."

The mistake here, of course, is that ATR has decided to lead with features and follow with benefits, which is just what they shouldn't do.

Moreover, they give you no incentive for immediate action, instead asking you (on the third inside panel) to send for information, but not providing any impetus for doing so.

Does this make sense?

Of course not. Brochures that stand alone succeed because they get the prospect to respond immediately. Because they pile on benefit upon benefit and motivate by loading anxiety upon anxiety. *And* by making the prospect an offer he simply cannot refuse.

This is not what's happening here. And if this is the kind of brochure you create, you will not pass "Go", will not collect $200, and will certainly *never* have a monopoly.

Brochures That Work In Tandem With Other Marketing Communications

The key to producing brochures that get prospects to respond is to think first and then create. How will you be using these materials:

- in response to ads;
- at sales meetings;
- after face-to-face meetings?

Decide.

A brochure is not a placebo, something to be placed in a prospect's hand merely because they want "information." Yet this is how too many brochures are used . . . and wasted. A brochure either works alone to get a prospect to respond . . . or works with other marketing materials to get a prospect to respond. When? *Immediately.*

You don't want prospects to read. You want them to respond. When do you want them to respond? NOW! A brochure . . . no matter how beautiful and expensively produced . . . that doesn't ask for action and doesn't focus rigorously on the prospect is a brochure that has failed in its essential mission.

A Look At Someone Who Tried . . . And Failed

Is this what Appex Lunayach Systems Corp, Waltham, MA, did in its grand three-color brochure? You decide.

Its opening panel simply says "Appex Lunayach Systems." Nothing more. And shows a picture of a car and a telephone. That's it.

The inside panel begins with eight words, two each on bright blue lines: "The People. The Services. The Products. The Company."

These are the headlines of insert pages. The first body copy you see comes under the words "The Company" and reads: "Appex Lunayach Systems Corp. (ALS) specializes in integrated software products and consulting services for meeting the information requirements of the cellular telephone and personal communications industries."

And what, pray, is the best response to this? "SO WHAT!"

This marketer has forgotten that a brochure is not an excuse to throw facts at a prospect, burying him in weighty information, but an opportunity for further persuasion . . . persuasion that should result in the prospect's taking immediate action to do something. And what should this something be? In this case, to request an appointment, since ALS Systems are a substantial investment.

Thus, this marketer should have set as his objective motivating the ALS prospect to call for an appointment. When systems cost $50,000 and up, that's the most likely thing the prospect will do . . . in Round 1.

But there's no evidence in this brochure of any strategy . . . or any prospect-centered objective. Ladies and gentlemen, you can't leave it to the prospect to decide what to do. You can't let him deduce your motivation . . . or your strategy. *You* have got to set your strategy: what is it you want to happen? When is it you want this thing to happen? What are you going to do to make this thing happen? And then you've got to use your marketing commununciations . . . in this case this expensive brochure . . . to achieve these objectives. The very thing that hasn't happened here.

The *best* thing (and it's pretty feeble) that can be said about this marketing package is that it is so designed, with its removable inserts, that a single panel can be updated without consigning all its panels to the scrap heap. Beyond that there's precious little good to say about this very expensively produced piece.

What You've Got To Keep In Mind
When Producing Your Brochure

Whatever you put into your brochure must be related to the interests of the buyer. Thus, if you expect to talk about "The Company", it must be clear how this information relates to the prospect. Mere facts will never be good enough . . . because facts don't sell. The *significance* of these facts to the prospect does.

Thus, your brochure must be composed of client-centered information. And what do prospects want to know?

- What can your product do for me? List all the ways it can help and (then) crucial information about components or parts.
- What can your service do for me? What can I expect to get from you? Then tell me how you work.
- What will your people do for me? Then tell me who they are.
- What kinds of specific successes have you had in the past that you can reasonably expect to replicate for me? Don't tell me where you've been. Tell me what you've done and what difference it made. Be specific.

In short, we're back to the "lead with benefit, follow with feature" mantra. And rightly so. For wherever the prospect's eye falls, he should always see some answer to the "what's in it for me?" question. Wherever.

Appex Lunayach forgets this in its desire to dazzle us with who they are. Here's their opening to "The Products" section of their brochure: "ALS offers integrated software solutions for information management in the cellular and personal communications industries." Well, what of it, we all say together? What does this have to do with me? What's in this sentence for me? In short, where are the benefits? There's nary a one in this handsomely produced testament to corporate narcissism.

Whether you are selling product or service, your brochure cannot work if you merely use it as a repository of facts . . . or, worse, assertions that you "know" to be facts, but don't bother to prove. Facts about who you are, where you went to school, your place in the industry, the names of products and services you produce. And all the other detritus that bedevils marketing communications.

Whenever you use these facts alone and unadorned, whenever you fail to describe their significance and tell your prospect why they're important to him and how he benefits from them, why, that's precisely where you have failed as a marketer. The presence of a compelling sell 'em cover letter doesn't change any of this. Why should it? If you don't follow this up with equally client-centered copy, it's like driving a car with only half a tank of gas. However many pieces there are in your sales kit is the exact number of documents in which you *sell*, for each document enables you to add reason after reason why and how your prospect benefits from your product or service.

Never forget this!

After you've written the first draft of your brochure, read it over . . . aloud. And slowly. After *each* sentence ask yourself one simple, pivotal question: "Is this line about me? Or is it about my prospect?" If you do this, you will see — and change — the kind of weak, self-centered copy that is the hallmark of today's business brochure. Copy that has no place in the active, client-centered marketing brochures you can now produce.

A Word About Fact Sheets

I cannot leave this section without a special word about Fact Sheets, usually separate 8 1/2" by 11" sheets that simply list key facts about a product or service.

The inept marketer, a patent literalist if there ever was one, simply uses this to stack facts, to add one item to another in an attempt to overwhelm the prospect into buying. This is exactly what doesn't work.

If you intend to use a Fact Sheet, (and with most products and services it's a very good idea), why, then, use it properly. Stop thinking of this as a storehouse of passive information . . . information about the product or service. And start thinking about yet another client-centered format. A chance for you to show the prospect what he gets from what you're offering.

Title the sheet not "Fact Sheet" but "Advantage" Or "Benefit" sheet. Or just plain "What you get when you use (name of product or service)." Now if you are listing plain old facts learn how to bridge to their significance. Use the words "so that". This bridge will lead you to the client-centered significance of the fact, the reason your prospect will buy.

Let's go back to my snakebite illustration. The marketer includes this line in his copy: "It describes a method of treatment of snakebite . . . that has been widely accepted and used throughout the world." This is about the product. It's a fact (although an unspecific one). Now transform it into a client-centered benefit with the magic words "so that".

You can now finish the sentence with a client-centered flourish: "that has been widely accepted and used throughout the world . . . so that when you get bitten by a rattler you'll know what to do to save your life." Get the idea?

In other words, don't stack facts in a fact sheet demanding (as you do) that the prospect figure out their significance. Marketers provide the significance, remembering that this significance is the motivation for prospect action.

And remember, everything has a client-centered significance . . . or it doesn't belong in a marketing document. A fact without client-centered significance has nothing whatsoever to do with marketing; that is, with getting a real person to take immediate action to acquire what you're offering.

Writing Proposals That Get You What You Want

All of us at some time have to write a proposal, a document that is our best attempt to persuade someone else to do something we want: give us a helper, authorize an expenditure, fund our request for a project or program. It doesn't matter if we are a nonprofit organization sending in a request for money to a local corporation or an employee intent on an office improvement, the key to a proposal — all proposals — is persuading someone to do something. In short, motivating action that's mutually beneficial for the giver . . . and for us. But stop for a minute and ask yourself, are you more likely to get what you want if you frame it as a benefit for you . . . or as a benefit for the person you want to motivate? It's obvious, isn't it?

Why, then, are so many proposals so selfish? And so unproductive?

Successfully getting your proposal authorized, whatever its objective, begins in a recognition that proposals are marketing documents and are as much subject to the rules of writing persuasive copy as any other marketing communication. Thus, to make your proposal successful:

- Identify your audience. Who is it that you want to take action?
- Be clear about what you want him to do. Precision is crucial to getting a proposal approved, both precision about results and precision about the means it takes to get these results.
- Be sure he can do it. Asking someone to do something he can't is a certain route to disaster.
- Write down the reasons why it is in *his* interest (not yours!) to do this thing. Your personal interest has no place in this proposal. Although your personal enthusiasm for getting the job done certainly does!
- Be clear that he can do this thing in the period you need it done. It's no good asking if, when you get what you want, it comes too late. Timing is everything.
- Ask yourself if he needs to do all of this thing alone, or can he be included as part of a team working to achieve the same objective.
- Write down what will happen if this proposal isn't approved. While there will certainly be benefits if the proposal is approved, there will also be adverse consequences if it isn't. Motivate your prospect by citing these.

Now recall your marketing mantra, "lead with benefits, follow with features."

Which do you think is a more compelling opening: "A Proposal Submitted To The Trustees Of The Alva Taft Foundation On Behalf Of Welfare House"? Or, "How The Trustees Of The Alva Taft Foundation Can Help Welfare House

Provide One Hot Meal A Day For Three Months To 80 Elderly People In Cambridge, Massachusetts"? Put this way, it's obvious isn't it? The former may be textbook perfect (yes, there are books that are so myopic), but it is pushing the steak, the dead meat; not the sizzle of helping real people achieve something significant.

Don't let this happen to you!

The real question is: once you've got your basic information, how do you put it into your proposal? Why, by using your questions to inform your presentation.

Lead with what the grantor will get when the request is approved. This is the benefit, the "what's in it for me?" for the grantor-prospect you must motivate. As usual, stay away from the flaccid, formless words like "a better community"; "more money"; or "fewer sick people." Be specific. Say instead, "one house out of an available three on Elm Street will be suitable for a family of four"; "you'll get an additional $88,000"; or "one community health nurse will make visits in our town every thirty days for six months to 13 elderly people."

Now, all these things may be worth accomplishing, but we must realize we live in a world of scarce resources where everything we want cannot be done. That's why we must always remember that our proposal, any proposal, is a case that always focuses on the benefits . . . and what must be done to get them. The basic structure of your proposal is this:

- benefit you (grantor), or those you represent, will derive from this proposal;
- why now is the time to do this;
- why person making request is best person to make this happen;
- how benefit will be reached;
- what happens if what is being asked for is not granted.

Other information can be added as necessary, such as what you have already done to achieve the desired result or who else is involved in helping bring this matter to fruition. If you can show the hoped-for grantor that he is not the only one being asked for assistance, do.

Like all marketing communications, the key to making a proposal work is to keep it squarely focused on the giver and to take yourself out of the proposition except insofar as including facts about yourself can be used as levers to induce immediate prospect action. But even these facts must be positioned so they are client-centered. Do you have some special credential, for instance, to help you achieve the objective? Don't list it; as such, it's nothing more than a fact. Instead, show how having this credential will enable you to achieve the objective and benefit the grantor-prospect.

That's marketing.

And remember this, in proposals, as in all marketing documents, establishing just the right tone is important. Coming across as high-and-mighty or sanctimonious won't help your cause, whoever you are. While it is certainly true that proposals are often approved just because of who makes the request (we *do* live in a political world, after all), more often it is the case itself — the reasons for immediate action now — that makes approval irresistible, with submitter selfishness and egotism getting in the way of a favorable response.

Creating Classified And Small Space Ads That Get Results

Book after book is written about advertising. Sometimes I wonder why. It is really a very simple thing . . . if you have the right reason for using it.

Recently I had occasion to work with a hospital that was spending a significant amount of money on ads in prestigious medical journals. Because they are an important hospital, they wouldn't ever consider taking anything less than a full-page, often the back page (one of the plum spots) and always daubed their copy with colors.

When I was retained as a marketing consultant, I blanched when I saw both the ads and the expenditures. Both appalled me. For my clients I had only one question, "Do these ads make you money?" "Oh, no," I was airily told. "But the boss likes to get his name in print."

And so month after month tens of thousands of dollars were simply thrown away. (I hasten to say, they now use many smaller ads, each costing a reasonable amount, repeat them often, and ensure that each ad features a reason for immediate action. And they are making money!!!)

Ads work for smaller advertisers because:

- they are rigorously targeted to precise groups who have the problem your product or service will solve;
- we can develop a long-standing customer relationship with the people who respond to our ads; even if we lose money on them initially, we know over the term of the relationship we shall profit;
- we can make additional revenue from renting the names we acquire;
- we repeat them sufficiently often so that the people who have the problem we solve *must* know we're available to solve it, and
- because every ad we run asks for an immediate response and makes an offer so blatantly in the prospect's interest he cannot refuse it.

Now, take these key points and review the ads in any marketing source. I'll give you a hint. The ads you see for retailing, where the marketers exist in a very competitive environment, will come closest to this standard. They, after all, are constantly fighting for the smallest advantage. All others . . . whatever they're selling . . . will fall farthest from the mark.

Having written this, I opened the current issue of *Boston Business* magazine and began to review its ads. The first one I encountered is for Miller Studio, Quincy, MA. The ad starts with its name at the top and then follows with this paltry copy: "The image of success. Photographers for the professional community." There is then an unmarked head photo of a young professional. The ad concludes with the studio's address and telephone number. And nothing more.

Now tell me: is this advertising? Yes, it most certainly is, as practiced by most marketers today; they consider that *placing* the ad is the same thing as *profiting* from the ad. But not you! And not me, either! *We* know that ads cost money. And *we* know we must make money from them, or the entire exercise is futile.

This is why we give our prospects a reason for immediate action.

And that's why I advise all marketers who are contemplating advertising to master the rules of writing classified ads. Because if you can write a winning classified . . . in 10 words or less . . . you can write a space ad that will make you money, too.

Using Classifieds

I advise you to start with classifieds because classifieds are relatively cheap. Generally, you get 10 words for a basic price. And in these 10 words, the shortest marketing copy you'll probably ever have to write, you must persuade someone, your prospect, to stop in his tracks to take immediate action. This is the objective. If he doesn't, you've wasted your money.

How can you do this? Start by including what you need to include: your address. In writing ads, don't focus on the hard stuff first (the benefits). Write the parts that are at once easy . . . and must be present. The address. Let's use mine.

Here is my complete address: 50 Follen St., Suite 507, Cambridge, MA 02138. If I used this complete address, as is, the magazine would charge me for either seven or eight words; (sometimes the state and zipcode count as one, sometimes as two, depending on the publication's policy.) So shorten . . . to the bare minimum. Because you're paying for *every* additional word. Thus, 50 Follen/ 507, Cambridge, MA 02138. This is now either four or five words. And cannot be shortened.

Do the same with your name. My company name is Jeffrey Lant Associates, Inc. Four words. Shorten to JLA.

Now add a code. A code enables you to show which publication it is and which month. This way you can gauge the success (or failure) of what you've done. Put the code on the name. Thus, "JLA/a".

We have now used either five or six words, depending on the publication's word-count policy. In the remaining space we must:

- provide an offer for action
- indicate to the prospect we're talking to him, and
- show him the benefit he gets when he acts.

Impossible? Not at all.

Start by writing down in everyday language what you want to occur. You must do this, or you cannot possibly make your ad a success.

"I want owners of small businesses to write immediately to get a free copy of my Sure-Fire Business Success Catalog, so they will make more money."

This is a sensible objective, because it enables me to "capture the name" and launch my own selling process, instead of trying to sell direct. In 10 words that is very, very difficult . . . and cannot be done for items costing more than a very few dollars.

Let's translate this into client-centered copy.

"Free" . . . the offer

"small business" . . . the targeted prospect

"profitable" . . . the benefit

"catalog" . . . the feature.

Now, make an action-inducing ad from these crucial elements:

"FREE PROFITABLE SMALL BUSINESS CATALOG, JLA/a, 50 Follen/ 507, Cambridge, MA 02138." 10 words (if you count state and zipcode as one word, 11 if you don't).

Note: consider how you can upgrade the feature. I send four catalogs during the course of a year (they're published quarterly) to each person who responds to an ad like this. Four catalogs constitute a subscription. And "subscription" is a stronger benefit word than catalog. So try this as your ad:

"FREE PROFITABLE SMALL BUSINESS SUBSCRIPTION" *etc*. Remember, your job is to get the prospect to respond. Would you rather get a catalog, which suggests two limitations: that you get it only once and will have to pay for something. Or would you rather get a "subscription" that suggests continuous information and has no suggestion of a fee?

While the first ad is perfectly acceptable, my experience shows the second draws even better. Your job as a marketer is always to find the word or combination of words that will produce the largest response NOW. And this means continually tinkering with your copy.

And don't forget: if your ad runs in a publication that's directed entirely to small businesses, you can drop the targeting words "small business" and put in other action inducers. Don't waste your money saying the obvious.

Now you try one and see how you do.

When you've finished, go on to write a space ad . . . using the same principles. Never forget the function of this ad: to get a human being to take immediate action to connect with you . . . either with a check. Or by requesting something that will enable you to further your sales process and, in due course, make the sale. Nothing else matters. Ads that do not succeed in making that human being do this are ads that should never have been run.

A Word About Post Card Decks

What I've just said about ads applies, too, to post card decks, which are nothing more than packages of ads printed on direct response post cards. In MONEY MAKING MARKETING, I've discussed how you can get these ads at rock-bottom prices. Here I'd simply like to remind you that your task is to capture the prospect's name, to get him to take immediate action. This means focusing on his benefits . . . and not yours.

As I write I'm currently getting just short of a continuing 4% response on my card deck advertising. This is *well over four times* the industry average . . . but a great disappointment and challenge to me. Despite the fact that I work continually to discover the means of inducing more people to take immediate action . . . by selling benefits to them (like a "free year's subscription" instead of a catalog) . . . more than 96 people in one hundred don't take action. To their detriment and mine. This is the kind of problem we marketers face nowadays . . . and we must work long and hard to ensure that our benefits are strongly and believably put before our prospects . . . while knowing, all the while, that most of them will *still* not respond. No wonder we all have discouraging days . . .

Using Your Annual Report To Influence The Future, Not Just Report The Past

For many, many years I've carried on a silent vendetta against annual reports: they are so big, so richly produced . . . so egotistical . . . so generally useless. Then I began to analyze the causes of my frustration and why this genre disturbs me so greatly. Now I know: most annual reports are about the past . . . and nothing more. But *all* marketing communications are about the present and future. Yet annual reports are somehow thought to be marketing documents. If this is true, we must rearrange their focus . . . and transform them into documents that help achieve some present or future objective.

Before you create an annual report, ask yourself why you're doing so. Sometimes there are legal reasons for creating it; certain requirements must be met. If this is your only reason, why, then, the report itself can be as simple and straightforward as possible. Most people, after all, don't need anything more elaborate.

But say you have other reasons (as you should): to induce investment counselors to think well of your financial possibilities so they'll recommend more people to buy stock, to persuade customers to buy your products, to get foundations and corporations to give you grant money. If these are your objectives, do you want your annual report to focus exclusively on the past . . . or to position the past so that it helps influence the future? The latter of course!

Just telling what happened in the past is passive. That's why you must set an objective for the future and use the past as a lever to achieve it. You do this by transforming your Annual Report into a Success Report.

A Success Report says in effect, "Here are the successes we achieved and here's who we achieved them for." This report doesn't merely tell about the debut of a new product. But about all the benefits that ensued . . . for each relevant group whose benefits it must consider . . . stockholders, say, or consumers; that is, for each group for whom the Success Report is written.

If funding sources will read the Success Report, you must talk about how wisely you used money previously given and what results you achieved . . . so that these same sources, or others influenced by the same reasoning, will be motivated to grant you still more funds. A Success Report does not look upon information passively . . . as a fact, say, that's just occurred and needs nothing more than to be stated to satisfy requirements. No, indeed!

Success Reports realize that all information is a lever . . . that can either work for or against you but is in no way neutral. Either it helps you achieve the objectives you have set for the report, or it doesn't. If it doesn't, it must either be repositioned so that it does. Or it must be dropped. But it must not merely be stated. Like all features it must be transformed into a client-centered benefit.

The marketer who wrote the annual report for the Strong Total Refund Fund, Inc., Milwaukee, WI, either didn't know this . . . or forgot it.

Strong is a mutual fund company and one that presumably wants its prospects and customers to invest more in its funds. But who'd know this from its 1987 Annual Report that begins with nothing more stirring than its name and the report period and the fact that it is, surprise!, an Annual Report? There's no marketing here.

Now, as you'll recall, 1987 was both a very good and a very bad year for stock funds. Moreover, after October's Black Monday, the year ended in terrible uncertainty and much investor paralysis. Strong knew this but took too long to use it in a report that begins: "December 31, 1987, marked the sixth anniversary of the Strong Total Return Fund." My response to this is "So what?" This is a classical marketing error: opening with yourself, not the client, in mind.

Movement begins in the second line of the main copy: "This Fund has generated positive returns each year since inception characterized by the investment results listed below." Ladies and gentlemen, remember what I said earlier: you can't bore anyone into action. And this copy is dull, dull, dull. Too many words. Passive voice. Jargon. Verbosity. What happened to keeping things simple, focused on the client . . . and what the client is interested in?

Thus, does it make sense, as Strong does, to lead off its list of returns with 1982 (admittedly a good Strong year) and force us to read through five years of data until they bring us to what we're interested in . . . 1987? Doubtful.

Only after we're well into the document do we begin to see marketing light, the kind of light that might induce an investor to stick with Strong (marketing objective #1) and invest even more (marketing objective #2): "The Strong Total Return Fund's compounded rate of return of plus 21.8 per cent for the six-year period ending December 31, 1987, ranks the Fund in the top three percent of the more than five hundred mutual funds rated by Lipper Analytical Services for this period."

Now if this is the best that can be said about this fund in the light of Black Monday, then the marketer should lead with this benefit . . . and follow with the feature. And not beg any questions (like what is Lipper Analytical Services).

I repeat: an annual report should not just look at the past. Because, as Shakespeare so well knew, the past is prologue — the lever that will induce someone to do something NOW. Such as, in this case, investing more.

Boring us to death with words doesn't help achieve this objective. Focusing squarely on the prospect's fears (considerable in this case) and aspirations (equally great) does. No amount of pompous verbiage, no matter how erudite, will ever be able to compete against these primal motivators.

I am going to tell you something here that I hope you never forget. Sadly, oh-so-many marketers do, constantly. Don't produce a marketing document for the sake of producing that document. Produce that document for the purpose of helping another human being by getting that person to take immediate action to acquire what he needs. In marketing, nothing else matters. Image doesn't matter. Prestige doesn't matter. Doing it because you've got to doesn't matter. Connecting with another person does matter . . . and doing *everything* you can to get that person to take immediate action.

If you keep this one simple fact in mind, you will produce far better, far more effective marketing communications. Help far more people . . . including yourself. And stop wasting an ocean of resources.

PLEASE!

Producing Media Kits That Get You
The Free Time And Space You Want

Though this chapter is growing overlong, I must say a few words about media kits, those marketing documents that induce people in the print and electronic media businesses to give you something of real value: their time and space.

Since I've written two books that deal either wholly or in part with this subject (namely THE UNABASHED SELF-PROMOTER'S GUIDE and MONEY MAKING MARKETING), I don't feel the need to give you more than a few hints here. But these few hints you shall have . . . with my recommendation to read my more complete treatments of the subject. For you do want to get this free time and space . . . and promote your products and services to your buyers for the least conceivable cost. The alternatives, after all, are getting no free time or space . . . or having to buy advertising space. Both questionable courses.

And how will you get this desirable result?

As always, by making the strongest possible case for what's in this for the media source you're approaching.

If you approach a media source and say "Hey, give me free time so I can sell my products and services," you'll be laughed off the lot, or (worse) told to buy paid advertising. Both are reasonable responses from the media's point of view. Why should they give you something of value to enable you to become richer?

That's why you must position yourself, and your media materials, as the solution to a pressing problem. To make this exercise work you must:

- identify that pressing problem. If you expect to get free time and space in the media, you must sell your problem. If your problem is of no interest to the media source you're approaching, your solution won't be of any interest either.

- make sure the media source connects with people who have this problem. The problem will not be of interest to the media source unless his audience has it, for *his* marketing problem (which he uses you to solve) is to interest this audience. If he fails to do so? Off with his head!

- sell your ability to solve the problem; actually, two problems. The problem, first, that the afflicted have . . . and the problem the media source has. And what is this latter problem? Why, his need for you to be a good, entertaining, informative, stimulating guest. Because if you cannot be this, it doesn't much matter you can solve the problems of the audience, because you're not going to get the chance.

As you see, I've included no mention here of details about your product and service. Those, after all, are features you cannot lead with. You must lead with the information that will get you the time and space you desire. So produce different marketing materials, all about a page in length (double-spaced, please), dealing with the three areas above. Give each a client-centered headline like this: "Four out of five of the small business people listening to your program will go out of business within the next three years. You can help them stay in business . . . or you can ignore them and hope for the best." Now follow with your supporting information that sells the importance of the problem.

Remember, this information is useless, unless there are small business people listening to or reading this media source. So now say, "These people look to you for help." How can you find this out? From your own familiarity with the kinds of material the source uses . . . or from information sent out by the source's own advertising department which continually surveys to find out about its prospects. The problem must be important, but it must also be a problem that this media source's audience needs to solve.

Your third sheet should indicate you can solve both the immediate prospect's problem (your media source) and your ultimate prospect's problem (the people who need your product or service.) But don't sell yourself (a feature). Sell your benefit.

"Help Your Small Business Listeners Stay In Business By Using Dr. Jeffrey Lant As A Guest On Your Show. He Provides The Step-By-Step Guidelines They Need To Profit . . . In A Way They Want To Listen To."

Here it is perfectly acceptable for you to talk about the information you've got to help the ultimate propect achieve his objective . . . which, of course, includes the benefits of your product or service. Face it: the media prospect knows what you're doing. He knows you want to sell products and services. And he needs guest experts. But he has to justify your appearance by your ability to provide useful problem-solving information and be an entertaining guest . . . not by giving you license to sell. So give him what he needs. From the beginning. And you'll get what you need: an opportunity to motivate your prospects to connect with you . . . and give them what they need to do so (your address and telephone number). This is now certain to happen, thanks to the media's third-party validation of you as a person who has the solution they need.

It is, however, an opportunity you'll get only if you lead with benefits . . . and follow with features.

Properly Using Free Newsletters

The advent of desk-top publishing has flooded the world with a run of the most thriftless marketing documents ever seen on this planet. I feel a bit like the Dutch boy at the dike . . . but I press on because all this waste nauseates me. Sadly, there's much of it in free client newsletters.

As a result of reviewing several hundred of these, I have come to the inescapable conclusion that the producers of these materials must think they are in the information disseminating business; that their job is to inform people, rather like the grand panjandrums of the mainline press. IF this is what you think, too, disabuse yourself of this foolish notion. Because the only purpose of these communications is to stimulate business.

Yes, the only purpose worth mentioning for creating a free client/prospect newsletter is because you think having it will get you more business. If this is your objective, fine. If it isn't, it ought to be.

But to get business, as we've already seen, means focusing the discussion rigorously on the prospect and the client. Which in this case means making the prospect salivate about what you can do for him . . . thanks in part to what you have done for others.

I have a friend, a copywriter, no less!, who has forgotten this. Each month he produces a very nice-looking single sheet newsletter, 8 1/2" by 11". Each issue focuses on one copywriting problem . . . and how to solve it. He always does a nice job on the information. But as far as his own marketing is concerned, he fails. Why? Because he never tells you he can help you solve the problem he's been discussing. Instead, he simply says, "here's information to use as you please." That's not marketing; that's publishing. And never the twain shall meet.

An article on how to write headlines that get people to buy what you're selling should *at the very least* conclude by saying, "These are the kinds of headlines I can write for you . . . headlines that get your prospects to respond . . . faster . . . and buy more sooner! Call me NOW so I can get started producing these kinds of headlines for you." Now *this* is marketing.

I find it incredible that a copywriter, skilled in the business of making people respond, wouldn't do this, but my hunch is that he finds it "unprofessional." Let me tell you something: where the choice is between stimulating business and appearing "professional", there isn't any choice. What do you say?

Nothing should appear in your newsletter that doesn't relate to two key factors: the benefit of the prospect and your ability to provide it. Explicitly. Thus, you should be providing articles about:

- your successes working with others . . . focusing on precise results attained . . . and making your prospects want them. Then tell them how to get these results, too: the first step being to pick up the phone and call you NOW.
- problems your prospects face . . . and how bad they are. While always letting the prospect know you're there to solve them. If only they act NOW.
- opportunities that are available to your prospect . . . and why NOW is the right time to act to get them. And giving them what they need so they can act NOW.

You get the idea. Again, I must reiterate: you are not in the business of providing information. You *are* in the business of stimulating action. NOW!

Your Newsletter Must Be Interactive: It Must Ask — Even Demand! — The Prospect To Do Things

Too many newsletter producers use the mainline press as both their inspiration and model and do not follow commonsense marketing principles. The mainline press disseminates information. Marketers ask for a response.

Just the other day I had occasion to take my august (and generally inert) local newspaper, *The Boston Globe*, to task about this. This paper is continually running articles that cry for the inclusion of follow-up information, like names, addresses and telephone numbers. Because they are a *news*paper, however, they don't bother to provide these crucial client-centered details, although it would be easy for them to do so and useful to the reader.

The particular article in question dealt with a group of individuals forming condominium owners protection groups. As a condo owner myself, the subject is of burning interest, and I wanted to follow the article up. But where were the necessary details? Not there. Not where they should have been. And so each individual reading the article had to do the paper's work alone . . . or (more likely) not do it at all.

This is sheer idiocy. Moreover, it's an almost daily occurrence everywhere in the nation. All because the producer doesn't think like a client-centered marketer or service provider.

But when you're producing your free client newsletter, you will. You'll make it as interactive as possible. You'll always ask — and make it possible for — the prospects to contact you. Give them an indication of the benefits they'll get when they contact you . . . and continually stimulate their desire to do so. While simultaneously ensuring that you've given them the means of doing so.

What do I mean? Take a look at the catalog in the back of this book, specifically the section where I ask people to contact me to get crucial details on selected advantages. Use your newsletter in the same way: to get your prospects to self-select. Once they do, you know they are real prospects and you can launch your thorough selling process. Because they've already told you they want what you can help them achieve.

And remember: the attention span of the average American is infinitesimal. That's why you've got to be ready for your prospect when your prospect is ready for you. If you can't handle the prospect after you've stimulated him to take action, you'll not only disappoint him, but reinforce his contrary feeling of skepticism and mistrust. All at your expense!

A Word About Tone

I cannot leave the important (and expensive) subject of free client newsletters without addressing, in just as few words, the important matter of the tone you should adopt. Don't try to write in the magisterial third person. Write in the second, that is, directly to your prospect. Talk to him. Provide information that relates to him. Bring benefits to his attention. And reinforce his anxieties. In short, act to move another human being. Use all the motivators available to you, always remembering that unless your prospect takes action your newsletter hasn't worked . . . for you. And while you can congratulate yourself for performing a valuable community service, you'll be able to take comfort from nothing else. You unfulfilled philanthropist you.

I call this tone the "Conversational Accessible", and it transforms your news-letter into a conversation between you and your prospect, not into a forbidding piece of written communication. Where can you find a good illustration of this tone? Why, look no further than this book, a sustained piece of work entirely written in an intimate, personal, conversational mode.

Psst! Want me to share a crucial secret with you? After people read my books and articles or listen to my tapes, all intimate and urgent, they call or write me as *friends*, not as "readers" or "listeners". And as friends they seek my advice on how to reach their objectives. The initial detachment and awkwardness so often present at first meetings between strangers doesn't happen here, thus enabling both of us to move to what we really want to accomplish and not waste time on inessentials. *This* is one of the crucial advantages of the Conversational Accessible mode of communications, one of the secrets of truly successful marketing.

Cashing In On Catalogs

I needn't detain you overlong on this important topic, for if you want an illustration of a profitable catalog, you have only to flip to the back of this book.

A few months ago a fellow marketer from Montana called to suggest I radically change my format. "Your catalog reads like a long personal letter" he said. "I'd like to change it into something that looks and sounds more like a standard catalog."

For once in my life I was virtually speechless. Obviously this fellow had glimpsed the intensely personal tone. It had even motivated him to contact me . . . so he could destroy it and return my catalog to standard fare. Truly, my thoughts about his suggestion were unprintable. What could he be thinking of!

I happen to be convinced that buyers:

- dislike dealing with institutions rather than individual people;
- want to connect with someone they can trust, who will give them fair value for their money and the benefit of candid advice;
- like to develop relationships with people who care, and
- will repay you with something approaching that now too-often-dormant concept, loyalty.

And, I assure you, dear friend, I am no Polyanna. But a businessman in good standing.

To achieve these objectives means:

- talking to people directly;
- making it easy for your customers to buy when they want to buy;
- standing behind what you sell;
- telling the good points (benefits) of what you're offering, and conceding the not-so-good;
- telling people you'll take care of their complaints promptly . . . and then doing just that;
- making yourself directly available to your customers, and not trying to hide.

These ought to be the precepts of every business. We know they're not, and we're personally frustrated by that fact every single day. I mean all of us!

But I tell you this: whatever others may do, when it comes to creating catalogs this must be what *you* do. Which does not involve listening to a half-baked expert who wants to do away with the very thing that has made my catalog so successful: its direct, candid, personal, conversational quality. What could he be thinking of!

To make your catalog successful, remember a few key precepts beyond my points above about tone and your business practices:

- always speak directly to your prospect;
- always lead with benefits, for every item, following with features;
- when running graphics, make sure they are focused on the prospect, and feature client-centered, benefit-rich captions;
- include practical, immediately useful information in the catalog. Your objective is to make sure your prospects keep it . . . and order from it immediately!
- give your prospects immediate reasons for action . . . offers they can't refuse;
- give them premiums for ordering more. People who are better customers should get something other people don't get.
- sell products at special prices before they exist (always assuming you can guarantee delivery at a fixed time) . . . just as you sell damaged and discontinued merchandise at a special price.

• use devices to get people to read and order from later pages, traditionally the less well used. All places in a catalog are not equal. Your job is to move people to areas where they ordinarily don't tarry.

Following these points will help. And so will connecting with a few mail order experts. So let me recommend:

• *The Direct Marketer's Legal Advisor.* If you're selling through the mail — or expect to — you're part of a regulated industry and had better know the law. Robert Posch gives it to you in 242 fact-filled pages. Get details on the 30-day rule; on comparative pricing methods; on how to use key words like "free", "new", even "sale". Find out how to run a sweepstakes . . . or how to run a simulated check promotion without getting a million dollar fine. Much more. *All* crucial.

• *Mailing List Strategies.* This book by Rose Harper is correctly subtitled "A Guide to Direct Mail Success." If you are going to be in the mail order business, you are going to have to master Harper's list selection techniques, since using the right list is one of the keys to mail order success. Don't rent another list until you master this book. Please!

• Then get Julian Simon's superb book *How To Start And Operate A Mail-Order Business.* This is frankly the best book ever written on mail order, and wherever you are — beginner or guru — you are going to profit from it. It's exhaustively detailed.

All these excellent books are published by McGraw-Hill.

Last Words

Now you've got the information you need about the major kinds of marketing documents you'll be using to induce people to act. If you need to construct others, the information you need is in this book. Just think before you act and know what you want your prospect to do. Have you *really* focused on that prospect and what he wants? Have you *really* made it easy for him to act? Because if you haven't, whatever format you use will not work. Believe me.

Chapter 15

Mastering The Writing Process

I'm including this chapter to deal with the pain so many people feel when they approach the matter of writing. For most Americans — and the odds are for you — writing is a hellish task, and the sooner it's over the better.

But if this is the way you feel, how to you expect to produce copy that is at once simple, graceful, and persuasive?

It will be very, very hard.

In fact, what most people write is not only wrong from a marketing stand-point (because it's self-centered); it's also wrong as writing. Being, as I can well affirm, stiff, wooden, and excruciatingly dull.

I cannot allow this situation to continue for *anyone* another moment — and certainly not for *you*, my friend, to whom I have an obligation to help produce the best in fluent client-centered marketing communications. That's why I'm including this chapter on the writing process and how you can master it, a subject that is crucial to both reducing your frustration and irritation to the absolute minimum . . . and producing winning cash copy. Sadly, I've never seen another book on copywriting deal with the writing process. This is a terrible, terrible mistake. But it's at least one I do not intend to make. . . .

Admit It: You Hate To Write

Being able to write client-centered cash copy begins with the realization that writing probably isn't your favorite topic. If it is, pardon me. But if you are one of those relatively rare individuals who finds the writing process easy, you must know how distinctive you are. Others do not have your facility. And these are the people I must speak to now.

Here's what I have to say to you: there's no shame in hating the writing process. Writing is not easy. It isn't fun. And it takes immense amounts of hard work and concentration. Moreover, it's something you have to do alone and (until you've written the Great American Novel) what you write can never be regarded as definitive, that is, beyond change. Certainly with marketing copy, you'll probably never be able to write *anything* that is incapable of being improved . . . or anything that won't have to be altered in the light of changing conditions and audiences.

So, you should be discouraged, right?

Wrong!

Marketing, as you now should surely be aware, is a game. A game that should have only winners: you and your prospects. Client-centered writing is one of the necessary tools you need so that you can win this game and sell your offering. Just because you don't like it is no reason to avoid it. And, frankly, your disliking the hard business of writing is a luxury you simply cannot afford in marketing.

Thus, you need an effort of will that may not come easily to you: you must resolve to master the basics of writing so that you can induce more people to take advantage of what you're selling.

Resolve this now. Now, while you're thinking about it. Don't put it off. Because if you do, you've stripped yourself of a crucial tool for your marketing success.

Practice Makes Perfect

There are, of course, many reasons why you've hated writing. Most Americans, with our ardently pragmatic leanings, need to see the purpose of what we're doing. When writing a high school English composition this purpose seemed unbearably elusive. And so we did what all good American children do: we resisted, often outwardly; sometimes from the depths of our intransigent souls. Well, I have this to say to you: do resist pointless writing but do not resist the writing process itself. *That* is foolish, indeed.

Secondly, we hate writing because we're not good at it, and we're not good at it because we don't do enough of it. If you want to be good at creating client-centered marketing communications you've got to write them regularly. And by regularly, I mean *daily*.

If you're groaning now, I feel sorry for you. Because foregoing writing is not an option for you any longer, whoever you are. Even when you are the Great Poobah, Lord of Ten Thousand Years, you will not be able to abandon marketing writing, because others will never understand the benefits of what you're selling as well as you do, and will certainly never have the investment in it that you do. Hence, you must stay involved . . . so long as the result is important to you.

Which means practicing.

What you need practice in, of course, should now be obvious: writing client-centered benefits, creating offers that get people to act NOW, using words to make people feel the motivating fears that get people to buy what you're selling.

And you must help others practice, too.

If you are a boss, listen for the way your employees talk about your products and services. Do they use short-hand, jargon, features? Of course, they do. Your job is to get your employees, sometimes the most lax of all in this regard, to present what you're selling in the most client-centered fashion. If they cannot — or will not — do this in your office, they will never do this in discussions with clients. Please believe me!

If you work alone, as I do, tape your conversations with others; tape your phone calls . . . and certainly tape your prospect meetings. And then listen to what you've said. I guarantee you that most times you present what you're selling in terms of yourself . . . and not in terms of your clients.

How, then, could it conceivably be easy for you to write client-centered marketing copy when the time comes (as it regularly does) for you to do so? It just isn't in the cards.

If you want to write facile client-centered marketing copy you must think and speak in these terms . . . and you must change the destructive egotistical framework of your mind that precludes your doing so now.

Remember Virginia Woolf: Get A Room Of Your Own

Ivan Petrovich Pavlov, as you certainly already know, was a Russian physiologist who is probably most remembered today for his work with dogs. All college students know the experiment he created using lightbulbs and hungry canines. For some time, every time a certain light went on, food was delivered to the expectant beast. Later, when Pavlov felt certain even his dogs (amiable, but not swift) had gotten the message, he failed to deliver the meat when the light went on. And the dogs? They duly salivated anyway. Which brings me to my point . . .

If you want to write, you need what the English author Virginia Woolf insisted upon: a room of your own. A special place. You must put yourself in the same place day after day, at the same time. Then, you trained dog, you, you'll soon find yourself writing. Continually. Here is where you write the copy that gets others to respond . . . without the crippling burden of waiting for inspiration.

Before I tell you how you can truly make this area your "writing place", let me address the dread subject of "inspiration." Personally, I don't believe in inspiration, and as a professional copywriter and author, I certainly cannot afford to be at its beck and call. Many, many years ago economist John Kenneth Galbraith told me the quality of his prose didn't vary from day to day, whatever the vicissitudes of his life. He reported that he had trained himself to *write* . . . and to avoid the influence of events. *Then* I had no way of knowing if this was true or not; perhaps it was nothing more than the bragging of a man inclined to a considerable self-esteem. But now I know: it is both a necessary insight into the writer's condition and perfectly true.

As a marketer and now, indeed, a copywriter, interested only in motivating your prospect to take action, you *cannot* wait for inspiration, whatever that is. You must produce . . . NOW. And you will . . . by firm resolution, training . . . and a little help from friends like me.

Arranging Your Writing Place

You can help yourself by surrounding yourself with encouragers. You're not obliged to write surrounded by white walls and boarded-up windows. Don't be silly. Help yourself with the following props:

- Keep a "compost heap" next to your typewriter or computer, a stack of both the very, very good marketing communications you've found . . . and the howlers. When you're depressed (or the day sunny and urging you to play) read the latter first. Remind yourself, by reviewing the foolishness that others have spent their money and time creating, that you can — and will — do better. I find nothing more satisfactory . . . and, yes, inspirational . . . than reviewing the stupid mistakes others have made and knowing that I shall not at least make these! *And neither will you.*

Now read through a few of the marketing masterpieces you've found. Years ago all art students used to spend a portion of their time copying the Old Masters in museums. Through this process, which I think a sensible one, they learned technique . . . what worked . . . what didn't . . . and why more seasoned hands than theirs had done what they did. All the great masters, whatever their fields, always know the basics. But they are great because they use these basics in new and exciting ways . . . and ultimately go beyond them.

If you're creating a cover letter for a product, read a half dozen good cover letters to see what makes them good. Examine them critically: how does this marketer use benefits, offers, testimonials, and all the rest? Now you do the same. At least it will get you started. . . .

Surround Yourself With Exhortation

In other books, I've talked about the value of Imaging . . . of putting the thing you wish to achieve in a picture in front of you with a date for when you want to achieve it. I've discussed the value of looking at this thing daily . . . several times a day . . . while doing what you can do *each day* to achieve it.

You can do the same with copy writing, and this book will help you.

Create some prompting posters for yourself with key cash copy concepts, and hang them where you can see them . . . constantly. Try these for a start:

- "Lead With Benefits, Follow With Features."
- "Have I REALLY Done *All* I Can To Make My Prospect Want To Respond . . . NOW!"
- "Today Have I Asked Someone Who's Happy With What I'm Selling For A Specific, Detailed Testimonial That Will Get Other People To Respond Faster?"
- "Don't Just *Talk* About Anxiety; Make The Prospect *Feel* The Anxiety."
- "I Must Stop Talking About What I'm Selling And Start Focusing On What My Prospect Wants To Buy. Over And Over And Over Again."
- "Make Sure Every Word In Every Thing I Create Is About The Prospect . . . And That Everything Relates To Him . . . Not To Me!"
- "Don't Use Complex Words When Simple Words Will Do. The Idea Is Not To Convince My Prospect That I'm Bright . . . But That I've Got Something Crucial For Him."

You get the idea.

You need to change your behavior . . . change your thinking patterns. This is difficult. You must give yourself all the help you can. So surround yourself with messages that state and reinforce the essentials of client-centered marketing.

But don't forget the Imaging messages, either. The pictures of what you want to achieve from this process. Is that the yacht? The million-dollar bank balance? The cover of *Time Magazine*? Then post graphic illustrations of your objectives. Remember: the more successful you are at reaching the objectives exemplified by your client-centered marketing posters . . . the more successful you will be at getting the things you want. Things you must never forget personally . . . but must never talk about in your marketing. After all, why should your prospects care about helping you? That is your concern; not theirs. But it is a concern *you* must never forget and always keep graphically before you.

Psych Yourself

There are days, believe me!, when I don't feel like writing client-centered marketing copy; when my care and concern for the human race are perilously low. And when abnegation seems to make more sense than being helpful. But I cannot afford to let this crotchety attitude persist, and neither can you.

You must psych yourself up for the great event of the day: striving to do all you can to connect with your prospect and motivate him to act . . . your daily motivation derby.

As you sit down to write, remember:

- if the world is going to be a better place, it starts being better with what you do NOW — not tomorrow;

- your prospects (who may never meet you) are nonetheless counting on you to get through to them . . . and to do what is necessary to bring your offer to their attention . . . and so make their lives better.

- your customers will be grateful because of what you do today. No, they won't always say so; most won't. (Thankfully, some actually do!) But even if all the prospects whose lives you improve fail to say a single commendatory word, *you* already know you have helped . . . already realize you are doing something fine.

Of course, if you do not believe in what you're selling. If you don't think people are better off because of what you're doing . . . you can't really get psyched up . . . ever. At best, you can only camouflage the problem. When people come to me for marketing assistance, and I discover that *this* is their problem, I tell them in all candor either to stop representing that product or service (by perhaps transferring to another in the same company) or to find another product or service altogether to represent . . . in some other company. Because lack of belief destroys your ability to perform and helps erode your faith in yourself. The worst conceivable consequence.

When you follow these rules — say them over and over until you know them by heart — you'll soon find yourself in the necessary mindset of the marketing missionary. Your blood will be roaring. Your chin will be up. Your fingers will fly over the keyboard . . . And no wonder. There is no feeling more satisfactory to us humans than the feeling that comes when we are helping someone else. Part of what's destroying our culture is that fewer and fewer people do what's necessary to experience this feeling, being instead so rigorously centered on what's good for themselves and themselves only. That is a sure *cul-de-sac* for each of us and a certain route to despair.

When you are really focused on helping your prospects by doing what you can so they'll profit from your offer, I guarantee you you'll be psyched up. But I'll also tell you this: like all feelings, all highs, if you will, this, too, will pass. One of those people you're trying to help will snub you. Another will ignore you. Still another will be outright rude.

Predictably, you'll get discouraged.

At this point, treat yourself to something you want. NOW! And remember, don't let the proliferating numbers of jerks in the world discourage you. They are everywhere. And they have the capacity to discourage you. But you must have the capacity to get beyond them . . . to focus on what's really important: the vast numbers of the truly "silent majority", silently grateful that you're helping them. These are the people you must always remember. Set against either the drain of daily life or the vividness of some unhappy incident happening now, it is easy to forget these people. However, you cannot succeed in marketing unless you learn to put them aside and concentrate on those who are benefitting from you. They are too often voiceless. Too seldom do they share their success stories and gratitude with us. But they are there. And we must never forget them. Their happiness and completeness (even if we must only imagine them) are the necessary fuel for us.

Write To A Friend

Much of the wooden, dull copy that currently exists would disappear if people wrote like they talked. This is precisely what I'm asking you to do. We live in a society where we are and have been constantly graded. We are constantly told that something is either right . . .or, more likely, wrong . . . because of some rule we may never fully understand. But in marketing only *one* rule matters, and it is easy to understand: you must do *everything* you can to get your prospect to respond to your offer . . . as soon as possible!

Consider what this really means. Perfect paragraphs don't matter. Until their imperfections destroy credibility and hence diminish the likelihood of response. Logical arguments don't matter . . . until illogical copy makes people think maybe you're not so smart after all and cannot help them. Your titles don't matter . . . unless you can convince your prospect that they constitute a reason for trust and immediate action. In truth, as in so many things in life, your job is to find the happy medium . . . while always remembering that that happy medium is only important if it facilitates the prospect's response. For that is all that matters.

When commencing to write client-centered marketing copy, imagine you *truly* care about this individual; that this individual is your friend. And that you have something of incredible importance to impart . . . something significant for this friend and for bettering his life. Not about you and yours.

Now, tell this person . . . in the most direct, simple and persuasive way . . . *exactly* what you've got to say. Don't worry about structure. Or sentences. Or paragraphs. Concern yourself only with "you", your friend, and why he should act now (the benefits he gets, the anxieties he avoids).

When you've finished, go back and put in the emphasising devices, the intonations, if you will. Make things that *are* important *be* important.

And ask yourself these questions:

- Have I clearly indicated to my friend, my prospect, what's in this for him?
- Have I communicated my fears for him in the anxiety information I've presented? Or will he just feel I'm crying "wolf" with words that have no impact?
- Have I communicated the benefits to him and the reasons why he should act NOW? Will he feel my passion, interest, and concern — or just that someone else is spitting out words at him as so many do, every single day of his life?
- Have I made him feel what's important by my emphasis of words, phrases, and ideas?
- Is what I've written simple and compelling, or does it bore even me? Am I sending out a piece whose offers and benefits excite me? Or am I hoping against hope that the boredom I feel will not be communicated to my poor prospect?

When you confront each piece of your marketing copy with these questions, you cannot help but make it better . . . cannot help but make it something of persuasive interest to your prospect. Which is just what you want.

It Helps To Read Aloud What You've Written

Many of the problems of marketing copy could be solved if marketers would only read aloud what they've written . Here are some telltale signs that what you've written isn't going to persuade anybody to do anything other than throw it away:

- You're falling over your words. Either the words are incomprehensible or they're jargon. Or sufficiently unfamiliar that they don't fall trippingly off the tongue. Marketing copy is simple copy, and simple copy is easy to read and comprehend. Always.

- By the same token, it's taking you too long to say the words. Words that require a breath are words that are too long. Sentences of more than 15 words are probably too long, too. Marketing copy is movement copy because marketing itself is about movement . . . about getting a person to take action to change his situation. Copy that doesn't move is copy that blocks the essential action of marketing.

- You're putting intonations into the copy that the copy itself doesn't have. Ever notice that when people read what they've written even mundane writing often comes alive? The reason, of course, is that the writer imparts through his voice and manner the significance that is not obvious in the words themselves. This is, of course, fatal in marketing.

In marketing *everything* you want the prospect to get out of the copy must already be *in* the copy when he gets it. You cannot ask the prospect to do anything. Thus, if you find yourself ascribing significance to your copy as you read it, breathing life into it through your intonation, you know you're not finished. Because your prospect is not going to do what you've just done. That's why you must.

Sadly, I'm one of the few people I know (though I regularly ask) who actually reads all my material aloud, articles . . . Special Reports . . . books . . . and all the client marketing communications I create. This is how I begin my day . . . *reading* over yesterday's production. Inevitably, I find a phrase that isn't quite balanced. A sentence that should be active into which I've allowed the passive voice to creep. A paragraph that's supposed to communicate excitement . . . but that succeeds in doing nothing more than using synonymns for enthusiasm. Reading aloud helps me find all these errors . . . and correct them . . . before I spend my money — and my client's — to send them out to real people whom I fervently wish to take immediate action.

Why, then, don't more people do this? There are, of course, several reasons:

- It takes time. The cliché of our age is that no one has time to do anything. We are so busy producing that we have no time to craft something that is worth producing.

- It seems foolish. Imagine, if someone were to hear you talking aloud. Why, they'd think you were in a certain stage of madness. But what do you care? Your job is not to appear universally sane; it's to persuade people to take immediate action. And you cannot allow trifling concerns about image to stand in the way of securing enhanced motivation.

- It means more work. Yes, yes, it does. I guarantee when you use this technique you will find, as I daily find, the marring imperfections of your work. And it is the elimination of these marring imperfections and their replacement with more action . . . more benefits . . . more truly client-centered language that gives you the competitive edge you want and the persuasive marketing documents that express it.

Stop Being Invested In Your Copy

One of my professors, whose wisdom has, in my memory, outlasted his name, once told me that the writing passages one most likes are the passages one should, as a matter of course, dispose of. "Invariably," he pronounced with New England sternness, "they are overwritten." I concur.

One of the key rules for writing persuasive marketing copy is to take yourself out of the equation: to approach the task with as much detachment as you can muster. To feel no obstructing investment in your ideas, your words, or how these words are expressed. Don't get me wrong! This doesn't mean transforming yourself into a spineless toady. Not at all. What it does mean is accepting that in the business of human persuasion you need to be committed to a single point only: that you will do everything you can to get this person to take immediate action. Nothing else, and certainly none of your golden syllables, is remotely as valuable.

Your task is to compare what you've written and intend to use against your one certain standard: on what it takes to get your prospect to respond faster and spend more. If what you've created is objectively the strongest way to achieve your fixed goal, why, then you must use it. And if it isn't, it must as assuredly be jettisoned. Without a second thought.

Clients consistently plead with me to be allowed to retain some (usually bloated) verbiage from past documents as we work to create new, more persuasive ones . . . rather like integrating the mantle from an old house into an improved version.

But I tell them what I've just shared with you: such lines are useless unless they are consummately useful . . . unless, that is, they are completely focused on the prospect and the benefits he gets from you. Mere sentiment, you see, has no place in the thoroughly utilitarian world of marketing.

Let Your Copy Repose Overnight Before Using It

The best marketers are prone to bouts of enthusiasm. Our ability to become enthused by what we're selling is an important part of what makes us so crucial to the marketing process. But it also has its negative aspect: we can easily project our enthusiasm onto others where there is, in fact, no such enthusiasm at all. Hence the need for calm reflection.

You must write marketing copy as frequently as you can. But you must also let it sit for a day or two, so you can come back to it fresh . . . and surgically critical . . . distanced from the state of excitement in which you may have created it.

Now scrutinize your creation closely. Were you excited by it just because you finished the project? Or were you excited because it is, indeed, superbly client-centered copy? Now, of course, you know enough to know the difference. The enthusiasm that comes because a project is finished will, when you return to that project, be gone. But the enthusiasm that emanates from the copy because it is rigorously focused on the prospect will be regenerated *each* time you review it . . . since it is about the prospect . . . not about you.

Get The Reactions Of Other People

Throughout this book, I've urged you not to make one of the crucial mistakes of marketing: do not assume you are your market. By definition a marketer and his market cannot be identical. This is why you must show what you've created to others . . .to get their opinions and, upon consideration, use what's valuable to alter your copy.

Almost none of the clients I work with likes this step. Since I'm a copywriter, they reason, and am supposed to know what I'm doing . . . and since the project has already taken too much time to finish (no matter how swiftly it has in fact been done), why must they add what they see as an additional, unnecessary step to the process . . . a step that takes more time and stands between them and their profit?

The answer, of course, is obvious. We must get the impressions of real people who won't spend hours, much less days, scrutinizing the copy from every conceivable angle. Oh, no! *These* people will make the kinds of snap judgments we all make in real life about the marketing copy we see and the products and services it represents. There is no subtlety in their reactions. It is either an immediate thumbs up (represented by the decision to read on, request information or buy now) . . . or thumbs down . . . and so into the trash.

Our job is to find out *what* our reviewers feel and *why* they feel that way. So that we can explain what they do . . . and decide if other people will react this way, too.

This is by no means a trivial process, and you skip it at your peril.

Finding Reviewers

One of the necessary components of this process, of course, is that you find other people to give you their opinion, *people who are in fact real prospects for what you're selling*. Note the crucial emphasis. This means you should not be using:

- family members;
- employees;
- adoring groupies.

For one reason and another, these people are not at all suitable for the job, not least because they know you want their approbation, not their honesty. Even more importantly, they're not people who will *buy* what you're selling, however much they can use it. They expect to get it free.

So your response group must be composed of real prospects, of people you are in business to serve and who may be induced to buy your offering.

And where, pray, do you find such very important people?

The best place to look is to the people you are already doing business with . . . or trying to: your prospects and buyers. Ask them. But give them an inducement . . . and make it easy for them.

Provide a brief questionnaire to accompany the materials you send. Ask them no more than ten questions, including:

- Have you ever bought a product or service like this before?
- If so, why? (If you like, marketer, you can include the answers and have your reviewer simply check off boxes that apply. Like, "☐ costs less ☐ needs little maintenance ☐ special sales discount.")
- Do you feel that our product/service offers you a better reason to buy from us instead of our competitor?
- If yes, say why.
- If no, say why not.
- Would you list at least three major benefits you feel you get from our product/service?
- Do you feel our product/service is missing some benefit you want?
- If yes, please say what you think is missing.
- Can you remember the offer we made to get you to buy the product/service now?
- Have you been persuaded to buy what we're selling as a result of this offer?
- If not, why not?
- Do our testimonials help persuade you to buy what we're selling?
- If not, why not?

Remember, you can ask your prospects these questions directly in person or on the telephone and write down their answers. Or you can simply send them your marketing materials and questionnaire in the mail with a stamped self-addressed envelop. It's up to you. The important thing, however, is that you get their response.

Now I hasten to say one thing here: what you hear from your prospects may not be accurate. It doesn't matter if it is. It matters what they think. A prospect's thoughts are a marketer's reality. The only real question you've got to answer is whether others share what you're heard. And you'll begin to know this as you compare one prospect's responses to others you've received. How many of these responses do you need? Twelve is a good, reasonable number. Marketing professionals may cavil at the limited number of people asked, but the truth is, I find it hard enough to get my clients to do even this. Asking them to do more risks having them do nothing at all. So, twelve is a compromise.

How To React To What You Hear And Learn

Face it, copywriters *are* human, and we do want our efforts to be applauded . . . as well as rewarded. That's natural. But it doesn't help much during this crucial review process.

One of the mistakes a copywriter makes as he listens to his reviewers' reactions is for him to defend what he's written . . . or attempt to explain it. Both are inappropriate responses.

Recently, a fellow running a lawn and garden supplies company in Ohio asked me to critique two of his marketing documents, a service I offer. When I reviewed them, I discovered the usual problems, now all too familiar to you: no benefits, a focus on features, no offer, all words equally weighted, *etc.* Without a second thought, I sent off my analysis to the client.

A few days later I received an outraged telephone call from a marketing representative of the parent company in Illinois. It seems the fellow who had hired me had sent what I said straight to the home offer. *Who*, she demanded, had given me permission to review their documents? What were my credentials for doing so? And still other insistent questions spat out so quickly there was no chance to respond to any. When reluctantly given the opportunity to provide a word or two, I explained my role in this situation and told her she had better ask her questions of the fellow who had originally contacted me. *He* must have felt the need for a professional review of the documents he was provided. Perhaps they weren't drawing very well. And, as I indicated, they could certainly stand general improvement for the reasons cited. I could tell that none of this was sinking in.

Through her outrage, however, I glimpsed the true heart of the matter: this woman had obviously written these documents and now felt under siege by some unknown "expert", whose findings jeopardized her position.

I concluded our brief, if poisonous, call by telling her that if she didn't like what I had to say she could throw my observations away. But, of course, I surmised that as others already knew about them, she could hardly so do.

And so the matter might well have rested . . . a typical illustration of a copywriter *defending* her work rather than *listening* to what a dispassionate authority had to say and attempting to benefit from it.

But, humans being what they are, the matter did not rest. No, indeed. The very next day she-who-must-have-revenge was back on the phone again now *demanding* I send her a letter explaining how I came to have any of this company's documents in the first place and include a resumé of my credentials for having the temerity to give my honest impression of what I saw.

Of course, the situation was by now absurd, and I could scarcely help from laughing at this poor creature's quite unnecessary rage and entirely ludicrous imperiousness. Now she clearly showed me she felt herself to be under siege at home and supposed she needed to strike out at the person who had, all inadvertently, placed her at risk. Quite, quite foolish. And so unnecessary.

Don't you be this way. Everything in marketing is expendable. Everyone in marketing is expendable. Except the thing that makes the prospect act NOW. And the person who can fashion this thing to produce this essential result.

By the way, I declined to write the letter in question and suggested she find my credentials for herself at the end of MONEY MAKING MARKETING, which her company's Ohio representative had purchased. Predictably, this smooth response infuriated her the more. And it is this fury which leads me to make this prediction, namely that this poor woman is not destined to become a pillar of the marketing community.

I find such incidents immeasurably interesting. Don't you?

Don't Forget To Thank Your Prospects

Even if what you're hearing discourages you, you've got to thank your prospects for taking time from their busy lives to share their feelings with you, even if you don't like hearing them. Give a free premium (don't forget those very useful Special Reports) . . . or some other benefit. Tell them in no uncertain terms just how grateful you are for what they've done. Even if you're hurting now.

Go Back To The Drawing Board

Most times what you hear is going to get you to modify your copy. Ordinarily, you'll discover the prospect hasn't either understood or, more likely, actually *felt* your benefits. More than anything else what forces us marketers to revise our documents is the lack of felt benefits . . . that is, the feeling of our prospects that they aren't getting enough from us and, therefore, don't want to buy what we're selling.

If this is what you learn from this important, though admittedly time-consuming step, then it's all been worth it. Because you've been given a reprieve . . . a chance to go back and improve what you're using to communicate with your prospects. You can now profit from what you've learned to improve what you're using to get more people to respond quicker. This is, after all, the name of the game.

Note: This review process is also very helpful in deciding which of two or more marketing tacks to take with your prospects. As a copywriter you don't always know which of two client-centered marketing gambits is likely to be the more compelling. Should you lead with fear? Or with benefit? Which offer is stronger? "Buy one, get one free"? Or "Buy two for the price of one?" These are very important questions and should not just be decided by flipping a coin. That's where your reviewers come in.

Marketers are necessarily superb listeners. And it is our job to perceive not just reality but what our prospects *regard* as reality . . . and to use what we hear and can deduce from it to motivate them to take action. *This* is why we ask our prospects to tell us what they think . . . so we can use it to motivate them — and others like them — to take action faster.

One Last Suggestion

Having now been in the motivational business for many years, I am certain that one of the essential enticers is communicating a sense of energy to your prospects . . . of motivating them by creating an atmosphere of excitement and enthusiasm. If a person is energized, he can be moved. Indeed, he wants to move.

Before I leave this chapter, then, and move to the matters of design and lay-out, I wish to provide you with a single thought. But first select just one of your marketing documents and read it. Is it dull? Is it flat? Is it passive? And sluggish? Why, then, this is no marketing document at all. It's precisely what you do not want to send to anyone. Because it will not motivate anyone to take action.

Look at your own life. Admit it: too much of what you do is routine. Too little is distinctive, different, exciting. Do you want to be around people who promise you more routine? More boredom? More of the same? Of course not . . . and neither do your prospects.

We humans are a notoriously restless breed. We are always looking, often desperately, for the things that will *really* make our lives better . . . that not only promise improvement . . . but deliver it. But we don't just want the things themselves . . . we want the sense of enthusiasm they engender in people who have them.

Thus, your job is clear. First, you must enthuse yourself about what you are selling. Then, you must communicate this enthusiasm to others. Because if you cannot communicate enthusiasm, you cannot write cash copy and will never succeed in motivating sufficient numbers of people. And without motivating these sufficient numbers, you cannot achieve your own grand objectives. So you see, what you must do is plain.

You must stop being "professional." Must stop merely retailing facts, no matter how correct. Must stop presenting what you're selling as if really it didn't matter if the prospect used it or not. And must start electrifying yourself with the possibility of what you have to offer . . . so you can electrify your prospects with all they have to gain. As we leave this chapter, remember Michelangelo's Sistine Chapel ceiling with the mosaic of God touching Adam. When you see this masterwork, you feel, hundreds of years after its creation, the terrific spark that is about to leap between the deity and his creation, the spark that will change the destiny of the universe.

In the marketing world, *you* supply that spark, you generate the enthusiasm, and you transmit it to people who will be motivated to act because they have felt the primal force emanating from you . . . the force that moves them to act so they get the benefits you offer. That force is an essential part of motivational marketing. And the basis for compelling cash copy. Without it you are just a peddler of things. . . . of things that will break, and get lost, and disappoint. Can you truly say this is the way you want to live your life?

I hope not. For the best marketers, the best copywriters, are in the business not just of selling things . . . but of transforming lives by communicating their own enthusiasm about how much better off the prospect can be . . . how very much better . . . if only he acts NOW.

For you see, we marketers are not in the service of things. We are in the service of human transformation, of improving the lives of more people by clearly communicating to them how much better off they must be when they take immediate action to secure the benefits which we have for them in such specific abundance.

We marketers are benefactors who, having done *everything* we can to get our prospects to act NOW and so make their lives better, can rest secure in the knowledge that we have done our share to make this a better world. For having done everything we can, the world must be better. We are, therefore, fully entitled to the ample rewards . . . and comfortable self-esteem . . . which is as much ours by right, as are the benefits for those we have motivated to acquire them.

Chapter 16

Cash Copy Lay-Out And Production Tips

You've now written your cash copy. And it's good. Client-centered. Packed with benefits that your prospects want. With an offer that will get even the most slothful to take immediate action.

Congratulate yourself. You're now a member of an elite group . . . you've got something every marketer wants . . . but which most never succeed in creating: copy that is rigorously focused on the prospect and which will motivate him to take lightning-fast action to acquire the benefit he knows he can get from you. My hat's off to you!

Don't blow it now.

The Role Of Design And Lay-Out In Inducing Immediate Prospect Action

Throughout this book, you've learned one thing, a thing I have driven home with sledge-hammer pounding: the only thing which matters in marketing is motivating your prospect to respond. To send in the coupon. NOW! To pick up the telephone and ask for more information. NOW! To take advantage of your offer by acquiring what you're selling. NOW! *Nothing else matters.*

Don't forget this crucial lesson as you approach the matter of design and lay-out.

Design and lay-out are a permissible expense only to the extent they help you secure the prospect's immediate response. They are a pointless waste of time, money and talent if you consider them from *any* other standpoint. Remember this . . . because your designer often does not.

As I write, I am thinking about all the marketing materials I have reviewed from designers . . . materials they have created for themselves: their own cover letters, brochures, ads, and all the rest. No more than other marketers are they aware of what copy should be doing, much less how it should be integrated into a marketing communication to secure the desired result.

Other factors weigh on designers, factors such as color, type face, graphics, and general presentation. I admit, these factors *are* important . . . but they are important for only one reason: because they can help get the quickest response. For any other reason . . . any reason whatsoever . . . they are pointless.

Keep this in mind. When you approach the matters of design, lay-out and copy presentation, you are simply taking the crucial matter of prospect response into a new domain, another area. The essential question remains the same: "Am I doing that which will induce a prospect to respond?" Or, are you wasting your resources producing something merely decorative?

How I wish a sometime client of mine had asked this question of herself before proceeding, all unbeknowst to me, with a designer and a very expensive brochure project. As I write I am looking at this luxurious creation: its fashionable burgundy cover containing four one-page 8 1/2" by 11" overlay inserts. These inserts carry on the color theme from the cover but are flecked with distinguished silver highlights. The paper is heavy, a thing of substance. The entire look is almost regal in its elegance, right from its imperial cover. (Could the marketer have known that such a color was the favorite of the last Tsarina of All the Russias?)

And well it should be, since *each* brochure cost about $6. Yes, $6 each!

For what? The general mailing in which most of these aristocratic beauties were shipped generated *no* responses whatsoever. Only the marketer's deep despair.

How much better would it have been to have rethought the strategy, to:

- focus on the copy, not the presentation;
- make sure the presentation did not overwhelm this copy

(which, after all, offered the benefits the prospect wanted) but accentuated it, and

- use the remaining (always limited) money to recontact the same group of prospects until they *had* to know the marketer's benefits and what she could do for them.

In short, to use lay-out and design as they must always be used in marketing: as important, though most decidedly ancillary factors, always of less importance than client-centered benefits and the copy that presents them. Always.

If this is the case, why do so many marketers forget it? There are at least two reasons.

1) When you're in business, it is easy to mistake any action as an action that helps generate business. Being busy can easily be justified to oneself as doing something that generates responses . . . that somehow connects (though one is hazy about just how) to the crucial matter of getting and retaining customers. Much of what happens between a marketer and his designer strikes me as this kind of self-deluding activity, busyness . . . not business.

The marketer doesn't demand that what the designer does be *entirely* devoted to help motivate a prospect to take action . . . and the designer doesn't bother to help the marketer reach an objective which has never been made starkly explicit. Instead, they focus on the decidedly peripheral issue of making something attractive, decorative, something that fulfills the marketer's self-image but has nothing to do with the central question at issue: "Does what is being created stimulate immediate prospect response?"

2) As court painters have known throughout the ages, design and lay-out and presentation involve image. And image involves the core of one's being: the question of how others will regard one. Subtly, designers can work on a marketer's ego, saying in effect: "Oh, Great One, because you are great, you must have this . . . and this . . . and this . . . and if you do not have this, this, and this, then you cannot be considered great."

This is an argument that sovereigns throughout the ages have been quite happy to accept . . . especially if they are without a fixed inner confidence about their abilities and place in the world. Truly great people are generally the simplest of all and find it easy to reject this line of reasoning as pointless. *These* people want to know if what is being proposed is necessary to enable them to reach their objectives. If not, it is pointless. *They* stay focused on the major point, in this case doing what is necessary to stimulate the prospect's prompt response. Everything else is jettisoned as thoroughly unnecessary.

Sadly, most of what transpires between a marketer and a designer doesn't involve the pivotal question of how best to stimulate prospect response. It is just pointless activity. Which is precisely what you must avoid. Otherwise, you will fall into the trap of too many marketers and too many of their design and lay-out associates.

Before we go on, I beg you remember this crucial point: design, lay-out and presentation of copy are only important insofar as they stimulate immediate prospect response. If they don't, they have failed you. This concerns you more than your consultant. What cares your designer? He, after all, has already banked his fee and advanced to his next project, whose marketer, all unawares, will again not challenge him to put design at the service of immediate-response marketing instead of decorative pleasantries.

To Have A Designer Or Not To Have A Designer, That Is The Question

You will understand, of course, that what I've just told you implies you will have a designer. That there is no other option. And in truth I suspect that for most of us . . . those with only the most rudimentary sense of color, texture, and presentation (whatever our pretensions) . . . there is no other alternative. For us, for me I might add, not having a designer is quite, quite unthinkable.

But not, perhaps, for you.

In considering the question of whether to retain a designer or not, you must ask yourself the following preliminary questions:

- Do I have the desire to learn to be a good designer and lay-out professional? That is, am I willing to do what it takes to master the skills of the design professional and place them at the service of my client-centered marketing efforts? If you have no desire, don't trifle with the exercise. Spend time instead finding the professional you need. (This is the category I fit in, and having made this decision I went happily to the necessary task of finding the professional I needed, the following questions now being superfluous.)

- If I have the desire, do I have the time it will take to master the essentials of design and presentation before I must use these skills? If you do not have the time, it doesn't matter if you have the desire. Find your design professional forthwith!

- If I have the time and desire, do I have the ability to learn and apply what is necessary to create designs and lay-outs that get my prospect to respond immediately? It doesn't matter, you see, if you have the desire and the time, if what you produce fails to do what is absolutely necessary: that is, to stimulate an immediate prospect response.

- If I have the time *and* desire *and* ability to create the necessary client-centered marketing designs, is the time I have *best* utilized by doing this work myself? Or, should I spend it doing what the marketer *must* do best (that is, working to generate immediate responses from prospects and clients) as opposed to what is merely desirable that the marketer do, namely creating client-centered lay-out and design? In other words, what is the opportunity cost of my doing this service for myself, even if I can do it quite satisfactorily?

If you decide that you do, indeed, have the time, desire and ability . . . *and* that that time is best spent creating your own materials, why, then, you are a unique person, whom I salute. You may approach this chapter as you do the others in this book: as a mine of golden information you can use directly.

The rest of us must approach it rather differently. We have to make sure not only that we understand what is being said here, but also that the design professional we employ understands it, since our objectives will only be realized working with and through this individual. Unfortunately, in my sad experience the designer is, at best, an unsophisticated marketer himself, not only for you but for himself.

Finding The Right Design Professional For Client-Centered Marketing

You now know what you're looking for, which helps considerably: an individual who will work hand in hand with you to use design in the service of immediate prospect response. As you meet candidates for this post, you'll be able, following the handy list of guidelines which is forthcoming, to evaluate them and decide if you should even consider working with them. But the first question, of course, is how do you even find the candidates . . .

Finding Candidates For Your Available Design Post

Would-be designers are everywhere. So where do you start?

- Check the yellow pages under "organizations" or "associations" and see if your city has a design club where professionals in the field regularly meet. Such a club may well maintain a list of available design consultants broken down into fields of expertise. They can also tell you if your city has what mine does, a superb directory entitled *Worksource: New England's Creative Source*. Published annually by Turnbull & Co., 15 Mt. Auburn St., Cambridge, MA 02138, this publication lists hundreds of designers, copywriters, photographers, and typographers for people seeking advertising and marketing assistance. There's even a list of their clubs . . . and the awards they can get for helping you!

- Failing such a directory, look through marketing materials you like . . . the ones that are clearly client-centered, that clearly draw you in, that make you WANT to respond immediately. Take the materials produced locally first (there is always an advantage to having your designer relatively close) and call the companies that produced them. Ask for the name of the designer. When asked why (officious secretaries must ask, don't you know) say you want to compliment the superb work. Flattery helps ease you through barriers that stop others.

One thing this approach will gain for you is some helpful information. If the designer isn't on staff, the secretary will have to give you his home or office address and telephone number.

And if he is on staff? No problem. Begin the conversation with a heartfelt compliment. All of us warm to praise . . . so dish some out. Then say, all innocence, "I bet what you created got a wonderful response, too." Make this half-way between a statement and a question. Now, listen closely. You are now gathering important intelligence. Information on how the design and copy you liked drew. How profitable it was. How worth while it will be for you to work with its creators . . . and perhaps even produce something similar.

If things turned out grimly, why, then, this may well be a situation worth considering just a little longer . . . he may be a person you don't want to work with after all. You can ring off politely. After all, you've committed yourself to nothing and have, by lavishing compliments galore, kept the lines of communication nicely open.

But if the response is enthusiastic, why, then you're ready to proceed. "I know you're on the staff of this company, but I wonder if you ever take on any freelance work?" *Everyone* can use extra money, and this approach may well yield you a designer whose work you already know capable of attracting people.

And, if it can't? Well, you'll probably get a referral out of this call to a person who can help you. By the way, it is perfectly permissible not only to ask for this referral but also to tell this designer what kind of person you want to work with: someone who's expert in creating immediate-response marketing communications. Nothing fancy. Just good old, excitation and motivation materials. Make sure he understands this. If he doesn't, he isn't the right person to be advising you.

Of course, I must say the odds of your finding the right designer on the first call are quite slight, just as you probably didn't find the love of your life on the first date. As the saying goes, "You've got to kiss a lot of frogs to find your prince." And so it is here. If the designer doesn't understand what you're trying to accomplish (be quite blunt about your objectives) and seems more concerned about peripheral design functions, then this is not your person. No matter how grand his connections. Or how many awards he's won. After all, unless his awards have come from projects that have made his clients money, those awards are things of trifling importance.

- If all this fails and you still don't have your designer . . . if calls to the design department of your local college haven't worked (oh, yes, all colleges employ designers these days both as teachers and for on-staff functions) or to colleagues whose marketing materials you've admired.

If, I say, these referrals haven't worked, and you cannot find the person you want near at hand, don't even think of worrying. Contact *my* designer, John Hamwey, ABC Publications, Inc., P.O. Box 162, 385 Weatherbee Dr., Westwood, MA 02090 (617-329-8811).

John is a conscientious professional, well aware of what client-centered marketing is all about, (after all, he hears about it constantly from me). *And*, if this is what you wish, he is quite prepared to show *me* your copy before embarking on the design stage to ensure that it is sufficiently persuasive. By the way, you might like having me do this review *whatever* designer you use since, while producing perhaps momentarily inconvenient results, it might well save you thousands of dollars in immediate expense and lost revenues. Just keep it in mind . . .

Selecting A Designer

Now you have candidates to select from. Remember what you are looking for: an individual who prizes your bottom line more than his chances of getting an advertising award. Who will do what is necessary . . . including *explain* what is necessary . . . to get your prospects to respond faster. His job is to make your life easier. A not inconsequential point.

How can you find this paragon . . . and avoid the plague of also-rans who abound? Get this kind of information from your designer candidate:

- Ask to review the designer's portfolio. Don't go "oooh" and "aaaah" when you see things either. Nor be fiercely critical. What you are looking for is evidence of client-centered design. And you *know* what that is: design that focuses on the prospect. That emphasizes benefits of real value to the prospect. That highlights offers to induce immediate action. And all the other things you have learned from this book.

Now, in all fairness, you may not see much of this . . . perhaps not any. And it may (I must be equitable) not be the fault of the designer. After all, it is the designer's job to render copy into a compelling presentation. But not to create the copy. Designers, after all, must work with what they've got. But you can inquire of your designer what he thinks of some of the copy he's worked with. If he doesn't know what client-centered cash copy is or why it's beneficial, you might have to have a brief tutorial on the subject (by all means recommend this book) . . . if you like the designs you see. If you don't, of course, there's no point.

Thus, either the design candidate understands client-centered marketing and has used his presentation skills to help create marketing communications that compel immediate action. Or, he doesn't understand the marketing . . . but has the skills to create such communications notwithstanding.

Given how much copy is produced that doesn't begin to take the client into account, you can't blame the designer unduly if you don't see in his portfolio evidence of client-centered marketing communications. But you *can* blame the designer if he isn't willing to listen to and understand your objective and isn't able to say how he'll help you achieve it. That is a person you *must* avoid.

So ask some pointed questions:

- What kinds of design elements have you found helpful for getting the prospect to open the envelope?
- What kinds of design factors help focus the prospect's eye on the offer, the offer that induces him to respond?
- What kinds of factors do you use to accentuate the benefits the prospect gets by responding to a format like this?
- How would you arrange the copy so the prospect must continue reading onto a second . . . or third . . . page?
- What colors do you find most attract prospects and make them want to respond? Is this your personal feeling . . . or do you have some evidence?
- What kinds of type faces have you found most compelling to get prospects to respond?

Get the idea?

For you see, *each* design element either works to get the prospect to respond . . . or it is pointless. And it is the designer's job, for all that he proclaims himself an artist, to know how each element works . . . and to make sure it works for you to get prospects to respond faster.

If your designer candidate isn't making sense on these issues . . . if he doesn't know what you're talking about . . . . or gives you vague responses . . . end the meeting. Because it's quite, quite pointless to continue.

The good designer knows:

- which type faces are more helpful in getting people to respond;

- what type sizes are too small and turn off prospects instead of motivating them to read on;
- if letters should have serifs . . . or not . . . and why;
- which colors attract more readers . . . and which repel;
- how to emphasize important words, the words that offer the greatest benefits to your prospects;
- how to position copy so that your prospects keep reading, deeper and deeper into the body of your text.

And all the rest.

Designers, you see, are crucial personnel in the marketing task force. But not because they tell you such and such a look is "contemporary". Or that this or that element looks "stylish". You should beware of designers that talk this tripe. The designer's one and only task, his only reason for being, is to find the design elements that are most likely to produce an immediate response. *And to fight to get you to use them.* Nothing else matters. You must understand this!

The good designer is a knowledgeable professional, armed with the necessary skills about how to use design to motivate prospects to respond faster. And an advocate who both explains what is necessary to you . . . and works hard to get you to use his ideas. He is not just a passive receptacle into which you pour your thoughts. He is a person who understands what you wish to achieve and does what is necessary to ensure that you reach your objective.

Can you honestly say that this is the kind of designer you have worked with in the past? I doubt it.

Which is one crucial reason why your marketing efforts have not been resoundingly successful.

Engaging Your Designer

At some point, you *will* get the answers you're looking for. You *will* find a designer who is interested in helping you achieve your objectives. In short, you *will* find a client-centered marketer who happens to approach the business of motivating prospect response through the elements of design. Before you engage him, however, check just a few more things.

- Will he give you references to clients you can ask about his work habits?
- Will he pick up and deliver copy if necessary?
- Does he provide you with both home and office telephones?
- Is his office conveniently located for you?
- Does he do the work himself, or subcontract it?

And, more importantly, does he guarantee your satisfaction?

I can assure you that getting the right answers to these questions is more important than what you're probably worrying about: how much he charges, and if he charges by the project or the hour.

Only if you get satisfactory answers to these questions should you consider engaging this paragon. For if his work is superb but he is difficult to work with, this may not be such a happy match after all.

What if you like most of what you hear — but not all? What then? Haggle. But don't haggle too hard if you're certain this is the person you want to work with, the person you feel confident can make your marketing communications successful by using design elements to motivate prospect response.

Still, *this* is the moment to find out how your fees can be reduced (for that's really what you're worried about, isn't it?). These days, with the advent of desk-top publishing and telecommunications, there are ways, ways you should be using, to cut your design bill.

Find out, for example, if inputting copy on your computer will save you money. Discover what kind of system your designer uses and see if it's compatible with yours. If not, don't worry . . . so long as your designer has access to a translating device, like a DaynaFile. Such a device enables computers to "talk" to each other by translating one computer's information into a form a non-compatible computer can read. Even if you and your designer are working on different systems — you IBM compatible, your designer on a Macintosh, as so often happens — so long as he has access to such a translating mechanism, you shouldn't have any problems. But find out how much this service costs anyway. Sometimes, on short jobs, it costs more to use this modern "convenience" than it does to reenter the text.

If your designer can take copy on diskette, get his style and format tips. Someday (and I hope it's soon) *all* designers will be able to give computerized marketers guidelines for how they'd like us to enter and arrange text. Guidelines they can give us *before* we've made a perfectly innocent and egregiously costly error. Someday . . . but since this commonsense epoch has not yet arrived, make sure your designer gives you the computer text guidelines you need to follow working with him. This should cut your expenses. You don't want to pay your designer for inputting text, after all, or doing things you might easily have done yourself . . . if you'd only known. You want to pay him for arranging what you've provided with all the design elements he has available so that people respond to his particular genius . . . and your compelling offer.

A Word About Modems

Assuming both you and your designer have computers *and* modems (that is, the device you need for telephone transmission of your data), you may well find this an easy way to transmit your copy quickly and inexpensively. But sometimes not easily. Some of my most frustrating moments in this age of dawning telecommunications have come when I've tried to follow some techie's advice about using "easy" modem communications.

To my sometimes not-so-secret satisfaction even computer jockies often fail to make this supposedly facile system work facilely. Yet, *when* it works, it *is* astonishingly helpful. That's why I recommend you get in touch with the Boston Computer Society (1 Center Plaza, Boston, MA 02108) and its Telecommunications Group. This group, for both advanced and basic users, provides tips on how to master the useful, if often irritating, art of modem communications. It also provides a helpful newsletter and, for just about $10, an online starter kit.

By the way, don't let the parochial name of this entirely worthy organization put you off paying its minimal fee (about $45 annually) for joining. It is the largest computer user group in the world, has members nationwide, and can provide you with useful computer information for whatever you're trying to do with your cyclopic machine.

Familiarizing Yourself With Design Basics

I am not, as anyone familiar with my books knows, an advocate of the "guru" school of consulting. By that I mean I do not approve and do not practice the kind of consulting that demands the client place himself fully and irrevocably in the hands of an all-knowing (and little-saying) consultant who may well solve the problem but doesn't bother to explain his decisions to his clients . . . much less involve that client in the problem-solving process.

We are all familiar with this school of consulting. It's the way old-fashioned medicine was practiced . . . and still is by the old-fashioned doctors, of whatever age, who continue this benighted operation today. Such people say, in effect, "You, client, don't need to know anything about what's going on. Or how I intend to solve your problem. Or even the difficulties I may be having. Just trust me, your god-like consultant."

As the true self-help master, believing in and daily practicing the art of human development, this attitude horrifies me. This is why I'm including this bit of advice on how to work with your designer: familiarize yourself, in at least general terms, with the kinds of issues he must resolve in your favor and the tools he has available to do so. The more you know about them, the more intelligently you can help him help you solve your problem: namely getting more people to respond faster. This necessitates some knowledge of design basics.

Now, as I hasten to add, I am not an expert in design, and don't claim to be. But, thanks to the work of at least two specialists whom I am happy to bring to your attention, I at least know the kinds of problems the designer confronts and must solve so that I can get what I want *and* what kinds of solutions the designer has available to solve them. I am therefore able to approach the designer as, if not an equal, at least an intelligent layman. This is absolutely crucial, because, in the last analysis, *I* am the marketer who must make the final decisions about how my dollars and resources are best utilized, not the designer; he doesn't begin to have the investment in the matter that I do. It is because of your investment . . . and your need to ensure that it is profitable for you . . . that you must familiarize yourself with design basics.

Let's begin.

Acknowledging My Experts

In this section, I am relying particularly on the work of two experts whom I heartily commend to you:

- Marlene Miller, author of *Business Guide To Print Promotion*, Iris Communication Group, 1278 Glenneyre, Suite 138, Laguna Beach, CA

92651. This book is an intelligent walk through three major subject areas: the world of print, including typesetting, paper, and the printing process; creative elements such as copywriting, photography and illustration, and design and art production; and key projects you're very likely to have: logo and stationery, brochures, and direct mail and print advertising.

- Judy E. Pickens, author of *The Copy-To-Press Handbook: Preparing Words and Art for Print*, John Wiley & Sons Publishers. In over 500 closely-written pages, Pickens offers a doggedly thorough approach to the *entire* matter of getting your marketing materials into print. You get crucial information on planning production specifications and the production budget and schedule; writing and editing copy, designing for print, selecting and using art, art sources, typesetting, preparing mechanical artwork, paper and ink, and much more.

When you have read these two books — and lived through one or two projects, I might add — you will have the basic information you need to deal comfortably with your designer so that you'll make intelligent decisions and not just be forced, because of your ignorance, to take the advice you're given, whether it's useful or not.

Having directed you to these twin sources of so much useful information, I would now like to deal with the subject in my own inimitable way . . . that is to say, from the jaundiced perspective of the hard-boiled marketer. Because, as I say yet again, not one word in even these superb books . . . or any other . . . matters unless it can be used to induce immediate prospect response.

With this key fact in mind, I should like to address myself to some important issues you must deal with.

The Type-Style You Use

The objective of *each* part of *each* marketing communication you produce is the same: to get the prospect to read on to the next part and to assist in producing an immediate response.

Since the year 114 A.D. when the great column of the Emperor Trajan was chiseled in imperial Rome, we have had available a style of type that assists you in doing this: it is called serif. Its opposite number, developed later, is called sans serif.

Serifs are hairlines, light lines or strokes projecting from the end of the main line of an individual letter of type. But, of course, it is easier to show you what they are. For that, you have only to look at the individual letters on this line. The serifs are the devices at the end of the letters that subtilely push you ahead to the next letter and so on to the next word. For, you see, the function of serifs is to move you through what you are reading . . . a direct marketing function.

Because serifs aid the movement of the eye, they are used wherever rapid communication is required . . . in books, for instance, like this one . . . and in your marketing communications.

Much, much later, in this century actually, the sans serif style of type was finalized, although people had been experimenting with it for some time. The idea, as particularly expressed by artists of the German Bauhaus movement, was to make typesetting more contemporary.

And so sans serif type was the result.

See the difference?

You don't need to know the history. But you do need to know this: the serif style is most likely what you'll select for your body copy, always remembering it helps move the eye through your text. However, you'll probably want to use a sans serif style for your headlines where you want the eye to linger, if only for a moment . . . because of the headline's benefit-rich message.

This is the kind of advice, you see, your designer should be giving you.

Using Type To Create Client-Centered Pages

How to get people to spend their time reading what you've produced is *the* marketing condundrum. Part of the solution to this perpetual puzzle lies in properly handling 5 essential matters:

- the choice of typeface
- the size of type
- the amount of space between lines (that is, the leading)
- the width of lines, and
- the format.

My intention here is not to give you definitive answers to these critical matters. But to remind you of what you and your designer should be thinking about when you confront the essential matter of how your products and services can best be presented to your prospects.

A Very Few Words About Each Of These Points

— On the matter of typeface

While it is certainly true that a typeface expresses the marketer, this expression is far less important that the critical matter of inducing the prospect to read and then to act. Your designer has access to a host of type faces from the exotic to the decidedly mundane. But when you discuss this matter with your designer, the only significant question should be: which type face is easiest for your prospect to read and offers him the fewest barriers to instant communication and action. This suggests a typeface that is at once clean, sharp, and energetic.

— On the size of your type

When you are a writer like I am, in love with the glory of words, you may well be inclined to overfeed your prospects, to want them to have every reason, to know every benefit. And because you have only limited space, you do what seems the only sensible thing: you cut the size of your type instead of the expanse of your copy. Don't. I beg you. On the matter of type size, as in all other matters, produce your document with the reader — and his tired eyes — in mind. And make sure you press your designer to advise you about what you've produced. Is it too small? Is it no longer easy to read?

— On the amount of space (that is leading) between lines

Ever notice how paragraphs in something you're reading tend to run together? This is largely a problem of the spacing, that is, the leading, between paragraphs. Watch out! As direct response authority Herschell Gordon Lewis says in his excellent book *More Than You Ever Wanted To Know About Mail Order Advertising* (Prentice Hall):

"Safety in readability lies in setting type as large as you can, solid. Add four to twelve points of lead between paragraphs, and your copy will be broken up into readable blocks, avoiding the gray look that makes a copy block seem formidable to the reader."

— On the width of lines

You want your reader to comprehend what you've got to say easily. Quickly. And move on to your other persuasive information. Line width helps.

Pioneer work done years ago by Professor Miles A. Tinker helped determine not only how long that should be but the correct size for type, too. The most readable line should be two times the length of the alphabet plus 8 additional characters, that is 60 characters total. More technically, a line of 8 to 13 centimeters allows for comprehension in a single eye scan, assuming Tinker's recommended 10 point type. Anything longer (or in smaller type) means your prospect has to work harder. This, of course, is not good for either your message or your marketing. (If you're interested in reviewing Tinker's other results, consult his book *Basics For Effective Reading*, University of Minnesota Press, 1965.)

— On the format you adopt

Format means presentation shape. There are three common formats: flush left, flush right and justified.

Flush left copy has a
straight left side and a
ragged right side.

Flush right copy is just
the reverse.

And justified copy has
both straight left and right
sides.

For what you're doing, conversational accessible marketing communications, you'll probably be using the first of these. Because this format gives the feeling of an informal personal letter, and hence, subtly, of something important from someone important. This is just the feeling you want your prospect to have.

As your designer makes his recommendations in each area, look him in the eye and say, slowly and deliberately: "Have you given me the best recommendation for getting my prospect to respond immediately?" Then wait for the answer. Now say, "Are you holding anything back? Would you use something different yourself? Do you have any further idea, any refinement, on how we can improve prospect response?" These are the key questions that ought to be asked of every designer and his recommendations. But almost never are.

Some Type Tips

Here are just a few key points to keep in mind that will help you when considering the matter of typesetting:

- Use client-centered subheadings to break up your copy.

Example? This book. It's littered with them! Why do I use them? For the same reason you will: because subheads — short benefit-rich, client-centered mini-headlines — draw your prospect in and make it easier for him to read a page of printing. Make sure you have some. And make sure they're always focused on the prospect and what he wants . . . or fears.

- Position your headlines for maximum meaning.

All headlines are not short. Some (I know!) extend over several lines. When they do, break your headlines for maximum meaning. That is, make sure *each* individual line conveys its own client-centered message, instead of leaving the reader to struggle over several lines to get the point. If you've got a point, make it fast. And make it *to* the reader.

- Keep your type selection simple.

Just because you *can* use lots of different type faces, doesn't mean you should. These days, with the advent of desk-top printing programs, I see a proliferation of type styles in a single marketing document. This is a mistake; it looks unsophisticated at best, irritating at worst. Try to use a single type style in a single marketing document, but if you want variety don't use more than two. In this case, try one for the body copy and another for your headlines. Remember: the objective is to get people to read what you're sending easily and respond quickly. Not to demonstrate how many typefaces you have access to.

- Plan for type in colored inks.

As authority Marlene Miller points out, type specimen catalogs show type in black. "If the type you order is going to be used in a different color, plan for the fact that it will appear lighter than the black sample." To compensate, you can order a heavier weight type or a large size, or both. Remember: the lighter the color of the ink, the more this adjustment is needed to retain good legibility.

Getting People To Turn The Page

Following this advice, you and your designer will produce compelling, interesting, client-centered pages. But I tell you this: don't treat each page as somehow separate, distinct from all the other pages. The objective, after all, is to get the prospect to read more and more. Not to come to a full stop at the end of a page. This means thinking about the crucial matter of how to get your prospect to keep reading, to keep turning pages, to read on. Right from the very first panel he sees . . . which may well, remember, be on the outer envelope! Here are some suggestions for achieving this crucial objective:

- Promise benefits ahead. If you want your prospect to read on, tell him what he gets by doing so. You can use this tactic on the outside of your envelope . . . or at the bottom of individual pages. But do make sure you deliver what you've promised.

- Complete sentences with an elipses (. . .) indicating there is more to come . . .

- Break sentences in half so that the person must turn the page to find how they end.

- Tell your prospect that you're not finished laying out benefits for him and invite him to turn the page to get more. Just because the prospect is already in the midst of your copy, doesn't mean you should forego the opportunity to urge him to continue to read on. Remember, your prospect can quit reading at any time. This is why you must keep urging him not to.

Obviously how you lay-out your pages will help facilitate the feeling that each page, each piece is not distinct unto itself but a part of a whole marketing message. Don't give the prospect the chance to feel at any point that he has reached the end . . . until he has reached the end you intend for him. Making sure he always feels there is more for him ahead is partly a copywriting problem, of course, but it is also a lay-out and design issue which your designer must help you solve.

Of Paper And Colors

You now have your copy, your type and your lay-out. You are moving ever closer to printing. It's therefore time to consider the kind of paper you'll use and the question of color.

Sadly, as you are surely aware, most people throw most marketing communications away without giving them much attention. You do this yourself. And everybody else does, too. It is because of this fact . . . the undeniable fact that in most circumstances over 9 out of 10 people receiving your marketing communication will throw them away without sustained consideration . . . that you need to give some attention to the matter of the quality of your paper. For here you may be able to save some money.

Perhaps my singular feelings about paper began when I was a child. My parsimonious father, you see, made all his children write their school work on the backs of scrap paper from his office. I didn't use completely clean sheets of paper until college and, when in my own business, quickly reverted to *pater*'s penny-pinching practice. Indeed, when one of my colleagues discovered I had written an entire book on the backs of out-of-date flyers, he was so astonished he bought me a ream of clean paper as a present. Still, I find that though I'm now over 40, my frugal paper habits haven't changed significantly.

Thus, I say to you from a lifetime of experience: find ways to keep your paper cost to the very rock-bottom.

You may argue that such a step will tarnish your image (you really mean your ego, of course), costing you prestige, sales, and your place as an Immortal of the *Académie Française*. Don't be silly. The drawing power of ivory laid rag bond is most decidedly overrated.

Each time you send a marketing document, see if you can reduce your costs by reducing the quality of your paper. Make this quality one of the marketing variables you test. I don't make this suggestion idly, either. For a long time I printed my catalog on 50-pound offset (this or the slightly heavier 60-pound is what you're probably using for your marketing materials). It looked good. But it also cost a good deal more than newsprint. I struggled with the issue of whether using that cheaper newsprint would cost me sales, hurt my image. Finally, I decided the potential of continued savings made the experiment worth the risk.

But, you see, there was no risk. For sales were not affected adversely in the slightest . . . which, of course, made the first newsprint catalog dramatically more profitable than the last 50-pound offset effort. All because of significantly reduced paper cost in a very large run of catalogs.

My message to you, then, about selecting a paper comes to this:

- Remember that most people will throw what you're sending them away without a glance. The money you invest in paper (along with everything else) is, therefore, largely wasted.

- Rather than put money into such fripperies as superior paper, put it into extra contacts with your prospects. Two hits with cheaper paper will, I guarantee you, produce a better result than just one hit with superior stock.

- Always experiment with less expensive papers and keep doing so until your response drops. This probably means you cannot make a paper selection for life, certainly not early in your business life. As in all other aspects of marketing, this one must not be set in cement, and certainly not before you've experimented with alternatives.

Here as elsewhere you must consult with your designer, the pertinent question being, "Can we use a cheaper stock, a less expensive paper quality? Or do you think this will adversely affect my response." Now listen closely. Designers, like everyone else, fall into habits of behavior. They recommend one thing over and over again, not necessarily because it is the best for achieving *your* objectives. But because it is what they know. Force them to evaluate their assumptions. Then see if what they do makes sense.

Using Color

Color improves response. I learned this in a dramatic way thanks to my dealings with a card deck company. My initial effort in black and white was 40% less effective than my subsequent use of color. In this case blue.

Remember, there are lots of ways to use color:

- You can use a single color and screen it to achieve the effect of different colors.

- You can use a colored stock (that is, paper) with black ink.
- You can use a colored ink.
- Or you can go whole-hog and use four-color printing.

My advice? Here, as always, I tell you to spend as little of your money as possible while pumping your designer for key information on how to use color to achieve what you want: to draw the prospect's attention to what you've created and hold it there sufficiently long until your client-centered copy begins to capture your prospect's more sustained interest.

For color, you see, is but a means to your necessary end of pulling the prospect in . . . and keeping him there until you can motivate him to act because of your copy.

For this purpose, you will find for the most part that a printer's stock colors (in both ink and paper) will work perfectly well. Other expense seems quite pointless to me . . . unless (because of the graphics you're using) you need superior color quality.

How will you know what he's got? The designer can assist you. And what assists him? The printer himself, of course, and the Pantone Matching System, swatchbooks of color samples that are virtually universally used throughout the printing industry. But remember as your eyes feast on this tonal riot that color always costs you more. Your objective is not to spend: but to attract the greatest number of prospects for the least conceivable cost. Thus, the question really becomes: how can you get the greatest benefit from color for the least conceivable expense?

This is where your designer must help and where you must be firm with him, especially if you harbor suspicions that he's more interested in the look of the piece than its ability to draw responses for the lowest possible price.

This means seeing what you can do with a single color. Now obviously this is not appropriate for many products where four-color printing is essential. But in the marketing of a large percentage of products and services a single color . . . with a color screen . . . will do nicely.

Where does this color go?

Color works best for you if you use it in connection with the internal message, namely those crucial client-centered benefits which cause the prospect to stop in his tracks to gather information about what you've got for him.

This means you'll want to use color to highlight:

- headlines
- offers
- buyer benefits
- action dates

Color, you see, should carry straight to the prospect's eyes the crucial pith of your client-centered message. If he reads nothing else, color should give him the necessary essentials of what's in this deal for him.

Color, then, must not be applied lavishly . . . but precisely, its end result being clear prospect comprehension about what he gets and why he must act NOW to get it.

Color, as I am discussing it here, must not be considered decorative. Instead, you must regard it as a helpful means of capturing the prospect's attention and holding it on key client-centered information, information that induces this prospect to read the remainder of the copy and to act. Moreover, you must attempt to achieve this crucial result for the least possible expense. Which is where you should focus your discussion of this subject with your designer.

A Word Or Two About Photographs

Before I leave this chapter, which I hope has focused your thinking about the role of design and lay-out in the marketing process and how you should be working with your designer, I should like to say a word or two about graphics, photographs and art work.

Various people can help you select something appropriate. You can follow the advice of Marlene Miller, for instance, and Judy Pickens. You can turn to the readily available books of clip-art produced by companies like Dover Publications, Inc., 180 Varick St., New York, NY 10014 (1-800-223-3130). Or you can use stock photographs.

A good person to check for stock photos is my friend Rohn Engh. He maintains a free stock photo service for subscribers. Contact him at PhotoSource International, Pine Lake Farm, Osceola, WI 54020. Or you can use a photographer to do custom work for your project. (Here resources like *Worksource* are invaluable in helping you find the talent you need.)

I find to my chagrin, however, there is far more written about how to find or create graphics than there is about how to use them wisely. Hence, I would like to end this chapter with a little advice about the use of graphics in marketing:

- A graphic is worth a thousand words if and only if it helps the prospect make up his mind to buy what you're selling that much faster than body copy. This means graphics should focus on the benefits you get (or anxieties you avoid) by using your product or service. The best graphics are involvement graphics . . . they draw the prospect in and allow him to experience the benefits of what you are selling. Again, as you won't be surprised to hear me say, they are about the prospect . . . not about you, the marketer.

This applies, too, to graphic captions. These captions, like all copy, *must* be about what your prospect gets when he uses what you're selling. Not about what you're selling.

Marketing, as you well know, is about movement . . . about getting a prospect to take immediate action to acquire the benefits you're offering. Your graphics must be active, too, not passive. They must establish a connection between your prospect and your product or service. And they must drive home benefits in the caption copy. Unless you can do this, don't waste your money on expensive graphics. Because they won't be doing what they're supposed to: motivating people to acquire what you're selling. This is what every aspect of graphics, design, typography and lay-out must work to accomplish. Or it has no reason for existing at all.

Chapter 17

How To Use Your Copy So You Get The Results You Want, Or Secrets Of Money-Making Marketing

Now you've got your cash copy and the lay-out that will bring it to your prospect's attention in the way that best ensures an immediate response. Right? If you're not sure, go back to the relevant chapters of this book until you are *absolutely certain* this is what you have to work with. If you are sure, you're now ready for the *next* hurdle: using this copy as part of a marketing strategy designed to get your prospect to respond.

What, you may be thinking, you mean I can't just write wonderful client-centered copy, arrange it for maximum impact, get it into my prospect's hands and sit back ready for the money to start rolling in like Ol' Man River?

Not quite.

Oh, to be sure, if you've written the kind of copy you are now capable of writing (you *have* been paying attention, haven't you?), your initial marketing activity *will* get responses. Perhaps quite a lot of responses. Yet it won't generate all the responses it could if you repeat the process. For remember . . . your prospects are beseiged with offers. In major urban areas, they get hit with thousands each week, all from people with products and services to sell. No wonder there are days when we consumers feel shell-shocked. We are!

Several things ensure that these consumers will respond to your offer rather than someone else's:

389

- They know you're talking to them. That is, your offer is clearly directed to them and no one else.
- You've thought through every conceivable benefit to your prospects and have brought them to their attention in a way that makes them want to respond NOW.
- You've taken the time to understand why your prospects might be anxious or nervous about you and what you're selling . . . and have fully and honestly answered every objection.
- You've made them an offer they can't possibly refuse . . . you've provided them, that is, with an immediate reason for action.

And you've resolved to be persistent . . . to keep bringing your benefits to their attention over and over and over again until they cannot conceivably fail to know who you are and what you can do for them.

Why such persistence? First, because you know your prospects have lots of other things on their minds and don't get the significance of things the first time they hear about them. You certainly don't. So why should they be different?

Second, because you've got a personal or business goal for yourself. You can only reach it by persuading increasingly large numbers of people to acquire the benefits you have for them. You can never reach your objective, understand, unless you help these large numbers get theirs. *Never.*

Finally, and importantly, you have benefits for your prospects which you will do anything to make sure they take advantage of. It must bother you . . . really bother you . . . that there are still people out in the world who aren't profiting from what you can do for them. Unless you are certain they are all flatworms, unlikely ever to take action, you must persist to bring your problem-solving products and services to their attention. Only afterwards can you rest.

How You Probably Feel When I Say This

Recently I was the speaker at a trade show in Boston. Both before and after my presentation, I worked the crowd from a booth in the exhibit area. I shared this booth with three other entrepreneurs. They hadn't had the advantage I did, the advantage, that is, of being able to place their materials directly into the hands of their prospects, as I did at my convention session. No, indeed. But they did have an incentive to act that I didn't have: they had paid for the booth and needed to get their money back.

I went to this trade show as I go to all such events: with a fixed objective in mind. In this case, I wanted to get a flyer about how to get a free year's subscription to my Sure-Fire Business Success Catalog into the hands of 300 people within three hours. That is, I wanted to connect with 300 people within 180 minutes with an offer they couldn't refuse. To do this, even when you have an audience to entrance and motivate, takes a lot of hustle. So upon arriving, I went to work inviting each person who passed our booth to take a coupon for the free year's subscription. Most did.

Occasionally during the time I was working the crowd, all potential prospects, I looked around the exhibit area and towards my booth colleagues. Without exception they hung back, afraid to reach out to the people passing by (people, I might add, who were in short supply compared to the number of exhibitors present). I was the *only* one actively passing out *anything*.

Finally one of my boothmates said, "I like your books. But they seem pushy to me. And here you are passing out flyers to everyone instead of waiting for the really interested people to come up and take what they want. I can't do this."

This is a common problem. A serious miscalculation. A devastating error.

Instead of saying so, however, I asked him some questions:

- Take a look at all the booths in our sector. How many of them actually have people at them? The answer: next to none.
- How many of these exhibitors have paid for their booths? The answer: all.
- How many of them want to make a profit from today? The answer: all, I guess.
- How many of them will make a profit if they connect with so few people. No answer. Instead, dawning awareness.

Instead of having an objective, a strategy, if you will, this entrepreneur kept hoping for lightning to strike; kept hoping that someone, anyone, would on his own volition approach his booth and make his investment profitable, instead of profoundly questionable.

I don't believe this. Instead I believe in the Rule of Seven, in the need, that is, to connect with your prospects again and again and again during a finite period of time with a precise client-centered message until at last they act. To make this work at this convention, where no list of attendees was provided (or, so I was later told to my consternation, even kept at all), I had to capture the names myself.

And I did. I handed out exactly 300 flyers with my special convention offer . . . and received back just over 100 either on the spot or in the mail. What if I had done this same thing with direct mail? How many, then, might I have received back? Maybe 10 or 12, a 3 to 4% response. On the spot hustle (and, admittedly, a convention slot to motivate people) gave me far more names to conjure with.

How many names did my lethargic boothmate, hemmed in by caution, fear of rejection and sloth, take away? Twelve, I think he said. Very costly name acquisition, indeed, given this activity had taken two days of his life and an investment of about $300 (his share of the cost of the booth). That's why I dedicate this section to him in the hopes he may finally get the message.

Understanding And Using The Rule of Seven

I have written about the Rule of Seven before, but no discussion of cash copy and how to use it effectively can overlook this crucial strategic point. The Rule of Seven is simple; because your prospects do not act the first time they are made aware of a benefit for themselves, you, the marketer, must connect with them a minimum of seven times in your attempt to stimulate their response. How long do you have in which to connect with them? Never more than 18 months . . . and often less, depending on the nature of your business.

Moreover, if you are not prepared to make the full effort it takes to stimulate prospect response, you should make no effort whatsoever. Why? Because marketing efforts less complete fall disproportionately short of success as a result of their lack of synergy, that is the combined and correlated client-centered force that finally induces the prospect to act. If this is confusing, it won't be in a minute, after we review some key components of this crucial marketing rule.

Realizing Why Your Prospects Don't Respond Immediately . . . Even When You Have Something Crucial For Their Betterment

One of the hardest things for most marketers to accept is how long it takes prospects to respond . . . even when you have something that, quite literally, transforms their lives. Sadly, whatever your offer, no matter how advantageous, most people hearing about it will not respond to what you're saying. By far the overwhelming majority. Why?

There are several reasons. For one thing, the human beast (and as a good Hobbesian I know this well) is an obstinate creature, slow to change, suspicious, often implacable in stupidity.

More understandably, we have just too many other things on our minds, too many other calls on our resources. As you already know, people are over-whelmed with marketing messages. As a result, we've simply learned to screen out what comes to our attention. We see or hear them, but we don't begin to perceive them.

Thus, instead of assuming that a prospect, however much he can benefit from what I'm selling, will act the first time he hears about the advantage I offer him, I assume the exact reverse. That, he will *not* respond, no matter the significance of what I have.

This necessarily means that successful marketers think far ahead. Plot, if you will, knowing that it is up to them to do what is necessary to get the prospect to respond. If this takes several connections with the must-be-motivated prospect, then that is what they must ensure, for that is their job. The successful marketers realize while there are those who have achieved substantial wealth quickly, the vast majority of wealthy people who have earned their money have not. This doesn't dishearten them; rather, they accept it as a necessary fact of life. And plan accordingly.

It Is Always Your Responsibility To Do What's Necessary To Get The Prospect To Move; Never The Prospect's.

My booth colleague from the trade show was a supremely passive marketer. Whether out of fear or pride or some lethal mixture of both, he felt it necessary to wait for his prospects to find him . . . for them to give him permission to connect with them. The successful marketer doesn't share this constraining viewpoint. No, indeed!

The successful marketer, following the guidelines of the Rule of Seven, understands it is *his* responsibility to do whatever is necessary to connect with the prospect. That the prospect has no responsibility whatever . . . except, in due and predictable course, to turn over his consideration as legitimate payment for the benefit you have for him. That is all. *You* must do the rest.

This means that marketing, as I've said repeatedly throughout this book and my other writings, is the quintessential action sport. Passivity has no place in this arena. Nor does a false pride that demands the prospect come to you, instead of your extending yourself to your prospect. Nor modesty. Nor anxiety about what the prospect will do to you if you approach him.

Face facts now. Despite the fact you have a benefit for your prospect, there will still be people who will treat you rudely, abrasively, thoughtlessly. That's the luck of the draw and the price we pay for living in vulgar, untutored times. Don't let it bother you.

If only one out of ten, just 10%, of your total market buys what you're selling, much less one out of 10 prospects in every market you approach, you will be wealthy. Which means that fully 9 out of 10 prospects can write you off as a nuisance, or worse.

Even this may not sit well with you, however, you who wish to be the bosom buddy of the world at large. Recently, one of my readers, an Ohio financial planner, came to town and called me. I invited him for a drink, as I often do with my readers. It became obvious that he had never, though well in his thirties, outgrown what I call the "high school syndrome" — the compulsive need to be liked by everyone.

I told him what I am telling you: grow up.

When you place yourself squarely in the path of your prospect and say unequivocally that you have something for him, some tangible, palpable, substantial advantage . . . why, there is every chance he'll reject you totally. Completely. Forever. As the French sagely say, "No good deed goes unpunished."

You'd be less than human, of course, if this rejection didn't cause at least a twinge of self-pity. But let it be nothing more than a twinge. *Nothing more.* And then remember these two things:

- the extent to which you are successful is a direct measure of the extent to which you have been rejected. The most successful people have been rejected the most often. They (I might say we) come to regard, must regard, rejection as nothing more than a facet of success; as something that is inevitably a part of success and cannot be separated from success. If you are to be successful, why, you *must* be rejected . . . and if you cannot, or will not, cope with the inevitability of rejection, there is no possibility that you can ever be truly successful.

- But if this argument fails to persuade you, consider this one: even if you are personally, directly, starkly rejected by someone every minute of your life, every minute of every hour, every hour of every day, every day of every week, every week of every month, every month of every year of your life. I say, even if this horrendous sequence occurs, even then you will still have *well over* 99% of the human race left to take advantage of all the good things you offer.

And if this doesn't cheer you up, you really do need professional help.

Thus, remember: it is always your responsibility, never your prospect's, to do what is necessary to get the prospect to respond. Instead of waiting for your prospect to find you, read your sign, overcome his nervousness, step over to you, ask questions and take your client-centered marketing communications on his own initiative, you must bring it to his attention in the way best calculated to get him to stop in his tracks and get the message that you've got something for him.

Write Down Your Objective

Do you want to achieve an objective? Then, you must write this objective down and (as we shall see) create a plan that helps you achieve it. As goals strategists are so fond of saying: if you don't know where you're going, you won't know when you get there . . . and probably won't make it anyway. This is true . . . and nowhere more so than in marketing, where a single attempt to connect with your prospect cannot and will not succeed in carrying you to your furthest goals.

This sounds obvious, doesn't it? But we live in the Age of Lottery Dreams, of wild hopes that a single sequence of numbers flashed one evening on a television screen will rescue us from the bad decisions, ineptitude, and organizational missteps of a lifetime. The lottery players in their mega-millions always assume they must be among the winners, that winning — and escape — is only a day away . . . despite a mountain of costly evidence to the contrary.

No, my friend, marketers have objectives: finite, precise, mathematically certain, attainable, but only after consideration and application. We can tell you . . . and can show you, for these objectives must be written down . . . how many clients we need in what period of time . . . how many widgets we must sell . . . to reach our objectives . . . and what we must do to achieve them. And we can tell you, too, how reaching this subsidiary set of prizes leads us on to the inevitable attainment of the grander prizes that follow.

We marketers know these things . . . and know the power of putting the subconscious mind to work for us by firmly setting attainable objectives and working daily to achieve them.

Targeting Specific Groups Of Prospects

Targeting, as you've often heard me say, is the essence of successful marketing. For with targeting comes our ability to understand, really understand, who we're talking to, what they want to achieve, what's bothering them, and what motivates them to act to acquire the benefit we offer.

This targeting is crucial to successfully using the Rule of Seven.

Too many marketers use the scattershot approach to marketing . . . hoping that if they throw out enough lures, some prospect will be caught. These people may just get by in running their businesses . . . but they can never be truly successful. Success means targeting. The ability, that is, to connect and connect again with the same group of people whose problems you can solve.

Do you remember my saying one of the great problems in marketing is that marketers try to be creative? Creativity is all very well and good but hitting home with a consistent, client-centered benefit, rich with advantages for the prospect is what marketing is all about. Hitting home once, twice, and again and again and again. But hitting home to the very same people . . . the people who will — finally! — understand you have something beneficial for them.

This suggests that as you begin a marketing gambit you must be certain you can reconnect with the *same* batch of people. Otherwise, you are making an investment in futility. If people don't respond the first time you bring your benefit to their attention but if you can't reconnect with them . . . why, then, much of what you've invested will necessarily be wasted. This is precisely what happens to most marketers and why so much money "invested" in marketing is actually just thrown away. Investment, you see, means follow-up. And follow-up means being able to get access to the same names . . . or following procedures the first time which enables you to "capture" the names of your prospects so you can, indeed, follow up yourself.

This means you must avoid what I call Thumbs Up, Thumbs Down marketing, terminology I took from the old Roman Coliseum where the plebs of the Eternal City were allowed to decide if some creature should live or die. As the creatures themselves might attest, this procedure offers far too many risks for comfort.

I feel most uncomfortable putting prospects in an either buy now . . . or don't buy now dilemma. Admittedly, for some things, it may well be appropriate. But it isn't always appropriate. That's because prospects fall out all along the line of interest and response possibilities. Some are keen to take action now. Some will never take action. Some need further persuasion. But many of these persuadables will take action to put themselves in touch with you . . . if they aren't being asked to do anything else. Yet.

Thus, when sending a catalog you could say, "Never seen this catalog before? We rented your name. Unless you let me know you want to keep receiving this catalog, you won't get (the benefit you're offering)." Admittedly, people who don't buy anything but just let you know they want to keep receiving your information are soft prospects. But having the names of these soft prospects enables you to keep targeting them and, by constant presentation of rigorously client-centered copy, persuade them to become buyers. If you don't give them the chance to identify themselves to you, you've lost them . . . and the investment you made in connecting with them initially.

This is what targeting is all about. It's about understanding that all prospects won't respond immediately. That Thumbs Up (Buy Now), Thumbs Down (Don't Buy Now) marketing isn't always sensible. That capturing the name so you can reconnect with this targeted prospect often is the most intelligent thing you can do.

Note: you can target dozens, if not hundreds, of different prospect groups at any one time. I do. There's nothing wrong with that . . . so long as you can stay on top of their wants and anxieties and continue to position yourself as having that which is crucial to their happiness.

Keeping Your Benefit Message Simple And Rigorously Focused On The Prospect And What He Wants

A key part of the Rule of Seven is what this book is about. But it won't hurt to mention it again here . . . namely, keeping your benefit message simple and rigorously focused on the prospect and what he wants.

Good marketing is simple marketing. Client-centered marketing. Marketing that hits home again and again and again about what you've got for your prospect.

Most marketers make the tragic error of expecting their prospects to be as interested in what they're selling as they are themselves. This will rarely, if ever, happen. Frankly, you can only expect your competitors . . . and the people who wish to emulate your success . . . to be as interested in your products and services (and other aspects of your business) as you are. If you assume that the rest of your prospects are interested only in themselves and what you can do for them now, you'll *never* go wrong.

Once you have determined who you are marketing to and what they want from you, you must think through your benefits. Once you have these benefits, you must hit home with them over and over and over again. Of course, this may bore you. Of course, you may wish for something new, exciting, different. You're an American, after all, and these are virtually patriotic buzz-words. But until your *prospects* show boredom, as evidenced by their less frequent response, your job is to keep pounding away with your profoundly simple, deeply client-centered message. Again. And again. And again.

I challenge you to find this kind of message in most of the marketing communications you receive and review. In 99 cases out of one hundred, it isn't there. What is there is self-centered copy, facts that have no significance to the prospect, impenetrable jargon, features of products and services that the marketer hasn't begun to excite you about . . . and a whole lot more rubbish. This isn't marketing: it's self-subsidized hara-kiri.

And what's in the marketer's follow-up materials? More of the same. That is, more waste, pointlessness, and consummate futility. All lavished on a rightly uncaring public by a marketer who feels certain that this batch of his ingenuity will certainly get the responses he wants. This is a marketer who honestly (if appallingly) has no idea why it all fails as miserably as his other efforts.

But *you* know. Don't you? And *you* won't make this mistake. Will you?

You'll keep all your marketing communications strictly focused on your buyer. You'll pound home the benefits he gets from your offer. And give him a reason to act now. You'll answer his objections. And make every fact you present directly relevant to this supremely important being who must be persuaded to act. For if he doesn't act both his world and yours remain comparatively impoverished and incomplete. A condition that should trouble you profoundly . . .

Figure How Much Time You Have To Persuade Your Prospects To Become Buyers

Some goods and services are perishable. They must be purchased by a certain time, or they have less value, perhaps no value whatsoever. In these situations the thing itself sets the time line. Other goods and services are hardy perennials. In these circumstances it is the need or want of the customer that dictates when the thing be purchased. There is no necessary or intrinsic reason within the thing itself why the prospect must buy it at any given time. Yet either way, you can use the the Rule of Seven to your benefit.

Perhaps here it would be useful to spend just a moment telling you how there came to be a Rule of Seven at all. The initial work in this area was done by movie marketers in the Great Depression of the 'thirties. They had to charm money out of people (many of whom had precious little) for what was most decidedly not an essential of life. And they had to do so quickly, because there was always another movie in the works which would shortly displace the current favorite as the object of their marketing activities.

These marketers, then, were looking for a formula, a formula to induce the most prospects to experience their product in the shortest period of time, so they could then get these same prospects to avail themselves of the next offering, again in the shortest period of time.

Out of this need the Rule of Seven was born.

What these marketers discovered was that a movie prospect had to hear about their film *at least seven positive times* before they could be certain he'd go to see it. *And* that this process was most effective if it took place within just 72 hours.

The means they used to achieve their objective were various and included newspaper reviews, write-ups on the stars, radio publicity, personal appearances, and various emanations from the publicity mill of the great age of Hollywood. Through these means — and satisfied customers as well, of course — they also counted on generating the most powerful marketing leverage of all: word of mouth promotion. Yet all these means were focused on a single objective: getting the maximum number of people to buy the product in the shortest period of time.

Now, very few people reading this book will be promoting first-run films. But all of us must be conscious of a deadline we're working towards . . . the deadline by which our prospects must respond. Either that deadline is built into the product, like Valentine cards, or it isn't, such as ongoing copywriting services for businesses. Either way the Rule of Seven applies.

And either way the marketer must work backwards from the date by which he wants his prospects to respond so that he can create the appropriate plan, featuring the minimum of seven prospect contacts. Here's an illustration.

I've had a client who buys distressed properties for a living, single-family houses whose owners have failed to make their mortgage payments and are therefore subject to mortgage foreclosure proceedings. According to the state where he practices his trade, once these properties fall subject to the legal foreclosure proceedings it is absolutely possible to determine which day they will be sold at public auction. At that exact moment his prospects lose control of what he wants and therefore cease to be his prospects.

Thus, this marketer must put the Rule of Seven to work for him between the day when the difficulties of the home owner are made public record (the first moment he learns who his prospects are) and the day when, given continuing non-payment by the prospect, his house is sold at public auction. That is this marketer's time-line, in this case about 100 days. It is during this period that he must connect with his prospect not once but a minimum of seven times with a simple, compelling, client-centered message and suitable offers that get this prospect to respond before he loses his right to do so.

As you see, here the marketing time period is obvious and fixed. Just as it is for many other products and services: seminars have dates when they'll take place; fruits and flowers have seasons when they must be sold; places have high seasons for visiting. In these cases, the marketing is geared to a precise objective at a precise time. And, therefore, is perfectly logical and inevitable.

But what of the rest of us, selling both products and services, where there is no such clear cut focus? Why, we must create one, of course. An artificial deadline.

In these cases, marketing is the business of creating perfectly artificial limits and working to persuade our prospects they are entirely real. Persuasive offers help.

Timed offers give us an artificial (but perfectly sensible) deadline on which to focus. Now you can use the Rule of Seven to sell the offer. By marketing the offer, you succeed in transforming a standard product or service into one that commands your prospect's especial attention and gets him to act NOW. And, importantly, in the act of selling this offer you also continue to market your company generally.

If you have only one target population, you must use your offers sparingly, or you'll cheapen their effectiveness. But if you, like me, have hundreds of different markets you regularly market to (which is, of course, what you should be striving for), your task is quite different. You, then, should *always* have an offer going, however artificial, so that you continually succeed in drawing enhanced attention to your products or services.

The key here is knowing how many different offers you can juggle simultaneously and how often you can bring an offer to the attention of any given market. Personally, I've found I can create a special offer once each year for *each* product that I sell to *each* specific market. I spend a considerable amount of time creating these offers . . . and selling them to the particular market. This keeps me very busy, but it does continually stimulate new business, business that I might never otherwise have received . . . and certainly wouldn't have received as fast. Of course, each offer in its own right is part of the general Rule of Seven for my firm in that market, a means, that is, of incessantly promoting my firm and what it can do for my prospects. A very neat system.

Create Your Rule Of Seven Plan

When people hear about The Rule of Seven they instinctively feel it makes sense. That much has never been in doubt. Anyone who's sat through just a single evening of television in which one of America's major advertisers has, in just a two- or three-hour period, rammed seven identical commercials down his throat knows this is the way things should be done. But when they set about promoting their own enterprises they most decidedly do not follow the rule.

Instead, most marketers create random marketing efforts, episodic, sporadic, individual in the worst sense of this word. Efforts, that is, that don't hammer home a simple, benefit-rich client-centered message over and over again to the same group. Because this is a terrible problem that will cost you your marketing shirt, I earnestly advise you to think through in advance of your first contact with your prospects just how you will succeed in connecting with them a minimum of seven times in the period of time you have chosen as your marketing window of opportunity, (never longer, of course, than 18 months).

First, of course, you must know the means that are available to you to connect with your prospects. I am *not* going to go through all of them with you again here. If you're truly serious about marketing, you'll put in a few hours of your time to really study my book MONEY MAKING MARKETING, a companion volume to this one. Suffice it to say, there are many ways you can reach your targeted markets including:

- package stuffers
- direct mail
- free publicity through radio, television, and print media
- paid advertising
- card decks
- trade shows
- telephone marketing
- workshops and other talk programs
- personal visits

- new buyer upgrade letters
- special past buyer contacts

Given the right circumstances, each of these — and all the other marketing opportunities available to you — can be appropriate.

But the trick is this: you *must* be certain you are reaching the *same* group of prospects . . . not one new group after another.

Recently in one of my marketing workshops, I asked each participant, all practicing business people, to write down each kind of marketing they were engaged in and who they were marketing do. Then I asked them to choose just one of the groups they wanted as customers and had been marketing to. Tell me, I said, how many times you have contacted this group within the last six months.

The results were sadly predictable. Not a single person in this group of 25 entrepreneurs, having invested in an initial contact with a targeted prospect group, had continued to attempt to get this *same* group to respond and become customers. Instead, despairing because of an almost universal initially poor response, they had invested their scarce resources in an initial attempt to get *another* body of prospects to respond and become buyers. With no better luck.

Now, admittedly, these marketers had other problems. They hadn't spent much time trying to identify a group of prospects who wanted what they were selling, nor were they masters of client-centered cash copy. Still, when we took time to look at what they were doing the disturbing trend became remarkably clear: they were looking for a magic formula, a single key, the open-sesame that would enable them to make a single marketing gambit sufficiently successful so they could joyfully abandon the costly and disheartening business of marketing. What madness!

You know, you *must* know, such thoughts are foolish. No single marketing gambit can end the need for further marketing. This is why you must plan . . . why you must commit yourself to doing all you can to make sure you can connect with the same targeted group again and again . . . and then do what is necessary so you do.

Let me give you an idea of what a plan is like, while advising you there are literally thousands of seven-step plans you can use to reach your *minimum* number of prospect connections:

Say I wanted to reach nonprofit organizations in the New England area. These are possible buyers of various consulting services I have available, workshops, books, and audio cassettes. In other words, I have many solutions available for their problems. With them as with other prospects, I have twin objectives: to hit them with a client-centered message a minimum of seven times in no more than 18 months and to keep my expenses in reaching them to an absolute minimum. These should be your objectives, too.

My first task in researching this market is to discover how to reach them for the lowest cost, an assignment in which superior marketers become expert. The existence of a publication I know about called *Contributions* helps; it reaches 15,000 New England nonprofit organizations. If I didn't know this publication existed how else could I learn about it?

- by asking people in the field;
- getting my name on various mailing lists, so I'd be the likely recipient of promotional literature;
- using the local library and following the steps in *Finding Facts Fast* to research the situation, or
- using the media directories we can both find in my book THE UNABASHED SELF-PROMOTER'S GUIDE.

Now that I have this crucial piece of information I can begin to formulate a plan.

1. See if *Contributions* will publish an article and run a Resource Box at the end inviting prospects to identify themselves as people with problems by getting them to call me. This Resource Box can sell hard offers and soft, by inviting prospects to get on my mailing list and be sent my catalog. If the publication will not run the Resource Box with follow-up information, see about swapping an article for ad-space. (This is what in fact occurred.)
2. Enter all names of people who respond to either my soft (information) or hard (buying) offer into my computer. Contact them quarterly.
3. Because their audience is also my product and service prospects, persuade the publication to have a workshop which it co-sponsors. Invite all those who cannot attend to request free business solutions (catalog) information. Add all names to catalog mailing list for regular follow-up.
4. Make product distribution deal with publication. Get them to review products (in this case books). This gives me further validation as the expert and constitutes another connection with my prospects. Have them publish their catalog of books (including mine) in their publication.

5. Since this publication is quarterly, propose an additional three articles on the same basis as the first . . . namely, swapping articles for ad-space.
6. Jointly create products of special interest to their audience . . . and my prospects. These products can include Special Reports and Audio Cassettes but must each include follow-up information both for how motivated prospects needing immediate assistance and soft prospects wanting further information can connect with me.

Of course, by the time you've implemented just these six steps, which you can easily do within 12 months, you must have connected with your prospects far more than the minimum 7 times. As a result, your prospects must know who you are, what you've got for them and how you can help. And you *must* have profited. Just as I have done. For what I have written above is exactly what happened in fact . . . and exactly what I do with dozens of publications and electronic data bases nationwide.

Before leaving this subject, I want to make a very simple point. No one is going to come to you and tell you how to make the Rule of Seven work for you. In each of the six steps above, I was *always* the persuading, motivating agent; in fact, at the beginning, even in this situation, my queries and suggestions were not always, much less inevitably, greeted enthusiastically, even though they were manifestly in the interests of the publication. No, indeed! But I am very clear about one crucial point: if what I am suggesting is in the mutual interest of my prospect (in this case the publication) and myself, then it is *my* obligation to persist . . . until I at last persuade him of what is, from the very beginning, so pellucidly clear to me.

For what is the alternative to this persistence? Spending my own money. Spending it on expensive paid ads that may or may not work. On costly direct mail that may not even be delivered! And in the process depleting my slender capital reserves. Instead of drawing from my major capital resource: my brain. As you must do.

You now know, you must see, that you need not only a plan . . . a plan that enables you to reconnect with your targeted prospects . . . but the gumption to seek out the least expensive alternatives (often financed by some one else's money) and use *them* to connect with those prospects. Don't be foolish like so many of the people who contact me with one expensive marketing idea after another . . . instead of just one shrewd, inexpensive one. Listen to me, reader, for in this area I am justifiably renowned. And, by the way, if you pick up most any issue of *Contributions*, you will find that no one gets as much ongoing publicity and marketing assistance from it as I do; the real problem is finding enough time to make good use of all the available opportunities. See for yourself, write Co-Publisher Jerry Cianciolo at 634 Commonwealth Ave., Suite 201, Newton Centre, MA 02159.

Work Your Plan Daily

Each morning when I get up I pass up the opportunity to use my exer-cycle without regret . . . for I know that shortly I shall be engaged in my daily dose of marketing aerobics. What's that? The business version of "reach-and-touch and reach-and-touch." You must do these, too. Reaching to touch prospects, not just your toes.

Marketing is like brushing your teeth. It's something you must do daily. Just as you wouldn't think of beginning the day without bathing (I hope), so you must not think of living a day without marketing.

Recently in meeting with some entrepreneurs, they told me they had no time for marketing; they were too enmeshed in the tiresome nitty-gritty of running a business. This sounds sadly familiar to me. Yet I, too, must run my business. May I remind you that I have (by choice) no employees to assist me. Yet you must never allow the daily necessities of running your business (or your life, for that matter) to interfere with the absolutely essential matter of marketing your products and services both to prospects and customers. This matter is crucial.

Thus, pick a time of the day (I do so at the very beginning) when you will contact at least five new prospects or follow-up on five pending prospects, or some combination. Make this a sacred trust for yourself . . . and for the betterment of your prospects. Obviously, having stock letters on computer will assist you in your task (you have read my Special Report on "Computer Assisted Marketing", haven't you?). Computerized or not, however, this is something you must do. Rain or shine. In sickness and in health. As long as your business shall live.

The end result of such persistent effort is that your prospects will:

- know you;
- be impressed by your assiduity and organization, and
- (being less intent on blocking you than you are on helping them) finally give in . . . and do what you want them to do, the thing that also happens to be in their own best interest.

I guarantee it.

But only if you have a plan, and work it.

Of course, despite the fact this advise is sensible, you'll find most marketers don't follow it. See for yourself. Ask the entrepreneurs you know how much marketing, really specific marketing, they do *each* day. You'll be as shocked as I constantly am. Virtually any other business activity takes priority over this one, and yet this is the *only* one putting you in meaningful contact with prospects and possible repeat buyers.

What I'm asking for, therefore, is nothing less than a radical transformation in your daily habits. I'm asking you to do your marketing before you do anything else. To do it . . . and to do it early. To make sure your marketing calls get made first. That your marketing letters catch the first post. That you mail regular releases and story possibilities to media sources who can bring you to the attention of even millions of possible prospects. That you propose cut-rate advertising deals with publications that can get you to your prospect's attention. And that you do all this — and all the rest that constitutes successful marketing — until it all becomes automatic.

Many people marvel at the amount of free publicity I get, of the constant exposure, the stories, the ads, the card decks, the inserts, and all the other marketing communications that add up to many millions of prospect hooks each year. Most importantly, these are arranged at a minimal cost no one in the nation comes even close to duplicating. The questions they ask me are always the same: how does this happen . . . and how can you do it without a staff?

It's no mystery, friend. No mystery at all. It's a system. A system that you can follow, too. If you make the commitment to your prospects and customers I have made to mine. However, you must think long and hard about how to reach them most often for the least possible expense . . . and do a constant amount *each* day to reach this necessary objective. You aren't doing this now. I know you're not. *But you can do it.* If only you decide to. Now.

When One Marketing Track's Started, Start Another

The other day I heard the president of Campbell Soup discuss his company's new and very aggressive marketing plans. He was positively messianic as he spoke about their approach to senior citizens, singles, and those with special dietary needs. "We're going to get people to eat soup again," he said enthusiastically. I believe him! Why? Because he's going after *every* conceivable market he can and focusing on the unique needs and circumstances of that market in an attempt to make soup prospect specific. This is what you have to do, too.

When I do my marketing workshops, I always get the participants to tell me who they're marketing to. At the beginning they offer such stunners as "the federal government", or "small business", or "women over 40." Ladies and gentlemen, I'm going to tell you now what I tell them: these aren't markets; these are collections of markets, conglomerates, if you will, in which there may well be thousands of smaller, prospect-specific subdivisions. Your job is to identify these subdivisions, the groups that all share common characteristics. The more compact and cohesive, the more similar the prospects within the groups, the more they share patterns of mind, behavior and organization, the more easy it will be for you to market to them.

We are now in the age of niche marketing, and it is your job as the consummate marketer to make the prospects in *each* niche feel you truly understand exactly what their problems are and can solve them to their advantage. Your success as a business person derives to a considerable extent from your ability to identify these coherent niches and to become clearly identified as the unique problem-solver for each. That is, not just being a seller of soup, but a seller of the particular kind of soup that each particular group needs.

Thus, once you start your Rule of Seven marketing in any given specific market, why, it is time to start a seven-step marketing sequence in another market of your choice, a market you can help and have made a commitment to serving. And when this is started? What then? You must continue marketing to the first group, continue marketing to the second, and start a third. And so on until you have penetrated all conceivable markets for all your products and services . . . or until you have reached your personal objectives. Which I predict will come first.

This may remind you of jugglers you have seen, who throw yet another ball or plate into the air . . . and then another . . . while continuing to manipulate what they already have. So it is. Yes, marketing is a lot like this. Only it's even more demanding than juggling, for here you must subtilely change each approach until the prospect you are talking to, in whatever market he exists, feels you are there solely and unconditionally for him alone. Whatever else you are doing . . . wherever else you are doing it . . . is unimportant. What matters is only that this single prospect in this single group always feels you can solve his particular problem. When the prospects in many distinct marketing groups come to feel this way about you, you know that you are indeed a marketer. You client-centered Proteus, you!

Don't Expect Too Much Too Soon

Without fail, the ingenue marketers expect miracles. They want miracles. They need a miracle. And so they await a miracle, rather than working diligently towards their objective. Old Aesop, with his fable of the Grasshopper and the Ant, would understand this situation. But he certainly didn't sympathize with the Grasshopper, did he?

And neither should you.

Your marketing objective should be two-fold: to turn every marketing gambit into a reasonable profit and to learn from each how to perfect the next. Indeed, even if you cannot always achieve the first of these goals, you *can* always achieve the second.

But only if you're patient.

Over the last decade of my practice I've encountered literally thousands of entrepreneurs in every kind of business, both in this country and abroad. Without exception, those who have no patience, and who are unwilling to follow the precise steps of success, are those who fail. They may, indeed, dazzle as today's comet. They are, however, soon forgotten as tomorrow's charred asteroid.

I think of one in our community. Out of kindness I won't give his name and when you hear his story, you'll see why. Now just 24 years old, he had worked hard to set up a computer data-processing firm. It was small but had potential. So far so good.

Sadly, its enterprising president couldn't wait for life's glittering prizes. He let personal considerations overwhelm business sense. Obese and unpopular in high school, he had gone to considerable lengths to change his personal image until he became svelt and attractive. But rage . . . and unhappiness . . . smouldered within. Soon they began to dictate his policy. He spent money he didn't have.

He borrowed wildly for the business, but used what he got for personal purposes. And he allowed himself the luxury of quarrelling with people who could do him good . . . of not answering his mail . . . of not tending to the business of business. And, finally, fatally, he gave an interview to *The Boston Globe* in which he lied both about his current wealth and the momentous prospects fast approaching for himself and his business.

Had he had the sense to have read THE UNABASHED SELF-PROMOTER'S GUIDE, he would never have lied to the media. For this, once found out, stimulates these furies like nothing else. Within days, aggrieved creditors loudly made known their complaints. A bank called in its life-supporting loan. And, having just turned 24, this entrepreneur found that his business, lifestyle and life had collapsed together. Bankrupt in every way, he tried unsuccessfully to commit suicide, a story the local media splashed across their front pages.

This story is tragic . . . but its moral is plain. Here was a man who wouldn't wait. Who expected too much, too soon . . . and wouldn't do what was necessary to achieve it. He saw a bright future for himself and lived in the less spectacular present as if he had already achieved all that he wanted. He misconstrued vision as reality, until reality obliterated that vision. Just this morning I see his dejected face, blank with incomprehension, caught at the moment of his courtroom arraignment staring out at me from the front page of today's newspaper.

This will not happen to you.

You will start small. And test. You will take whatever success you achieve, no matter how limited, and leverage it to achieve more. You will use your new wisdom to do even better next time. Remember what Ronald Reagan said to Mikhail Gorbachov at the 1988 Moscow Summit, "It was born. It was not rushed." This is exactly what I'm talking about. Let your success be certain. Not abrupt. This means that until you are a seasoned marketing specialist, don't commit serious resources to what you're doing. Admit that you don't know it all, recognize that your resources are limited and must be wisely used, and act accordingly.

Don't Get Discouraged

Do you think all this is easy? Effortless? It isn't! It takes regular work on your part . . . and continuing thought. I despise the "get-rich-quick" types who think there's a lazy man's way to riches. There isn't. The wealthy people I know who earned their money — and I know many — got their money in lots of ways, but, without fail, each of them encountered great difficulties along the way. But they persisted . . . and they thought, tinkered, and remained both patient and certain of their inevitable success, despite often desperate situations.

These people got discouraged, to be sure . . . they're only human after all . . . but they did not let their momentary circumstances and consequent discouragement dictate their policy. No, indeed. Instead, they sought to extract what benefit they could from the predicament in which they found themselves. How could they turn even this situation into a benefit? It was present reality. It would be history. But for them, it would never become precedent.

For the developing marketer even failure can be a source of enlightenment as he seeks to learn what happened, why it happened, and avoid having it happen ever again.

Besides, amidst such failures (which happen to all of us) the successful marketer doesn't make a quintessentially American mistake: allowing the failure to undercut your own humanity and sense of personal worth. Because you've made a marketing mistake — even a big one — doesn't make you less worthy as a person. Sadly, in a society where you are what you're worth, it's often easy to forget this essential fact of life.

You cannot.

At the moment of discouragement, remember one essential point: you are dedicated to your prospect's welfare and betterment. While you may have erred in your approach to this individual *this time* and in your presentation of the benefits you have available, you stand secure in the knowledge you have the two essential things you must have to succeed in marketing: you are firmly focused on improving your prospect's life and have, in your product or service, the means to do just that.

It is unfortunate this prospect doesn't see this now. But see it he will . . . because you are determined to do everything you can to make sure he does. This includes shrugging off your all-too-human feelings of discouragement and self-doubt.

And, if necessary, going back to the drawing board. There you can perfect your cash copy until even the slowest . . . least responsive . . . prospect knows just how much you have for him. And is motivated to take the action you've always known he must take to be better off.

Chapter 18

Tinkering With Your Copy, Or Looking For Ways To Improve Your Response

You have now finished your cash copy.

That is, you've finished transforming every feature into at least one benefit. You've finished creating an offer that will get your prospect to respond. You've finished getting testimonials from satisfied customers to reassure your prospect and let him know what he can get from what you're selling. And you've finished designing your marketing format for maximum impact on your prospect.

Now your prospect *must* know you're talking to him. *Must* know you've got factual, believable, meaningful benefits he wants. And an irresistible offer he cannot refuse.

Thus, you are ready to distribute your marketing piece and get it into his hands.

But wait!

If, at this moment, most marketers would just review what they're about to disseminate they'd go back to the drawing board.

Remember, the object of the marketing game . . . and of the cash copy you're creating . . . is not just to get something into your prospect's hands. But to put something in his hand that will induce him to make an immediate response. To get him to request the further information he must review to be persuaded to buy.

Or to send in a coupon . . . pick up the telephone . . . or walk into your establishment NOW to buy what you're selling!

Read your marketing piece out loud. Show it to someone who does not have a vested interest in the success of what you're doing. In short, scrutinize what you're about to distribute to make sure it should be.

When a marketing gambit fails, its failure is virtually always predictable. Either it:

- isn't addressed to a targeted, coherent, compact unit of prospects who share the same wants and anxieties, or
- it doesn't have specific, believable benefits that are measurably better for the prospect than he can get elsewhere . . . or these benefits aren't convincingly presented, or
- there's no offer, no reason, that is, for the prospect to take immediate action.

If you'd approach what you're about to distribute in a totally detached, objective fashion and ask yourself if these three key conditions were being met, you'd save yourself a lot of grief. Sure, if you had to recast your marketing communication now, it would be bothersome. You would have lost time and money and maybe your ego would be bruised. But at least you wouldn't waste more time and money and face the still greater jolt you're bound to receive if what you distribute fails to generate inquiries and buyers.

So, I therefore beg you: review whatever marketing materials you are about to use with what you've come to learn from this book. If you don't feel you can be entirely objective about them (a very severe problem), then let an outside authority be so objective. If you can't find one near at hand, then send your documents to me, and I'll happily review them for you with complete candor using one standard only: is what you're about to use likely to get an immediate response from a qualified prospect or certain buyer? Or are you wasting your money?

Let me say something about this review: it must be thorough. *Each* component must be checked using one rigorous standard: does what you plan to use assist in getting your prospect to respond . . . or it is just words that have no point beyond filling up space?

Be hard on yourself . . . because your market is going to be very hard on you.

If you don't succeed in reaching the right market . . . don't succeed in piling one wanted, believable benefit on another for your prospects and making them want what you've got . . . if you don't make them act to acquire your offer and your benefits, why, then, your marketing communications go into the trash with excruciating speed. You're out the time, trouble and treasure it took to create them. This is a prety bleak prospect, and one you should be doing everything possible to avoid.

I know you're not doing this kind of thorough review now. From long experience, I know you're probably just creating marketing materials because you need marketing materials. A brochure because everyone else has one. A flyer because you've got to mail something right away. An ad because you've got an ad budget. STOP THIS NONSENSE!

For one thing, you should be a responsible citizen and stop wasting resources and adding to the general pollution of our time. Resolve to market only when you have something important to say and are willing to do *everything*, and I do mean everything, so that your prospects understand the benefits of what you've got for them . . . and have been effectively persuaded to take action to acquire them. Any other approach to marketing is irresponsible.

Let me make one of my famous predictions: if you scrutinize your intended marketing documents in the way I'm suggesting, I bet you'll decide to spend more time perfecting them. To take the necessary time and trouble to make them truly speak to your prospect . . . and truly convince him you've got something of real value for him . . . that he needs to act NOW to acquire. Oh, yes, you'll grumble. You won't like taking this extra time and trouble. Who does?

But by taking this time and trouble, by doing what is necessary to create truly client-centered marketing documents, you're doing several good things.

1) You're training yourself to become a better marketer. Do you think it's easy to continually create client-centered marketing documents? It isn't. Even the smartest people at the beginning of their marketing careers find it very difficult to write cash copy. Sure, they know what they're doing in their business. Sure, they've created a wonderful product or service. But all that's about them. Cash copy is about prospects. It involves a complete reorientation of your perspective. This isn't easy and takes time. That's why the kind of training I'm suggesting is so important.

2) You're enhancing the likelihood that the money you invest in your marketing will pay off. It often strikes me that many marketers are

insufficiently concerned about whether the investment they're about to make in approaching their prospects actually makes them money or not. Do you think this odd? I certainly do!

Personally, as an hereditary Scotsman in good standing, I spend much time and trouble ensuring that I will get back — with a healthy profit — the money I originally spent in any marketing endeavor. My objective is to make sure *everything* I do makes money, and I work to make sure it does. When I first went into business years ago I thought this was how everybody operated, but I have long since come to know something astonishingly different: many people market because they feel they're supposed to market. Develop and send out materials because every one else is. And don't truly care if these materials make them a profit . . . and get their products and services into the hands of their prospects, thereby enabling them to transform their lives.

In other words, these people approach the business of marketing as they would a lottery . . . being hopeful about a good result, but not overly concerned when it doesn't happen. I cannot tell you how mind-boggling I find this most prevalent attitude and how inimicable to your success.

3) You're ensuring that your prospects get products and services that will help them. Personally, it bothers me a good deal when people who would be better off using one of my products and services (and who have the money to acquire them), fail to get and use them.

Part of me, of course, wants to blame them . . . for their short-sightedness . . . foolishness . . . even stupidity. In weaker moments, I want to strike out at them for failing to see that I have something which is so manifestly in their interest. But this is my flawed humanity speaking.

In truth, when a prospect fails to buy what I'm selling . . . and has the means available to do so . . . and has not so far been firmly identified as a flatworm . . . it is not his problem that he doesn't do so. It is mine. I have somehow failed and must work to rectify this situation and get the prospect to respond.

Now, as egotistical as the next fellow, I don't like admitting that I have made a mistake. But the marketer in me compels this humbling admission. If the prospect doesn't buy, it is for a very good reason:

- He isn't a prospect at all (either because he doesn't have the problem I can solve, doesn't have the means available to

purchase a solution, or, being a flatworm, has no intention of solving it);
- He doesn't know I can really help him. Something about my presentation has failed to convince him I've got real, believable, meaningful benefits he can't get elsewhere, or can't get elsewhere on the same favorable terms;
- He isn't persuaded by my offer to take action, isn't convinced it provides any benefit or that moving to take advantage of it makes more sense than just letting it go by.

When the prospect feels this way . . . whether he is justified in so feeling or not . . . it is *my* fault . . . not his. It is *my* problem . . . not his. I must therefore work to correct this situation.

Given this marketer's perspective on how you should feel when a prospect declines to take advantage of your benefits and offer, it is no wonder I become most angry when I hear people with products or services abusing their customers for their shortcomings.

This attitude, which I see constantly, is suicidal. When I see it in young people, who are notoriously self-centered, I can understand, if not condone, it. But when I see it in adult marketers, I boil with fury. Berating one's prospects for their failings is pointless . . . especially when most marketers have not yet mastered the necessary components of the cash copy that induces an immediate prospect response. When you feel yourself giving way to this kind of mindless condemnation of your prospects, remember it is your lesser self speaking. As a marketer you should be ashamed.

4) Finally, you are cutting the marketing pollution of our times. One of the reasons why the recent postal rate increase went through so easily, despite the vehement objections of direct-mail marketers, was because most people felt this was a way of cutting the intrusion into their lives of material that has no value to them. They call this "junk mail", but the problem is really broader than mail and might be called "junk marketing."

If people really felt that marketers were offering them information of value about products and services that would improve their lives, they'd want more . . . not less . . . of it. The fact that so much that is disconnected to prospects is distributed only makes it easier to attack all of us marketers and allow dramatic increases in the cost of our doing business to take place without serious opposition.

I say this to you, therefore, in all earnestness. Do you really want to bear the responsibility for polluting our burdened world with marketing materials that aren't rigorously focused on the prospect and which don't clearly offer them products and services to improve their lives?

Do you want to have trees cut down for such a futile purpose?

Do you want to have people waste their lives — including your life — writing pointless copy, designing pointless marketing materials, delivering pointless communications . . . to people who will only throw them away, because they don't see in them the benefit for themselves and the means for improving their lives?

Do you want to spend all this money for no purpose whatsoever?

These fruitless acts strike me as existential absurdity, as the very definition of sterility and the basis for "is-this-all-there-is?" despair.

If you are not prepared to do all you can to let your prospects know what you've got for them . . . if you are not prepared to do all you can to get them to respond as quickly as possible . . . if you are not prepared, that is, to behave like a marketer, get out of this business and leave it to those of us who are!

At Last Your Marketing Communications Have Been Sent To Your Prospects. Now You Must Play The Waiting Game.

When you have finished your final review of your marketing materials . . . and made the revisions you've deemed necessary, it's time to distribute them. By mail. By hand. Through publications. Whatever you've decided.

You've decided you cannot, for now, speak more directly to your prospects than you have. You've concluded the benefits you offer them are really superior to those they can get elsewhere and will improve their lives, and you've told your prospects so — in the most persuasive way you know how. Finally, you've made them an irresistible offer that will cause even the most slothful to take immediate action.

Now what?

Now, you wait.

And because marketing is the quintessentially action game, this is probably the hardest thing to do, of all the hard things you must do.

Having done all you can, it is now time for others to do their jobs. For postal workers to sort and deliver the mail. For publishers to print and distribute their latest issue. For the fulfillment house to cut and paste your cheshire labels and get your mailing piece out for delivery. *And* for the prospect to read, understand, and act on the benefit you have for him.

This is a long and trying process. Personally, it's one I never handle easily. I am a man of action. And this is a period of passivity during which I, who have done so much, can now do no more.

When this happens to you, you're bound to feel frustrated, too.

Your job, however, is scarcely over. For now is the moment you should be preparing to gather the data you need to ascertain what really happened (when it happens), so you'll know what to do next. Because there definitely will be a "next". Either, you'll be:

- going back to the same prospects with the same benefits and the same offer because your initial endeavor was profitable, or
- because your initial gambit was profitable, you'll want to expand your marketing with the same benefits and the same offer to a larger group of the same type of people, or
- because your initial move suggested other target groups you should be approaching, you'll be going to an entirely new group of prospects with the same benefits and the same offer, or
- because your initial maneuver provided insight into what really motivates your prospects, you'll be returning to the same group of prospects with new benefits and a new offer, or
- because your initial action gave you the information you needed to refine your approach, you'll be going to an ex- panded group of similar prospects with new benefits and a new offer, or
- because your initial activity indicated that there's no point in returning to that targeted group, you'll be going to an entirely new group of prospects with new benefits and a new offer.

Or, sadly, you'll either rest on the laurels of your first marketing operation, exulting in your success, or give way to deep despair because this enterprise didn't produce the results you wanted and expected. It goes without saying, I regard either of these two alternatives as most inappropriate.

Instead, you must approach the next phase of your marketing with the calm and perfect detachment and objectivity of the skilled scientist. You need to know what happened, why it happened, and allow the data you discover to influence what you'll do next.

This is precisely what most marketers don't do.

Most marketers use a scattershot approach to their work. They try an ad. Then they try a cover letter. Then they try a radio show. Then a card deck. Then something else altogether. They never really know what works, and so they don't really know where they should be investing their scarce resources.

This must not happen to you. *You must know.*

Marketing resources are always scarce, particularly so for the kinds of people I'm especially addressing in this book — small businesses, independent professionals and nonprofit organizations. Because you have comparatively little to spend on your marketing and because what you do spend has to produce a disproportionately superior result, you must think about where you'll spend your money. This means you must gather data.

What You Need To Know And How To Find It

You can't succeed in knowing where to invest your scarce resources unless you have basic data about the people you're marketing to. Sometimes the information you'll be working with is direct: who responded and why? Sometimes, it's indirect. You must act like Sherlock Holmes to discern why people didn't respond and what this suggests for your future marketing.

Both direct and indirect information are important to you and may enable you to make crucial decisions about what to do next. So, let's look into how you can gather the data you need.

Gathering Direct Data

The essence of marketing is testing. You are testing for a purpose; you are trying to discover what kind of people constitute the best market for what you're selling, how you can reach them for the least possible cost, what benefits they most respond to, and how to get them to respond fastest. Substantial data from your buyers and the ability to make intelligent deductions about those who didn't buy are crucial to answering these pivotal queries.

To begin with, set yourself up to gather data. You don't need to be terribly sophisticated about this at the beginning. But you do need to start. Create filing folders for your responses, or, if you use something like card decks (as I do), where there is likely to be a good-sized return, put your data in a shoe box. Don't worry that this doesn't look like the way they do it at IBM. Even this rudimentary way of gathering information will put you in the relatively small group of marketers who don't just send out materials but actually review what they got back . . . and why. Make sure that along with all your data you keep a copy of the marketing communication you used: letter, flyer, *etc.*, so you know what generated the response in the first place.

You need to review these data to determine if you should return to this marketing source, what kind of marketing communication you should use, if you should expand your marketing to a larger comparable group, approach a related group, or go in another direction altogether.

It will help you to create a data sheet, a single page with categories into which you can enter your information as it arrives. Much can be entered in hatching fashion. Here are some areas that may be pertinent for you to know about:

- sex of respondent/buyer
- geographical location
- professional position
- dollar value of purchase
- item purchased
- when purchased

Let's take a look at some actual data and see where they could lead you.

Sex of respondent/buyer

30 women bought

80 women inquired

10 men bought

30 men inquired

Geographical location

60 responses from the East

20 from the South

30 from the Midwest

40 from the West

75% from large cities.

Professional position

60% of respondents indicated no professional position. (100% of men indicated professional position but only 40% of women.)

Dollar value of purchase

30 women purchased $900 worth of products

10 men purchased $400 worth of products.

Item(s) purchased

list purchases here

When purchased

80% of respondents purchased in first four weeks, or by offer deadline. Remainder up to 90 days later.

Other Information You Need

Before you can draw any conclusions and make any decisions based on these data, you need to take a look at how you approached this group and how much it cost. Let's say that between the cost of your marketing piece, product cost and fulfillment, you spent $1000. So far your total revenues are $1,300.

I've selected this situation because it is typical in marketing. In other words, there is a small, marginal profit and no clear-cut indication of what you should do. That's why you need data. Now, here are the steps you take.

To begin with, convert the people who asked for additional information into buyers.

In this illustration, the most immediate profit lies in converting the qualified prospects, those who have requested information, into buyers. This is Priority One. Thus, your first task is to develop a strong follow-up marketing piece. As you come to know your market, you'll probably want to develop this strong follow-up piece at the same time you're working on your initial marketing activity.

Until you know your market, however, there is some advantage to waiting until you see who's responding. Here, since a clear majority of your respondents are women without employment outside the home, you may wish to slant your copy in that direction. If you hadn't expected this response, waiting would have been advantageous . . . so long as you don't dilly-dally about developing your copy and getting your response out promptly. In marketing, you must strike while your prospect's interest is high.

Your second priority (though it should take place simultaneously with the first) is to upgrade the people who bought from you. That is, when you fulfill their order you should attempt to sell them something else, something related to either what they've now purchased or the problem their purchase indicates they want to solve.

The upgrade letter you develop (which I discuss at length in MONEY MAKING MARKETING) is an important cash copy document. It is targeted to people who have already made an investment in you, whose resistance is lower than those who haven't yet bought, who can be approached in a candid, direct, friendly manner, and about whom you have further information, knowing, as you do, the level of their interest in solving a given problem. You must, therefore, devote some of your cash copy talents to developing a strong, personal letter to them replete with additional benefits . . . and an offer that induces them to buy again in a very short time.

With the numbers given above and using both follow-up letters to proven buyers and qualified prospects, this marketing gambit should be profitable. Indeed, even if your initial return were even 20-25% *below* your costs, by following up in this fashion, you should be able to return a profit (though a small one) on this activity.

If you don't return a profit at this point, it is for one of several reasons, reasons you already know:

- If you have targeted the right group, with meaningful benefits and an irresistible offer, and you haven't been able to make a profit . . . or come close enough to justify further investment, then you are able to deduce that this is a group you should avoid.

- If, on the other hand, your copy is weak . . . you present features and not benefits . . . and there is no inducement for immediate prospect action, you need to rewrite and do your test again since the results prove nothing.

Thus, as you can see, making sure you have produced superior copy, packed with benefits, and an inducement for immediate action is crucial to determining what you should do next.

Now, assuming you have written this kind of copy and the response is sufficiently profitable (or nearly so) to justify continuing, you must decide what to do.

In my illustration above, given the numbers I've provided and the prospect of additional profit from upgrade sales and converting prospects into buyers, it makes sense to repeat this particular marketing gambit, be it an ad, mailing, or whatever. This means you will start benefitting from the synergy of the Rule of Seven. Given the marginal response from the first marketing activity, however, you will want to do two things:

1) See if you can find out who is doing well from using the marketing source you're employing, and

2) pay very close attention to subsequent results to see just how much potential profit there is in this market.

As to the first point, it always pays to find out who's using this marketing source profitably. If you've used a publication, call the advertising department and find out. They aren't in a position to tell you exact numbers, but they can tell you who's reported a good response . . . and who keeps using their publication. You can then review their ads — and the demographics of the publication — to see what makes them profitable.

By the same token, you can ask a list broker about who uses a particular list successfully. Then you can get yourself on that marketer's mailing list so you can review their marketing communications.

In short, you can try to emulate the winners and see how much of what they do is applicable to your marketing and making it more profitable.

Secondly, you must keep close tabs on subsequent results. It is impossible, without this kind of constant monitoring, to really know how profitable any given market is for you . . . and how worthy of your further time and investment. That's why you must pay attention to results.

Quo Vadis?

The profile of those who have responded also suggests other places you should consider for your marketing, and you must review these results carefully to establish trends. When you review your responses, do patterns emerge? Demographic information that suggests where you really should be directing your marketing and to whom you should be speaking in your cash copy?

In my illustration above, having reviewed the data, you'll want to discover mailing lists, publications and other marketing sources that connect with primarily urban, non-professional women outside the South with a proven track record of spending at least $30 on a purchase using the marketing means you have used (like direct mail). This information will help you find just the right marketing vehicle for you. It will enable you to write just the right kind of targeted cash copy . . . so you can get more of these prospects to respond. Only by reviewing the data could you possibly have drawn this conclusion . . . a conclusion that effectively points you in the direction you should go next . . . and tells you how to position your copy.

Now, you're developing a market niche. You *know* one coherent, unified, identifiable group of targeted prospects who, your initial research suggests, are perfect targets for what you're offering. Congratulations! You now have the basis for a real one-on-one, benefit-laden conversation with a person whose wants you either know or can logically deduce . . .and so strengthen your copy accordingly. You're on your way to making real money.

And For Indirect Data?
Put Sherlock Holmes At Your Service!

Sometimes what you're not able to gather directly is as important as what you are. Which is why you must learn to think like my investigative hero Mr. Sherlock Holmes.

The ineluctable Holmes can help you in several ways.

On the one hand, by following his methods, you'll learn to deduce what your prospects really want and how you should be trying to motivate them.

In the illustration above, we have factually discovered that most of the women live in large cities outside the South and are not employed outside the home. We can now begin to make deductions about them which will help future marketing:

- Ease and convenience is important to them. Unless we have asked them to walk into our establishment, we can conclude that they want us to do as much work as possible . . . make things as easy as possible for them. Your marketing must show your prospect just how easy and convenient you are.

- Despite the fact they live in large cities, where they could presumably get a competitive item, quality is important for these buyers. Thus, your marketing should stress this.

- If we are selling an item for the women themselves of utility only to them, by buying it they indicate that personal indulgence is acceptable. Our marketing can motivate them accordingly.

- Price may not be a consideration. If we know that our buyers can get the item for less money closer to home, we know this is a relatively price-insensitive market. These are people who will pay for things like service, personal attention, and our trouble. We therefore must stress other matters than price; that can be treated as a relative afterthought, because these people will buy what they want, regardless of price.

In short, from just a few facts like these (and I have by no means drawn all the inferences), we can begin to deduce a complete profile of our buyer . . . a profile that will enable us to create just the right kind of client-centered marketing. This marketing, in turn, must result in this prospect's saying, to herself and, shortly, to us, "I felt you were talking to me." When buyer after buyer says this to you (as they certainly will if you follow these guidelines), you can be sure you're on the right track.

With his deductive skills, another of the questions Holmes can help you answer is whether your offer helped your response. Unless you ask all your buyers (and, of course, you can) *why* they bought from you at a given time, you have to make a deduction about why they did. That's why you need to track *when* they bought. Obviously, offers are an expense to you. And, logically, you'd like to do away with them if you could and so increase your profit. The only reason for making an offer is not to be a generous person, but to increase response. If an offer doesn't work to do that, then it is an expense, not an investment.

When we peruse the numbers above, seeing when our buyers bought, we find that 80% of them responded during the offer period. We must therefore conclude that the offer was an important motivator in getting the prospect to act faster and that it makes sense to use it, despite its expense.

Obviously, there is only one way to really test this. And that is to do some controlled marketing to the same prospect group without the offer. But, frankly, with numbers like these, I wouldn't recommend it. The data are too clear as they stand.

However, I still must say a few words about testing. As you won't be surprised to hear me say, all marketing is a test, because you can never be absolutely certain what will happen, and must always evaluate both what happened and why — so you can decide what to do next. This means your whole life in marketing is one big test.

Thus, you must track such variables as:

- offer used. Did it matter what the offer was? For how long the offer was valid? Or what conditions were imposed on the offer?
- benefits cited. Which benefits seemed to produce the best prospect response?
- client-centered headlines. Which headlines (with what benefits) got a better response?
- paid response envelope versus unstamped response envelope. Did incurring the extra expense of business-reply mail make a sufficient difference to justify the cost?
- design factors. Did it matter how the benefits and offer were visually presented to the prospects?

As you look at this list and consider these, and other, marketing variables (like targeted audience), you may become quite glum. Don't. You can't test all these variables at one time. And in fact in any given marketing gambit, it's advisable only to test for one.

Other marketing authors speak grandly about testing, but I know that with all your other responsibilities this is one that may be pushed to the background, to be forgotten altogether. Don't let this happen.

Do gather information from each of your marketing gambits. Do find out who responded, when they responded, how many bought versus inquired, *etc.* You can't write truly client-centered cash copy without this information.

Do take the time to figure out what the data you've received — as well as what you didn't hear from the silent people who have not responded to your marketing — are trying to tell you. Remember, data are always trying to speak to you; it's your job to figure out what they're saying.

Do test various marketing variables. In marketing, everything counts. You've just got to figure out what's helping you . . . and what isn't.

Do let your discoveries influence how you spend your scarce marketing dollars. You're not as rich as Croesus, and you should be concerned that you get the biggest bang for your buck.

And *do* let these discoveries influence the cash copy you create. You don't test because a few authorities think it's a good idea. You test because only through testing can you craft your cash copy and all your marketing activities to be sure you are talking directly to the people who most want what you have for them. So you can pile on the benefits that are most appealing and motivating for them. And can create the offers that are most likely to get them to respond.

There isn't any other reason for what otherwise is a perfectly academic (and hence futile) exercise.

Your Discoveries Will Mean Changing Your Copy. Be Prepared!

As you find out more about your real market and about what causes people to respond to your marketing communications, you're going to have to make changes in your copy. You'd better be prepared for this! What I'm going to tell you now will keep you prepared and make sure you have the information on hand you need to redraft your cash copy and make it more client-centered.

This brings us right back to where we started on the road to developing client-centered cash copy . . . to keeping information files. These crucial information files not only enable you to create superb client-centered cash copy to begin with . . . but to improve your copy as you discover more and more about your core market(s); the people you're really selling to and who really want (and need) what you've got.

You don't need a super-sophisticated filing system to maintain this information. But you do need a system. If you have to use shoe boxes, do. But keep these kinds of data. You need a:

Pain File

As you know, pain motivates people to buy solutions that make them well. Thus, make sure you maintain a file with as much information about how your prospects' hurt as you can find. The more specific this information is, the better.

Want File

What is it your prospects really want to achieve? When do they want to (or must they) achieve it? Be specific!

Feature/Benefit File

List all the features of every product or service you sell and make sure you have at least one benefit for each feature. Remember, if the feature has no benefit, it has no place in marketing. The more you know about your targeted markets and listen to what they're telling you, the more specific you can make these benefits; the more specific they are, the more believable — and hence desirable — they'll be to your prospects.

Testimonial File

Who has used your product or service successfully? What specific benefits did they achieve? If your product or service is as good as you say it is (it is, isn't it?), then people are deriving substantial benefits from it regularly. What these people get motivates others who are still skeptical to buy . . . but only if you use these testimonials for their marketing leverage.

Offer File

How do you intend to induce an immediate response from your prospects? List your offers here . . . and the results they produced when used to a particular target group.

Swipe File

Collect illustrations of motivating client-centered marketing components:

- envelope teasers
- headlines
- offers
- testimonials
- benefit charts
- response coupons
- lift letters (which beg a prospect to reconsider a decision not to buy)

And all the rest.

There's no reason why you have to reinvent the wheel. It's absurd not to learn from other people's marketing, and while good illustrations of client-centered marketing are not always easy to find, they should be the more prized by you as a result. It always pays to learn from the best . . .

And from the worst. So, for the days when you need cheering up, collect illustrations of marketing documents that are ludicrously substandard. You *know* you can do better than that!

I'm not spending a lot of time on these files, because you already know you need them. Indeed, by now, I hope you've already started collecting information for them.

But I would remind you to spend the time you need to gather this information. And to store it for easy access.

If you're computerized, it will be easier. Open up a file for each category. As you see useful information, store it. If you compose on a computer as I do, you'll find it incredibly helpful to have this information a button or two away, instantly available to be used in the creation of your marketing communications and their subsequent improvement.

Remember, marketing is an organic process. It involves people, and people's wants and needs change constantly. You must be prepared for this, or your marketing will clearly lose its impact. Just imagine how poor a response you'd get if today you re-used even the best marketing materials from a decade ago. At best, you'd look woefully out of touch.

Is That All There Is?

Now that we've finished 18 chapters of this book together, you may be shaking your head in dismay. If you see the utility of what I've advocated, you may still wonder how you can possibly do it all yourself . . . especially given all your other activities. And the fact you occasionally like to do things entirely removed from your business (imagine!).

True, when you really approach marketing . . . and the creation of client-centered cash copy . . . with the seriousness it deserves, it is a task that demands time and your full consideration. But let me cheer you up a bit. First, much that you create can be reused.

So long as your benefits are truly client-centered . . . so long as your offers do stimulate an immediate response . . . so long as you are presenting your product or service in such a way that your prospect is excited by what it can do for him . . . why, there's no reason why you can't reuse large pieces of what you create.

Moreover with a computer, it's wonderfully easy to remove whole sections of documents and, in an instant, make them the building blocks for new successful marketing communications . . . and integrate new material from your ongoing data files. So, don't despair.

Moreover, if you want or need help, there are plenty of people who can assist you to create cash copy. In my final chapter, I want to tell you how to make sure you find one who can really help . . . and doesn't just provoke and impoverish you; something which has sadly happened to many who have, with such high hopes, availed themselves of this service.

Chapter 19

Finding And Working With
A Cash Copywriting Consultant

Now that you've come this far with me, you know what a lot of work there is to creating cash copy. There's no point denying it: it's considerable.

For the best of reasons, you may not want to do some or all of this work yourself.

- You may not have the time to create the cash copy you need.
- You may not have the inclination.
- You may not, despite all my help!, have the talent.

Thus, you're going to need assistance. That's fine, so long as you don't become a marketing ostrich, burying your head in the sand.

What do I mean? Too many people with products and services to sell, don't bother to familiarize themselves with the essential components of cash copy. Instead, abdicating all responsibility, they seek a copywriting White Knight who'll do everything for them — including think. I am unalterably opposed to this approach.

Even if you don't have the time or inclination (or, even, the talent) to compose cash copy yourself, you must familiarize yourself with its basics so you're in a position to evaluate what a copywriter does for you. Otherwise, how are you going to know that what you're getting is going to help you generate the immediate responses you need?

433

The truth of this point was carried home to me again just the other day when a financial planner and his assistant came calling on me with their new brochures; brochures they were very eager to have complimented.

With the merest glance, I knew these brochures wouldn't be of any assistance to them whatsoever. Why, the bloated sentences didn't even make sense, much less offer client benefits.

I did what I often do in these circumstances: I asked my visitors to pretend they were their own client prospects, and then I read them their own words. As I did, they winced. "Hadn't anyone else commented on the brochure before?" I asked. "Oh, yes, one of our clients said he couldn't understand it. But . . ." (and here's the punchline), "they were done by the best firm in Cleveland." And, of course, that firm, being "the best" had to produce something exemplary, even if clients couldn't understand the point.

Net result? Over $8,000 wasted; some hundreds of brochures created that were quite, quite useless; a batch of client prospects scratching their heads wondering what was in that brochure (and in the company that sent it) for them, and two very abashed entrepreneurs, surely sadder, hopefully wiser. All because they didn't have the foggiest idea about the rudiments of cash copy . . . and so were in no position to evaluate what was proposed to them.

This, of course, cannot happen to you. You've not only read but studied this book and know the essentials of creating cash copy. If you don't have the time or inclination to create such copy yourself, you at least know it when you see it. Right?

For you, therefore, the real problem is finding the right copywriter, the person who can write the kind of copy you know you need and insist upon having: copy that generates an immediate response from your prospect. Since you have to organize a search, you'd better know just what you're looking for.

What Is A Copywriter?

Unless you already know a creature of this ilk, you may have a very limited idea of what a copywriter is and what a copywriter does. Most people (including my new clients, who are quickly disabused of their notions) think a copywriter is a person who magically sits down at a typewriter or word-processor and writes word-perfect copy off the top of his head. To them, hiring a copywriter is rather like buying a ready-made suit off the rack: all they have to say to this perfect machine is "write" and write it does . . . so many words per minute, so many pages per hour. And that's that. Indeed, even if the actual seller of the product or service doesn't understand his market, he supposes his copywriter will. Astonishing!

Need I say this is both a misguided and even insulting idea of the work of a copywriter?

In fact, a copywriter may perform at least ten crucial roles in helping you sell your products and services. Inventing word-perfect copy off the top of his head isn't one of them.

The Ten Pivotal Roles Of The Copywriter

A copywriter is at once:

- *a strategist.* He helps you decide to whom you should be talking and what you should be saying; helps you, that is, maximize limited resources so that what you do is profitable. While a copywriter is the master of the little things, he never loses sight of the big picture. A copywriter will know right away if you are muddled in your thinking. The good copywriter tells you so and helps you create a more focused strategy; the bad copywriter just follows your lead . . . and asks for his money promptly, before the disastrous marketing results get tabulated.

- *a tactician.* The good copywriter not only sees the big picture but, importantly, examines the relative impact of all the smaller components to make sure that each part of what he creates helps to persuade the prospect to take immediate action. A good copywriter knows that *everything* must help . . . or there is no point in having it at all.

Even if you forget what your copy is supposed to do (*i.e.* generate responses), the good copywriter never does. He is quite capable of asking you one insistent question when you present your ideas: "Will this help get us more responses?" That's the only thing he cares about, and he'll keep urging you to think this way, too. All tactics are used in the service of this single objective.

- *a conceptualizer.* The copywriter helps you develop a basic concept about who you are and what you're really doing. But even more significantly, he works to discover who your prospects are and what they're trying to do. The copywriter realizes that the best concepts are about prospects and not about marketers. He wants to hear from you if you have information about your prospects and what they want, but he'll give what you say relatively short shrift if what you want is focused on you and what you're selling.

The good copywriter realizes that the role of copy is generating sales, not massaging the marketer's ego. Bad copywriters, who don't care about the end result, will do that massaging and do it gladly; the good ones will fight you every step of the way until you're willing to focus on the people who really count in copywriting . . . your prospects.

- *a master of timing.* Or, should I say, a master of two different kinds of timing: how long a project takes to create and the best time for launching it?

The good copywriter acts like a bridle for the headstrong marketer. He knows that most marketers, visualizing the avalanche of sales just around the corner, focus less on the marketing communication than on the result that communication must generate. Such marketers tend to be careless about the crucial details involved in creating a profitable marketing project. Not the copywriter. His job is to remind the marketer how long each task takes . . . and to make sure that that task is allotted the necessary time, and not rushed.

The seasoned copywriter knows it takes time to gather key facts about a market, time to understand that market, time to transform features into benefits, time to think up the best approach, and time to do all the technical work involved in that approach. With the marketer pressing for immediate release, the copywriter focuses on what needs to be done to assure the desired result. He is willing to risk the wrath of the marketer, if necessary, to ensure the success both want.

Too, the good copywriter realizes that all moments of time are not equal. He knows what periods are best for your marketing gambit, and which should be avoided. Being insistent, too many marketers are cavalier about timing; to them one moment for launching their marketing is as good as another. But the good copywriter is a connoisseur of timing. Listen to him. He can afford to be dispassionate and objective. He doesn't have your ego investment in the project . . . an investment that often fuels headlong behavior.

- *a damage-control specialist.* Being objective, the good copywriter can assess what you're selling without bias. He knows what's superior . . . and what isn't. He knows why your product or service is really worth buying. And why other products and services might be better. Face it, most products and services are not the best of their kind. But that doesn't mean they cannot be sold. That's where the experienced copywriter comes in. He can help position what you're selling for faster sale, despite the fact that it may not be the best. A damage-control specialist, he knows what to emphasize, how to emphasize, and when to say nothing at all. The good copywriter is the master of positive accentuation.

- *a wordsmith.* The job of the copywriter is to select words that will motivate prospects to take immediate action . . . and to eliminate words that just take up space or impede the prospect's movement through the copy and decision to act. The good copywriter is acutely aware of the subtleties of language and is always weighing, weighing, weighing each word . . . each phrase . . . each sentence . . . each paragraph, attempting to discover if it offers sufficient motivation to the prospect. Or is merely dead weight.

At the same moment, the copywriter is vividly aware of the power of individual words . . . and of the overall effect of the entire marketing communication. If the latter is to be successful, the former must focus on the prospect. The master copywriter is not casual; he is not lax . . . he doesn't utter the most infuriating word of our age — "whatever" — when asked about one choice versus another. He knows that things matter. And he carefully considers each choice against his constant objective: getting the prospect to respond. He is the master of discernment.

- *a representative of both the prospect and the marketer.* The job of the copywriter is to stand between both prospect and marketer and to work to connect them so that the interests of each will be realized. He must think like the prospect (and so discover how to motivate him) . . . as well as the marketer . . . and so discern how to get from that marketer that which will motivate the prospect.

The expert copywriter constantly prods the marketer to discover if all the benefits he has for the prospect have yet been revealed. In this role, he continually asks for more. "Tell me more," he insists, "about what you have . . . what you can do for your prospect." This copywriter has a seasoned sense of how much he needs to be able to motivate a prospect whose difficulty of arousing he never underestimates. And he will not relent until he has the more that he needs.

By the same token, he works to understand the mind, the hopes, the dreams, the anxieties, the entire condition of the prospect. He works to center the marketing process where it must be centered to succeed: on the prospect. He strives to gather the insight into the mind and circumstances of the prospect that will enable the copywriter, as the representative of the marketer, to touch that prospect . . . and motivate him to act. He has twin motives for wanting this action: on the one hand, he knows that getting the prospect to act will be beneficial for the marketer. On the other, he never forgets that, if the product or service is indeed beneficial, the prospect must be better off using it than going without.

- *a candid friend.* A good copywriter must be candid . . . must be willing to fight any notion that doesn't lead to client-centered marketing. He must be willing — and able — to tell his client that the marketer's idea is without merit and will not bring about the response he says he desires.

Too many copywriters, like too many people generally, are time-servers. Either they do not know the truth and cannot say it; or they know it, and will not say it. Whether ignorant or prevaricating, the result is the same: their client doesn't have the benefit of ringing candor. The good copywriter is, of necessity, outspoken. Having one objective and one objective only, namely getting the prospect to respond as quickly as possible, he is bound to attack all that works against this end. As politely as possible, but as directly as necessary, this copywriter works resolutely to ensure that no lesser goal is even considered.

The ego of his client means nothing against the importance of the objective. Neither does the outrage of the flatworms, who always find the copywriter's client-centered directness affronting. All that matters is doing what will get the prospect to respond. If the tested copywriter will not allow himself to deviate from this essential standard, there isn't the slightest chance he'll allow you to do so, either.

- *an organizer.* The good copywriter is a good organizer. He must be. He has to find people with information, get the information from them, store it and have it ready when necessary. His job is to oversee the process that provides the information and, while being a worker in the process as well, to coordinate the process that results in the final marketing communications being created by copywriter, designer, printer — and, of course, the marketer himself. The good copywriter is acutely aware of who should be involved in the process of producing superior marketing communications and just when critical tasks must be completed. Knowing this, he will not let you forget.

- *an editor.* Finally, a good copywriter is not only the master of writing . . . but of rewriting. The master copywriter is always willing to rewrite material so long as it will enhance achievement of the one critical objective: getting the prospect to respond NOW. If the copywriter can be shown that what is suggested will help reach this goal, then he is entirely willing to make changes. A rigid defensiveness on behalf of what he's written is not part of the make-up of the experienced copywriter, though, on behalf of an essential client-centered idea he is necessarily tenacious.

The copywriter understands he is making compelling words to measure . . . that they must fit the space available . . . and achieve only one task. If this means rewriting, he is happy to do it. And if some of his words, indeed many of his words, end up on the cutting-room floor . . . but the project is successful . . . then he is content. For, after all, his is the art of motivation, and if the words used have motivated prospects to act, then they are the right words in the right order, no matter what literary canons have been broken.

Will such a paragon be easy to find? Of course, not. Paragons never are. But you will be able to find such a person if you understand the different approaches copywriters take to their jobs. You see, all copywriters, even the paragons, are not the same. And they don't work the same way. The trick is finding just the right one for you and your situation.

Understanding The Four Different Kinds of Copywriters

Speaking broadly, there are four different kinds of copywriters:

- Some copywriters specialize in a particular industry.
- Others (like me) are generalists who will work on any interesting project.
- Some copywriters do everything. They find all the information, and they write the copy.
- Others (like me) use a less expensive system whereby we assume the role not only of copywriter but of project

coordinator, assigning certain research and writing tasks to the product/service marketer while being responsible for the end-result.

Let's look at the pros and cons of each situation.

Specialist *vs* Generalist

A copywriting specialist knows the issues in your industry. He knows who the prospects are, what their current interests and anxieties are, who else is marketing to them, in what way, and, perhaps, with what result. Having created other marketing communications (which he may or may not be at liberty to share), he'll be able to steer you in the right direction . . . towards marketing activities, formats, language and offers that draw well . . . and away from those that do not. When you work with such a specialist, you're paying for his years of experience as well as the actual time he spends on your project. There is always value to working with a copywriting specialist who really knows your business. There could also be risks.

It's easy to become provincial when you're a specialist, to stop looking outside your industry for inspiration. The best specialist is not only thoroughly familiar with what happens in an industry and with what kinds of marketing are working . . . but allows himself to look beyond this industry for ideas. In other words, he will take, create or use *any* idea to generate immediate prospect response. He will not be limited by what is usually done or not done in an industry. Too often specialists can become unthinkingly conservative and narrow in their approach, worrying about what others in the industry will think and say about them.

Remember, the only thing that matters in marketing and in copywriting is getting the prospect to respond. If you've found a copywriter who's forgotten this, don't use him. How will you know? By checking his samples and reviewing his approach.

The Generalist

I speak from experience when I say people become generalists because they have active, inventive minds and enjoy working on lots of projects with lots of different products and services. The best generalists are magpies, taking ideas from one industry (or inventing their own) and using them in another. They remember that getting the immediate prospect response is all that matters. They need the creative stimulation that comes from confronting new projects and problems and not just focusing on one thing or another in a rather narrow range. The best generalists are quite likely to tell you something you didn't know . . . and to suggest something you'd never thought of before.

Unlike the copywriting specialist, they may very well not know much, if anything, about the particular prospects in your industry, or the current issues, marketing campaigns, and the like. This doesn't bother him for a minute . . . and, if he's good at creating client-centered copy that draws responses, it shouldn't bother you, either. A generalist isn't worried about not knowing; he worries about not finding out and not being able to get the information he needs to motivate the response.

Your risk, of course, is that the generalist you work with may be incapable of understanding your industry and situation and unable to produce the necessary client-centered copy. How can you tell? The good generalist knows he doesn't know and isn't afraid to ask the basic, probing questions that mark his approach to his work. He knows he needs specific information and takes nothing for granted. The mediocre generalist will be less willing to admit that he doesn't know; the vagueness of his answers will tip you off, however, to an ignorance he fears admitting.

Working with the superior generalist, you'll find yourself constantly prodded to come up with information that's more and more specific about your prospects, their circumstances, and the benefits of what you're selling. The generalist is under no illusions that he knows everything in your industry; you may be. Thus, you may find yourself getting irked when he presses you. Don't be. Getting prodded by your copywriter is a very good thing and should result in client-centered copy that gets results.

The Do-Everything Copywriter *vs* The Coordinating Copywriter

The do-everything copywriter does both the research and writing associated with the creation of cash copy. For instance, he draws up a list of the features associated with any given product or service and then finds out, from any relevant personnel and materials, just what the benefits actually are.

This person may end up questioning the inventor, reading relevant trade publications, speaking with sales repsentatives, and anyone else who may have information about what prospects want and what the product or service benefits are.

This process, while undoubtedly convenient, is undoubtedly expensive. Indeed, because good copywriters can easily charge $100 or more per hour, this process is beyond the reach of many businesses.

Which is where the coordinating copywriter comes in. I speak with real enthusiasm about this model, because it's one I use myself and have pioneered. This copywriter understands that the client's resources are decidedly limited . . . but his need for cash copy isn't. In other words, he must achieve superior results for minimum investment.

There is only way to do this: to institute a process that enables the copywriter, who knows what he needs to produce persuasive marketing communications, to oversee the gathering of the information he must have. In other words, in addition to actually writing copy, he oversees and coordinates the process that produces the crucial information he needs to create that copy.

Thus, instead of doing all the work himself to transform product and service features into benefits, to check out the competition, to create offers, to gather testimonials — and all the other things that must be done — he instructs the marketer how to gather this information so that the copywriter gets exactly what he needs to create cash copy.

You can clearly see the benefit of this process. Here, the copywriter-coordinator becomes a sort of marketing mentor. He knows, because he must create the cash copy, exactly what the seller should be finding . . . and provides guidelines on how and where to find it. He both clearly outlines the objective, the tasks needed to reach this objective, and provides regular guidance to the marketer as he gathers the necessary information in the most efficient way possible.

A very neat system.

And much less expensive for you.

I like to think of this system as a how-to book on copywriting come to life. Only, unlike a book, you don't just get guidelines (however thorough); you get ongoing assistance and continuing direction as problems arise, so you don't waste any time and get the maximum benefit for your limited marketing investment.

There's one more benefit I should point out in this how-to system. You get trained in the essentials of producing cash copy.

People who use do-everything copywriters often (but not always) get superior work, work that makes them money. This is all to the good. Unfortunately, they can't replicate the process themselves. Each time they want this kind of result, they have to hire someone to do it for them. Unless you have unlimited resources, this is not a good thing.

The good marketer, after all, is always seeking to do two things: limit the cost of reaching his prospects and increase the number of prospects who respond. Buying cash copy is a cost, and therefore, all entrepreneurs should consider how they can limit it, thereby minimizing their investment in any single marketing project, and, one hopes, increasing their profit.

Under the Coordinating Copywriter system, you learn how to produce your own cash copy. Given that I'm a how-to and human-development fanatic, you won't be surprised to learn I far prefer this system, because it leads to the marketer being able to help himself and do what is necessary for him to produce his own cash copy when he needs it, not just when a hired gun can provide it.

Frankly, I've never seen the copywriting universe broken down into what I regard as these crucial categories. Now you know what's available, and you have a decision to make: what kind of copywriter — and resulting experience — do you want. Obviously, your available resources will play a part in this decision. But don't even start looking for a copywriter until you know what you're looking for and know how much work (if any) you want and are prepared to do. Or if you want someone else to do it all. When you've made this first crucial decision, you're ready to start hunting for the right copywriter for your situation.

The Search

The search for the right copywriter moves along the same lines as the search for the right designer . . . and, indeed, you can use several of the same sources, although it is very unlikely your designer and copywriter will be the same person.

Here are some places to look for a copywriter:

- Review local resource directories (like Boston's *Worksource*, already cited);
- Check the yellow pages under "Advertising" to start with;
- Check advertisements in your local business newspaper;
- Save copy (letters, ads, flyers, *etc.*) you like and approach the writer who did it. (You can ask for his telephone number and address from the company promoted in the copy.)
- Ask publications in which you intend to advertise for referrals to their best copywriters;
- Ask colleagues whose marketing you admire to provide you with referrals.
- Use me. This is what I do for a living, after all!

Now start your review process.

At this point, you should already have decided which of the four different kinds of copywriters you want, specialist or generalist; do-everything or coordinating copywriter. While different copywriters may well use different names to describe themselves, all fit into one or another of these categories. Remember, the clearer you are about what you want, the easier it will be both to find the right copywriter and to work with him.

One thing is obvious, however: whichever kind of copywriter you decide to work with, you are still seeking the same objective. You want evidence he can produce copy that gets people to respond NOW! Having read this book, you know what to look for as you review the portfolios of your candidates:

- envelope teasers that get you to open the envelope;
- headlines that speak directly to you and get you to read the copy;
- an offer that leads off the copy and motivates you to take immediate action;
- benefit-rich copy that tells you exactly what you're going to get;
- copy where the features have been banished;
- testimonials that tell you about specific results achieved by satisfied buyers;
- "lift letters" that are so compelling that even the most reluctant to buy are motivated to do so.

Ask to see what your candidate regards as his best work. He should show you not only superior copy but copy that elicited a profitable response for the marketer.

You've got to understand that the copywriter is not entirely responsible for that response, of course. It is the prime marketer who selects the list and, in the final analysis, is responsible for the offer, even though he may have received advice on it from the copywriter. By the same token, remember the copywriter is also not a designer and is not responsible for the design. So pay attention to his particular area of expertise: the rendering of the words.

Be critical. You want to see how successful the copywriter has been . . . not just in writing copy . . . but in writing copy that has actually sold products and services.

At your interview with the prospective copywriter, find out how he works and what he needs from you. The good copywriter has a system, a way of working that gives him what he needs when he needs it. Find out what this system is.

Expect the good copywriter to want to know as much about you and your project as you want to know about him and his experience. He'll want answers to questions like these:

- What marketing document(s) do you want to create?
- When do you want them to be finished?
- Besides me, the copywriter, do you have anyone in your company to help you with this project?
- Who is he/are they?
- What is your budget for this task? (This should be cited in a range, from a low figure to the absolute maximum that can be spent.)
- Who are your (the product or service seller's) prospects?
- Do you have information about how your competitors sell this product or service?
- What are the specific benefits of using your product or service?
- Do you have testimonials available from satisfied customers?
- Have you considered what offer to use to induce an immediate response?

Marketer: a good copywriter at this point can tell if you are at all realistic or not. If you tell him you want to produce a new six-panel brochure for just $300 but have no information and want the copywriter to gather it, write the copy, edit it and review the final result before production, he is very likely to laugh in your face. Certainly, he'll know you have no experience in the realities of what must be done and how long it takes.

Obviously, the marketer wants to pay the least amount of money for the job, and the copywriter wants to get the highest fee conceivable. That's business. But no relationship between marketer and copywriter will work unless each is absolutely clear on what the other is supposed to do and when each is supposed to do it. And unless each trusts the other to follow through professionally.

My experience has taught me that problems in a business relationship are almost immediately apparent, right from the first meeting; that the way things start is a good indication of what will happen in the relationship.

Therefore, marketer, if you have an unsettled feeling about the copywriter at the first meeting, either because you don't feel he can deliver the cash copy you require when you need it, because you don't like him personally, or because you think he's disorganized, don't go any further with this relationship. *Find someone else.*

By the same token, copywriter, if you find the marketer demanding about what he wants and not understanding about the constraints and necessities of your business; if he niggles too much on small points and can give you no assurance about how you will get the information you need, when you need it, then this is probably a relationship you don't want, either.

Years ago, when I was a new consultant, a wise man told me something worth sharing. "You'll know," he said, "you're an established consultant and not just an ingenue, when you start turning down clients who won't do what's necessary, in a pleasant and professional way, to achieve the superior results you're capable of giving them." It's excellent advice, and I find it has helped me decline a client without regret, when I decided that the relationship would not be a happy or productive one.

Before Starting Your Relationship: Call People Who Have Worked With This Copywriter Before

Before you make your final decision about your copywriting candidate, check out two or three of his references. A good copywriter will be happy to provide you with this information. Personally, I'm always happy to have past customers help me get new clients!

Telephoning these references makes by far the most sense. Not only is it faster, but you can catch the nuances in the person's voice, and ask necessary follow-up questions. Here's what you want to know:

- Did the copywriter produce copy that sold your product or service? Were you happy with your investment?
- Did you feel his fee was reasonable given the results and the way the work was handled?
- Was his estimate of costs accurate?
- Was the copywriter clear about what he needed from you, why he needed it, and when he needed it?
- Did the copywriter meet deadlines?
- Did he make constructive suggestions about how to improve the copy?
- Was he easy to work with?
- Was he willing to explain his decisions and recommendations to you?
- Would you hire this copywriter again?

Listen carefully! These calls shouldn't take any more than 8–12 minutes. But they are very important and can spare you a lot of grief. Remember, often what isn't said is as important as what is, so pay close attention.

Entering Into A Relationship With Your Copywriter

Now you should know enough about your candidates to make the right choice. Let me say one final thing before you enter into any formal relationship: look for someone who can be enthusiastic about what you're selling. As should be manifestly apparent to you from reading this book, I regard the ability to transmit enthusiasm and even passion to prospects as crucial for cash copy.

If your copywriter cannot get interested in and enthusiastic about what you're selling . . . he's the wrong choice, no matter what his technical qualifications. As committed as you are to selling your product or service, it is not too much to ask that those you employ, whether hired guns or not, share at least some portion of your vision and your excitement and stand ready to place it at your disposal.

Following these guidelines, you should find the cash copywriter you need. You are now ready to enter into a formal, contractual relationship. This need not be complicated or difficult. A simple letter of intent with both parties signing will do nicely. This letter should:

- clearly indicate who is to do what and when they are to do it;
- indicate whether the copywriter is being paid by the project or the hour;
- detail what consideration is being paid and how it is to be rendered;
- show what happens if this consideration, as outlined, is not paid;
- discuss how disputes between the parties are to be resolved;
- indicate how parties to the contract may leave the agreement;
- express that both parties to the relationship must agree before it can be altered, and
- show which state law is applicable should the contract be litigated.

This is simple and sufficient. If you'd like to have a ready-made sample, you can get one in my book THE CONSULTANT'S KIT, which, of course, deals with independent contractor relationships between consultants and their clients.

At this point, both some marketers and copywriters may feel a bit queasy. Both can and do tell me horror stories about relationships that went awry, about substandard and shoddy work given to the marketer and about copywriters oppressed by overly demanding and slow-paying clients.

But, you see, I live by Robert Frost's rules, where "good fences make good neighbors." If you work hard to select your copywriter and make sure your expectations — and his — are written into even a simple contract, you won't have these kinds of problems. I speak from experience.

The Importance Of The First Draft

The work is now ready to begin. Assuming it has been decided who is to gather the necessary information (either the copywriter will do so himself or the marketer will do so under the copywriter's direction), the next crucial stage is the production of the first draft of the copy.

This is an important development because it enables the marketer to see if the copywriter has grasped what's important about his product or service and has presented it in such a way to motivate quick response, and shows both parties how much more information is needed before the task can be completed.

Personally, I try to produce a first draft for a client as quickly as possible after the information's been gathered. Only when this draft is produced do I know, and can the marketer know, how we're coming along. We both need to know this as soon as possible.

The draft clearly indicates where there are gaps to be filled and how sharp the client-centered features of the copy really are. In my experience, there are always gaps to be filled . . . and always work to be done sharpening the reasons why the prospect should respond NOW and the benefits he gets by doing so.

What both marketer and copywriter should be trying to do at this moment is plain: all effort should be turned to producing specific and believable benefits, benefits which compel immediate prospect action.

At this stage, the poor copywriter will be content to turn in the kinds of weak and unspecific "benefits" I've been decrying throughout this book. If he *knows* they are unspecific and need more work, fair enough. This is the moment to do it. But if he doesn't know how to produce the kind of specific and believable benefits that cause prospects to take immediate action, and the marketer doesn't demand this high standard of him, then you are on the road to disaster.

Now is the moment for both you and your copywriter to make certain you are doing all you can to produce cash copy . . . not just passive, feature-laden copy.

If you don't think your copywriter is doing this . . . or are just not certain why the copywriter has presented things in a particular way . . . ask! You are the one making the investment. Read the copy aloud. Does it move actively across the page? Or does it drag? Are there masses of undigested words in the copy? Are there features but no benefits? Do you feel that what has been produced speaks to you and gives you an incentive to take immediate action?

Now, now!, is the moment to be severely critical and to subject each word, each phrase, each headline . . . each individual element of the copy . . . to intense scrutiny. For I remind you: the market is apathetic and difficult to motivate. Each day billions of dollars worth of marketing materials are instantly and irrevocably tossed away by prospects to whom they do not speak and never persuade. To avoid this fate, pay close attention to this first draft. Understand what the copywriter is doing, why he is doing it, and review what has been done by putting yourself in the shoes of your prospects. Does what has been produced persuade? Does it motivate? Does it excite? Or does it merely inundate with selfish words and lethal marketer-centered features?

If only all the ads and flyers and brochures and cover letters and annual reports . . . and all the other marketing communications produced so profusely in this nation . . . were subjected to this client-centered review at *this* point — by both marketer and copywriter — much that is so pointlessly created could be transformed from profligate waste to action-generating marketing.

Marketer, here are the questions you must use to review the first draft of the copy:

- Is the copy about you, or is it about your prospect?
- Is it full of features, or client-centered benefits?
- Are the benefits believable?
- Does it speak directly to your prospect, or pontificate in the third person?
- Does it offer your prospect an immediate incentive for action?
- Are the testimonials packed with specific, believable benefits?
- Do the headlines offer benefits that are developed and con-firmed in the copy?
- Does the copy move quickly . . . is it something your pros-pects want to read . . . or something which takes a lot of time and attention to get through because it's complicated, full of jargon, and leaden language?

- Is there an indication of what will happen to the prospect if he doesn't act?

With questions like these, and others you can draw from this book, you'll be able to do a thorough, detailed review of the copywriter's first draft and know if it's on the right track.

If it isn't, *now* is the moment to make changes. In the copy, of course, and, if the first draft is disastrously wrong, perhaps even in the copywriter himself.

Listening To Your Copywriter

A good copywriter knows the state the copy is in and knows what he must have to produce the cash copy you need. Having completed a first draft, he should be prepared to tell you where he thinks you are and how things are going. Listen to him. Up until now much was speculative: could you get the information? Could you do the job? How might a relationship be handled? Now, however, the copywriter has experience he didn't have before . . . and has begun to produce material for you. He should have an opinion, and that opinion is now very much worth listening to.

Listen to him as he tells you about the quality of information he's found:

- Have the features really been transformed into specific, believable benefits?
- Are the benefits too vague and unspecific?
- Is he having trouble getting information he needs from you and your employees?
- How does he feel you are now positioned against your competitors? Are you really making the best case for what you're selling . . . and have you dealt in the best possible way with your weak points?
- Are the testimonials too general; do they need more specific benefit information?
- Is the offer strongly motivational? Or weak?

These are the kinds of questions your copywriter should now be raising . . . and giving the guidance you need to answer them! You will be evaluating his work, of course. But he'll also be evaluating how well you've provided him with what he needs to produce superior cash copy.

You must listen to each other.

Listen — and not get defensive.

At this point, it is a good idea for each of you, individually and together, to reaffirm your objective: producing cash copy that generates the quickest and biggest prospect response.

It is good to reaffirm your mutual commitment to this common objective, because it is easy for both parties to become defensive at this moment. The marketer can easily be made to feel, under the constant questioning of the copywriter, that he really doesn't know his business, a business he may well be devoting both days and nights to. As the copywriter shows him that the marketer really doesn't know how his product or service stands *vis-à-vis* his competitors; doesn't really understand the specific benefits he has to offer, or the needs and wants of his prospects, the marketer may well get defensive or angry.

Hold it!

The copywriter is asking these insistent questions for a reason. He needs this information to help produce the cash copy you need. If this process is occasionally irritating, it is better that this happen now, in the cash copy development stage, than that the unyielding marketplace be left to do its obliterating work.

By the same token, the copywriter can come to feel defensive as the marketer prods him. "Why," says the marketer, "did you write the copy this way? Why did you position the offer here? Why this headline? Why did you lead with this line . . . and not something else?"

The copywriter can easily get defensive and resentful if the marketer asks him for explanations which, as an established professional, the copywriter may well feel are beneath him.

Hold it!

The marketer has a right to ask these questions. He is paying the freight on this marketing activity. It is his name . . . or his product's or service's . . . that appears in every ad . . . on every brochure. He's the one on the line, and he has a right to make sure the copywriter is doing *everything* possible to produce more prospect responses. And that what is done is done for a reason, not in a fit of absent-mindedness . . . or because the copywriter "always does it this way."

Neither party can abdicate his responsibility at this crucial stage. Both must be fully alert to the importance of what is being done and expect, indeed encourage, the other to exercise his right to evaluate and push for perfection. This is what an engaged professional relationship is all about, after all. It is entirely appropriate that it take place at this moment and entirely wrong that either party feel affronted by it, so long as it is handled in a professional manner. After all, both parties are committed to the same objective: producing the greatest prospect response as fast as possible.

As a result of this draft and the discussions that follow, both parties will probably find themselves with more work to do. Fortunately this work, very focused and precise, is relatively easy. After all, unless this first draft is egregiously wrong, there is now something to work from . . . and improve. As a result, the copywriter should be able to produce the second draft quickly, and have it be very close to the final product.

Of course this draft, like the first, must be reviewed to make certain the copy is client-centered . . . packed with believable, specific benefits . . . and an incentive for immediate action. You know how to do this now, too, or at least how to recognize such copy when you see it! That's why this stage doesn't take very long . . . and doesn't produce nearly the fireworks between marketer and copywriter that the first sometimes does.

When this review is finished, much, but not all, of the copywriter's work is complete. It cannot, however, be considered final until the designer lays out the copy . . . and both copywriter and marketer review the designer's effort with marketing precepts in mind.

As you know, I have already discussed the role of the designer in this marketing process. But let me say one thing again, very clearly: cash copy is *always* more important than design and must never be subordinated to design. Never. Design helps attract prospect interest and may help retain prospect interest, but it is copy — and copy only — that gets the prospect to respond. You must never forget this, because your designer — whose first love is rarely marketing — often does.

That is why, once the copy has been laid out, both copywriter and marketer must again review it with their constant standard in mind: does what has been created help capture and hold the prospect and help motivate him to respond? Or does it in any way obstruct or impede this response? In other words, they must ensure that marketing has priority over design. Design, in this context, is only relevant to the extent that it promotes and induces immediate prospect response. Here, it has no other purpose whatsoever.

Keeping this objective in mind, once the copywriter has seen the copy laid out, he may well wish to make changes in either the design . . . or the copy. If copywriter and marketer agree on the suitability of the copy as a prospect motivator, then design changes must be made. By the same token, a strongly market-centered designer may have good reason to suggest certain changes in the copy . . . its volume, for instance . . . to ensure a better response. In other words, there will be dickering at this point; so, expect it. The expert worth listening to, however, is the one who presents his argument with your prospects in mind and what it takes to get them to respond. He, at least, is attempting to answer the right question.

Towards Completion

Following these steps, your copy will move briskly towards completion . . . and towards being the kind of copy with the kind of presentation that must induce prospects to respond. Before you sign off on it, however, read it aloud; show it to prospects for their opinion. And inspect each component. Does it help motivate a prospect to respond? Or is it just dead weight that serves no marketing purpose at all?

Ask your copywriter, too, for his candid opinion of what is now a virtually complete project. The good copywriter knows that in the service of speed, and in the needs of business, it is not always possible to produce perfect cash copy; for better or for worse, perfection is often sacrificed to the needs of the moment. But, while lamenting this fact, your copywriter can tell you where this copy falls down and what you should do now to improve it for next time. In other words, if it is necessary for you to use something that is less than perfect, there is no reason to use it more than once.

When all this is done, conclude this project. It is now time to send it into the world and see what happens. Even if it is, perhaps, not quite perfect, if you and your copywriter have followed these guidelines, it should still be the best marketing material you have ever distributed. That being the case, thank your copywriter. There may have been some tense moments in your relationship, but, if he has consistently acted in your best interest, recognize it . . . and say so. This is not the moment for a testimonial letter to your copywriter . . . that comes after the results of this marketing activity are in . . . but a sincere word of appreciation is very much in order — and a sample of the marketing materials for his portfolio.

On Building A Relationship With Your Copywriter

If your relationship with this copywriter has been upbeat and professional and (a more important condition) if what he produces for you makes money, then this is a relationship you should foster. Do so.

There are many copywriters in the world. But many fewer competent ones. Once you have found one who works well for you, do your part to build your relationship:

- Share the results of this marketing activity with your copywriter. If things went well, if you made money, compliment him for his part. If things went less well than you'd like, share your prospect and customer feed-back and your own opinions; even the best copywriter wants to be better. And there isn't one of us who can't improve.

- Use your copywriter regularly. The more often you use him, the more he'll know about you and your business, and the less time it'll take him to create a strong client-centered document. Once he knows you and your business and understands crucial aspects of both, you'll find your cost decreasing and the value of his services increasing.

- Take it upon yourself to recommend his services when you can. A good word won't cost you anything . . . and, through the golden ties of gratitude (not quite dead in this country) . . . probably get you preferred service.

- Finally, when the strong results come in based on the cash copy your copywriter helped create, write the kind of testimonial you know, from mastering this book, that he can use in the development of his own business, one with specific results that will stimulate new prospects to sign up for his services. When you send it to your copywriter (without being asked to do so), let him know you're available to confirm his value to these prospects by telephone.

If you want to be one of those people who always gets preferred treatment, try this. It is not only one way to make the world just a little bit more pleasant . . . but may, perhaps, be just the thing to ensure that your copywriter goes just a little bit further for you, so you get both service and copy that is superior to what he gives anyone else.

And isn't this what you, as a marketer, really want? To get the competitive advantage in all things?

You know it is.

Conclusion

Are you exhilarated now?

You should be!

Think of how much money you now spend . . . you have spent . . . on producing marketing documents of every kind. Consider your expenditures on flyers . . . cover letters . . . ads . . . brochures . . . annual reports . . . and everything else you use to bring your important messages to your prospects.

Admit it, these numbers add up to truly astonishing figures. And to generally depressing ones, when you contemplate how many people dispose of what you send them instead of acting on it.

This needn't happen to you again. And that is cause for excitement, indeed.

Now you know what to do to transform your marketing communications into the most compelling and persuasive of documents. Never again will you produce materials that speak about you . . . that pile one leaden feature on another . . . that fail to give your prospects an immediate incentive for action.

Never again will you use weak testimonials . . . or fail to use testimonials at all. Your happy buyers will now be a potent marketing corps motivating prospects to respond.

Never again will you pretend it doesn't matter when your prospects respond . . . or leave matters exclusively to their discretion as to when they do. You know that you want them to respond NOW!, and you know how to get them to.

Of course, all this takes work. Of course, until you're in your stride, this work is difficult. Of course, you will make mistakes. Why pretend otherwise? But why allow mistakes and early imperfections to deter you?

You have a superior product or service, do you not? You know it can transform your prospects' lives and make them better, do you not? And you know that as more and more of your prospects use what you're selling, your own life will improve.

Therefore, your task is plain: you must master the art of cash copy . . . and do everything you can so that the largest number of people benefit from what you have available. This is your commission.

And now you have what it takes to achieve it.

The next time, today!, you sit down to communicate with your prospects and buyers, remember the constant message of this guide: it is your responsibility to do everything you can to let your audience know just what you can do for them . . . how much you have for them . . . how many benefits are available for them . . . and how easy it is for them to get these benefits . . . if only they act NOW!

If your marketing is to succeed, you must fully focus on the prospect and what you can do for him . . . and show him, to the furthest extent possible, just how far you will go to make his life easier. Then to this already potent formula, add the last crucial ingredient: your passion.

Do not act impersonally . . . indifferently . . . with cool reserve. Act as if what you're doing matters. Act as if it matters to you that the life of each of your prospects is improved . . . and that you will do what is necessary so it will be. Act as if *each* contact with *each* prospect counts . . . as if every one is of very real consequence. As indeed it must be.

You are the one, with your product and service, who can change a life. Through your marketing communications *you* are the one who can indicate just how that life will be changed . . . and how much better it will be . . . if only the prospect will act. And *you* are the one who must show . . . in every conceivable way . . . that what you are doing is important and matters; not just that you are going through the motions, peddling a product or service of no importance, to an individual about whom you are apathetic, in a way that clearly indicates just how bored and indifferent you are to anything but your own betterment.

This is the fault of most of today's marketing.

The best marketing is communication between just two people . . . a person who has a want or an anxiety. And a person, you!, who can solve that problem. It is intensely personal. Always intimate. Never apathetic. It is vital! Committed! Engaged!

Just as your marketing communications will be now . . . now that you know how to create cash copy and motivate your prospects to respond immediately.

Soon you will set to work to produce this copy. Yes, you will experience frustrations and difficulties in doing so; it is always difficult going beyond yourself and focusing on someone else. But very soon, you will produce and then distribute the best and most compelling marketing materials you ever have.

As your results come back . . . results superior to anything you have previously had . . . take a moment to congratulate yourself. What you have done is a fine and worthy thing, and your achievement is justly deserved.

Then take a moment to share your triumph with an old friend who may have helped you produce these significant results. Share your triumph with me. You see, I never doubted it would happen and am delighted to know it is only the beginning.

I look forward to having this most welcome news very soon,

Jeffrey

About the Author

Over the last several years, Dr. Jeffrey Lant has emerged as one of America's most well-known business authorities. His provocative and information-packed articles on a wide variety of business development topics (under the title "Sure Fire Business Success") are now carried by over 100 publications nationwide and abroad. Major electronic databases like CompuServe (U.S. Entrepreneurs Network and Working from Home), GEnie (Ephote), Delphi, and Boston Citinet also carry his articles. Well over a million and a half people monthly get their business get-ahead information from Jeffrey!

Unlike most writers, Jeffrey's telephone number runs along with these articles, so that his readers can call for additional information, hints, and the "kick where it helps" that all of us occasionally need.

A practicing marketing consultant for the last 10 years, Jeffrey is president of Jeffrey Lant Associates, Inc. Based in Cambridge, Massachusetts, he works nationally. Some of his work includes creating marketing plans, developing information products, and writing brochures, cover letters, ads, and response coupons for a wide variety of both individuals and organizations which want to sell their products and services faster. He also provides fund raising assistance to nonprofit organizations and public relations consultation. His practice is distinguished by his own distinctive brand of enthusiasm, excitement and positive problem-solving skills.

A well-known speaker on such topics as establishing a successful consulting practice, effective marketing, publishing profitable books, succeeding in your own mail order business, running a profitable home-based business, and many other topics, Jeffrey ranges the country giving speeches, workshops and conference presentations. An animated and often electrifying platform speaker,

461

Jeffrey never merely talks to an audience, but also seeks to involve them in his presentation. Intellectually demanding of himself, Jeffrey demands no less of his audiences!

Over the past 10 years, Jeffrey has written a book each year. His titles include the seven volumes in his well-known "Get Ahead" Series, including THE CONSULTANT'S KIT: ESTABLISHING AND OPERATING YOUR SUCCESSFUL CONSULTING BUSINESS (now in an 8th printing); THE UN-ABASHED SELF-PROMOTER'S GUIDE: WHAT EVERY MAN, WOMAN, CHILD AND ORGANIZATION IN AMERICA NEEDS TO KNOW ABOUT GETTING AHEAD BY EXPLOITING THE MEDIA; MONEY TALKS: THE COMPLETE GUIDE TO CREATING A PROFITABLE WORKSHOP OR SEMINAR IN ANY FIELD; TRICKS OF THE TRADE: THE COMPLETE GUIDE TO SUCCEEDING IN THE ADVICE BUSINESS; MONEY MAK-ING MARKETING: FINDING THE PEOPLE WHO NEED WHAT YOU'RE SELLING AND MAKING SURE THEY BUY IT, and CASH COPY: HOW TO OFFER YOUR PRODUCTS AND SERVICES SO YOUR PROSPECTS BUY THEM . . . NOW! His latest book is HOW TO MAKE A WHOLE LOT MORE THAN $1,000,000 WRITING, COMMISSIONING, PUBLISHING AND SELLING 'HOW TO' INFORMATION. Major media sources nation-wide and critics have hailed these books as unrelentingly thorough, models of what a "how-to" book should be. This thoroughness and the complete practical-ity of the information he provides have become Jeffrey's trademarks.

His other titles include DEVELOPMENT TODAY: A FUND RAISING GUIDE FOR NONPROFIT ORGANIZATIONS; INSUBSTANTIAL PAG-EANT: CEREMONY AND CONFUSION AT QUEEN VICTORIA'S COURT; and (as Editor) OUR HARVARD: REFLECTIONS ON COLLEGE LIFE BY TWENTY-TWO DISTINGUISHED GRADUATES.

Jeffrey has also produced a series of 60-minute audio cassettes on topics like "How To Get Free Time On Radio And T.V. And Use It To Get Your Prospects To Buy What You're Selling" and "How To Create Marketing Documents That Get Your Prospects To Buy What You're Selling . . . NOW!" Books In Motion in Spokane, WA the same company that produces tapes for the Stanford Univ. Continuing Education Program, has produced Jeffrey's books MONEY MAKING MARKETING and CASH COPY in multi-cassette albums.

Jeffrey, his work, and innovative ideas are also featured in many books including *What Color Is Your Parachute?*, *The Harvard Guide To Careers*, *1001 Ways To Market Your Books*, *Create Your Own Career Opportunities*,

How To Succeed As An Independent Consultant, The Complete Guide To Self Publishing, Maverick: Succeeding As A Free-Lance Entrepreneur, Playing Hardball With Soft Skills, Cash In On Today's Educational Market, Win Them Over: A Survival Guide For Corporate Consultant Relations Programs, Marketing To The Fortune 500, How To Get Happily Published, Homemade Money, The Consultant's Guide to Winning Clients, The Do-It-Yourself Publicity Kit, Writing For Fun And Money, How To Get The Prospects You Need So That You Make At Least $100,000 Every Year Selling Real Estate!, How To Make Money Buying Pre-Foreclosure Properties Before They Hit The County Courthouse Steps, 148 Great Ways To Make Money On The Side, Street Smart Marketing, and many others. His credentials and achievements are also featured in over 18 different biographical guides from *Who's Who In Finance & Industry* to *The International Who's Who Of Intellectuals.*

His achievements have been recognized by many organizations, including the Boston and Cambridge City Councils; twice by the House of Representatives of the State of Massachusetts, by two Governors of Massachusetts, by the State of Texas, and by the cities of Charleston, South Carolina; Cape May, New Jersey; Virginia Beach, VA and Eureka, California. In 1987 he received special recognition from the Governor of Massachusetts upon the completion of the first five volumes of his "Get Ahead" Series.

Jeffrey is a graduate of the University of California, Santa Barbara (B.A. *summa cum laude* '69); Northeastern University, Boston (Certificate of Advanced Graduate Studies in Higher Education Administration, '76); and Harvard University (M.A.'70 and Ph.D.'75). He has never had a business course in his entire career!

Among Jeffrey's many official positions are: member, National Advisory Board, National Association of Independent Publishers and Editorial Advisory Board Member, *Limited Partnership Investment Review.*

Jeffrey is 42 years old and currently lives in Cambridge, Massachusetts, surrounded by mountains of paper, an underused exercise machine, and a computer and telephone which connect him to millions of people striving to build strong businesses of every kind. You can reach him at 50 Follen St., Suite 507, Cambridge, MA 02138 or by calling (617) 547-6372.

Jeffrey Lant's
SURE-FIRE BUSINESS SUCCESS CATALOG

FALL, 1989

Dear Friend,

Let's not kid each other. You want to make more money faster, don't you? Candidly, I can help you. That's why you need this Sure-Fire Business Success Catalog.

This edition is packed with over 125 ways for you to make more money and solve business problems. Not tomorrow. Not next week. BUT RIGHT NOW.

What's more, if you act NOW, I'll load you up with profit-making freebies.

If you order just $220 from this catalog by January 1, 1990, you can select any one of my giant money-making books absolutely free. Take your pick from:

- THE CONSULTANT'S KIT: ESTABLISHING AND OPERATING YOUR SUCCESSFUL CONSULTING BUSINESS
- THE UNABASHED SELF-PROMOTER'S GUIDE: WHAT EVERY MAN, WOMAN, CHILD AND ORGANIZATION IN AMERICA NEEDS TO KNOW ABOUT GETTING AHEAD BY EXPLOITING THE MEDIA
- MONEY TALKS: THE COMPLETE GUIDE TO CREATING A PROFITABLE WORKSHOP OR SEMINAR IN ANY FIELD
- TRICKS OF THE TRADE: THE COMPLETE GUIDE TO SUCCEEDING IN THE ADVICE BUSINESS
- MONEY MAKING MARKETING: FINDING THE PEOPLE WHO NEED WHAT YOU'RE SELLING AND MAKING SURE THEY BUY IT
- CASH COPY: HOW TO OFFER YOUR PRODUCTS AND SERVICES SO YOUR PROSPECTS BUY THEM...NOW!
- Or select my latest book HOW TO MAKE A WHOLE LOT MORE THAN $1,000,000 WRITING, COMMISSIONING, PUBLISHING AND SELLING "HOW-TO" INFORMATION

Your free money-making guide, packed with step-by-step guidelines to achieve its objectives, is valued at between $27.95–$34. But it's yours absolutely free!

That's not all, when your order totals at least $220, you also get any one of my three 60-minute audio cassettes. Get money-making details on getting free radio and television time to sell your products... or how to create ads, flyers, brochures and cover letters that get your prospects to respond immediately... or what you've really got to do to successfully market your products and services every day. A $14 retail value, you get your audio cassette free — if you act by 01/01/90. That's right, order at least $220 from this catalog, and you get over $40 worth of money-making gifts from me!

Another Bonus: Ordering less this time? No problem! Get at least $150 from this catalog, and you can select with my compliments any one of my three 60-minute audio cassettes. You decide.

This catalog launches my 11th year in the business of helping you make more money faster. Most new businesses bite the dust within a couple of years. There's a good reason this one has lasted: the best money-making products and services presented in the most straightforward manner. When you really want to sell your products and services faster, send in your order or call me at (617) 547-6372... twenty-four hours a day... 365 days a year. I mean it!

Your personal profit-maker,

P.S. If there's a ** next to your name on the mailing panel it means you're about to be zapped off the mailing list. Better buy something, or I can't help you make any money.

All prices include shipping!

Fall Selection #1

New! HOW TO MAKE A WHOLE LOT MORE THAN $1,000,000 WRITING, COMMISSIONING, PUBLISHING AND SELLING "HOW-TO" INFORMATION

Want to learn how to make a fortune creating and selling "how-to" products like books, booklets, audio cassettes and Special Reports? Wonder no more... thanks to Jeffrey's latest book. Here in over 500 pages, you get the exact step-by-step details you need so you can:

- create information products people want to buy;
- learn how to profit from them now — and for years to come;
- produce your products fast and accurately;
- make tens of thousands of dollars more with end-of-product catalogs;
- save money — and avoid hassles — by following Jeffrey's product production guidelines;
- learn to cut your personnel costs... get to more prospects faster and get more buyers to spend more... by using a personal computer;
- get other people to produce money-making info-products for you... so you can make your million-dollar fortune faster;
- get all the free publicity you'll want so you can sell your products for the least cost... and most profit;
- master the essentials of direct response marketing... so you bring your info-products right to the people who can buy them... and get them to buy IMMEDIATELY;
- make big money through talk programs, bookstores, libraries, overseas rights, exhibits... and more. Dozens of alternatives are fully presented... so you can start making money right away from your products.

Jeffrey's written this new book for one reason and one reason only: to make you an information product millionaire. No one in America's as qualified as Jeffrey to "tell it like it is" about exactly what you've got to do to make a fortune creating and selling information products. Here's where he lays it on the line... in easy-to-read, easy-to-profit from steps. Jeffrey guarantees there's no resource remotely like this one on the planet... You just can't get these guidelines anywhere else.

Helping make your business more profitable since 1979

465

SPECIAL PRE-PUBLICATION PRICE. Act by January 1, 1990 and the cost of this book is just $30 postpaid. Your autographed copy — packed with Jeffrey's characteristically detailed guidelines and hundreds of resources you need to build your million-dollar information empire — will be sent in December. Warning: beginning 01/01/90 the price of this money-making resource is going up to $38.50 postpaid. *No special price orders will be honored after the deadline.* So act now. Dealers: Your discount does not apply on this pre-publication offer. To get your copy, send $30 postpaid. Don't forget — if your order totals at least $220, you can select this as your gift book!

"Your book CASH COPY is the best book I've ever read on advertising! WOW — it boggles the mind with all the information you've included. I'd pay $100 for a book like this anytime. It's a bargain at $27.95." **Harry Weyandt, Norwalk, CA**

#2

CASH COPY: HOW TO OFFER YOUR PRODUCTS AND SERVICES SO YOUR PROSPECTS BUY THEM... NOW! You're spending thousands... maybe even tens of thousands of dollars... producing your marketing communications... flyers, ads, cover letters, brochures, proposals, annual reports, *etc.* You know what happens to over 98% of them: THEY'RE TRASHED IMMEDIATELY. You can keep hoping this madness will stop... or you can get CASH COPY. For just $27.95 postpaid, you find out *exactly* what you need to know to get your marketing communications to do what they're supposed to do: turn prospects into buyers and buyers into repeat buyers NOW... not tomorrow, not next week. You get the low-down on:

- all the stupid mistakes you're making... so you can stop;
- how to stop producing selfish marketing that talks about you... and learn how to put the focus exactly where it belongs: on your prospect;
- *every* component of *every* marketing document you'll ever produce. Each

word, each sentence, every paragraph is either working to make you money... or it's useless. Learn what it takes to make all your marketing materials make money;

- how to produce every single kind of marketing communication you'll ever use;
- offers that get people to respond immediately;
- testimonials that motivate sales... and reduce buyer anxiety.

And much, much more.

Not only has CASH COPY been recommended by the American Library Association for every American library, but it's now a Special Selection of one of the prestigious Writer's Digest Book Clubs. I'll tell you why: there has never been a book like this one, a book that tells you *exactly* what to do to stop wasting your money on marketing materials that get thrown away.

Act today. If you don't like this resource, return it within 30 days... just like everything else in this catalog. But get it. Or keep wasting your money on marketing documents that are just plain pointless. 480 pages $27.95

JEFFREY'S CHALLENGE: If you have the slightest doubt that CASH COPY is for you, call me right this minute at (617) 547-6372 and read me the first three sentences of any one of your marketing communications. I'll prove to you that you're wasting big bucks producing junk that won't get anybody to do anything except throw your marketing materials away.

#3

MONEY MAKING MARKETING AUDIO CASSETTE PROGRAM After all these years as a marketing consultant, I'll tell you something: you're probably a lousy marketer. You don't have a marketing plan; don't have fixed cash objectives for yourself.

"Thank you for writing CASH COPY, such a thorough and informative book. I consider your book a goldmine of practical information, and I hope with all my heart that my competitors don't read it!" **Lili O'Day, Palos Park, IL**

Don't have a clear grasp of your various markets. Don't understand what they want from you. Don't know how to translate the features of what you're selling into the benefits your prospects want to buy. Don't understand the Rule of Seven, so you bring those benefits to their attention sufficiently often to generate a sale. And don't understand specific marketing formats like direct mail, telemarketing, card decks, co-op advertising, classified and small space ads, *etc.*

In short, you're wasting your marketing dollars. Every single day!

Now there's just no excuse for that. The most detailed audio marketing program ever created is now available. It's 12 ninety-minute cassettes (18 hours in all!) all based on my book MONEY MAKING MARKETING. While riding in your car or home in your study, you can slip in a tape and be immediately surrounded by the insistent guidelines of a relentless marketer.

If you're happy with your business as it is, don't bother with these tapes. But if you want to make more money and sell more of your products and services, don't waste another minute. Get them ... and tune in the step-by-step marketing details that ensure you more money.
12 cassette package. $125.

#4

MONEY MAKING MARKETING: FINDING THE PEOPLE WHO NEED WHAT YOU'RE SELLING AND MAKING SURE THEY BUY IT. This is the 285-page book on which the tapes are based. Using the tapes in your car or office, you hear and understand what you need to do. With the book, you get to read the guidelines and get samples you can immediately put to use.

MONEY MAKING MARKETING book alone. $34 postpaid.

#5

MONEY MAKING MARKETING AUDIO CASSETTE AND BOOK SPECIAL OFFER. Get the complete MONEY MAKING MARKETING package including 18 hours of audio cassettes and book. Just $144.95. You save $20!!!

#6

THE CONSULTANT'S KIT: ESTAB-LISHING AND OPERATING YOUR SUCCESSFUL CONSULTING BUSINESS. The one book specifically recommended by the U.S. Small Business Administration to new and aspiring consultants in *any* field tells you exactly what you need to know to make a success of your new consulting business. If you're thinking about consulting or have been in business under a year, this is the resource you need. It's the only resource on consulting recommended by *What Color Is Your Parachute?* (the best-selling career guide of all time) because it provides you with exactly what you need to launch a profitable consulting business. 203 pages $34

#7

TRICKS OF THE TRADE: THE COMPLETE GUIDE TO SUC-CEEDING IN THE ADVICE BUSI-NESS. This book is designed for people who want to build at least a six-figure annual income. If you follow these guidelines, we guarantee you'll get it! Specifically for people who *really* want to squeeze the last drop of profit from their problem-solving information. Here's where you get complete details on the Mobile-Mini Conglomerate: 10 steps that you'll use to get the utmost benefit from your problem-solving information. Tells you how to get clients, how to work with clients, how to get the results you want, how to build long-term relation-ships, even how to work with Flat-worms, people who say they want results, but really want to obstruct. It's all here. Herman Holtz, himself a master of the consulting genre, said this may be the most important book ever written on consulting. 315 pages $34

#8

MONEY TALKS: THE COMPLETE GUIDE TO CREATING A PROFIT-ABLE WORKSHOP OR SEMINAR IN ANY FIELD. Brand new edition!!! Just out!!! If you want to make money with talk programs of any kind, find out how to use these programs to get clients and publicity, then you need the new Second Revised Edition of this well-known book. It's got everything you need to start making money — really big money — on the talk circuit

with workshops, lectures, seminars — every kind of talk program. Find out how to get sponsors — or sponsor programs yourself; make money from "back of the room" sales, even when you don't have a product. And when you do. The Most Complete Book Ever Written On This Subject. 308 pages. $34

#9

THE UNABASHED SELF-PRO-MOTER'S GUIDE: WHAT EVERY MAN, WOMAN, CHILD AND ORGANIZATION IN AMERICA NEEDS TO KNOW ABOUT GET-TING AHEAD BY EXPLOITING THE MEDIA. A recent review said this may be the "most important single book on promotion ever written." We agree! Stop paying money for paid ads. Find out how to get as much free publicity as you can, whenever you need it. This book is exhaustive. You'll use it for the rest of your business career whatever you're selling: product, service, organization or idea. Step-by-step guidelines for getting you and what you're promot-ing continuing media attention. *The Levison Letter* calls this "The best business book ever written." If you're really interested in getting free media time and space, we think you'll agree. 366 pages. $34

"I cannot express how pleased I am with THE UN-ABASHED SELF-PRO-MOTER'S GUIDE. It termi-nates a month-long search to find a book like it... I am awed by the concentration, organization and intelligence of your book; I must say, I've rarely encountered a 'how-to' book on so complex a subject, that is so readily applicable, generous and spiritual."
**Harold Herbstman
New York, NY**

"I've read MONEY MAKING MARKETING and listened to your cassette album of the same title. I think both the program and book are terrific. They do indeed offer unrelentingly practical advice."
Berkeley Fleming, Entrepreneur's Guild, Mountain Lakes, NJ

#10

... for the success-minded consultant

Want to succeed as a part-time or full-time consultant in any field? Get a deal on **THE CONSULTANT'S KIT** and **TRICKS OF THE TRADE.** $55 for the pair. Save $13.

#11

...when you want to sell more of your products and services

Now benefit from Jeffrey's step-by-step marketing advice and learn how to sell more of your products and services for the least possible cost. Get a deal on **THE UNABASHED SELF-PRO-MOTER'S GUIDE, MONEY MAK-ING MARKETING** and **CASH COPY.** $80 for all three. You save $15.95.

#12

... when you want to master all the master's profit-making techniques

Get all six books in Jeffrey's "Get Ahead" series, including **CASH COPY, THE CONSULTANT'S KIT, THE UNABASHED SELF-PRO-MOTER'S GUIDE, MONEY TALKS, TRICKS OF THE TRADE** and **MONEY MAKING MARKETING.** Over 2,000 pages of detailed step-by-step guidelines on achieving success by selling products and services. *No other specialist — anywhere — has written such complete instructions on what it takes to make money — lots of money.* We'll be flabbergasted if you don't make back the cost of this package many hundreds of times.

Get all six for just $175. *Save $27.45.*

Jeffrey Lant's 60-Minute Audio-Cassette Series

#13

HOW TO GET FREE TIME ON RADIO AND T.V. AND USE IT TO GET YOUR PROSPECTS TO BUY WHAT YOU'RE SELLING. Listen as Jeffrey gives you the secrets of getting valuable free time on radio and television so you can sell your products and services without spending any of your money. Getting on *just one* program could return your investment dozens of times! $14

#14

HOW TO CREATE MARKETING DOCUMENTS THAT GET YOUR PROSPECTS TO BUY WHAT YOU'RE SELLING ... NOW! Since you spend thousands of dollars on your marketing documents, don't you think you should know what will get people to respond to them faster ... to buy what you're selling **NOW**? Here's just what you need to know. $14

#15

ESSENTIALS OF MONEY MAKING MARKETING: WHAT YOU'VE REALLY GOT TO DO TO SELL YOUR PRODUCTS AND SERVICES, EVERY DAY! Jeffrey shares his secrets of successful marketing, what you've got to do, when and how you've got to do it to sell your products and services. $14.

#16

Get all three of Jeffrey's new 60-minute audio-cassettes for just $35. That's **three hours** of precise profit-making consultation for less than 20% of Jeffrey's regular hourly fee! You can't beat this value. And if your order totals at least $150, select one **free.**

> *"I think your book MONEY MAKING MARKETING is the BEST I've ever read on marketing! I can't believe all you have packed into one USEFUL book."* **Berniece Good, Longview, WA**

Real busy? Can't seem to find the time to learn all the things you need to know to stay on the cutting edge? You need Jeffrey Lant's unique Special Reports (#17–55) ... highly concentrated information in an easy-to-read five-page format. Sent first class the day you order so you can start using the information you need ... fast! Just $4 each. $10 for any group of three!!!

#17

New! WHY MOST CONSULTANTS CAN NEVER MAKE AT LEAST $100,000 A YEAR... AND WHAT TO DO SO YOU WILL. Jeffrey shows you why most consultants fail to make at least $100,000 a year... and provides the specific steps to follow so you will. $4.

#18

New! HOW TO GET FREE AND LOW-COST SOFTWARE FOR YOUR IBM AND IBM-COMPATIBLE COMPUTER. Jeffrey interviews John Gliedman, author of the new book *Tips And Techniques for Using Low-Cost And Public Domain Software* on how to get your hands on some of the stupendous amount of free and low-cost software currently available for IBM and IBM-compatible personal computers. Gliedman provides the names, addresses and phone numbers of just where to go to save big money on your software and techniques on how to use it effectively. $4.

#19

New! HOW TO CREATE CLASSIFIED AND SMALL SPACE ADS THAT GET YOUR PROSPECTS TO RESPOND... AND WHAT TO DO WHEN THEY DO! Jeffrey gives you the low-down on how to create classified and small space ads that get people to respond... and how to create

an effective, profit-making program so you can turn your new prospects into buyers... fast! $4.

#20

New! HOW TO MAKE MONEY BUYING PRE-FORECLOSURE PROPERTIES BEFORE THEY HIT THE COURTHOUSE STEPS. Jeffrey interviews property investment advisor Tom Lucier, author of the new book *How To Make Money Buying Pre-Foreclosure Properties Before They Hit The Courthouse Steps* on just what it takes to make big money in pre-foreclosure properties. New workshops have sprung up recently charging as much as $5000 for a week-end providing this kind of advice. Why pay 5G's when specialist Tom Lucier provides the detailed steps right here? $4.

#21

HOW TO DEVELOP AND USE A CLIENT-CENTERED QUESTIONNAIRE THAT GETS YOUR PROSPECTS TO TELL YOU WHAT THEY WANT ... SO YOU CAN SELL IT TO THEM. Here, Jeffrey helps people who hate making cold calls ... and can't figure out how to get their prospects to tell them what they want. If you can solve this problem, you can sell *any* product or service. With these guidelines, you create the unique client-centered prospecting questionnaire ... and find out how to use it. When you do, your prospects start telling you precisely what they want ... all you have to do is give it to them. $4

#22

HOW TO DO "HOW-TO" (BOOKLETS AND BOOKS, THAT IS). Here Jeffrey tells you exactly how to produce a how-to booklet or book that really tells your readers how to do what your title promises. Most how-to products are dismal failures. They don't provide the details your readers need to achieve what they want. If they don't use your product, they don't refer it to others, don't buy other products you sell, don't make use of your services ... and in general make sure you don't get the benefits of the product you've created. Don't let this happen to you. Learn what it takes to create a truly useful client-centered how-to product. $4

#23
HOW TO MAKE OVER $100,000 EVERY YEAR WITH YOUR OWN CATALOG SELLING PROBLEM-SOLVING INFORMATION PRODUCTS. Most people in mail order try to make a big kill from a single problem-solving information product ... or just a few. Here Jeffrey shows you why that's futile ... and how to go about establishing a client-centered catalog selling how-to information products that will make you at least $100,000 every year ... and maybe a whole lot more. $4

#24
HOW TO USE JOB ADS TO LAND THE JOB YOU *REALLY* WANT. If you've ever tried to get a job using classified job ads you know how time consuming and frustrating it is. Here Jeffrey interviews jobs-finding specialist Kenton Elderkin, author of the new book *How To Get Interviews From Job Ads: Where To Look, What To Select, Who To Write, What To Say, When To Follow-Up, How To Save Time.* With these techniques, answering job ads *can* lead to the interviews you need ... and the good job you want. $4

#25
YOUR WORST FEARS REALIZED, OR WHAT TO DO WHEN THE CORPORATION OR FOUNDATION DECLINES YOUR PROPOSAL. The competition for corporate and foundation dollars for nonprofit organizations has never been greater ... and will get worse. You can count on getting turned down, often. What you do next determines whether your organization will ever get the money it needs from these sources. Here are Jeffrey's guidelines for turning a no into a yes, for doing what it takes to build a lucrative relationship with a funding source which has just turned you down. Since this will happen to you (if it isn't happening already), prepare for it now. $4

Yes, you can see Jeffrey's books (and Debra Ashton's, published by Jeffrey) in book stores and libraries nationwide. But you only get the special deals on them here!

26
HOW TO CREATE A BROCHURE AND COVER LETTER YOUR PROSPECTS WILL RESPOND TO ... NOW! In honor of his new book **CASH COPY: HOW TO OFFER YOUR PRODUCTS AND SERVICES SO YOUR PROSPECTS BUY THEM ... NOW!,** Jeffrey tells you how to solve one of the most basic marketing problems of any business: what it takes to create a brochure and cover letter that get people to respond, instead of being tossed. $4

#27
HOW TO USE HUMOR TO MAKE YOUR NEXT BUSINESS SPEECH A SUCCESS. Jeffrey teams up with communications specialist Michael Iapoce to give you tips on how to use humor to make your business presentations successful. The information provided here won't turn you into a Las Vegas comic, but it *will* help you break down your audience's barriers, get them to like you, and help you make more sales faster. And isn't that just what you want? $4

#28
HOW TO RAISE MONEY FOR YOUR NONPROFIT ORGANIZATION WITH AN ANNUAL PHON-A-THON. Jeffrey tells you what you've got to do to use telemarketing to raise money for your nonprofit organization ... when you've got to work with community volunteers and can't afford professional help. $4

#29
HOW TO BRING ORDER TO DESK CHAOS, OR ESSENTIALS OF ORGANIZING YOURSELF. Jeffrey talks to organizational specialist Kate Kelly, author (along with Ronni Eisenberg) of the best-selling book

ORGANIZE YOURSELF!, about what you've got to do to control clutter and get all those papers in your business life under control. $4

#30
HOW TO AVOID DESKTOP DISAPPOINTMENT, OR WHAT YOU'VE *REALLY* GOT TO KNOW TO MAKE DESKTOP PUBLISHING WORK FOR YOU. Jeffrey interviews desktop design specialist Roger Parker, author of *Looking Good In Print,* on what to do to avoid the pitfalls of desktop publishing and use design to create compelling marketing communications. $4

#31
IT ISN'T JUST SAYING THE RIGHT THING THAT MAKES A SUCCESSFUL PRESENTATION ... OR WHAT YOU'VE REALLY GOT TO DO TO CONNECT WITH YOUR AUDIENCE AND PERSUADE THEM TO LISTEN TO YOU. This isn't a Special Report about speech content ... it's a Special Report about how to deal with your audience so they like you and want to listen to what you have to say. Verbal presentations aren't just about imparting information; they're about persuading people to do things. Here's what you've got to do to achieve this crucial objective. $4

#32
HOW TO CREATE A MARKETING PLAN THAT SELLS YOUR SERVICE FOR THE LEAST COST AND MAKES THE BIGGEST PROFIT. Most people selling a service are "winging it", with predictable results: their marketing is episodic, spasmodic ... unproductive. Jeffrey tells you how to create a marketing plan that will sell a service for the least possible cost and greatest results. $4

#33
HOW TO CREATE A PROPOSAL THAT A CORPORATION OR FOUNDATION WILL FUND. Jeffrey tells you and your nonprofit organization what it takes to create a proposal that a corporate or foundation funding source will give money to support. $4

#34
TELESELLING: HOW TO GET THROUGH THE SCREEN THAT'S KEEPING YOU FROM YOUR PROSPECT. Jeffrey and telemarketing expert Art Sobczak, editor of *Telephone Selling Report*, provide tips on what you've got to do to get through your prospect's screens … switchboard operators, secretaries … anybody who stands between you and your next sale. $4

#35
HOW TO OPEN A TELEPHONE SALES CALL WITH EITHER A PROSPECT OR A CUSTOMER … SO YOU GET THE BUSINESS. Jeffrey again talks to Art Sobczak, editor of *Telephone Selling Report*, on what to say during those crucial opening sentences with a telephone prospect … and how to develop and build profitable relationships by phone with existing customers. $4

#36
WHAT YOU HAVE TO DO TO SELL YOUR PRODUCTS AND SERVICES THROUGH A FREE CLIENT NEWSLETTER. Jeffrey tells you how to produce free client newsletters that get your prospects to buy your products and services. $4

#37
HOW TO CREATE INEXPENSIVE, EFFECTIVE AUDIO CASSETTES TO GET MORE OF YOUR PROSPECTS TO RESPOND FASTER … AND MAKE EXTRA MONEY, TOO. Jeffrey tells you how to create inexpensive 60-minute audio cassettes in your home or office, use them to induce more and faster sales … and sell profitably, too. $4

#38
HOW TO PROFIT BY INVESTING IN NEW AND BRUISED HOUSES. Jeffrey gets step-by-step advice from Florida author and investor Thomas Lucier on how to make money in real estate through affordable used and bruised houses, one of today's smart investments for people with a moderate amount to spend. $4

#39
HOW TO USE WORKSHOPS AND OTHER TALK PROGRAMS TO GET CLIENTS. In honor of the publication of the new Second Edition of his well-known book **MONEY TALKS: THE COMPLETE GUIDE TO CREATING A PROFITABLE WORKSHOP OR SEMINAR IN ANY FIELD**, Jeffrey tells you how to use lectures and talk programs to get clients. $4

#40
THINKING ON YOUR FEET, ANSWERING QUESTIONS WELL WHETHER YOU KNOW THE ANSWER — OR NOT. People who can't deal effectively with questions present a poor self-image and can harm a company. Here Jeffrey interviews Marian Woodall, author of a new book on the subject, about how people can master the crucial "thinking on your feet" strategies. $4

#41
WHY YOU NEED SPECIAL REPORTS: HOW TO WRITE THEM, USE THEM TO GET PEOPLE TO BUY WHAT YOU'RE SELLING NOW, TO PUBLICIZE YOUR BUSINESS, AND MAKE MONEY! The secret to successful marketing is making people take action NOW to get what you're selling. Jeffrey shows you how to create inexpensive but powerful Special Reports and how to turn them into compelling marketing tools that get your prospects to respond **NOW**, and that you can also sell profitably. $4

#42
YOUR GRAND OPENING: HOW TO START YOUR MARKETING DOCUMENTS SO PEOPLE BUY WHAT YOU'RE SELLING. If your marketing documents don't draw people in immediately, you — and your next sale — are lost. Jeffrey tells you precisely what to do to begin documents so your prospects read what you have to say — and buy what you have to sell. $4

#43
COPY FLAWS THAT DOOM YOUR EXPENSIVE MARKETING DOCUMENTS TO LINE BIRDCAGES IN SAINT LOUIS. Jeffrey tells you just what you need to know to write marketing copy that gets people to buy. Key rules of profit-making copy. $4

#44
COMPUTER-ASSISTED MARKETING: HOW TO INCREASE YOUR PRODUCTIVITY AND MAKE EVERY PROSPECT AND CUSTOMER FEEL YOU'RE DELIVERING *EXACTLY* WHAT HE WANTS. People have computers but aren't using them effectively. Now learn to turn the computer into your best marketing tool. You'll read things here you've never seen before and increase your marketing productivity astonishingly. $4

#45
MONEY MAKING MAIL, OR HOW TO AVOID THE TEN BIGGEST MAIL ORDER MISTAKES. Every day I get deluged with mail order offers that make me weep for the trees that have died. What rubbish! There are rules to succeed in mail order. Here's what you should avoid — and what you should do. $4

#46
HOW TO CREATE AND USE OFFERS YOUR PROSPECTS FIND IRRESISTIBLE. The trick to marketing is to create and sell offers — not products and services. Here's

---

Remember, you can call in your order 24 hours a day (617) 547-6372, or send it to Dr. Jeffrey Lant, 50 Follen St., Suite 507, Cambridge, MA 02138.

Your cover letters, brochures, ads, free client newsletters, proposals, catalogs ... and all your other marketing communications are not getting you all the business you want. Most people getting them throw them away instantly ... costing you money every day. You can stop this foolishness — and get more people to buy from you faster — with one simple phone call to Jeffrey Lant, one of America's top marketers. Call (617) 547-6372 today ... or resign yourself to wasting your precious dollars.

what you need to know about offers, how to create them and use them so that your prospects will buy. (Example? Three of these reports for just $10). $4

#47
KNOWING WHAT TO DO WHEN PEOPLE OWE YOU MONEY, OR HOW TO GET PAYMENT IN FULL. Don't give way to the rage and frustration of being owed money by deadbeats. Get what you're owed. Here's what you need to do in practical detail. $4

#48
HOW TO USE THE YELLOW PAGES TO GET THE GREEN STUFF. If you're in the yellow pages now — and want to learn how to increase the return on your investment — or want to avoid the mistakes of yellow pages advertising before you make them, use the guidelines in this Special Report. $4

#49
TELESMARTS: EFFECTIVELY USING TELEMARKETING TO SELL YOUR PRODUCTS AND SERVICES. Most people are hideously ill-equipped to use the phone to sell anything. Here's the basics (and some advanced tips, too) on how you can turn the phone into a profitable business tool. Have I reached out and touched you? $4

#50
HOW TO OVERCOME SALES OBJECTIONS, INCLUDING THE BIGGEST ONE OF ALL: "YOUR PRICE IS TOO HIGH!" If you're in sales (and if you're reading this, you are), you've got to learn how to deal with objections. Here's what you need to know so that you can. But if you say "The price is too high" about this, I'll scream. $4

#51
TESTIMONIALS FOR YOUR PRODUCT OR SERVICE: WHY YOU NEED THEM, HOW TO GET THEM, HOW TO USE THEM. If you aren't using testimonials now, you are missing a prime marketing device. If you are, make sure you're doing it right! $4

#52
UNDERSTANDING AND PROFITING FROM THE RULE OF SEVEN: CONNECTING WITH YOUR BUYERS AND CONNECTING WITH THEM AGAIN UNTIL THEY BUY WHAT YOU'RE SELLING. Most marketing gambits don't work. In part this is because you don't hit your prospects sufficiently often to interest them in what you're selling. Now learn how you can. The Rule of Seven is the prime rule of marketing. $4

#53
WHAT TO DO WHEN YOUR PROSPECT SAYS NO. We all get turned down. Now what? Tears? Rage? No! Use Jeffrey's step-by-step guidelines to get the sale after all — or do what it takes to get the next one! $4

#54
ESSENTIALS OF MONEY MAKING MARKETING. Successful marketing is the key to business success. Now learn precisely what you have to do to improve your marketing. Follow these steps; sell more. $4

#55
WHY YOU NEED A BUSINESS PLAN, WHY YOU RESIST CREATING ONE. Makes a clear case for why you must have a business plan to succeed, how to overcome your resistance to creating one, and what should go in it. A must, particularly for new and struggling entrepreneurs. $4

*Three Report Special. Get any **THREE** of these Special Reports for just $10 (#17–#55). Note: if you want this special price you must order in multiples of **THREE**. Three Special Reports cost $10. Six cost $20. If you order other amounts, you pay $4 each!!!*

NONPROFIT RESOURCE CENTER

Running a nonprofit organization that needs money? We can help. Use:

#56
DEVELOPMENT TODAY: A FUND RAISING GUIDE FOR NON-PROFIT ORGANIZATIONS. This is your one essential resource for raising capital, project, and operating funds. Complete details on successful fundraising planning, who to involve and what they do, how to get best results from your Board, how to target the right corporations and foundations, how to raise money in your community, how to profitably use direct mail — even what to do when your proposal gets turned down. Comes complete with a Samples Section of ready-to-use documents, just like all Jeffrey's books. 276 pages. $28.95

#57
THE COMPLETE GUIDE TO PLANNED GIVING: EVERYTHING YOU NEED TO KNOW TO COMPETE SUCCESSFULLY FOR MAJOR GIFTS. This book by Debra Ashton is the most complete resource ever produced on planned giving. Planned giving is the fastest-growing

area of fund raising. Here's what you need to know to profit from it. Based on current tax laws, **THE COMPLETE GUIDE TO PLANNED GIVING** contains step-by-step techniques so you can profit from every aspect of the subject. We have never seen a book with this much information on planned giving, so lucid and easy to use. That's why Attorney Lynda Moerschbaecher, Editor of *Charitable Gift Planning News* says, "I give this superb book my unqualified recommendation." 407 pages. $38.50

#58

Get a special price on **DEVELOPMENT TODAY** and **THE COMPLETE GUIDE TO PLANNED GIVING**. Learn exactly what you need to know to raise capital, project, operating and endowment funds from corporations, foundations, and individuals. Up-to-date, ready-to-use. Both books just $55. Save $10.95.

#59

New! STARTING & MANAGING A NONPROFIT ORGANIZATION: A LEGAL GUIDE. I get questions regularly from people who want to start a nonprofit organization and manage it right. I direct them all to Bruce Hopkins, the doyen of this highly specialized field. Here's his new book on the subject, and as usual it's packed with just what you need to know to launch your nonprofit organization legally and efficiently and run it well. You can't go wrong with Hopkins. 264 pages. $47.50

WRITE DOWN THESE NUMBERS ON PAGE 16 AND COMPLETE DETAILS WILL BE SENT ...

#60

Dealers: if you're already selling my products and want to add the **MONEY MAKING MARKETING** audio cassette series to your profit-making line, let me know, and I'll send you the camera-ready art you need for this big money-maker. **Everybody else**: if you're not a dealer yet and want to make money from all my products, write and request the free Dealer Information Kit.

#61

Jeffrey will write every marketing communication you need ... cover letters, brochures, flyers, media releases, fund raising proposals, annual reports, ads ... you name it! He's inexpensive and fast ... and what's most important: what he writes gets your prospects and customers to react the way you want them to. Now! Ask for the details.

#62

Bring Jeffrey to your organization. Are you involved in a continuing education program or trade or professional organization that needs superb speakers? Then ask for the details on how you can get Jeffrey to do a speech or workshop for your group. He travels nationwide at reasonable rates and always to top reviews.

#63

Distribute this catalog. If you're offering programs, why not give your participants this catalog and introduce them to some of the best "how-to" materials in existence. Just tell us how many catalogs you need, for what group, and when.... *We'll ship them right away.* Note: you don't get any of the proceeds from any sales made this way ... just the credit for thinking of your audience. If you want to benefit directly, you've got to become a distributor. See #60.

#64

Publishers & Authors: if you want your business development books, booklets and audio cassettes featured in this catalog, send me a copy right away! And don't forget to ask for details about how your materials can be featured in my Sure-Fire Business Success Column and reach at least 1,500,000 people!!!

#65

Articles available. Have you got a newsletter or other publication that needs good material...or are you reading a publication that could be improved with articles on the kinds of subjects I handle in my Special Reports? I can help! Over 1.5 million people currently read my *Sure-Fire Business Success* Columns monthly. Write this number and I'll send you details on how you can get them...*free!*

#66

Great business development and motivational tapes. We've got a new mini-catalog of 40 of the best business and motivational tapes now available. If you'd like a copy, request it.

#67 & #68

#67 Would you like to get free time on radio shows nationwide and use it to sell your products and services? Send $2 for the information on how to do that.

#68 And would you like to have your product or service featured in a nationally-syndicated story that goes out regularly to 1,200 (mostly weekly) newspapers? Send another 2 bucks.

Get A Professional Evaluation Of Your Marketing Materials!

#69

Get Jeffrey's detailed, written critique of your marketing documents. Find out if you are doing all you can to get your prospects to respond **NOW. Send any two** of the marketing documents you're now using and just $45. Stop wasting your money on unproductive marketing. Get help **NOW!**

Developing And Protecting Ideas And Products

#70

New! FROM CONCEPT TO MARKET. Gary Lynn's just published book tells you how to protect your idea without submitting a patent, how to license a new idea, market your innovation, start your own company, raise money, build a prototype, write a business plan and price your product. Developing a product is one of the best ways to get really rich there is. Making a small investment in Lynn's extensive research tells you how to develop it right and launch it fast. 243 pages $22.95.

#71

PATENT IT YOURSELF. This is the most breathtakingly thorough book ever written on how to patent your baby. It's written by an author (Patent Attorney David Pressman) who really understands precisely what you've got to do. Subtitled "A Complete Legal Guide For Inventors", you should have this volume on hand if you're even thinking of developing a new product. Cheap at $32.95. **Just updated!!!**

Getting Organized

#72

Here it is, the book you've been waiting for to organize your personal and business lives. ORGANIZE YOURSELF! is replete with shrewd observations and guidelines on bringing order to desks, calendars, bookshelves, taxes, travel, investments, medical payments, personal inventory control, job searches, budgeting, filing systems and more. If you're the kind of person who will lose this catalog within moments of getting it, do yourself a favor. Send $11.45 now.

"I got your book MONEY TALKS from the library and must say I was impressed. It's very complete, accurate and easy to understand." Bob Schafer, Olympia, WA

Working With Your Accountant, Setting Up Your Corporation Or Partnership

#73

New! THE ACCOUNTANT AS BUSINESS ADVISOR. Every business start-up and management book I've ever read tells you you should use your accountant as a business guide. But not a single one has ever provided the kind of useful information that this resource does. Edited by William Grollman, here you get just what you need to know about financing, taxes, insurance, computers, mergers, and more. I spend a lot of money every year on my accountants, and I read this book real, real closely to see how I could use them better and profit more. I predict you'll do the same. 469 pages $67.95

#74

THE PARTNERSHIP BOOK: HOW TO WRITE YOUR OWN SMALL BUSINESS PARTNERSHIP AGREEMENT. After a very long search, I'm quite prepared to dub this the best book now available on putting together a mutually-satisfying partnership agreement. A partnership is a business marriage and is subject to terrible consequences if it doesn't go right. With this book in hand, you'll minimize the chances for partnership failure. Exhaustively detailed. $21.95

#75

INC. YOURSELF: HOW TO PROFIT BY SETTING UP YOUR OWN CORPORATION. This classic 205-page book by Judith McQuown is back ... and better than ever in its just published 6th edition. McQuown has sensible information on the preparation you've got to do to incorporate, how to handle the necessary forms and paperwork, what you've got to do about Subchapter S, insurance, medical benefits ... there's even a special section for women ... and one dedicated to the ins and outs of hiring. You get state requirements, sample corporate minutes and bylaws, a model profit-sharing plan, crucial tax information. And much, much more. Read this before you do anything. $22.45

Creating An Effective Business Plan

#76

You know you need a *written* business plan, and you know you don't have one. That's why you need THE BUSINESS PLANNING GUIDE. It's not just a book. It's your basic business tool and roadmap. Packed with forms, checklists and immediately usable examples, this will give you exactly what you need: a specific, written business plan. In about 130 pages, you'll get your MBA in small business management. Over 200,000 businesses already have. Now it's your turn. $21.45

First Steps To Being A Millionaire

#77

New! HOW TO BUILD A MILLION DOLLAR FORTUNE: THE 14-DAY NO-NONSENSE PROGRAM TO START YOU ON THE ROAD TO RICHES. People just love Ty Hicks' books, and this one will be no exception. Here this intelligent financial guru tells you just what it takes to become a millionaire and gives you a step-by-step 14-day program to get you started in the right way. No, you're not going to be a millionaire in 14 days... but you're going to have just what you need to start the trek to the objective you've always wanted to have. Over 2,000,000 people have profited from Ty's books. You really ought to take a look at what he's got to say to you. 259 pages. $20.95.

Getting Credit & Loans

#78

New! FINDING PRIVATE VENTURE CAPITAL FOR YOUR FIRM. This new book by Robert Gaston tells you just what you need to do to get private venture capital for your business. Presently, about $56 billion is invested annually in new and expanding firms by private investors. This book gives you the details so you can get your share. 260 pages. $54.95

If you're ordering materials produced by multiple publishers, they will come in multiple packages. So don't call if you only get a partial shipment. The rest is on its way...

#79
HOW TO GET CREDIT AND LOANS: A PRACTICAL GUIDE.
Author Christopher James has packed an enormous amount of information in these 179 pages. You find out how to get and protect your credit through checking accounts, security deposits, merchant credit, and credit cards. You'll learn what you need to know about retail credit reports and personal financial statements and get the low-down on where to bank, what bankers need to know about you and how to negotiate loan terms and conditions. There are even specific sections on vested interest loans, consumer loans, student financial aid and home loans. If borrowing money is in your future, get this resource first. $12.45

#80
SUCCESSFUL BUSINESS BORROWING: HOW TO PLAN AND NEGOTIATE A LOAN.
Kenneth Sparks' book deals with one of the crucial things every business person needs to know: how to borrow money. Face it, as your business grows you have to know the details on how to get money fast and at the lowest possible rate. Sparks can tell you. By the way, the last time I had to borrow money, my banker shaved 1/4 point off the bank's charge because he said I was such a nice person. This not only saved me some money, but has ensured my being even nicer to him in the future. $22.95

#81
SBA LOANS: A STEP-BY-STEP GUIDE.
At last, Patrick O'Hara has written the definitive book on how to get money from the Small Business

Administration. Here are the loan terms, collateral requirements, step-by-step application process, typical loan package examples, business plan guidelines, loan evaluation guidelines and eligibility requirements. If you want your Uncle to lend you the money, read this first. $19.95

#82
THE MONEY RAISER'S DIRECTORY OF BANK CREDIT CARD PROGRAMS.
This amazing book is correctly subtitled "The Insider's Guide to Multiple Bankcards". It tells you just what you need to know before you apply for a major bank credit card, just what any specific bank requires before they'll grant you credit. In addition to the requirements of nearly 1000 financial card programs, you also learn where the lowest credit card interest rates are (you can still actually get credit cards that only charge 8% interest!), which banks have "gold" card requirements so easy you can qualify even if you've been turned down for a "regular" bank credit card ... what banks charge for cardholder fees and how to obtain multiple credit cards ... with over $100,000 in unsecured credit! And much, much more. If you want more credit fast ... everything you need is right here. Only $32.95

Writing Proposals That Get You What You Want

#83
HOW TO WRITE WINNING PROPOSALS FOR YOUR COMPANY OR CLIENT.
In this just published book, 19 expert proposal writers tell you everything you need to know to get what you want using proposals. Here are the details you need on how to get decision makers on your side before the decision; what it takes to succeed with a government RFP or RFQ; how to overcome opposition to your proposal. Find out how to write government proposals and proposals that win in the private sector. Why, there's even a section about voice proposals ... when and how to make them. Whether you're selling a product or service, you've got to master the art of creating effective proposals. Here's where you start. 265 pages. $44.95

Essential Marketing Books, (In Addition To MONEY MAKING MARKETING, Of Course!)

Marketing books are a dime a dozen. Most are severely disappointing. These, I think, are worth paying close attention to not only because of the specific techniques they provide but also because of the mind-set towards successful marketing they'll help you create.

#84
New! DO-IT-YOURSELF MARKETING RESEARCH. The new Third Edition of this excellent book by Breen & Blankenship is now available. I've recommended its previous editions, and I'm glad to recommend this one, too. Use it when you've got little money... but absolutely must get information about your potential markets. One of the key variables in successful marketing is getting your product/service to just the right people. This book shows you how to do your absolutely necessary research. 261 pages. $42.95

#85
STREETFIGHTING: LOW-COST ADVERTISING/PROMOTION STRATEGIES FOR YOUR SMALL BUSINESS is an ingenious book. It needs to be read and thought about. Jeff Slutsky understands that small businesses need a different approach to marketing than big businesses and that this approach starts in the streetfighting mentality. Get it. $32.45

Getting Rich On Other People's Money

#86
HOW TO GET RICH ON OTHER PEOPLE'S MONEY.
Author Ty Hicks subtitles his new book "Going from Flat Broke to Great Wealth with Creative Financing", and I believe him! It's always instructive to find out what this world-class financial maven has to say. This time he supplies the information you need on such crucial topics as how and where to get fast,

hard cash now; where and how to find unique products to turn quick profits; how to become a money-making importer with little or no money; how to discover low-interest loans and grants to fund your business; how to make big money in real estate without owning property. It's all here — and a whole lot more — told in Ty's usual factual, down-to-earth, eminently practical style. Take advantage of this man's brain and expertise ... for just $20.45.

Making Money With Your Micro, Getting Free Software

#87

New! HOW TO MAKE MONEY WITH YOUR MICRO. Here's another great book from Herman Holtz, that "how-to" workhorse. This time Herman, who's got to be the most prolific computer-based writer today, tells you just what you need to know so you can set up a computer-based business, market your products and services and where to get all the information you need to get started. Herman knows what he's talking about. After all, he's made a bundle with his micro! Listen up. 270 pages. $19.95

#88

New! ALFRED GLOSSBREN- NER'S MASTER GUIDE TO FREE SOFTWARE FOR IBMS AND COMPATIBLE COMPUTERS. Glossbrenner is the free software genie. His publisher calls this book "The authoritative guide to the best public domain and shareware pro- grams for PCs, PS/2s, and com- patibles." I agree. If you want to save hundreds of dollars on top-quality, high-performance software of every kind, including the best word process- ing, spreadsheet, database, communi- cations, and accounting programs, get this book. Packed with user-groups, mail order, and online services. 530 pages $21.45

Selling On The Telephone, Overcoming Call Reluctance

#89

James Porterfield's SELLING ON THE PHONE: A SELF-TEACHING GUIDE is concise, detailed, and intelligent. Use it to find how a telemarketing sale works, how to project product knowledge over the phone, conceive your basic sales-call strategy, prospect, grab attention, analyze the needs of your prospects, answer objections, ask for the order, and close. Porterfield will help you create a positive mental attitude for phone work, use words that sell, listen effectively, and use your voice the right way. $19.45. Don't forget you can call in your order (617) 547-6372.

#90

Millions of people suffer from call reluctance. I got a vivid picture of just how bad this problem was when I ran an article about it and about this book's excellent suggestions on how to overcome it. My telephone rang for days. If you suffer from call reluctance and sometimes just cannot bring yourself to make that next important sales call, suffer no more. Get THE PSYCHOLOGY OF CALL RELUCTANCE: HOW TO OVER- COME THE FEAR OF SELF- PROMOTION. $22.45

Advertising In the Yellow Pages

#91

ADVERTISING IN THE YELLOW PAGES: HOW TO BOOST PROF- ITS AND AVOID PITFALLS. If you're in the yellow pages now or even thinking of advertising there, get this new book by W.F. Wagner. It's got the exact information you need to cut your cost, deal with sales reps, get the right position, and write the right copy. With Wagner, if you're in the yellow (pages), you'll get the green. $16.45

Collection Techniques For The Small Business

#92

You've got uncollected and uncollect- ible invoices sitting in your drawer right now. If you used the techniques in PAYMENT IN FULL: A GUIDE TO SUCCESSFUL BILL COL- LECTING, some of them wouldn't be there. If you'd use it now, you can still collect on some of them. $27.95 is also a pretty fair price to pay to cut the anger you feel about the deadbeats who're ripping you off.

Making Sure You've Got The Right Insurance... And Pay The Least For It

#93

New! THE LIFE INSURANCE BUYER'S GUIDE by William Brownlie. Just the other day I was called in by one of my clients to advise on how to assist the widow of a 35-year old man who was left with three children. My first question was "Did he have life insurance?" The answer was no. As a result, he left his wife and three yound children impoverished... totally at the mercy of events and the charity of their neighbors. This thought sickens me and it ought to sicken you. That's why you need life insurance... and this guide to the most sensible ways to acquire it and the protection you need. 248 pages. $27.95

#94

101 WAYS TO CUT YOUR BUSI- NESS INSURANCE COSTS WITHOUT SACRIFICING PRO- TECTION. Specialists McIntyre and Gibson provide what you need to know about how you can reduce your cost for property, liability and workers compensation insurance. Use this as your basic reference on *all* business insurance and as your handy desk-top advisor on saving money on insurance premiums. $23.95

Each month, lots more than 1,500,000 people—people running businesses, professional practices, and non-profit organizations—either read my books and Special Reports, order from this catalog, attend one of my workshop programs, listen to my audio cassettes, and/or read my Sure-Fire Business Success column in one of the more than 100 print and electronic data base sources carrying it. What's more, I'm still the only major business source in America who answers my own phone and doesn't put any barriers between you and me. I don't need to. I like my friendly customers.

#95
THE COMPLETE GUIDE TO HEALTH INSURANCE: HOW TO BEAT THE HIGH COST OF BEING SICK. This new book by Hugue, Jensen & Urban comes at just the right time ... as health costs are zooming out of sight. In 353 pages, you get good, solid information on health insurance policies, hospitalization, medical/surgical coverage, self-insurance, health maintenance organizations, claims, coordination of benefits, special insurance needs like catastrophes and nursing homes, and medicare. Whatever your age, you need good solid health insurance information. If you're not healthy, you can't make money. And if you're over 65, you really need the specialized information available here. $32.45

Buying A Business With Nothing Down, Getting The Most Money When You Sell Your Business
#96
New! **THE RIGHT PRICE FOR YOUR BUSINESS.** At some point, you're going to want to sell your baby, er business. When you do, you need this step-by-step guide by Morris Nunes so you get the most money you can with the fewest problems. Don't even think of selling your business without it! 175 pages. $44.95.

#97
New! **HOW TO BUY A GREAT BUSINESS WITH NO CASH DOWN.** Arnold Goldstein's back with a new book on another subject I'm constantly asked about: "How can I acquire a business when I don't have any money?" Arnold knows, and here he tells you just what you need to know. Subjects include: how to find the no-cash deals you need, how to find out what the business is really worth, how to get partners who will put up the money, how to get financing from the seller, and much, much more. 294 pages $44.95.

How To Get Lucrative Contracts From The Feds
#98
New! **GETTING STARTED IN FEDERAL CONTRACTING.** Author Barry McVay, once a Dept of Defense contracting officer, bills this book as a "guide through the federal procurement maze." He's right. There's an awful lot of money to be made selling to the government... but you've got to know just how to do it. That's where Barry comes in with 318 pages of easy-to-read, technically precise advice on how to know what to do so your contract gets approved. $24.95.

Better Barter
#99
New! Year's subscription to the quarterly BARTER NEWS. I'm including this new item because I love to barter, use it all the time... and am glad there's a publication that gives you regular tips on how to do it successfully and lots of leads to people who want to do it, too. One year. $40.

Key Business Problems And How To Solve Them
— How to publish effective newsletters

#100
Howard Penn Hudson is America's newsletter guru. If there's something to be known about newsletters, he knows it. That's why you should use PUBLISHING NEWSLETERS: A COMPLETE GUIDE TO MARKETS, EDITORIAL CONTENT, DESIGN, PRINTING, SUBSCRIPTIONS, AND MANAGEMENT. Take my word for it: this is the best book on newsletters ever written. $15.95

— Producing goodlooking marketing materials.
#101
LOOKING GOOD IN PRINT: A GUIDE TO BASIC DESIGN FOR DESKTOP PUBLISHING. After you've mastered my new book CASH COPY (so you've got the right *content* to attract buyers), you need Roger Parker's ultra-intelligent book on desktop publishing design. Use it to turn your spiffy copy into compelling newsletters, ads, brochures, manuals, letters ... and all the rest of your marketing materials. I love this book ... and your new buyers will be glad you used it! 221 pages $26.45

— How to pay less for office supplies.
#102
OFFICE PURCHASING GUIDE. Tod Snodgrass' handy little book tells you how to buy better, easier, and save up to 50% on office supplies and furniture, business forms and printing, office machines and equipment. This book has just been revised, and I can't think of an office in America that wouldn't profit from having it. Most people just buy office supplies and equipment without a second thought. But I started giving Tod's techniques a lot more thought when my own bills started soaring. Now I do just what he says. I still pay a lot ... but a lot less than I was before. So will you. Just $17.95

— Training your secretary.
#103
THE SECRETARY'S FRIEND. Just today I received a letter featuring a secretary's initial at the bottom. It was full of typographical errors, spelling mistakes, execrable grammar. What a mess! This book, subtitled "The Office Management Manual" is for this poor creature ... and any secretaries you know. It's packed with crucial information every secretary needs about the secretary's role in office planning, production, and oral and written communications. It's got key information on spelling, punctuation, grammar, diction, even titles. Had some nitwit secretary read this wonderful resource, I wouldn't have

gotten a letter beginning, "Deer Dr. Jeffery". ARGH! A very small investment for so much payback. $17.95

— Learning how to network.

#104

IS YOUR 'NET' WORKING? Anne Boe's new book deals with a crucial business problem: how to develop meaningful contacts with people who don't know you by leveraging connections with people who do. This is called networking. We all do it, but most of us are pretty haphazard about it. Not any more. Now you can get this "Complete Guide to Building Contacts And Career Visibility." Boe details how networking works and can benefit the self-employed; how to build a sales and customer service network whether you work for yourself or someone else; how to develop a networking plan to keep track of the favors and information you give; how to get job referrals ... even overcoming networking rejection. Comes complete with a list of professional organizations useful for your network. $27.95

How The Government Can Help You!

#105

U.S. GOVERNMENT SURPLUS: A COMPLETE BUYER'S MANUAL. Here's exactly what you need to know to buy incredible things at astonishingly low prices from Uncle Sam ... including office supplies, industrial, commercial, residential, recreational and personal goods. You can even find out how to get things donated to you! I met author Jim Senay on a t.v. show in New York and was immediately impressed by his knowledge and by the startling bargains in his easy-to-read 120 page guide. Just $10.50

#106

FREE HELP FROM UNCLE SAM TO START YOUR OWN BUSINESS (OR EXPAND THE ONE YOU HAVE). William Alarid's 158 page book is packed with ways for you to get money for your business from the government ... 20 loan programs, 14 loan guarantees, 8 direct payment programs, 20 grant programs, 26 information services, 11 counseling services ... and much, much more.

Are you thinking of developing a "how-to" booklet or book and need some help? First, get Jeffrey's new book HOW TO MAKE A WHOLE LOT MORE THAN $1,000,000 WRITING, COMMISSIONING, PUBLISHING AND SELLING "HOW-TO" INFORMATION. Then, call Jeffrey for some direct consulting help. Don't create the kind of product that leaves your readers in the lurch without the useful information they need. And don't spend your money producing a product that can't make you money for years to come. Let Jeffrey help you.

This book is so inexpensive and so packed with information, you'd be crazy not to use it to see how much you can get your hands on. Just $13.95

#107

THE OFFICIAL U.S. DEPARTMENT OF COMMERCE GUIDE TO EXPORTING FROM THE UNITED STATES. This 148-page book is billed as "The indispensable handbook for selling products and services abroad." I agree. It's got the low-down on how to assess your product's export potential; where to receive free expert advice; how to conduct market research abroad; methods of exporting; how to adapt your product for an overseas market, how to brand, label and package ... and much, much more. Don't wait until the dollar goes sky-high again. Learn how to export now!!! Just $12.45

#108

THE OFFICIAL U.S. CUSTOMS SERVICE GUIDE TO IMPORTING INTO THE UNITED STATES. "The indispensable handbook to the millions of business owners and collectors who buy or want to buy overseas." Find out how to enter goods into the U.S.; how to prepare invoices; how duty is assessed; what goods are dutiable; how to get refunds on duty; how to deal with currency conversions; how to deal with import quotas; forms needed for importing, etc. 85 info-packed pages. $10.45

Finding Facts And People Fast

#109

All of us are dependent on information, knowing where to find it and where to

find it fast. That's why you need FINDING FACTS FAST, the best little book ever written on quick, economical information gathering. $7.45

#110

If you've lost touch with a loved one or friend or just want to track down the animal who's skipped town on your bill, use Eugene Ferraro's book YOU CAN FIND ANYONE: A COMPLETE GUIDE ON HOW TO LOCATE MISSING PERSONS. $17.45

#111

HOW TO OBTAIN BIRTH, DEATH, MARRIAGE, DIVORCE & ADOPTION RECORDS. Eugene Ferraro's books are always good value. This one is no exception. This book tells you how to get important records about yourself and members of your family. $12.45

#112

One of the most perplexing problems business people have is how much to charge for their services. Wonder no more. Kate Kelly tells you HOW TO SET YOUR FEES AND GET THEM. Her guidebook is filled with information and examples of how to charge the right rates for your services. $19.50

Making Money From Mail Order

#113

SELL IT BY MAIL: MAKING YOUR PRODUCT THE ONE THEY BUY. If you're selling a product by mail, you'd better get James Lumley's intelligent, step-by-step guide to direct marketing techniques. What's great

"What happened to my order?" Your order can be delayed by a number of factors, including the fact you sent a check with a post office box as return address. Unless these checks are guaranteed with a MC or Visa, we hold them until they clear. The post office is not always reliable . . . shipping clerks take orders in sequence . . . books sometimes go out of stock and have to be reprinted. People make mistakes. Give me the benefit of the doubt. Inquire before you scream. I'll work out your problem. But I'll also remember how you treat me . . .

about this book is that it's studded with Key Points and Caution Notes, the things you've got to know and keep in mind to sell your products by mail. $27.95

#114

Then get Julian Simon's superb book **HOW TO START AND OPERATE A MAIL-ORDER BUSINESS.** This is frankly the best book ever written on mail order, and wherever you are — beginner or guru — you are going to profit from it. It's exhaustively detailed. $42.50 New Edition!

Developing & Preserving Your Wealth & Estate

#115

𝓝𝓮𝔀! LIES YOUR BROKER TELLS YOU. Thomas Saler, a former stock broker himself, tells you what you've got to look out for with your broker and still achieve financial security. Americans are currently paying over $50 billion (yes, billion!) for investment advise. If you're handing over fees (like I am) you'll read this book with as much interest as I did... so you can protect yourself from the charlatans (and the merely inept) and get on with the business of developing your wealth. Don't invest without this 251 page guide to safer wealth development. $22.45

"Jeffrey, I've been reading and appreciating your stuff for years. Thanks for sharing yourself and your experience with us."
    Ron Keller, Minneapolis, MN

#116

𝓝𝓮𝔀! PREPARE YOUR OWN LAST WILL AND TESTAMENT WITHOUT A LAWYER. Are you one of the 80% of Americans who don't currently have a will? If so, you're gambling with your family's security and giving your state the legal right to dispose of all the good stuff you've accumulated. Is this what you really want? I certainly don't. That's why I recommend this new, sensible book by Attorney Daniel Sitarz to you. Dan knows what he's talking about. 160 pages $17.95

#117

𝓝𝓮𝔀! FINANCIAL FREEDOM ON $5 A DAY. This little 170 page paperback is billed as "a step-by-step strategy for small investors." I agree. Author Dr. Chuck Chakrapani gives you an intelligent strategy for building and maximizing wealth based on as small an investment as just $5 each day. America's a hellish place to be poor in. You need capital. Spend just $11.45 here to find out how you can begin to develop it now with just a few dollars a day.

Successfully Working At Home

#118

Master this essential resource by Barbara Brabec, one of the brightest and most thorough experts in the business. Get her book **HOME MADE MONEY.** It's simply stuffed with useful information. I read every page and have profited mightily from the lady's insight. $19.95

#119

Then use Tyler Hicks' book **HOW TO START YOUR OWN BUSINESS ON A SHOESTRING AND MAKE UP TO $500,000 A YEAR.** Ty Hicks is one smart cookie. In addition to a lot of sensible advice about what it takes to start and run a business, he includes a list of over 1,000 businesses you can run from your home. $12.95

Winning Your Small Claims Cases

#120

If you are running a business, you are going to be the plaintiff in a small claims action. So you'd better plan for it. That's why you need **EVERYBODY'S GUIDE TO SMALL CLAIMS COURT: HOW TO WIN YOUR CASE, COLLECT YOUR MONEY, AND SMILE ALL THE WAY HOME.** It's the best book ever written on what it takes to win your action and get your money. $17.95

Being a Successful International Consultant

#121

THE INTERNATIONAL CONSULTANT. So many people have asked me about the nitty-gritty of functioning as an international consultant that I'm delighted Peter Guttmann's book on the subject has just come out in an updated edition. Find out from this well-known authority how to pursue foreign prospects, write proposals, negotiate contracts, administer overseas work, handle liability, and much, much more. Don't leave home without it. $27.95

For You Inventors

#122

THE INVENTOR'S NOTEBOOK. For those of you who long to create something new, here's the book you need. It's a real inventor's workbook ... complete with information on how to record your conception, preserve information about its building and testing, distinctive design information and then the key facts you need about legal protection, trademarks, marketing and financing. Don't start your next invention without this crucial workbook. When you've completed it, you'll have just what you need to get your baby off to a good start. $22.95

The Help You Need, The Fun You Need

#123

New! NANNIES, MAIDS & MORE: THE COMPLETE GUIDE FOR HIRING HOUSEHOLD HELP. I don't know about you, but I just can't handle everything by myself any more. If you're in the same boat and want to get some household and child help, get Linda Radke's new book. It's packed with intelligent advice on just how to find and work with the help you need. If you're not at the point of needing help yet, keep this reference on hand. As your business grows, you're going to need it! 113 pages. $17.45.

#124

New! INSIDER'S GUIDE TO CRUISE DISCOUNTS. Captain Bill Miller's new book comes at just the right moment. You know you're working too hard, know you need a vacation. Now go to some of the world's most desirable places — the Caribbean, European river cruises, Hawaii — and save lots of money. Bill's packed this helpful 128-page book with the exact details and tactics you need to save big money on personal & family cruises. I used techniques like these to get a free Caribbean cruise on Windjammer. You'll use them, too, to go to some of the world's top pleasure

spots for pennies on the dollar — or even free! Just $11.95.

Turning Paper Into Gold

#125

New! TURNING PAPER TO GOLD: HOW TO MAKE MONEY WITH OLD BOOKS, MAGAZINES, COMICS, SHEET MUSIC, AND OTHER PRINTED PAPER COLLECTIBLES. I'm including this new book by Joseph LeFontaine (which includes the current prices of over 3000 collectible books) because I'm a collector fanatic myself... along with millions of other Americans. Like you, I want to know how to find what's valuable, how to get it for the least price, and where to sell it (and for how much) when I'm ready. LeFontaine's a fountain head of useful information on all these topics and his 285-page book's a real bargain at just $20.95. (By the way, have you thought of collecting autographed copies of my books? When you order, just tell me what you'd like me to write. I'm happy to oblige.)

Renovating Your Home For Maximum Profit

#126

New! RENOVATING YOUR HOME FOR MAXIMUM PROFIT. If you're thinking of selling your home, get this new book by Lieberman and Hoffman. They tell you in no uncertain terms how you can reap $4000 in profit for every $1000 you invest in your home. You can't do anywhere near that well on Wall Street. Your home is

probably your largest single investment. Use this 390 page guide to get the most money for it you can. $25.45.

What You Need To Find A Regular Job

#127

New! THE PERFECT COVER LETTER by Richard Beatty. If you're still in the job market, chances are you'll be looking for a new job before long. Thus, you'll need to know exactly how to write the perfect cover letter to accompany your credentials and give you the best chance for getting an interview. Remember, no interview, no job. No PERFECT COVER LETTER, no interview. Help your chances. Spend just $14.95 here. 179 pages.

#128

New! SUPER JOB SEARCH: THE COMPLETE MANUAL FOR JOB-SEEKERS AND CAREER-CHANGERS. Peter Studner's giant, oversized 325-page book has become must reading for people who are really serious about getting a job. I'll tell you why: Peter lays down a sensible, step-by-step program that enables you to become an outstanding job candidate in just 7 days. This book is so crammed with useful information, I hardly know what to single out about it: its getting started guidelines, how to present your accomplishment, networking strategies, telemarketing tips, or negotiating tactics. A terrific value packed with information so that your job search is faster and more productive than the last one you ran yourself. $25.95

Your books and information will be sent to the name and address on the mailing label on page 16, unless you fill out the coupon below.

Send items to: Name _____

Company _____

Street Address _____

City/Town _____ State _____ Zip _____

Day Telephone ( ) _____

If you haven't seen this catalog before and didn't request it, you are not on the mailing list. Even if you're not buying anything now but want to keep getting the catalog, check 'mailing list' here ☐, complete coupon above (or make sure I have your mailing label). I'll make sure you keep getting it!

Order Form

Complete 30-Day Money-Back Guarantee!

Photocopy or return this page to: Dr. Jeffrey Lant, Jeffrey Lant Associates
50 Follen St., #507, Cambridge, MA 02138

CLEARLY write down the number(s) of the items you are ordering. Some items in the catalog involve information being sent you. Write these numbers down here, too.

____, ____, ____, ____, ____, ____, ____, ____, ____, ____, ____, ____, ____, ____, ____, ____, ____, ____,

Remember, if you are ordering my Special Reports (see pages 4–7), you get **any three for $10.** If you don't order in multiples of three, each is $4. No exceptions.

Total your order here $ _____. Are you a Massachusetts resident? ☐ Yes   ☐ No

If so, add 5% sales tax here $ _____.   Total enclosed $ _____.

Shipping. If you are ordering books and Special Reports by Dr. Jeffrey Lant, they are sent the day you order (unless you are using a post office box address that is not guaranteed by a MC/VISA). Other books are sent to you direct from their publishers by fourth class/book rate shipping. Allow four-six weeks. If you want them faster, add $3 per item for first class or UPS shipping. Remember: to ship UPS, I must have a street address!

Canada and overseas. If you want your items shipped to Canada, add $1 for *each* item ordered and $1 to the total for our bank's fees, even if you pay in U.S. dollars. If you want shipment to any other country, you must pay by credit card. I'll charge your account surface or air shipping, as you like. Check ☐ surface ☐ air.

Premiums. If your order totals at least $150, you can select any one of my three 60 minute audio cassettes as my gift to you. The three titles are listed on page 4. Write down the one you want here # _____. If your order totals over $220, you get your free audio cassette and any one of my seven "Get Ahead" books (#1, 2, 4, 6–9). List the number of the one you want here _____.

Payment & Billing. Unless you are a government agency, college, library or other official public organization (in which case, include your Purchase Order # here _____), COMPLETE PAYMENT MUST ACCOMPANY YOUR ORDER. I cannot invoice individuals and private businesses. If paying by check, make it payable to Jeffrey Lant Associates, Inc. If you are using a post office box number for shipment, I require a Master Card/VISA number and expiration date to guarantee your check, or else I wait for the check to clear. Sadly, several rip-off artists use post office boxes to defraud reputable merchants like me, so I have to inconvenience good people like you.

If paying by credit card (or using a post office box for shipment):

✓ ☐ MasterCard ☐ Visa. #_____

Expiration date_____ Signature_____

For faster service, place your order by telephone twenty-four hours a day at (617) 547-6372. (Yes, I really do answer my own phone). Before calling make sure your credit card is handy. The order tape doesn't last forever!

**Your books and materials will be sent to the address on the shipping label below, unless you indicate otherwise.
Please be clear about where you want your items sent.**